Analytics Stories

Analytics Stories

Using Data to Make Good Things Happen

Wayne Winston

WILEY

Analytics Stories: Using Data to Make Good Things Happen

Published by
John Wiley & Sons, Inc.
10475 Crosspoint Boulevard
Indianapolis, IN 46256
www.wiley.com

Copyright © 2021 by John Wiley & Sons, Inc., Indianapolis, Indiana
Published simultaneously in Canada

ISBN: 978-1-119-64603-7
ISBN: 978-1-119-64605-1 (ebk)
ISBN: 978-1-119-64604-4 (ebk)

Manufactured in the United States of America

For general information on our other products and services please contact our Customer Care Department within the United States at (877) 762-2974, outside the United States at (317) 572-3993 or fax (317) 572-4002.

Wiley publishes in a variety of print and electronic formats and by print-on-demand. Some material included with standard print versions of this book may not be included in e-books or in print-on-demand. If this book refers to media such as a CD or DVD that is not included in the version you purchased, you may download this material at http://booksupport.wiley.com. For more information about Wiley products, visit www.wiley.com.

Library of Congress Control Number: 2020939801

SKY10050088_070323

To my lovely and talented wife Vivian and my wonderful children, Gregory and Jennifer. All three of you light up my life!

About the Author

Dr. Wayne Winston is a Professor Emeritus of Decision Sciences at the Kelley School of Business at Indiana University. He holds a bachelor of science degree in mathematics from M.I.T. and a PhD in operations research from Yale. He has won more than 40 teaching awards at Indiana University and has written more than a dozen books, including *Marketing Analytics: Data-Driven Techniques with Microsoft Excel* (Wiley, 2014), *Business Analytics: Data Analytics & Decision Making* (Cengage Learning, 2016), *Operations Research: Applications and Algorithms* (Cengage Learning, 2003), *Practical Management Science* (Cengage Learning, 2016), *Excel 2019 Data Analysis and Business Modeling* (Wiley, 2019), and *Mathletics: How Gamblers, Managers, and Sports Enthusiasts Use Mathematics in Baseball, Basketball, and Football* (Princeton University Press, 2012). Dr. Winston has taught classes and consulted for many leading global organizations. He also is a two-time *Jeopardy!* champion and has consulted for the NBA's Dallas Mavericks and New York Knicks.

About the Technical Editor

Joyce J. Nielsen has worked in the publishing industry for more than 25 years as an author, technical editor, development editor, and project manager, specializing in Microsoft Office, Windows, Internet, and general technology titles for leading educational and retail publishers. Prior to her work in publishing, Joyce was a research analyst for Simon Property Group in Indianapolis. Joyce holds a bachelor of science degree in quantitative business analysis from Indiana University's Kelley School of Business in Bloomington, Indiana. She currently resides in Tucson, Arizona.

Acknowledgments

Wiley Publishing made the writing of this a book a pleasure and as easy as possible. Thanks to Associate Publisher Jim Minatel for having faith in my ideas for the book and fine-tuning them. Project Editor John Sleeva did a fantastic job, finding many errors and suggesting many rewrites that greatly improved the final product. Technical Editor Joyce Nielsen did an amazing job double-checking every reference and correcting errors in the original manuscript. Copy Editor Liz Welch did a great job finalizing the manuscript for the production process, which was handled brilliantly by Production Editor Saravanan Dakshinamurthy, and to Evelyn Wellborn for proofreading the book minutely.

Contents at a Glance

Contents

Introduction

In March 2007, Tom Davenport and Jeanne Harris wrote the groundbreaking book *Competing on Analytics* (Wiley, 2007). Google Trends (discussed in Chapter 36) tells us that Internet searches for the word *analytics* tripled by May 2011! If you have picked up or downloaded this book, I am pretty sure you have heard the word analytics in the workplace or in the media.

A great description of analytics is given on the SAS Institute website (see www .sas.com/en_us/insights/analytics/what-is-analytics.html). Simply stated, analytics is the use of mathematics and/or statistics to transform data and/or mathematical models into a better understanding of the world. Most applications of analytics involve answering at least one of the following questions:

- What happened?
- Why did it happen?
- What will happen?
- How do we make good things happen?

In my 40+ years of teaching MBAs, I have won over 40 teaching awards and leaned heavily on teaching concepts by example. This book is no exception. Through a discussion of over 60 analytics applications (most successful, some unsuccessful), we will enhance your understanding of analytics. You can perform all calculations discussed in Microsoft Excel. In order to not disrupt the discussion flow in our stories, we placed Excel instructions for most examples at the end of the chapter. In each story, we focus on the following issues:

- State the problem of interest.
- What data, if any, is needed to attack the problem?

- How do we analyze the data or develop the relevant mathematical model?
- How does our model solve (or not solve) the problem of interest?

Below we give a preview of some or all our analytics stories.

What Happened?

In many situations, it is not clear what happened. In Part I, "What Happened?," we describe analytics techniques that can be used to illuminate what happened in many well-known situations. For example, since not all votes were counted, more than 20 years after the 2000 Gore-Bush U.S. presidential election, it is not clear who won the election. In Chapter 3, we give you the pro-Bush and pro-Gore arguments and let you decide.

What Will Happen?

We all want to know if the stock market will go up or down next year, whether our favorite sports team will win the championship (if it's the Knicks, they won't), how many units our company's top product will sell next year, and so forth. The use of analytics to predict what will happen is known as *predictive analytics*. In Part II, "What Will Happen?," we give many applications of predictive analytics, such as a discussion (see Chapter 22) of whether the past success of an investment fund is predictive of its future success.

Why Did It Happen?

Often, we know what happened, but we want to know why it happened. In Part III, "Why Did It Happen," we try to determine the cause of the outcomes in many well-known situations. For example, children raised in neighborhoods only a mile apart often have vastly different life outcomes. In Chapter 44, we attempt to explain this important phenomenon.

How Do I Make Good Things Happen?

Prescriptive analytics helps us "prescribe" solutions to a problem that drive a situation towards a desired outcome. In Part IV, "How Do I Make Good Things Happen?," we discuss many important applications of prescriptive analytics. For example, Chapter 54 describes how the 2012 Obama and 2016 Trump campaigns used analytics to win the presidency.

How to Read This Book

If you have taken a basic statistics course, you should be able to read most of the chapters in any order. If not, then the book will provide you with a needed primer on basic statistics. The book might be useful as a supplementary text for statistics, basic analytics, or management science courses.

I hope you will have gained the following after reading the book:

- An appreciation of how analytics has changed (and will continue to change) the world

- Intuition for the appropriate data needed for a successful application of analytics

- An intuitive understanding of the most commonly used analytics techniques.

Most chapters close with an "Excel Calculations" section that describes how I used Excel to conduct each chapter's analysis. I have failed you if you need to read these sections to understand the essence of the analysis.

Finally, I hope you enjoy reading this book half as much as I enjoyed writing it! Feel free to email me at `Winston@indiana.edu` with any comments. I would love to hear from you!

Reader Support for This Book

Companion Download Files

You can download the book's Excel files from `www.wiley.com/go/analyticsstories.com`.

How to Contact the Publisher

If you believe you've found a mistake in this book, please bring it to our attention. At John Wiley & Sons, we understand how important it is to provide our customers with accurate content, but even with our best efforts an error may occur.

In order to submit your possible errata, please email it to our Customer Service Team at `wileysupport@wiley.com` with the subject line "Possible Book Errata Submission."

What Happened?

In This Part

Preliminaries

Most applications of analytics involve looking at data relevant to the problem at hand and analyzing uncertainty inherent in the given situation. Although we are not emphasizing advanced analytics in this book, you will need an elementary grounding in probability and statistics. This chapter introduces basic ideas in statistics and probability.

Basic Concepts in Data Analysis

If you want to understand how analytics is relevant to a particular situation, you absolutely need to understand what data is needed to solve the problem at hand. Here are some examples of data that will be discussed in this book:

- If you want to understand why Bernie Madoff should have been spotted as a fraud long before he was exposed, you need to understand the "reported" monthly returns on Madoff's investments.
- If you want to understand how good an NBA player is, you can't just look at box score statistics; you need to understand how his team's margin moves when he is in and out of the game.
- If you want to understand gerrymandering, you need to look at the number of Republican and Democratic votes in each of a state's congressional districts.

■ If you want to understand how income inequality varies between countries, you need to understand the distribution of income in countries. For example, what fraction of income is earned by the top 1%? What fraction is earned by the bottom 20%?

In this chapter we will focus on four questions you should ask about any data set:

■ What is a typical value for the data?

■ How spread out is the data?

■ If we plot the data in a column graph (called a *histogram* by analytics professionals), can we easily describe the nature of the histogram?

■ How do we identify unusual data points?

To address these issues, we will look at the two data sets listed in the file `StatesAndHeights.xlsx`. As shown in Figure 1.1, the Populations worksheet contains a subset of the 2018 populations of U.S. states (and the District of Columbia).

	A	B
	State/federal district/territory/Division/region	2018population
3	California	39557045
4	Texas	28701845
5	Florida	21299325
6	New York	19542209
7	Pennsylvania	12807060
8	Illinois	12741080
9	Ohio	11689442
10	Georgia	10519475
11	North Carolina	10383620
12	Michigan	9995915
13	New Jersey	8908520
14	Virginia	8517685
15	Washington	7535591
16	Arizona	7171646
17	Massachusetts	6902149
18	Tennessee	6770010
19	Indiana	6691878

Figure 1.1: U.S. state populations

The Heights worksheet (see Figure 1.2) gives the heights of 200 adult U.S. females.

	B	C
4	Female	Height
5	1	61.05
6	2	59.54
7	3	64.93
8	4	65.63
9	5	60.20
10	6	59.96
11	7	66.41
12	8	61.49
13	9	65.89
14	10	61.35
15	11	67.80
16	12	62.64
17	13	67.61
18	14	64.75
19	15	71.44
20	16	67.49
21	17	66.87
22	18	69.58
23	19	68.11

Figure 1.2: Heights of 200 adult U.S. women

Looking at Histograms and Describing the Shape of the Data

A *histogram* is a column graph in which the height of each column tells us how many data points lie in each range, or bin. Usually, we create 5–15 bins of equal length, with the bin boundaries being round numbers. Figure 1.3 shows a histogram of state populations, and Figure 1.4 shows a histogram of women's heights (in inches). Figure 1.3 makes it clear that most states have populations between 1 million and 9 million, with four states having much larger populations in excess of 19 million. When a histogram shows bars that extend much further to the right of the largest bar, we say the histogram or data set is *positively skewed* or *skewed right*.

Figure 1.4 shows that the histogram of adult women heights is *symmetric*, because the bars to the left of the highest bar look roughly the same as the bars to the right of the highest bar. Other shapes for histograms occur, but in most of our stories, a histogram of the relevant data would be either positively skewed or symmetric.

There is also a mathematical formula to summarize the skewness of a data set. This formula yields a skewness of 2.7 for state populations and 0.4 for women's heights. A skewness measure greater than +1 corresponds to positive skewness, a skewness between –1 and +1 corresponds to a symmetric data set, and a skewness less than –1 (a rarity) corresponds to negative skewness (meaning bars extend further to the left of the highest bar than to the right of the highest bar).

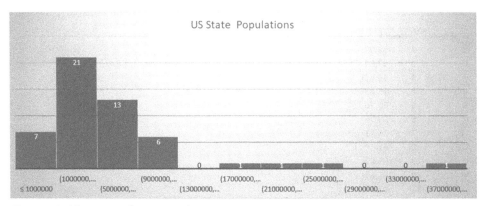

Figure 1.3: Histogram of state populations

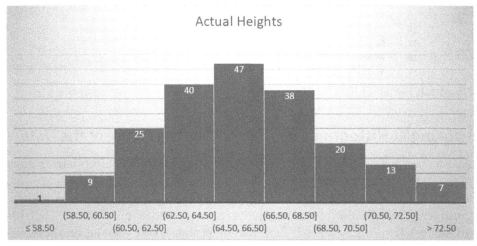

Figure 1.4: Histogram of women's heights

What Is a Typical Value for a Data Set?

It is human nature to try to summarize data with a single number. Usually, the typical value for a data set is taken to be the *mean* (simply the average) of the members of the data set or the *median* (the 50th percentile of the data set, meaning half the data is larger than the median and half the data is smaller than the median). When the data set is symmetric, we use the mean as a typical value for the data set, and when the data exhibits positive or negative skewness, we use the median as a measure of a typical value. For example, U.S. family income is very skewed, so the government reports median income. The Census Bureau analysis of income (www.census.gov/library/publica-tions/2018/demo/p60-263.html) does not even mention the word *average* but lets us know that median family income in 2017 was $61,372. Try an Internet search for mean U.S. family income, and you will probably not find anything!

After searching for 30 minutes, I found that mean family income for 2017 was $100,400 (fred.stlouisfed.org/series/MAFAINUSA672N)! This is because high-income families exhibit an undue influence on the mean but not the median. By the way, the FRED (Federal Reserve of St. Louis) website (fred.stlouisfed.org) is a treasure trove of economic data that is easily downloadable.

For another example where the median is a better measure of a typical value than the mean, suppose a university graduates 10 geography majors, with 9 having an income of $20,000 and one having an income of $820,000. The mean income is $100,000 and the median income is $20,000. Clearly, for geography majors, the median is a better measure of typical income than the mean. By the way, in 1984 geography majors at the University of North Carolina had the highest mean salary but not the highest median salary; Michael Jordan was a geography major and his high salary certainly pushed the mean far above the median!

What measure of typical value should we use for state populations or a woman's height? Since state populations exhibit extreme positive skewness, we would report a typical state population as the median population (4,468,402). The mean population (6,415,047) is over 40% larger than the median population! The mean state population is skewed by the large populations of California, Texas, and Florida. Since our sample of women's heights exhibits symmetry, we may summarize a typical woman's height with the mean height of 65.76 inches. The median height of 65.68 inches is virtually identical to the mean height.

How Spread Out Is the Data?

Suppose you live in a location where the average temperature every day is 60 degrees Fahrenheit, and your mother lives in a location where half the days average 0 degrees and half the days average 120 degrees. Both locations have an average temperature of 60 degrees, but the second location has a large spread (or *variability*) about the mean, whereas the first population has no spread about the mean. The usual measure of spread about the mean is the *standard deviation*. There are two formulas for standard deviation: population standard deviation and sample standard deviation. To avoid unnecessary technical complications, we will always use the sample standard deviation. Following are the steps needed to compute a sample standard deviation. We assume we have n data points.

1. Compute the mean of the n data points.
2. Compute the square of the deviation of each data point from the mean and add these squared deviations.
3. Divide the sum of the squared deviations by $n - 1$. This yields the sample variance (which we will simply refer to as *variance*).

The *sample standard deviation* (which we refer to as *standard deviation* or *sigma*) is simply the square root of the variance.

As an example of the computation of variance, consider the data set 1, 3, 5. To compute the standard deviation, we proceed as follows:

1. The mean is 9 / 3 = 3.
2. The sum of the squared deviations from the mean is $(1-3)^2 + (3-3)^2 + (5-3)^2 = 8$.
3. Dividing 8 by 2 yields a variance of 4.

The square root of 4 equals 2, so the standard deviation of this data set equals 2.

If we simply add up the deviations from the mean for a data set, positive and negative deviations *always* cancel out and we get 0. By squaring deviations from the mean, positive and negative deviations do not cancel out.

To illustrate the importance of looking at the spread about the mean, the file `Investments.xlsx` gives annual percentage returns on stocks, Treasury bills (T-bills), and 10-year bonds for the years 1928–2018 (see Figure 1.5).

	D	E	F	G
2	mean	11.36%	3.43%	5.10%
3	std dev	19.58%	3.04%	7.70%

Figure 1.5: Histogram of annual investment returns

We find that the mean annual return on stocks is more than triple the annual return on Treasury bills. Yet many portfolio managers hold T-bills along with stocks. The reason is that the annual standard deviation of stock returns is more than six times as large as the standard deviation of T-bill returns. Therefore, holding some T-bills will reduce the risk in your portfolio.

How Do We Identify Unusual Data Points?

For most data sets (except those with a large amount of skewness), it is usually true that

- 68% of the data is within one standard deviation of the mean.
- 95% of the data is within two standard deviations of the mean.

We call an "unusual data point" an *outlier*. There are more complex definitions of outliers, but we will simply define an outlier to be any data point that is more than two standard deviations from the mean.

For state populations, our criteria labels a population below −8.27 million or above 21 million as an outlier. Therefore, California, Texas, and Florida (6% of the states) are outliers. For our women's heights, our outlier criteria labels any woman shorter than 58.9 inches or taller than 72.6 inches as an outlier. We find that 7 of 200 women (3.5%) are outliers. For our annual stock returns, 4 years (1931, 1937, 1954, and 2008) were outliers. Therefore, 4 / 91 = 4.4% of all years were outliers. As you will see in later chapters, identifying why an outlier occurred can often help us better understand a data set.

Z-Scores: How Unusual Is a Data Point?

Often, we want a simple measure of "the unusualness" of a data point. Statisticians commonly use the concept of a *Z-score* to measure the unusualness of a data point. The Z-score for a data point is simply the number of standard deviations that the point is above or below average. For example, California's population has a Z-score of 4.5 ((39.6 − 6.4) / 7.3). The 2008 return on stocks has a Z-score of −2.45 ((−36.55 − 11.36) / 19.58). Of course, our outlier definition corresponds to a point with a Z-score greater than or equal to 2 or less than or equal to −2.

What Is a Random Variable?

Any situation in which the outcome is uncertain is an *experiment*. The value of a *random variable* emerges from the outcome of an experiment. In most of our stories, the value of a random variable or the outcome of an experiment will play a key role. Some examples follow:

- Each year the NBA finals is an experiment. The number of games won by the Eastern or Western Conference team in the best of seven series is a random variable that takes on one of the following values: 0, 1, 2, 3, or 4.
- A PSA (prostate-specific antigen) test designed to detect prostate cancer is an experiment, and the score on the PSA test is a random variable.
- Your arrival at a TSA (Transportation Security Administration) checkpoint is an experiment, and a random variable of interest is the time between your arrival and your passage through the checkpoint.
- Whatever happens to the U.S. economy in 2025 is an experiment. A random variable of interest is the percentage return on the Dow in 2025.

Discrete Random Variables

For our purposes, a random variable is *discrete* if the random variable can assume a finite number of values. Here are some examples of a discrete random variable:

- The number of games won (0, 1, 2, 3, or 4) by the Eastern or Western Conference in the NBA finals
- If two men with scurvy are given citrus juice, the number of men who recover (0, 1, or 2)
- The number of electoral votes received by the incumbent party in a U.S. presidential election

A discrete random variable is specified by a *probability mass function*, which gives the probability (P) of occurrence for each possible value. Of course, these probabilities must add to 1. For example, if we let X = number of games won by the Eastern Conference in the NBA finals and we assume that each possible value is equally likely, then the mass function would be given by $P(X = 0) = P(X = 1) = P(X = 2) = P(X = 3) = P(X = 4) = 0.2$.

Continuous Random Variables

A *continuous random variable* is a random variable that can assume a very large number, or to all intents and purposes, an infinite number of values including all values on some interval. The following are some examples of continuous random variables:

- The number of people watching an episode of *Game of Thrones*
- The fraction of men with a PSA of 10 who have prostate cancer
- The percentage return on the Dow Index during the year 2025
- The height of an adult American woman

When a discrete random variable can assume many values, we often approximate the discrete random variable by a continuous random variable. For example, the margin of victory for the AFC team in the Super Bowl might assume any integer between, say, −40 and +40, and it is convenient to assume this margin of victory is a continuous rather than a discrete random variable. We also note that the probability that a continuous random variable assumes an exact value is 0. For example, the probability that a woman is exactly 66 inches tall is 0, because 66 inches tall is, to all intents and purposes, equivalent to being 66.00000000000000000 inches tall.

Since a continuous random variable can assume an infinite number of values, we cannot list the probability of occurrence for each possible value. Instead, we describe a continuous random variable by a *probability density function* (PDF). For example, the PDF for a randomly chosen American woman's height is shown in Figure 1.6. This PDF is an example of the *normal random variable*, which often accurately describes a continuous random variable. Note the PDF is symmetric about the mean of 65.5 inches.

A PDF has the following properties:

- The value of the PDF is always non-negative.
- The area under the PDF equals 1.
- The height of the PDF for a value x of a random variable is proportional to the likelihood that the random variable assumes a value near x. For example, the height of the density near 61.4 inches is half the height of the PDF at 65.5 inches. Also, because the PDF peaks at 65.5 inches, the most likely height for an American woman is 65.5 inches.

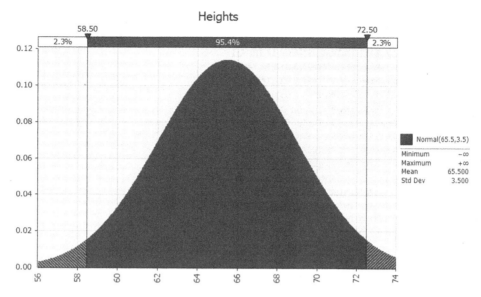

Figure 1.6: PDF for height of American woman

- The probability that a continuous random variable assumes a range of values equals the corresponding area under the PDF. For example, as shown in Figure 1.6, a total of 95.4% of the women have heights between 58.5 and 72.5 inches. Note that for this normal random variable (and any normal random variable!) there is approximately a 95% chance that the random variable assumes a value within 2 standard deviations of its mean. This is the rationale for our definition of an outlier.

As shown in Figure 1.6, the normal density is symmetric about its mean, so there is a 50% chance the random variable is less than its mean. This implies that for a normal random variable, the mean equals the median.

Computing Normal Probabilities

Throughout the book we will have to compute probabilities for a normal random variable. As shown in the "Excel Calculations" section in a moment, the NORM.DIST function can be used to easily compute normal probabilities. For example, let's compute the chance that a given team wins the Super Bowl. Suppose that the mean margin of the game is approximately the Las Vegas point spread, and the standard deviation of the mean margin is almost exactly 14 points. Figure 1.7, from the NORMAL Probabilities worksheet in the StatesAndHeights.xlsx workbook, shows how the chance of a team losing depends on the point spread.

	D	E	F
8	Point Spread	Chance of Losing	
9	-10	0.762475	=NORMDIST(0,D9,14,TRUE)
10	-9	0.739842	=NORMDIST(0,D10,14,TRUE)
11	-8	0.716145	=NORMDIST(0,D11,14,TRUE)
12	-7	0.691462	=NORMDIST(0,D12,14,TRUE)
13	-6	0.665882	=NORMDIST(0,D13,14,TRUE)
14	-5	0.639508	=NORMDIST(0,D14,14,TRUE)
15	-4	0.612452	=NORMDIST(0,D15,14,TRUE)
16	-3	0.584838	=NORMDIST(0,D16,14,TRUE)
17	-2	0.556798	=NORMDIST(0,D17,14,TRUE)
18	-1	0.528472	=NORMDIST(0,D18,14,TRUE)
19	0	0.5	=NORMDIST(0,D19,14,TRUE)
20	1	0.471528	=NORMDIST(0,D20,14,TRUE)
21	2	0.443202	=NORMDIST(0,D21,14,TRUE)
22	3	0.415162	=NORMDIST(0,D22,14,TRUE)
23	4	0.387548	=NORMDIST(0,D23,14,TRUE)
24	5	0.360492	=NORMDIST(0,D24,14,TRUE)
25	6	0.334118	=NORMDIST(0,D25,14,TRUE)
26	7	0.308538	=NORMDIST(0,D26,14,TRUE)
27	8	0.283855	=NORMDIST(0,D27,14,TRUE)
28	9	0.260158	=NORMDIST(0,D28,14,TRUE)
29	10	0.237525	=NORMDIST(0,D29,14,TRUE)

Figure 1.7: Chance of winning the Super Bowl

For example, a 10-point favorite has a 24% chance of losing, whereas a 5-point underdog has a 64% chance of losing.

Independent Random Variables

A set of random variables is *independent* if knowledge of the value of any of their subsets tells you nothing about the values of the other random variables. For example, the number of soccer matches won by Real Madrid in a year is independent of the percentage return on the Dow Index during the same year. This is because knowing how Real Madrid performed would not change your view of how the Dow would perform during the same year. On the other hand, the annual return on the NASDAQ and the Dow Index are not independent, because if you knew that the Dow had a good year, then in all likelihood the NASDAQ index also performed well.

We can now understand why many real-life random variables follow a normal random variable. The *Central Limit Theorem* (CLT) states that if you add together many (usually 30 is sufficient) independent random variables, then even if each independent random variable is not normal, the sum will be approximately normal. For example, the number of half-gallons of milk sold at your local supermarket on a given day will probably follow a normal random variable, because it is the sum of the number of half-gallons bought that day by each of the store's customers. *This is true even though each customer's purchases are not normal because each customer probably buys 0, 1, or 2 half-gallons.*

Excel Calculations

In most chapters, we will include the "Excel Calculations" section to explain the way we used Microsoft Excel to perform the calculations and create the figures discussed in the chapter. With these explanations, you should be able to easily duplicate our work. All the Excel workbooks discussed in the book can be found at wiley.com/go/analyticsstories.com.

Creating Histograms

To create the histogram of women's heights in the Heights worksheet, shown in Figure 1.2, proceed as follows:

1. Select the data in the range C4:C204.

2. From the Insert tab, select the Insert Statistic Chart icon shown in Figure 1.8, and then select the Histogram chart, as shown in Figure 1.9.

3. With your cursor in the chart, select the third choice (showing the numerical labels) from the Chart Styles group on the Chart Design tab.

4. With your cursor on the x-axis of the chart, right-click the x-axis, select Format Axis, and choose the settings shown in Figure 1.10. These settings ensure that heights less than or equal to 58.5 inches or above 72.5 inches are grouped in a single bin and that each bin has a width of 2 inches.

Figure 1.8: Statistical chart icon

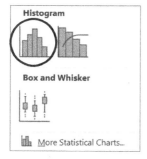

Figure 1.9: Histogram chart icon

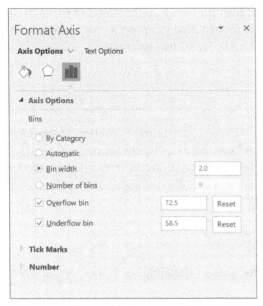

Figure 1.10: Settings for histogram bin ranges

Computing Descriptive Statistics

As shown in Figure 1.11, we compute the appropriate descriptive statistics in the Populations worksheet by simply applying the MEDIAN, AVERAGE, STDEV, and SKEW functions to the data range (B3:B53).

	H	I	J
3	Median	4468402	=MEDIAN(B3:B53)
4	Mean	6415047.73	=AVERAGE(B3:B53)
5	Standard Deviation	7343307.89	=STDEV(B3:B53)
6	Lower Outlier	-8271568.1	=I4-2*I5
7	Upper Outlier	21101663.5	=I4+2*I5
8	Skewness	2.69479768	=SKEW(B3:B53)

Figure 1.11: Computing descriptive statistics

In the workbook Investments.xlsx, we computed the mean return on each investment by copying from E2 to F2:G2 the formula =AVERAGE(E5:E95). We computed the standard deviation for each investment by copying from E3 to F3:G3 the formula =STDEV(E5:E95).

Counting Outliers

The incredibly useful COUNTIF function counts the number of cells in a range that meet a given criterion. This function makes it easy to count the number of outliers in a data set. In cell H10 of the Heights worksheet of `StatesAndHeights` `.xlsx`, we compute the number of outliers (2) on the low side with the formula `=COUNTIF(height,"<="&J7)`. We named the range C5:C204 Height by selecting the range C4:C204 and from the Formulas tab choosing Create From Selection. Now anywhere in the workbook using Height in a formula refers to the named range. The portion of the formula `"<="&J7` ensures that the formula counts only the heights at least two standard deviations below the mean. Similarly, the formula `=COUNTIF(height,">="&J8)` in cell H11 counts the number of outliers (5) on the high side.

Computing Normal Probabilities

If you want to compute the probability that a normal random variable with a given mean and standard deviation assumes a value less than or equal to (or less than) x, simply use the formula

```
=NORM.DIST(x,Mean,Standard Deviation,True)
```

For example, as shown in Figure 1.7, the chance that a normal random variable with mean 10 and standard deviation 14 is less than or equal to 0 is computed with the formula

```
=NORM.DIST(0,10,14,True)
```

CHAPTER 2

Was the 1969 Draft Lottery Fair?

In 1969, the unpopular Vietnam War was raging, and the United States needed soldiers to fight the war. To equalize the chance of young men (born in years 1944–1950) being drafted, a draft lottery based on a man's birthday was held. A total of 366 pieces of paper (one for each possible date, including February 29) were mixed in a shoebox and placed in capsules that were placed in a large glass jar. Then the capsules were selected, and the order of selection determined a man's priority for being drafted. September 14 was chosen first, so that date was assigned #1, April 24 was drawn next, assigned #2, and so on. Men with draft numbers up to 195 were drafted. The lottery numbers for each date are listed in column G of the Data worksheet of the file `DraftData.xlsx`.

Statisticians quickly noticed (see `www.nytimes.com/1970/01/04/archives/ statisticians-charge-draft-lottery-was-not-random.html`) that lottery numbers for the last few months of the year seemed to be suspiciously low, meaning that men with late-year birthdays were more likely to be drafted. Were the statisticians correct?

The Data

All we need are the lottery numbers for each calendar date. As you will see, there were likely problems with the 1969 lottery method. A different selection method was used in the July 1, 1970 lottery (for men with 1951 birthdays), and that data is included in Column H of the Data worksheet of the file `DraftData.xlsx`.

The Analysis

To examine whether later months tended to have lower lottery numbers, we simply charted the average draft lottery numbers for each month for the 1969 lottery (see Figure 2.1). We also charted the average 1969 lottery number, 183.5 (the average of 1 and 366), as well as the average lottery numbers by month for the 1970 lottery.

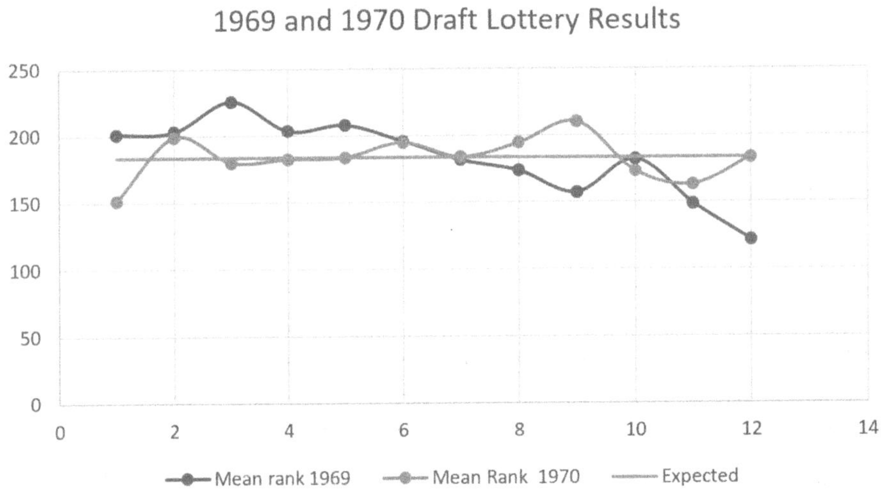

1969 and 1970 Draft Lottery Results

Figure 2.1: Average draft lottery number by month

A cursory exam of Figure 2.1 indicates that the average 1969 lottery numbers for the later months appear to drop off substantially and that for 1970 this is not the case. *The question is whether the late year decrease in the 1969 lottery numbers could have reasonably occurred by chance.* After all, even if each date in the 1969 lottery had a 1/366 chance of being #1, #2, . . . #365, #366, then the December lottery numbers could theoretically have come out as #1, #2, . . ., #31. This is where a key analytics idea, *hypothesis testing*, enters the fray. Often, we have two competing hypotheses: a *null hypothesis* that we wish to overturn with overwhelming evidence and an *alternative hypothesis*. When faced with these two competing hypotheses, the analytics expert pulls out the relevant hypothesis test and computes the appropriate *probability value* (*p-value* for short). Probably the easiest hypothesis testing approach to our problem is to group the lottery numbers into two groups: lottery numbers for January 1–June 30 and July 1–December 31. Then our null and alternative hypotheses would be as follows:

- **Null hypothesis**—The average 1969 lottery number for January 1–June 30 equals the average 1969 lottery number for July 1–December 31.

- **Alternative hypothesis**—The average 1969 lottery number for January 1–June 30 does not equal the average 1969 lottery number for July 1–December 31.

A hypothesis test has a test statistic that is random. Here the test statistic equals (January 1– June 30 average rank) – (July 1–December 31 average rank).

Each time lottery numbers were drawn, a different set of lottery numbers for each date would likely be drawn.

The appropriate hypothesis test (in this case, the t-Test: Two-Sample Assuming Equal Variances) is now used to compute a p-value between 0 and 1. The p-value gives the probability that, given the null hypothesis is true, a value exceeding the test statistic would occur. As shown in Figure 2.2 and the Difference Between Means worksheet, the mean lottery number in the 1969 lottery for the first six months was 206.3 and the mean lottery number for the last six months was 160.9. Note the Excel results give both a one-tailed and a two-tailed p-value. We use the two-tailed p-value here because both large positive and very negative values of the test statistic indicate inconsistency with the null hypothesis. The p-value given by Excel is 3.4E-05, which is 3 chances in 100,000. This means that if the null hypothesis is true, the chance of seeing a difference in the average lottery numbers exceeding |206.3 – 160.9| = 45.4 is around 3 in 100,000. Since this probability is so small, we reject the null hypothesis and conclude that there is a significant difference in lottery numbers for the two halves of the year.

The t-statistic of 4.2, shown in Figure 2.2, is virtually equivalent to a Z-score of 4.2, which indicates the observed difference in average lottery numbers is not likely to be due to chance. Therefore, the end-year decrease in lottery numbers *cannot reasonably be attributed to chance*. Perhaps the shoebox did not sufficiently mix the capsules and the later-in-year capsules tended to stay on top.

J	K	L	M	N	O	P
1 t-Test: Two-Sample Assuming Equal Variances				t-Test: Two-Sample Assuming Equal Variances		
2						
3	*1969 Jan-June*	*1969 July-Dec*			*1970 Jan-June*	*1970 July-Dec*
4 Mean	206.3241758	160.923913		Mean	181.4364641	184.5380435
5 Variance	11266.48549	10151.91768		Variance	10444.24733	11865.50674
6 Observations	182	184		Observations	181	184
7 Pooled Variance	10706.13958			Pooled Variance	11160.75001	
8 Hypothesized Mean Difference	0			Hypothesized Mean Difference	0	
9 df	364			df	363	
10 t Stat	4.19706774			t Stat	-0.280438722	
11 P(T<=t) one-tail	1.70098E-05			P(T<=t) one-tail	0.389650344	
12 t Critical one-tail	1.649050545			t Critical one-tail	1.649062137	
13 P(T<=t) two-tail	3.40196E-05			P(T<=t) two-tail	0.779300687	
14 t Critical two-tail	1.966502569			t Critical two-tail	1.966520641	

Figure 2.2: Results of two-sample Z-test

For the July 1, 1970 lottery, the selection method was changed. For each of the 365 possible birthdates (no February 29 for 1951 birthdays), the date was written on a piece of paper and placed in a capsule. The capsules were placed in a random order and then put in a drum that was rotated for an hour. Then the same process was used with the numbers 1 through 365. (Due to technical issues, this drum was rotated for only 30 minutes.) Then a date and a number were simultaneously drawn. For example, if January 1 and the number 133 were drawn at the same time, then January 1 was assigned the lottery number 133. As shown in Figure 2.2, the average lottery number of the first half of the year was 181.4 and the average lottery number for the second half of the year was 184.5. The p-value for the t-test was 0.78. This means that if the average of the lottery numbers for the two halves of the year were equal, then 78% of the time an absolute difference of at least 3.1 in average rank would occur. This gives us no reason to doubt that the 1970 procedure resulted in lottery numbers that showed little or no dependence on the portion of a year in which a man was born.

Excel Calculations

We now explain how we created the figures and calculations discussed in this chapter. Refer also to `wiley.com/go/analyticsstories.com`.

Charting the Average Lottery Number by Month

As shown in Figure 2.3, copying from K6 to K6:L17 the formula

```
= AVERAGEIF($E$6:$E$371,$J6,G$6:G$371)
```

computes the average lottery number for each month during the 1969 and 1970 lotteries.

After selecting the range J6:M17, choose the second Scatter chart option from the Insert tab to see the results shown in Figure 2.1.

Conducting the t-Test: Two-Sample Assuming Equal Variances

To conduct the hypothesis tests that created the output shown in Figure 2.2 and the Difference Between Means worksheet, perform the following steps:

1. Choose File ➪ Options ➪ Add-ins, select Go, check Analysis ToolPak (the first option), and then click OK. You will now see the Data Analysis option on the right-hand side of the Data tab.

	J	K	L	M	N	O
3						
4						
5	Monthly Means	Mean rank 1969	Mean Rank 1970	Expected		
6	1	201.161	151.8387	183.5	=AVERAGEIF($E$6:$E$371,$J6,G$6:G$371)	
7	2	202.966	198.8929	183.5	=AVERAGEIF($E$6:$E$371,$J7,G$6:G$371)	
8	3	225.806	179.7742	183.5	=AVERAGEIF($E$6:$E$371,$J8,G$6:G$371)	
9	4	203.667	182.1667	183.5	=AVERAGEIF($E$6:$E$371,$J9,G$6:G$371)	
10	5	207.968	183.5161	183.5	=AVERAGEIF($E$6:$E$371,$J10,G$6:G$371)	
11	6	195.733	194.5667	183.5	=AVERAGEIF($E$6:$E$371,$J11,G$6:G$371)	
12	7	181.548	183.5806	183.5	=AVERAGEIF($E$6:$E$371,$J12,G$6:G$371)	
13	8	173.452	194.3548	183.5	=AVERAGEIF($E$6:$E$371,$J13,G$6:G$371)	
14	9	157.3	209.8667	183.5	=AVERAGEIF($E$6:$E$371,$J14,G$6:G$371)	
15	10	182.452	172.9677	183.5	=AVERAGEIF($E$6:$E$371,$J15,G$6:G$371)	
16	11	148.733	163.1333	183.5	=AVERAGEIF($E$6:$E$371,$J16,G$6:G$371)	
17	12	121.548	183.4516	183.5	=AVERAGEIF($E$6:$E$371,$J17,G$6:G$371)	

Figure 2.3: Computing average lottery number by month

2. Click Data Analysis on the Data tab, select t-test: Two-Sample Assuming Equal Variances, and then click OK. Fill in the dialog box as shown in Figure 2.4. After clicking OK, you will see the results shown in Figure 2.2.

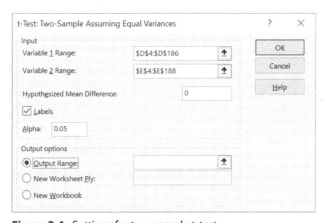

Figure 2.4: Settings for two-sample t-test

Who Won the 2000 Election: Bush or Gore?

The November 7, 2000 presidential election is still a controversial topic. On December 12, 2000, the U.S. Supreme Court declared Bush the winner, but the outcome is still a subject of great debate. By early morning November 8, Gore had locked in 255 electoral votes and Bush had locked in 246 electoral votes. Florida's 25 electoral votes were in doubt. Whoever won Florida would have the 270 electoral votes needed to become president. When the final vote was completed, Bush was ahead by 1,784 votes out of nearly 6 million total votes (a 0.03% margin—the smallest state percentage difference in U.S. history). Of course, a recount began. In counties with voting machines, the machine recount was completed on November 10 and Bush's margin shrank to a mere 327 votes. Then the fun and legal machinations began. Most of the controversy centered around the 61,000 undervotes (ballots in which legally you could not determine if the voter chose any presidential candidate) and the 113,000 overvotes (ballots on which it appeared that the voter selected more than one presidential candidate). Attempts to clarify the winner continued until December 12, 2000, when the Supreme Court decided in a controversial 5-4 decision (with the justices dividing along party lines) to stop the recount and declare Bush the winner of Florida's 25 electoral votes by 537 votes (a mere 0.01%). This decision was criticized on legal grounds (see Toobin, Jeffrey, *Too Close to Call*, Random House 2001).

Since there is no way a manual recount could be completed before Florida's electors needed to be certified, we will focus on how analytics could have been used to project how the uncounted undervotes, the infamous "butterfly ballot," and overvotes would have ended up if a recount had been completed.

Projecting the Undervotes

Michael O. Finkelstein and Bruce Levin (F&L) (*Statistics for Lawyers,* Springer 2015) describe a plausible method to project how the undervote would have come out if every undervote had been examined. Here is the procedure they followed:

- Based on counties already counted, they assumed that counties with punch card machines would have 26% of undervotes recovered, whereas counties with optical scanners (similar to Scantron's used to grade standardized tests) would have 5% of undervotes recovered. They also assumed that on average the undervote would break in an identical fashion to the already counted votes.

- They estimated the net gain for Gore from the undervotes in a county as follows:

   (fraction recovered)*(Undervote)*(Net margin for Gore as a fraction of
      already recorded votes)

- Then they summed these estimated net gains over all counties and added them to the prior Gore margin (–195 votes). For example, in Miami-Dade County (a Gore stronghold) punch card machines were used, and among recorded votes Gore, was ahead by 39,461 votes out of 625,985 cast. There were 8,845 undervotes so F&L estimated that Gore would pick up (39,461 / 625,985) * (0.26) * 8,845 = 145 undervotes.

Summing up the estimated gains for Gore over all counties, F&L estimated Gore would have lost 617 votes in a complete count of the undervotes. Since Gore started 195 votes behind, F&L estimated that after undervotes were counted, Gore would have lost by 812 votes. Of course, 812 is simply an estimate of how many votes Gore would have been behind. Through a complex calculation, F&L computed the standard deviation of the actual number of votes Gore would have lost equals 99. By the Central Limit Theorem, the number of votes Gore would really be behind after a complete undercount follows a normal random variable with Mean = 812 and Standard Deviation = 99. Then the chance Bush would have been behind after a complete recount of the undervotes can be computed with the following Excel formula:

```
=NORM.DIST(0,812,99,True)
```

This yields a (really small!) 0.00000000000000012 chance that Bush would be behind.

What Happened with the Overvotes?

USA Today and several other media outlets conducted a postelection analysis (it took 5 months) of 60,647 undervotes and 111,261 overvotes (*USA Today*, Revisiting the Florida Vote: Final Tally, May 11, 2001). They concluded (as did F&L) that if only undervotes were manually recounted, then Bush would have won and that under the most widely used standards that define a legal vote, even if all undervotes and overvotes were recounted, Bush still would have won. *They also concluded that more voters intended to vote for Gore.* (More on this when we discuss the infamous butterfly ballot in the next section.)

Anthony Salvanto, CBS News' director of Elections and Surveys, concluded that only 3% of the overvotes could have been converted into a *legal vote*. Salvanto concluded, however, that if Gore supporters had not made unintentional overvote errors, Gore would have gained at least 15,000 votes. To illustrate the problems with the overvotes, we now discuss the infamous Palm Beach County butterfly ballot.

The Butterfly Did It!

Figure 3.1 shows the infamous butterfly ballot that was used on Election Day in Palm Beach County. The ballot was spread out over two pages to make it easier for older voters to see their choices. The ballot is called a butterfly ballot because the two pages correspond to a butterfly's wings. Punching hole 3 would be registered as a Bush vote, punching hole 4 would be registered as a vote for third-party candidate Pat Buchanan, and punching hole 5 would be registered as a vote for Gore. Looking at the ballot, it is easy to see how someone who was for Gore might have punched hole 4 in lieu of hole 5. As you will see, there is overwhelming evidence that enough Gore voters mistakenly voted for Buchanan to turn the election to Bush.

Kosuke Imai (*Quantitative Social Science: An Introduction*, Princeton University Press, 2018) tried to predict for each county the 2000 Buchanan vote from the 1996 third-party vote for Ross Perot. This data is in the All Counties worksheet of the file `PalmBeachRegression.xlsx`. Plotting the Buchanan vote on the y-axis and the Perot vote on the x-axis yields the graph shown in Figure 3.2. The straight line shown is the line that best fits the data. This figure shows (from the R^2 values of 0.51) that the Perot vote explains 51% of the variation in the Buchanan vote. *Note, however, the one point way above the line. This point is Palm Beach County and is clearly an outlier, which indicates that in Palm Beach County, Buchanan received an abnormally high number of votes.* Figure 3.3 (see the worksheet No Palm Beach) shows the relevant chart when Palm Beach County is omitted from the analysis. When Palm Beach County is omitted, the line appears to fit all the points well,

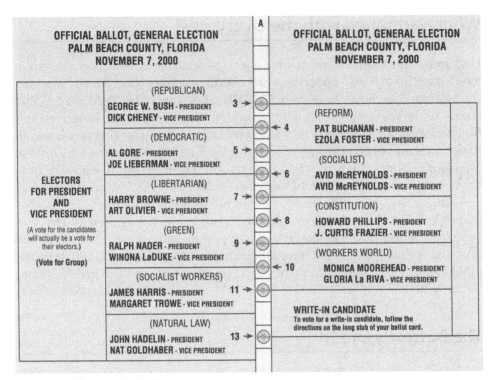

Figure 3.1: The butterfly ballot

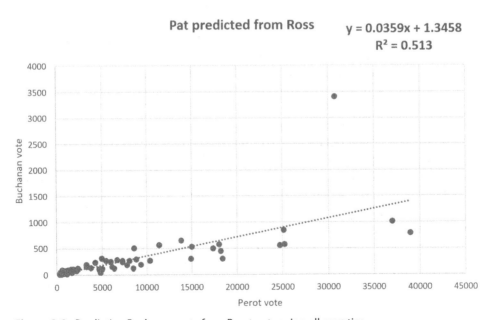

Figure 3.2: Predicting Buchanan vote from Perot vote using all counties

Pat predicted from Ross No Palm Beachy = 0.0244x + 45.842
$$R^2 = 0.8512$$

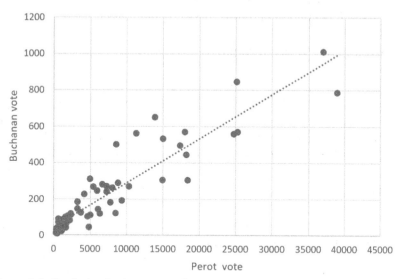

Figure 3.3: Predicting Buchanan vote from Perot vote omitting Palm Beach County

and now the Perot vote explains 85% of the variation in the non–Palm Beach County Buchanan votes. These two charts make it clear that Buchanan received many more votes than expected in Palm Beach County, and the layout of the butterfly ballot provides a plausible explanation for this anomaly.

A more sophisticated analysis was provided by Jonathan N. Wand et al. ("The Butterfly Did It". *American Political Science Review*, vol. 95, no. 4, December 2001, pages 793–809). Wand et al. looked at Palm Beach County absentee ballots. *These were not butterfly ballots, so confusion could not have caused voters to have mistakenly voted for Buchanan.* The authors found that Buchanan got 8.5 of 1,000 votes on Election Day but only 2.2 of 1,000 absentee votes. There were 387,356 Palm Beach County presidential votes cast on Election Day, so a reasonable guess would be that there were (.0085 − .0022) * 387,356 = 2,440 accidental Buchanan votes on Election Day.

The authors also looked at who voters chose for senator. There was no reason for confusion on the senatorial ballot. Ninety percent of absentee voters who voted for the Democratic senate candidate Bill Nelson voted for Gore. On Election Day, 10.2 of 1,000 Nelson voters voted for Buchanan, whereas in absentee ballots 1.7 of 1,000 Nelson voters voted for Buchanan. This indicates that around 8.5 of every 1,000 Nelson voters mistakenly voted for Buchanan. Nelson received 269,835 Election Day votes, so it is reasonable to estimate that (.0102 − .0017) * 269,835 * .9 = 2,064 voters intended to vote for Gore and were not recorded as Gore votes. These votes were far more than were needed to reverse the Florida vote and the entire presidential election! The fraction of voters who voted for the GOP senatorial candidate (Joel Deckard) on Election Day and absentee ballots showed no significant difference, so it does not appear that the butterfly ballot caused Bush to lose any votes. Therefore, it seems that Wand et al.'s conclusion that the "butterfly did it" is valid.

Salvanto also found that Duval County's strange ballot cost Gore around 2,600 more votes.

The astute reader might argue that the Palm Beach County absentee voters differed significantly from the Election Day Palm Beach County voters. Although the absentee voting population usually includes more military personnel, Wand et al. showed that the difference between the Election Day and absentee Buchanan votes in Palm Beach County was far more significant than the vote difference in any other county. This knocks out the objection that (with regard to their views on Buchanan) Palm Beach County absentee voters differed significantly from Palm Beach County Election Day voters.

It is important to note that, as we previously discussed, there was no legal reason to reverse most Palm Beach County and Duval County votes, so the *USA Today* conclusion that Bush should have legally been declared the winner but more people intended to vote for Gore, appears to be correct.

Excel Calculations

We now show you how we found the best fitting lines shown in Figure 3.2 and Figure 3.3.

How to Find the Best Fitting Line

To find the best fitting line that could be used to predict each county's 2000 Buchanan vote from each county's 1996 Perot vote, as shown in Figure 3.2, complete the following steps:

1. Put the data that goes on the x-axis to the left of the data that goes on the y-axis. Therefore, the Perot votes are placed in Column B and the Buchanan votes in Column C.

2. Select the range B1:C68 in the All Counties worksheet and from the Insert tab, choose the first Scatter chart option (Scatter).

3. Right-click any of the points and select Add Trendline.

4. Choose the Linear option and select Display R-squared Value On Chart and Display Equation On Chart to obtain the best fitting line, the equation of the line, and the R^2 value of 0.51. This shows that 51% of the variation in county Buchanan vote is explained by variation in the county Perot vote.

In the No Palm Beach worksheet, we deleted the Palm Beach data (in Row 51, not Area 51) from the data. Then we charted the range B1:C67 to obtain the least squares line predicting the variation in the county Buchanan vote from the variation in the county Perot vote. Since the Palm Beach data was inconsistent with the other county data, removing the Palm Beach data greatly increases the fraction of county variation in the Buchanan vote explained by the fraction in the county that voted for Perot.

Was Liverpool Over Barcelona the Greatest Upset in Sports History?

On May 7, 2019, Liverpool played Barcelona with a slim (most people thought nil) chance to make the Champions League Final. Having lost previously to Barcelona 3-0, Liverpool needed to win the match by at least four goals to advance. Amazingly, Liverpool won the match 4-0 and then went on to defeat Tottenham 2-0 in the Champions League Final. In this chapter, we will place this great upset in proper perspective relative to other great sports upsets.

How Should We Rank Upsets?

Let's rank upsets by the chance of the upset occurring. For each sporting event, we could try to build a sophisticated math model to predict the likelihood of the upset happening, but the bookmakers have done the work for us. Betting markets estimate the probability of an event happening. As we will see in Chapter 23 "How well does Vegas predict the outcome of sporting events?" betting markets usually create *unbiased forecasts*. For example, if the oddsmakers declare a team has a 90% chance to win a game, then on average, these 90% favorites win 90% of the time.

The odds on Liverpool advancing past Barcelona were 18-1 (www.fanduel .com/theduel/posts/liverpool-s-odds-to-advance-to-champions-league-final-over-fc-barcelona-were-astronomical-01daa13vzxn8). To understand how this implies a probability that Liverpool would advance, let's assume for the moment (we will later relax this assumption) that the oddsmakers set "fair odds" that yield on average a profit of 0 on a Liverpool bet. The odds of 18-1 mean that if you bet \$1 on Liverpool, then if they advance, you win \$18 and if Liverpool does not advance, you lose \$1. Let p = chance Liverpool advances. If (1 − p) * (−1) + p * 18 = 0, then a \$1 bet on Liverpool on average breaks even. Solving this equation yields p = 1 / (1 + 18) = 5.3%. In general, if the odds pay \$x if the event happens and −\$1 if the event does not happen, then the bet is fair if p = 1 / (1 + x). With this background, we will analyze the likelihood of other famous upsets. We will find, like Laura in the underrated musical *High Fidelity* (listen to www.youtube.com/watch?v=p4PJFFFbwog), that Liverpool doesn't even make the Top 5!

Leicester Wins the 2015–2016 Premier League

During the 2014–2015 Premier League soccer season, Leicester had a 13-game streak during which they did not win a game. Then in 2015–2016, Leicester stunned the soccer world by winning the Premier League. Before the 2015–2016 Premier League season, the "Money Line" for each team winning the Premier League is listed in the file `Leicester.xlsx`. See Figure 4.1 and www.sports insights.com/blog/2015-16-premier-league-title-odds/.

Team	Odds	Money Line Probability	True Prob
Chelsea	1850	0.0512821	0.04787938
Manchester City	-125	0.5555556	0.518693279
Manchester United	610	0.1408451	0.131499705
Arsenal	240	0.2941176	0.274602324
Liverpool	6500	0.0151515	0.01414618
Tottenham	15000	0.0066225	0.006183099
Everton	75000	0.0013316	0.001243206
Southampton	75000	0.0013316	0.001243206
Swansea City	150000	0.0006662	0.000622017
Stoke City	250000	0.0003998	0.00037331
Crystal Palace	100000	0.000999	0.000932715
West Ham United	100000	0.000999	0.000932715
Newcastle	750000	0.0001333	0.00012447
West Brom Albion	500000	0.0002	0.000186692
Aston Villa	750000	0.0001333	0.00012447
Leicester City	150000	0.0006662	0.000622017

Sum Money Line Probabilities: 1.07106758

https://www.sportsinsights.com/blog/2015-16-premier-league-title-odds/

Figure 4.1: 2015–2016 Premier League Odds

For all teams except Manchester City, the number in Column D is the number of dollars you'd win if you bet $100 on the team in Column C, and they won the Premier League. For example, if you'd bet $100 on Arsenal to win the Premier League and they won, you'd win $240; otherwise, you'd lose $100. If we let P = Probability that Arsenal wins the Premier League, then this is a fair bet if P * 240 + (1– P) * –100 = 0 or P = 100 / (100 + 240) = 29.4%.

For Manchester City (or any team with a negative number), you need to bet the absolute value of the negative number to win $100. Thus, you can bet $125 on Manchester City to win $100. If P = Probability that Manchester City wins the league, then this bet is fair if –125 * (1 – P) + 100 * P = 0 or P = 125 / (100 + 125) = 55.6%. Column E computes the probability of winning the league implied by the Money Line. The problem is that these probabilities add to 1.07, not 1. This ensures that the bookmakers will, on average, make a profit. In Column F we obtain "fair probabilities" implied by the Money Line by dividing the Column E probabilities by 1.07. From cell F22, we see that the oddsmakers' implied probability of Leicester winning the Premier League was 6 in 10,000—much smaller than Liverpool's implied chance of making it to the Champions League Final.

#16 Seed UMBC Beats #1 Seed Virginia

In the NCAA men's basketball tournament from 1985 to 2017, #16 seeds lost to #1 seeds in all 132 games between a #16 and a #1 seed. Then in 2018, #16 seed University of Maryland, Baltimore County (UMBC) Retrievers, shocked the basketball world by beating #1 seed Virginia Cavaliers. (Virginia rebounded from this stunning upset and won the 2019 championship.) On average, #16 seeds lost to #1 seeds by 25 points. The standard deviation of college basketball scores about the oddsmakers' prediction is 11 points. A normal random variable closely approximates the margin of victory in basketball games. Therefore, we can approximate the chance that a #16 seed loses to a #1 seed with the following formula:

```
=NORM.DIST(0,25,11,TRUE)
```

This yields 1.1%, a much smaller percentage than the probability of Liverpool advancing.

The Jets Win Super Bowl III

In 1969, Joe Namath promised that the upstart New York Jets would defeat the mighty Baltimore Colts in Super Bowl III. The Colts were 18-point favorites. The standard deviation of the margin in an NFL game about the point spread is 14 points, and the margin of victory is again approximated by a normal random variable. Therefore, the chance the Jets would win can be computed as 10% with the following formula:

```
=NORM.DIST(0,18,14,TRUE)
```

Other Big Upsets

A great article in the *Atlantic Monthly* (`www.theatlantic.com/entertainment/archive/2016/05/leicester-city-premier-league/480918/`) gave the following odds on some great upsets:

- Buster Douglas was a 42-1 underdog when he beat Mike Tyson in 1990.
- In 2017 you could get 2,000-1 odds that Elvis was still alive.
- The 1969 New York Mets were 100-1 shots to win the World Series.
- The 1980 U.S. Hockey Team was 1,000-1 to win the Olympic Gold Medal. (Do you believe in miracles?)
- Rulon Gardner was a 2,000-1 underdog to defeat Russian Alexander Karelin in the 2000 Olympic Greco-Roman wrestling competition.

Again, not to diminish Liverpool's great upset, but it was not as unlikely as many other amazing sports upsets.

How Did Bernie Madoff Keep His Fund Going?

A *Ponzi scheme* is a form of fraud in which the fraudster promises a higher-than-average level of returns with low risk. Investors are attracted by this no-risk, get-rich-fast promise and quickly deposit funds. Then more and more people deposit funds. When early investors want to withdraw some of their money (from real deposits and/or fake profits), the fraudster uses deposits by later investors to give the earlier investors their money. As we will soon show, things can run smoothly until the withdrawal demands suddenly increase. Bernie Madoff's investment fund turned out to be a Ponzi scheme. The original Ponzi scheme was created by Charles Ponzi in 1920. Ponzi promised a 50% return in 45 days or a 100% return in 90 days. The purported profits were to be obtained by buying "postal reply coupons" in foreign countries and redeeming them for a profit in the United States. The problem was that to earn the promised profits, Ponzi needed 160 million postal reply coupons when only 27,000 existed! By the end of 1920, Ponzi's scheme had collapsed, and he pleaded guilty to mail fraud.

Bernie Madoff's investment fund also turned out to be a giant Ponzi scheme. Investors put in $18 billion, and when Madoff was arrested in December 2008, the fund on paper was worth $65 billion. Amazingly, as of this writing it appears that the original $18 billion deposited with Madoff will be recovered. In this chapter we will explore the following issues:

- The mathematics of Ponzi schemes.

- How Harry Markopolos (watch the 60 Minutes segment www.youtube .com/watch?v=s68FR1MXT8Q) or read Harry's great book (*No One Would Listen*, Wiley, 1999) spotted Madoff as a fraud in 1999, and reported the fraud to the Securities and Exchange Commission (SEC). Markopolos watched in horror as the SEC ignored his warnings.

- How the mathematics of Benford's law indicated Madoff's returns were "made up."

- Why Madoff's purported investment strategy could not have been real.

- How the widely used risk adjusted return concept of the *Sharpe ratio* indicated that Madoff's fund was a fraud.

The Mathematics of Ponzi Schemes

The file Ponzi.xlsx (see Figure 5.1) contains a simple model of a Ponzi scheme. We make the following assumptions:

- At the beginning of each of years 1–15, our fund gets 1,000 new investors who each deposit $10,000. No customers ever leave the fund.

- We entice investors by always reporting an annual rate of return of 10%, but we simply invest our money in T-bills that always return 3%.

- During years 1–5, customers withdraw 12% of the amount they "think" their account is worth.

- In year 16, the economy tanks and panic ensues, causing investors to ask to withdraw 55% of what they think their account is worth.

As you can see from cell I27, at the end of year 16, the fund has negative cash and is out of business. This is because the fund does not have enough money to cover the unexpectedly large year 16 withdrawals. The "Excel Calculations" section later in this chapter explains the spreadsheet's logic.

	B	C	D	E	F	G	H	I
2	Ponzi							
3	initial cash	$1,000,000.00						
4	newcustomers	1000						
5	deposit	$10,000.00						
6	promisedreturn	10.00%						
7	actualreturn	3.00%						
8	fractionwithdrawn	0.12						
9	panic fraction	0.55						
10	initial cash	$100,000.00						
11	Year	Start customers	New customers	End Customers	Start cash	Payout	Liability	End Cash
12	1	0	1000	1000	$100,000.00	$0.00	$10,000,000.00	$10,100,000.00
13	2	1000	1000	2000	$10,403,000.00	$1,200,000.00	$19,680,000.00	$19,203,000.00
14	3	2000	1000	3000	$19,779,090.00	$2,361,600.00	$29,050,240.00	$27,417,490.00
15	4	3000	1000	4000	$28,240,014.70	$3,486,028.80	$38,120,632.32	$34,753,985.90
16	5	4000	1000	5000	$35,796,605.48	$4,574,475.88	$46,900,772.09	$41,222,129.60
17	6	5000	1000	6000	$42,458,793.49	$5,628,092.65	$55,399,947.38	$46,830,700.84
18	7	6000	1000	7000	$48,235,621.86	$6,647,993.69	$63,627,149.06	$51,587,628.18
19	8	7000	1000	8000	$53,135,257.02	$7,635,257.89	$71,591,080.29	$55,499,999.13
20	9	8000	1000	9000	$57,164,999.11	$8,590,929.64	$79,300,165.72	$58,574,069.47
21	10	9000	1000	10000	$60,331,291.56	$9,516,019.89	$86,762,560.42	$60,815,271.67
22	11	10000	1000	11000	$62,639,729.82	$10,411,507.25	$93,986,158.49	$62,228,222.57
23	12	11000	1000	12000	$64,095,069.25	$11,278,339.02	$100,978,601.42	$62,816,730.23
24	13	12000	1000	13000	$64,701,232.13	$12,117,432.17	$107,747,286.17	$62,583,799.97
25	14	13000	1000	14000	$64,461,313.96	$12,929,674.34	$114,299,373.01	$61,531,639.62
26	15	14000	1000	15000	$63,377,588.81	$13,715,924.76	$120,641,793.08	$59,661,664.05
27	16	15000	0	15000	$61,451,513.97	$66,352,986.19	$59,717,687.57	-$4,901,472.22

Figure 5.1: Ponzi scheme model

Madoff's Purported Strategy

The monthly returns reported by Madoff averaged 10% per year, with the worst month incurring a small loss of 0.64%. Harry Markopolos realized that having no significant negative monthly returns was unrealistic. (Refer to the file `NewMadoff.xlsx`.) After describing how call and put options work, we will explain the strategy that Madoff said he used to create his amazingly large, low-risk monthly returns.

Call and Put Options

Suppose a stock today sells for $30. Consider a six-month European *call option* on the stock with an exercise price of $33. The payoff from this call option is based solely on the value of the stock at the expiration date (in six months) of the option. The option is worthless if the index in six months is at $33 or less. Every dollar the price at expiration exceeds $33 results in a $1 call payout. So, if the stock sells for $34, the call pays $1; if the stock sells for $35, the stock sells for $2, and so on. For a stock of average risk, the famous *Black–Scholes* option pricing formula gives $0.87 as a fair price. This $0.87 price allows you to make a lot of money if the stock price increases by more than 10%, but otherwise you receive nothing.

The Black–Scholes option pricing model was developed in 1968 by Fischer Black and Myron Scholes. They developed a formula that computes a fair price for an option based on the following inputs:

- Current stock price
- Exercise price
- Duration of option
- Current interest rate on treasury bills (T-bills)
- Percentage *volatility* or risk associated with the stock

If you're interested in learning more about option pricing, check out John Hull's classic text (*Options, Futures, and Other Derivatives*, Pearson, 2018).

Suppose a stock today sells for $30. Consider a six-month European *put option* on the stock with an exercise price of $27. The payoff from this put option is based solely on the value of the index at the expiration date (in six months) of the option. The option is worthless if the stock in six months is at $27 or more. Every dollar that the price at expiration is less than $27 results in a $1 put payout. So, if the stock sells for $26, the put pays $1; if the stock sells for $25, the put pays $2, and so on. For a stock of average risk, the Black–Scholes option pricing formula gives $0.39 as a fair price. This $0.39 price allows you to make a lot of money if the stock price decreases more than 10%, but otherwise you receive nothing.

Madoff's Split-Strike Strategy

An important reason why Madoff continued to pull in new investors was that his strategy seemed like a reasonable method to gain fairly high returns with much lower risk than the market. As you will see, Madoff's Split-Strike strategy required buying puts and calls. As Markopolos and others (Carole Bernard and Phelim Boyle, "Mr. Madoff's Amazing Returns: An Analysis of the Split-Strike Conversion Strategy, *Journal of Derivatives*, vol. 17, no. 1, 2009, pages 62–76) discovered, a successful execution of Madoff's strategy would require more options than existed!

Here is a brief explanation of Madoff's Split-Strike strategy:

- Buy a basket of around 30 "high-performing stocks" that are highly correlated with the market. For simplicity, assume all stocks purchased sell for $30.
- Sell a lot of out of the money calls on your stocks (say, exercise price = $33). Unless the market goes up a lot, you keep the price of these calls. If

the market goes up a lot, your stocks make a lot of money, and you are happy. This part of the strategy generates return if the market does not move much.

- Buy a lot of out of the money puts (say, exercise price = $27). These puts don't cost that much, and if stocks crash, the puts will greatly cushion your downside risk.

If enough puts and calls could be bought to carry out this strategy and Madoff was a good stock picker, then he would have greatly lessened market risk and generated high-average, low-risk returns similar to those he reported. It is unconscionable that the SEC ignored Markopolos's valid critique of Madoff's strategy.

The Sharpe Ratio Proves Madoff Was a Fraud

Suppose that you are running an investment firm and want to determine each trader's end-of-the-year bonus. Would you give the largest bonus to the trader who had the highest average monthly return? If you do, you are ignoring the possibility that this trader generated their high average return by taking on lots of risk. If so, it is likely that this trader will eventually bring down the firm. Read Nassim Taleb's great book *Fooled by Randomness* (Random House, 2005), and you will see how taking on lots of risk is a good idea until it isn't.

Many investing firms evaluate traders based on the *Sharpe ratio*. The Sharpe ratio is:

(Average Annual Return – Risk Free Return) / (Standard Deviation of AnnualReturn)

Essentially, the Sharpe ratio measures the average annual excess return per unit of risk. As pointed out on www.marginofsaving.com/whats-your-sharpe-ratio/, a long-term Sharpe ratio above 2 is fantastic. The website www.investmentnews.com/gallery/20180801/FREE/801009999/PH/10-funds-with-the-greatest-sharpe-ratios&Params=Itemnr=11 claims that the PSGAX's fund had the best Sharpe ratio (1.76) for the short period, June 2017–June 2018.

As you will soon see, over 1990–2008, Madoff's reported returns yielded an amazing Sharpe ratio of 2.51. This amazing reported risk-adjusted performance was another factor that aroused Markopolos's suspicions.

To compute Madoff's annualized Sharpe ratio, we compute:

- Annual Mean Return = 12*Monthly Average Return = 10.1%
- Annual Standard Deviation = Sqrt(12) * Monthly Standard Deviation = 2.45%
- Annual T-Bill Return 1990–2008 = 3.95%.

Then Madoff's Sharpe ratio is computed as (.101 − .0395) / (.0245) = 2.51.

Benford's Law and Madoff's Fraud

What fraction of the populations of world countries do you think begin with a first digit of 1–4? A number can begin with any of the nine digits 1–9. If you assume that each first digit is equally likely, then 4 / 9 = 44% of all country populations should begin with 1–4. Actually (see file `CountryPop.xlsx` and Figure 5.2), 69% of country populations begin with a first digit of 1–4. This is an example of Benford's law, which states that for many sets of real-world numbers the chance that the first digit is less than or equal to x (see Figure 5.2) is approximately given by $Log_{10}(x + 1)$. Then the chance the first digit is 1 is approximately $Log_{10}(2) = 30.1\%$. Note the amazing agreement between Benford's law prediction and the actual fraction of country populations having each first digit.

	G	H	I	J	K
2	First	Fraction	Theoretical	Cumulative Theory	
3	1	30.04%	30.10%	30.10%	=LOG10(G3+1)
4	2	15.88%	17.61%	47.71%	=LOG10(G4+1)
5	3	11.16%	12.49%	60.21%	=LOG10(G5+1)
6	4	11.59%	9.69%	69.90%	=LOG10(G6+1)
7	5	9.87%	7.92%	77.82%	=LOG10(G7+1)
8	6	6.87%	6.69%	84.51%	=LOG10(G8+1)
9	7	3.43%	5.80%	90.31%	=LOG10(G9+1)
10	8	6.01%	5.12%	95.42%	=LOG10(G10+1)
11	9	5.15%	4.58%	100.00%	=LOG10(G11+1)

Figure 5.2: Benford's law for country populations

The file `BenfordSim.xlsx` will help you understand why Benford's law holds for many real-world data sets. Many quantities (such as population and a company's sales revenue) grow by a similar percentage (say, 10%) each year. If this is the case, and the first digit is a 1, it may take several years to get to a first digit of 2. If your first digit is 8 or 9, however, growing at 10% will quickly send you back to a first digit of 1. This explains why smaller first digits are more likely than larger first digits.

In the file `BenfordSim.xlsx`, pressing the F9 key will place a random integer between 1 and 9,000,000 in cell K2 as the starting value for, say, Sales Revenue and will place a random annual growth percentage between 1% and 50% in cell K3. Then, based on these two numbers, Column C generates 500 years of revenue. Finally, Columns I and J compare the theoretical fraction for each first digit to the simulated fraction. You will see that, whenever you press F9, the simulated and theoretical fractions are virtually identical!

In the file `NewMadoff.xlsx`, we multiplied each of Madoff's monthly returns by 10,000 to ensure that each monthly return had a first digit. As shown in

Figure 5.3, we used a PivotTable (see the "Excel Calculations" section) to determine the fraction of monthly returns beginning with each first digit.

	L	M	N
2			
3	Row Labels	Count of First Digit	Percentages
4	0	1	0.47%
5	1	84	39.07%
6	2	29	13.49%
7	3	20	9.30%
8	4	13	6.05%
9	5	11	5.12%
10	6	17	7.91%
11	7	14	6.51%
12	8	15	6.98%
13	9	11	5.12%
14	Grand Total	215	100.00%

Figure 5.3: Benford's law and Madoff returns

Note that 84 of 215 monthly returns (39%) have a first digit of 1. Is this significantly more than the Benford's law theoretical 30% percentage? Here, we need to know the mean and standard deviation of the number of successes, given

- N = number of observations
- P = fraction of successes (a success = first digit of 1)

In this situation, the Mean Number of Successes = N * P and the Standard Deviation of Successes = SQRT(N * P * (1 – P).

Therefore, Benford's law predicts an average of .30 * 215 = 64.5 first digits of 1 with a standard deviation of SQRT(215 * .3 * (1 – .3)) = 6.7.

We observed 84 successes, which corresponds to a Z-score of

$$(84 - 64.5) / 6.7 = 2.91$$

This indicates that substantially more first digits of Madoff returns are 1 than Benford's law predicts. This is yet another indication of "made-up" or fraudulent reporting of returns.

Excel Calculations

In this section we explain the logic of the `Ponzi.xlsx` spreadsheet, how we applied Benford's law to country populations in the workbook `Countrypop.xlsx`, the intuition behind Benford's law shown in the workbook `BenfordSim.xlsx`, and our calculations in the worksheet returns of the workbook `NewMadoff.xlsx` that were used to show that Madoff was a fraud.

Logic of the Ponzi Scheme Spreadsheet

We now explain the logic of the `Ponzi.xlsx` spreadsheet, which shows how a Ponzi scheme can collapse:

1. In Column C, we compute Start Year t Customers = End Year t – 1 Customers.

2. In Column D for years 1–15, we enter the same number of new customers.

3. In Column E, we compute End Year t Customers = Start Year t Customers + New Year t Customers. We are assuming that no customers leave the fund.

4. In Column F, we compute Year t + 1 Start Cash = (1 + actual return) * Year t End Cash.

5. In Column G, we compute Year t Payout = (Year t – 1 Liability) * Fraction Withdrawn.

6. In Column H, we compute Year t Liability = (Year t New customers) * (Deposit per customer) + (Year t –1 Liability – Year t Payout)*(1 + Promised Return).

7. In Column I, we compute Year t End Cash = (Deposit) * (Year t New Customers) + Year t Start Cash – Year t Payout.

8. In year 16, we change the withdrawal rate to 55%, and we see that at the end of year 16 the fund is out of money!

Benford's Law and Country Populations

We now explain how in the file `CountryPop.xlsx` we showed that country populations closely follow Benford's law:

1. Copying from D2 to D2:D234 the formula =VALUE(LEFT(C2,1)) extracts the first digit of each country's population.

2. Copying from H3 to H4:H12 the formula =COUNTIF($D$2:$D$234,G3)/$G$14 computes the fraction of country population whose first digit starts with 1–9.

3. Copying from J3 to J4:J12 the formula =LOG10(G3+1) computes $Log_{10}(2)$, $Log_{10}(3)$, . . . $Log_{10}(10)$. This gives the theoretical percentage of first digits, which Benford's law states should be < = 1, < 2, . . .< = 9.

4. The theoretical percentage of first digits that should begin with 2–9 is computed by copying from J4 to J5:J12 the formula =LOG10(G3+1).

Intuition Behind Benford's Law

In the workbook BenfordSim.xlsx (sim is short for simulation), we demonstrate how Benford's law arises when a company starts with a random revenue and its annual revenue grows for 500 years at a random percentage rate:

1. In cell K2 the formula =RANDBETWEEN(1,9000000) generates a year 1 revenue equally likely to be any integer between 1 and 9 million.

2. In cell K3 the formula =RANDBETWEEN(1,50)/100 generates an annual growth rate in revenue that is equally likely to be anywhere between 1% and 50%.

3. Cell C4 simply copies the first-year revenue from cell K2.

4. Copying from C5 to C6:C503 the formula =C4*(1+growth) generates revenues for years 2–500.

5. Copying from D4 to D5:D503 the formula =VALUE(LEFT(C4,1)) extracts the first digit of each year's revenue.

6. Copying from I7 to I8:I16 the formula =COUNTIF(First __ Digit,H7)/500 computes the fraction of years whose revenue begin with 1–9. Note the amazingly close agreement with Benford's Law.

Benford's Law and Madoff's Return

We now explain how we determined in the worksheet returns of the workbook NewMadoff.xlsx the nonconformity of Madoff's reported monthly returns with Benford's law:

1. To find the first digit of each month's returns, we begin in Column F by multiplying the monthly returns in Column E by 10,000.

2. In Column G, copying the formula =VALUE(CLEAN(LEFT(F3,1))) from G3 to G4:G217 extracts the first digit for each month. The CLEAN function removes spaces and invisible characters. The LEFT function extracts the first digit from Column F, and the VALUE function converts text to a number.

3. After selecting the range G2:G217, we select PivotTable from the Insert tab and choose cell L3 as the upper-left corner of the PivotTable. Then, we drag First Digit to the Rows field area and drag First Digit twice to the Values area. With the cursor in Column M and then Column N of the PivotTable, we right-click and select Summarize Values By and change Sum to Count.

4. Finally, with the cursor in Column N, we right-click and select Show Values As and choose % Of Column Total. Now we see the number and percentage of months beginning with each possible first digit.

CHAPTER 6

Is the Lot of the American Worker Improving?

Many political observers believe that Donald Trump won the 2016 election in large part because the lot of the "average" American worker was not improving. America has been built on the view that your children will be better off than you were. It is important to be able to determine whether the lot of the typical American is improving. As discussed in Chapter 1, "Preliminaries," the typical value for a highly skewed data set is the median rather than the mean. In this chapter, we will use data from FRED (Federal Reserve of St. Louis website, `fred.stlouisfed.org`) to examine trends in the well-being of the American worker.

Is U.S. Family Income Skewed?

The data for each U.S. family's income is not available, so I cannot exactly determine the skewness of family income. I did, however, find the salaries of 2019 Major League Baseball players (see the file `BaseballSalaries2019.xlsx`). The salaries exhibit high positive skewness (skewness = 2.21). Therefore, we should use the median salary of $1.4 million as a measure of a typical salary. The mean salary of $4.5 million is more than triple the median! The top 4% of the players make 23% of the money, and this causes the highly paid players to greatly distort the mean salary. Since the U.S. government emphasizes median income, we will use median household income (adjusted for cost of living) as our primary measure of economic well-being.

Median Income and Politics

Whether you agree with Ronald Reagan's politics or not (C-SPAN ranks Reagan as our 9th best president), he had a way with phrases. "Mr. Gorbachev, tear down this wall" will live forever in history. In my opinion, Reagan won the 2000 election against Jimmy Carter when in a presidential debate, he asked the voters, "Are you better off than you were four years ago?" The economy performed poorly under Carter, and Reagan won. As shown in Table 6.1, median family income adjusted for the cost of living tells the story.

Table 6.1: Real household median income 1977–1980

YEAR	MEDIAN INCOME IN 2017 DOLLARS
1977	$59,153
1978	$60,997
1979	$61,863
1980	$59,711

Table 6.1 shows that between 1978 and 1980 the purchasing power of the typical (50th percentile) household dropped 2%.

In January 2012, at the Republican presidential debate, Mitt Romney decried the state of the U.S. economy by claiming that during the last four years median income dropped 10%. Table 6.2 contains relevant information to fact-check Romney's claim.

Table 6.2: Median income 2007–2012

YEAR	MEDIAN INCOME IN 2017 DOLLARS
2007	$72,716
2008	$70,215
2012	$66,515

We see that from 2007 to 2012, median income dropped 9%, and from 2008 to 2012, median income dropped 6%.

Are the Rich Getting Richer?

Beginning with Thomas Piketty's best-selling book *Capital in the 21st Century* (Belknap Press, 2017), increasing income inequality in the United States (and other countries) has come under increased scrutiny. Using U.S. Census data, we can look at recent trends in U.S. income inequality with a simple chart that shows the trend in the share of U.S. income that is earned by the top 5%, top 20%, middle 40%, and bottom 20%. Figure 6.1 summarizes these trends (see also the `IncomeShare.xlsx` workbook and the "Excel Calculations" section at the end of this chapter).

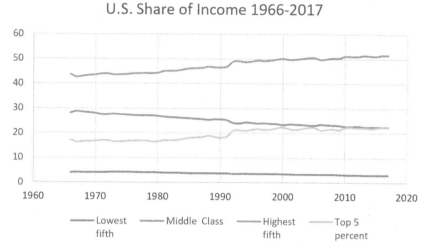

Figure 6.1: Trends in U.S. income inequality

This chart shows us so much more than gazing at the sea of numbers in the file `IncomeShare.xlsx`:

- The bottom 20%'s share of income has stayed steady at 3%.
- The middle 40% of the population's share of income has dropped from 28% to 22%, which essentially is the same as the current share of income earned by the top 5%.
- The top 20% of the population now earns over half the income. (The gains coming mainly at the expense of the "vanishing" middle class.)

In Chapter 7, we will discuss three other measures of income inequality: the Gini index, the Palm index, and the Atkinson index.

In the 2020 Democratic debates, claims of increased inequality were brought up in every debate, with most of the candidates advocating a wealth tax or more progressive income tax as a measure to reduce America's increased income inequality.

Causes of Increasing U.S. Income Inequality

Disentangling the many causes of the increase in U.S. income inequality is difficult. We recommend Timothy Noah's excellent book *The Great Divergence* (Bloomsbury Press, 2012) as a primer on this subject. This section gives a brief discussion of commonly cited causes of increased U.S. income inequality.

The Winner-Take-All Society

Robert Frank and Philip Cook (*The Winner-Take-All Society*, Penguin Books, 1996) were the first to popularize the idea of winner-take-all markets. The idea is that a product (or a person like a CEO) can just be a little bit better than their competitors and still earn a lot more money than their competitors. For an example of the winner-take-all nature of American society (see www.theguardian.com/business/2018/aug/16/ceo-versus-worker-wage-american-companies-pay-gap-study-2018), look at the trend in the ratio of CEO pay to median worker pay. In 1965, this ratio was 20:1; in 1989, the ratio was 58:1; in 2000, the ratio was 344:1, and in 2017, 312:1.

The Education Premium

It is well known that college graduates with a bachelor's degree earn on average more money than high school grads and that holders of advanced degrees earn, on average more than grads with only a bachelor's degree. These differences are known as the *education premium*. According to the Hamilton Project (www.hamiltonproject.org/charts/the_education_wage_premium_contributes_to_wage_inequality) in 1979, bachelor's degrees earned a 35% premium over high school grads and advanced degree holders earned a premium of 53% over high schools grads. By 2016, the bachelor's degree premium had nearly doubled to 68%, and the advanced degree premium had more than doubled to 113%. Noah (2012) argues that these increases in the education premium are driven by the fact that demand for college and advanced degree grads is increasing faster than supply. It is clear that this increase in the educational premium would increase the fraction of income earned by the top 10%. In fact, the fraction of the people in the top 20% on income with a college degree doubled between 1979 and 2016. Claudia Golden and Lawrence Katz (www.nber.org/papers/w12984) conclude that 60% of the increase in income inequality between 1973 and 2005 is due to the education premium.

Increased Trade

The populist movement in the United States and other developed nations has been largely driven by the belief that globalization and increased trade with underdeveloped countries has increased income inequality. You can find articles that support and oppose this view. We will focus on the work of Andoni and Yusuf Barusman ("The Impact of International Trade on Income Inequality in the United States since 1970's," *European Research Studies Journal*, vol. 20, issue 4A, 2017, pages 35–50). The authors refer to the famous Stolper-Samuelson (SS) theorem (see `en.wikipedia.org/wiki/Stolper%E2%80%93Samuelson_theorem`). Consider a country with two factors of production (say, capital and labor). The SS theorem implies that the factor of production that is relatively scarce will lose in trade, whereas the factor of production that is relatively abundant will gain in trade. Compared to China, for example, the United States is abundant in capital and scarce in labor, so SS implies that capital (more associated with top-income people) will gain relative to labor (more associated with lower- and middle-income people). The authors' complex analysis shows that even after adjusting for government expenditures and inflation, an increase in the ratio of imports to GNP (gross national product) significantly increases inequality. Their work shows there is less than a 2 in 10,000 chance that an increase in the import/GNP ratio does not increase income inequality.

In my opinion, this conclusion is eminently reasonable. More dependence on imports may lower the costs of products to most of the population, but many middle-class workers will lose their jobs to lower-paid workers overseas. I can speak only for my "small town" of Bloomington, Indiana. In the 1970s, we had large GE, Otis Elevator, Westinghouse, Ford Component, and RCA plants. Workers at these plants were certainly in the middle class (or higher). Now all these companies have moved to Mexico or Asia.

Tax Policy

The United States has a progressive tax rate structure. Before the new tax law was passed in 2018, the top marginal tax rate was 39.6%, and some workers received money back from the government from the Earned Income Tax credit. You would expect that this progressive tax structure would mitigate income inequality. According to `www.taxpolicycenter.org/briefing-book/how-do-taxes-affect-income-inequality`, in 2018 the top 20% of people had 52% of the total before-tax income. After taxes, the top 20% income still had 49% of the income, so it does not appear that our current tax structure does much to lessen inequality.

Share Buybacks

In 2018 (`www.cnbc.com/2018/12/18/stock-buybacks-hit-a-record-1point1-trillion-and-the-years-not-over.html`), companies (partially motivated by the new tax law) spent $1.1 trillion buying back their stock. This reduces the number of outstanding shares and therefore increases earnings per share and drives up stock prices. Since the richest 10% of Americans own 84% of the stocks (`money.cnn.com/2018/03/05/investing/stock-buybacks-inequality-tax-law/index.html`), it seems that share buybacks will increase income inequality. For a defense of share buybacks, check out `hbr.org/2018/03/are-buybacks-really-shortchanging-investment`.

Money Isn't Everything: The Human Development Index

We have all heard versions of the quote "Money isn't everything" or "Money can't buy happiness." The Human Development Index (HDI) is an attempt to measure the quality of life in a country based primarily on three attributes (see `hdr.undp.org/en/content/human-development-index-hdi` for a full discussion of the computation of a nation's HDI):

- Life expectancy
- Education
- Economic well-being

When measuring any quantity (like a nation's well-being) that depends on multiple attributes, a key question is how you weigh the different attributes. We refer you to `hdr.undp.org/sites/default/files/hdr2018_technical_notes.pdf` for a discussion of this complex issue.

In the worksheet named Selected in the workbook `HumanDevelopmentIndex.xlsx`, we summarize the trend in HDI for 1980–2017 for eight countries (see Figure 6.2).

The HDI is always between 0 and 1. The great improvement in China's and India's HDI (well over 2 billion people!) is extremely gratifying. I am also surprised that despite two wars, Iraq's HDI has substantially increased.

Create Your Own Ranking of Well-Being

Everybody has a different opinion of the relative importance of different attributes to a country's well-being. So why not create a website that allows the user to define the relative importance of the following attributes and then rank countries based on the user-defined weights?

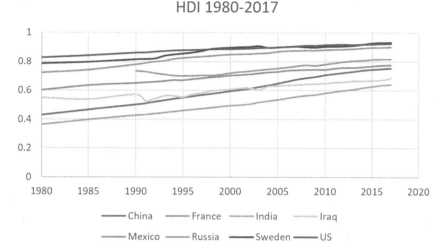

Figure 6.2: HDI indices 1980–2017

- Housing
- Income
- Jobs
- Community
- Education
- Environment
- Civic engagement
- Health
- Life satisfaction
- Safety
- Work-life balance

Fortunately, the Organisation for Economic Co-operation and Development (OECD) has created such a website: www.oecdbetterlifeindex.org/#/23232213222.

Based on the relative weights that I defined (see Figure 6.3), the top five countries were Norway, Iceland, Switzerland, Australia, and Canada, with the United States ranking 8th.

Are Other Countries Catching Up to the U.S.?

Hall of Fame pitcher Leroy "Satchel" Paige once said, "Don't look back, something might be gaining on you." If we look back at past mean incomes

Figure 6.3: Attribute ranks for ranking countries

(I could not find past median incomes) in different countries, as shown in the file MeanIncomeByCountry.xlsx (data.worldbank.org/indicator/NY.ADJ.NNTY .PC.KD) and Figure 6.4, we are given the ratio of mean per capita income in 2010 dollars for countries divided by U.S. mean income over the period 1995–2017. Most notably from this figure, we see that since 1995 China has quadrupled their per capita income from 3% to 12% of U.S. mean income, whereas India and Russia have doubled their per capita income relative to the United States.

	A	B	C	D	E	F	G
15	Country Name	1995	2000	2005	2010	2015	2017
16	Brazil	22.86%	18.55%	18.61%	22.82%	21.28%	20.15%
17	China	2.69%	3.31%	5.01%	8.46%	10.67%	11.78%
18	Germany	91.06%	81.80%	79.45%	85.72%	84.91%	86.16%
19	India	1.73%	1.76%	2.10%	2.87%	3.31%	3.59%
20	Japan	104.02%	89.98%	87.75%	85.76%	83.80%	84.52%
21	Qatar			76.70%	102.33%	94.51%	92.00%
22	Russian Federation	8.11%	11.84%	16.28%	20.60%	19.53%	18.85%
23	Sweden	104.10%	100.55%	103.25%	109.28%	103.14%	103.04%

Figure 6-4: Ratio of national mean incomes to U.S.

Excel Calculations

We created Figure 6.1 and Figure 6.2 with a simple scatter chart. For example, to create Figure 6.1, perform the following steps:

1. Select the range E6:I58 from the workbook IncomeShare.xlsx.

2. From the Insert tab, select the Insert Scatter (X, Y) option and then choose the third option (Scatter With Smooth Lines).

3. If you want to change a chart's type, right-click the chart, select Change Chart Type, and then select your desired chart.

Measuring Income Inequality with the Gini, Palm, and Atkinson Indices

Increased income inequality is known to be correlated with increased crime (see `siteresources.worldbank.org/DEC/Resources/Crime%26Inequality.pdf`) and increased poverty (see `www.odi.org/sites/odi.org.uk/files/odi-assets/publications-opinion-files/3876.pdf`). Part of human nature is the desire to boil down a complex concept like inequality to a single number. In this chapter, we will discuss three widely measures of income inequality—the Gini index, the Palm index, and the Atkinson index—that facilitate easy comparison between the degree of inequality between countries.

The Gini Index

In 1912, Italian statistician Corrado Gini developed the *Gini index* for use in measuring the degree of inequality in a country's income distribution. To explain the calculation of the Gini index, we will assume all countries consist of 20 people. As a benchmark, we consider a country (named Equal) with complete income equality in which each resident has an annual income of 5 units. As shown in the worksheet named Typical in the workbook `GiniTheory.xlsx` (see Figure 7.1), consider another country (named Unequal) in which the income of individual n is proportional to n and we normalize the incomes to add up to 100. For example, Individual 1 has an income of .48, Individual 2 an income of .95, . . . Individual 20 has an income of 9.52. As shown in our example, computation of the Gini index requires the individual incomes to be listed in ascending order.

	C	D	E	F	G	H	I
1						Gini	Area Under
2						0.26666667	0.3666667
3							
4		Person	Equal	Unequal	Cumulative Equal	Cumulative Unequal	Area Under Orange
5	1	0.05	5	0.48	5.00%	0.48%	0.000
6	2	0.1	5	0.95	10.00%	1.43%	0.001
7	3	0.15	5	1.43	15.00%	2.86%	0.001
8	4	0.2	5	1.90	20.00%	4.76%	0.002
9	5	0.25	5	2.38	25.00%	7.14%	0.004
10	6	0.3	5	2.86	30.00%	10.00%	0.005
11	7	0.35	5	3.33	35.00%	13.33%	0.007
12	8	0.4	5	3.81	40.00%	17.14%	0.009
13	9	0.45	5	4.29	45.00%	21.43%	0.011
14	10	0.5	5	4.76	50.00%	26.19%	0.013
15	11	0.55	5	5.24	55.00%	31.43%	0.016
16	12	0.6	5	5.71	60.00%	37.14%	0.019
17	13	0.65	5	6.19	65.00%	43.33%	0.022
18	14	0.7	5	6.67	70.00%	50.00%	0.025
19	15	0.75	5	7.14	75.00%	57.14%	0.029
20	16	0.8	5	7.62	80.00%	64.76%	0.032
21	17	0.85	5	8.10	85.00%	72.86%	0.036
22	18	0.9	5	8.57	90.00%	81.43%	0.041
23	19	0.95	5	9.05	95.00%	90.48%	0.045
24	20	1	5	9.52	100.00%	100.00%	0.050

Figure 7.1: Data for computing the Gini index

In columns G and H, we compute for each country the cumulative income for individuals 1, 2, . . . n. For example, the first 10 individuals in Equal have a cumulative income of 50%, whereas the first 10 individuals in Unequal have a cumulative income of only 26.19%. To compute the Gini index, we create a graph (see Figure 7.2) in which the x-axis represents the cumulative fraction of the population (for n = 1, 5%; n = 2, 10%; etc.), and the y-axis represents for each country the cumulative fraction of income earned by individuals 1 through n.

In Figure 7.3, we created an analogous chart for the country of Plutocracy having complete inequality: 19 people with zero income and 1 person with 100 units of income. The curves representing the income distribution in the countries Unequal and Plutocracy are called *Lorenz curves*. Looking at Figures 7.2 and 7.3, we see that for Plutocracy there is a much larger area between the 45-degree line representing complete income equality and the Lorenz curve than there is in the country Unequal. Motivated by this observation, Gini defined the Gini index to equal the area between the 45-degree line and the Lorenz curve as a fraction of the total area (0.5) below the 45-degree line. If Excel had drawn Figure 7.3 properly, the orange curve would have been 0 for x less than one and then suddenly jumped up to one. Then the area between the Lorenz curve and the 45-degree line would have been .5, and the Gini index for Plutocracy would equal one. For the country Equal, the area between the 45-degree line and the Lorenz curve is 0 because they are the same. Therefore, we see the Gini index will always be between 0 and 1, with a larger Gini index indicating more inequality. Calculations in the worksheet Typical show that the area under the Lorenz curve for the country Unequal is approximately 0.367. Therefore, the area between the Lorenz curve and the 45-degree line is 0.5 – 0.367 = 0.133, and the Gini index for country Unequal is 0.133 / .5 = 0.267.

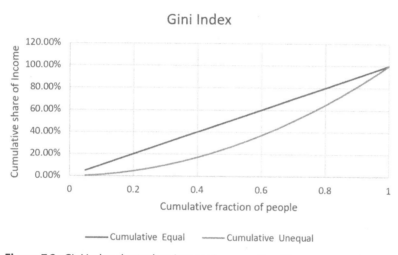

Figure 7.2: Gini index chart when income is proportional to n

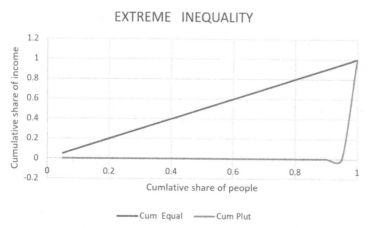

Figure 7.3: Gini index chart with complete inequality

Figure 7.4 shows the 2020 Gini Indices for selected countries see https:// worldpopulationreview.com/countries/gini-coefficient-by-country/. We see that South Africa has the largest Gini Index and Slovenia and Slovakia have the smallest Gini Indices. We note that the US Gini Index has increased from 0.405 in 2004 to 0.48 in 2020.

Figure 7.4: 2020 Gini indices

The Palma Index

The Gini index is the most widely used measure of income inequality, but it has several shortcomings (see `www.hsrc.ac.za/en/review/hsrc-review-november-2014/ limitations-of-gini-index`), including the following:

- ▪ It is too sensitive to changes in middle income, rather than those with very high or low incomes.

- ▪ If absolute income increases but the number of people in poverty decreases, then the Gini index may increase.

Many other indices have been suggested (see `www.ncbi.nlm.nih.gov/pmc/arti-cles/PMC2652960/`). Perhaps the simplest alternative is the *Palma index*, proposed by Chilean economist José Gabriel Palma (see `datatopics.worldbank.org/gmr/ palma-index.html`). The Palma index is computed by simply taking the ratio of the income of the top 10% divided by the income of the bottom 40%. Figure 7.5 shows the Palma index in 2014–2015 for different countries (see `datatopics .worldbank.org/gmr/palma-index.html`). We see, for example, the top 10% in income of people in Qatar have 9.2 times as much income as the bottom 40%. In the United States, the top 10% have 1.9 times as much income as the bottom 40%.

By focusing on the top and bottom of the income distribution, the Palma index reduces the Gini index's excessive sensitivity to middle class income. On the other hand, by not using everyone's income, the Palma index throws away a lot of information.

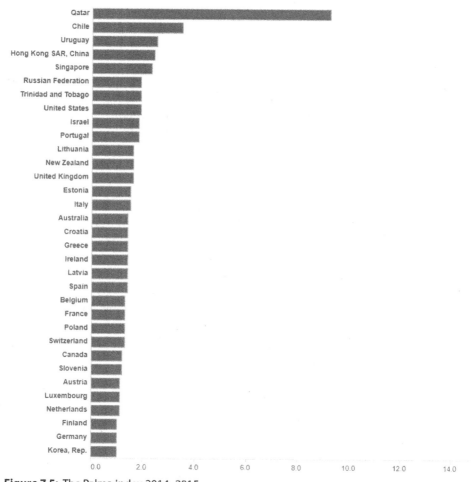

Figure 7.5: The Palma Index 2014–2015

The Atkinson Index

Given the income of each household or individual, the Palma and Gini indices crank out a number that measures a nation's degree of inequality. The *Atkinson index* measures inequality and also gives you a normative foundation to evaluate how changes in a nation's income inequality modify the country's level of welfare. The late Anthony Atkinson (1944–2017) was a great British economist who worked nearly 40 years studying poverty and inequality. If you want to be an educated citizen of the world, Atkinson's book *Inequality: What Can Be Done?* (Harvard University Press, 2015) should be on your reading list. Atkinson begins by assuming that society defines a utility function U(y), which measures the benefit to society when an individual has an income y. U(y) depends on a nonnegative parameter ε. If ε = 0, the society does not think inequality matters while for larger values of ε inequality matters more to society. U(y) is defined for non-negative ε not equal to 1 as

$$U(y) = \frac{y^{1-\varepsilon}}{1-\varepsilon}$$

For ε=1 U(y) = Log y.

U(y) is increasing in y (more income, more utility). U(y) also ensures that each additional dollar you give an individual yields diminishing extra (marginal) utility. Given a choice of ε, and a country with N individuals and individual i has income y_i, the Atkinson index is computed from the following equation:

$$1 - \frac{1}{\mu}(\frac{1}{N}(\sum_i y_i^{1-\varepsilon})^{1/(1-\varepsilon)}$$

Suppose a nation wants to ensure that each individual has the same income. What fraction of the country's total income can the nation give up and keep their total utility the same? The answer is the Atkinson index.

For a country consisting of five individuals with respective incomes of 1000, 2000, 3000, 4000, and 5000, and ε = 3, worksheet Unequal of the file AtkinsonIndex.xlsx (see Figure 7.6) computes the Atkinson index to equal 0.384. Cell H11 computes the nation's total utility –7.3E-07. (The E-07 means divide by 10^7 = 10 million, so total utility is –0.00000073.) The formulas used to compute the Atkinson index are shown in Figure 7.6. The ^ symbol is used to raise numbers to a power. For example, the formula =4^3 returns 64.

D	E	F	G	H	I	J
2 mean	3000		Atkinson			
3				0.38390044 =1-(1/E2)*G12		Give up 38% of income
4						to make everyone equal
5	Person	Income	Income^(1-epilison)	Utility		
6	1	1000	0.000001	-0.0000005 =(F6)^(1-epsilon)	=(1/(1-epsilon))*F6^(1-epsilon)
7	2	2000	0.00000025	-0.000000125 =(F7)^(1-epsilon)	=(1/(1-epsilon))*F7^(1-epsilon)
8	3	3000	1.11111E-07	-5.55556E-08 =(F8)^(1-epsilon)	=(1/(1-epsilon))*F8^(1-epsilon)
9	4	4000	6.25E-08	-3.125E-08 =(F9)^(1-epsilon)	=(1/(1-epsilon))*F9^(1-epsilon)
10	5	5000	0.00000004	-0.00000002 =(F10)^(1-epsilon)	=(1/(1-epsilon))*F10^(1-epsilon)
11			2.92722E-07	-7.31806E-07 =SUM(G6:G10)/5	=SUM(H6:H10)
12			1848.29868		=G11^(1/(1-epsilon))

Figure 7.6: Computation of the Atkinson index

In the worksheet Equal, we reduced the total national income by 38.4%. Then each individual's income will equal (1 – 0.384) * 15,000 / 5 = $1848. The worksheet Equal shows that even though the nation has substantially less income, equalizing the income kept the nation's total well-being the same! Using Atkinson's approach, economists can estimate whether government programs will change national well-being.

Excel Calculations

In this section, we explain the calculations involved in our Gini index examples.

Once we have the cumulative fraction of income earned by the n poorest people, we multiply this fraction for person n by .05 and sum up these values to approximate the area under the orange curve. We created the chart shown in Figure 7.2 by selecting the range D4:D24 and then holding down the Ctrl key to select the noncontiguous range G4:H24. We selected the Scatter Plot option and then Smooth Lines And Markers.

CHAPTER 8

Modeling Relationships Between Two Variables

In many analytics applications, we need to try to determine how two variables are related. This chapter is a primer on how analysts can determine the relationship between two variables.

Examples of Relationships Between Two Variables

Often, we want to predict a dependent variable (call it Y) from an independent variable (call it X). Table 8.1 lists some examples of business relationships you might want to estimate.

Table 8.1: Examples of relationships between two variables

X (INDEPENDENT VARIABLE)	Y (DEPENDENT VARIABLE)
Units produced by a plant in a month	Monthly cost of operating plant
Monthly dollars spent on advertising	Monthly sales
Number of employees	Monthly travel expenses
Company annual revenue	Number of employees
Monthly return on the stock market	Monthly return on a mutual fund or stock
Square feet in home	Home price
Price of product	Units sold of product

Finding the Best-Fitting (Least Squares) Line

The first step in determining how two variables are related is to create a scatterplot graph where each data point, the value of X is on the horizontal axis, and the value of Y is on the vertical axis. If your graph indicates that a straight line is a reasonable fit to the data, you can use the Excel Trendline feature (or Excel functions) to find the straight line that best fits the points. The "Excel Calculations" section at the end of the chapter describes how to find the straight line that best fits the points.

For example, suppose we are given the price for a box of cereal charged each week and also given weekly sales as shown in the file Demand.xlsx (see Figure 8.1). From the scatterplot, we see that a straight-line fit is reasonable. Excel reports the best straight-line fit to this data is Demand = 20.54 – 2.12 * Price. For example, if Price = $3.00, then we predict demand to equal 20.54 – 2.12 * 3 = 14.18.

How does Excel find the best-fitting line? For each possible straight line, we find the squared distance of the point for the line. The best-fitting (or *least squares line*) is the line that minimizes the sum of the squared distances of the points from the line. We square the distances so that positive and negative distances do not cancel out.

Here are some important facts about the least squares line:

- The reported R^2 value of 0.87 means that changes in price explain 87% of the change in demand, with 13% of the change in demand explained by other factors.

- In cell I1, we see that Standard Error of the regression is 0.79. This means that approximately 95% of the demand values will be within 2 * 0.79 = 1.58 units of the line. Any point more than 1.58 units off the line is an outlier. Column H shows the error (actual demand – predicted demand) for each point. We see there are no outliers.

- The least squares line "splits the points in half" in the sense that the sum of the errors equals 0. This means the sum of the distances of the points above the line from the line equals the sum of the distances of the points below the line from the line.

- Even if a line fits observed data well, beware of extrapolating the line to make predictions based on values of X not near the observed data. For example, it would be unreasonable to use our line to predict demand for a price of $10. (You would get a negative demand prediction, which clearly is unreasonable!)

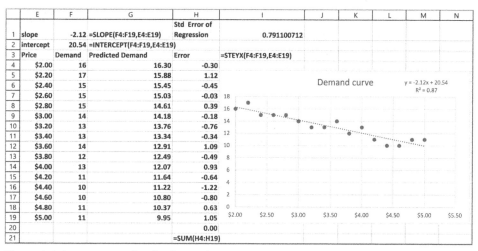

Figure 8.1: Least squares line for demand

Computing the Beta of a Stock

An important concept in finance is the *beta* of a stock or investment fund. Beta is the slope of the least squares line in which X = monthly or annual return on a market index and Y = monthly or annual return on the stock or investment fund. On July 4, 2019, in the file Betas.xlsx, we used Office 365's new Data Type feature (see Figure 8.2 and the "Excel Calculations" section) to find the following betas.

	B	C
7		Beta
8	🏛 International Business Machines Corp (XNYS:IBM)	1.28
9	🏛 Microsoft Corp (XNAS:MSFT)	1.22
10	🏛 Pfizer Inc (XNYS:PFE)	0.63
11	🏛 Walmart Inc (XNYS:WMT)	0.42
12	🏛 Kroger Co (XNYS:KR)	0.62
13	🏛 Target Corp (XNYS:TGT)	0.61
14	🏛 Alphabet Inc (XNAS:GOOG)	0.97

Figure 8.2: Betas July 2019

A larger beta means the stock is more sensitive to changes in the market. For the listed stocks, Walmart is least sensitive to market changes. A 1% increase in the market is predicted to yield a 0.42% increase in the price of Walmart. IBM is the most sensitive to the market, with a 1% increase in the market predicted to result in a 1.28% increase in the price of IBM.

In the file `MadoffBeta.xlsx`, we used the Trendline feature (see Figure 8.3) to estimate the beta of annual returns for Madoff's made-up data. We found a remarkably low beta of 0.08. Thus, Madoff's reported returns made it look as if he had indeed hedged away most of the market risk.

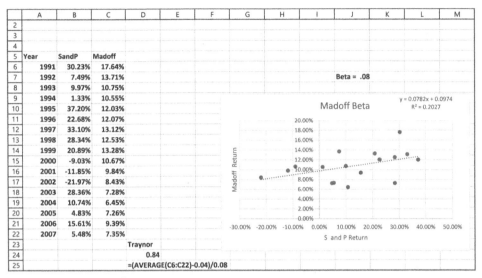

Figure 8.3: Beta Madoff returns

Recall that in Chapter 5, "How Did Bernie Madoff Keep His Fund Going?" we showed that Madoff's reported returns should have been suspect based on the unreasonably high Sharpe ratio. Another measure of risk adjusted return, the *Treynor ratio*, makes Madoff's returns look even more suspect. The Treynor ratio on annual returns is

$$\left[\left(\text{Mean annual investment Return}\right) - \left(\text{Risk free rate}\right)\right] / \text{Beta}$$

Thus, the Treynor ratio is the excess return earned per unit of market risk, with beta defined as market risk.

As shown in cell D24, Madoff's returns yielded a Treynor ratio of 0.84. The website `www.styleadvisor.com/resources/statfacts/treynor-ratio` shows that a Treynor ratio of 0.21 is incredibly good, so the amazingly high Treynor ratio makes Madoff's returns even more suspect.

What Is a Good R²?

If I had a dollar for every time a student asked me what is a good R^2, I would be rich. The answer is, it depends on the situation. To illustrate the idea, consider the daily returns from 2009–2019 on the Dow Index in the file `Dow.xlsx`. Some bright know-it-all says I can predict Y = Dow Index today from X = Dow Index on last trading day. Using Excel's `RSQ` function (see the "Excel Calculations" section), we obtained an $R^2 = 99.9\%$, which means that knowing the Dow Index on the last trading day explains 99.9% of the variation in the trading index on the next day. Does this mean we can beat the market? Of course not; all it means is at closing today, the Dow will be close to its closing value on the previous trading day.

What we really want to do is predict Y = Percentage change in Dow today. You can use any information known at the start of the trading day. As shown by John Campbell and Samuel Thompson (`pdfs.semanticscholar.org/3706/3e21ba30f903af7a640792fde281867c9014.pdf`), it is incredibly hard to get an R^2 of even 1% when predicting *monthly* (much less daily) stock returns. This illustrates the *efficient-market hypothesis*, which states current stock prices incorporate all relevant information about future stock returns, making it very hard to predict future returns. Check out `en.wikipedia.org/wiki/Efficient-market_hypothesis` for a balanced evaluation of the efficient-market hypothesis.

Correlation and R^2

Given any two variables X and Y, the *sample correlation* (referred to as r) is a unit measure of the strength of the linear relationship between X and Y. By a linear relationship, we mean how well the best least squares line of the form Y = a + bX (a = Intercept, b = Slope) fits the data. As shown in the "Excel Calculations" section, the `CORREL` function can be used to easily determine the correlation between two variables.

The sample correlation is always between –1 and +1 and can be interpreted as a *unit-free* measure of the strength of the linear relationship between X and Y.

- A correlation near +1 implies that when X is much larger than average, we expect Y to be much larger than average.

- A correlation near –1 implies that when X is much larger than average, we expect Y to be much smaller than average.

- A correlation near 0 implies there is a weak linear relationship between X and Y.

As shown in the range K14:N20 of the file `Galton.xlsx`, correlation does not capture nonlinear relationships. The points shown in Figure 8.4 satisfy the relationship $Y = X^2$, a nonlinear relationship, but the five points shown have r = 0.

Figure 8.4 contains data collected by the famous eugenicist Sir Francis Galton on the height of parents and their children.

	A	B	C	D	E	F	G	H	I	J	K	L	M	N	O	P	Q
1	family	father	mother	gender	height	kids	male	female									
2	1	78.5	67	M	73.2	4	1	0									
3	2	75.5	66.5	M	73.5	4	1	0		0.391317	male with father		{=CORREL(IF(male=1,father,""),IF(male=1,height,""))}				
4	2	75.5	66.5	M	72.5	4	1	0		0.458761	female with father		{=CORREL(IF(male=0,father,""),IF(male=0,height,""))}				
5	3	75	64	M	71	2	1	0		0.334131	male with mother		{=CORREL(IF(male=1,mother,""),IF(male=1,height,""))}				
6	4	75	64	M	70.5	5	1	0		0.313698	female with mother		{=CORREL(IF(male=0,mother,""),IF(male=0,height,""))}				
7	4	75	64	M	68.5	5	1	0									
8	5	75	58.5	M	72	6	1	0									
9	5	75	58.5	M	69	6	1	0			0.3913174	correlation male child height with father's height					
10	5	75	58.5	M	68	6	1	0		=CORREL(E2:E466,B2:B466)							
11	7	74	68	M	76.5	6	1	0			0.3341309	correlation mother height with male child					
12	7	74	68	M	74	6	1	0		=CORREL(C2:C466,E2:E466)							
13	7	74	68	M	73	6	1	0									
14	7	74	68	M	73	6	1	0		X	Y		Y=X²				
15	11	74	62	M	74	8	1	0			0	0					
16	11	74	62	M	70	8	1	0			1	1					
17	14	73	67	M	68	2	1	0			-1	1					
18	14	73	67	M	67	2	1	0			2	4					
19	15	73	66.5	M	71	3	1	0			-2	4					
20	15	73	66.5	M	70.5	3	1	0							0 =CORREL(L15:L19,K15:K19)		

Figure 8.4: Galton height data

Note that a 1 in the Male column indicates the child was male, and a 1 in the Female column indicates the child was female. Based on the data in Galton.xlsx, the correlations between the height of a parent and a child were as shown in Table 8.2. (See the "Excel Calculations" section for an explanation of how these correlations were computed.)

Table 8.2: Galton height correlations

PARENT	GENDER OF CHILD	CORRELATION
Father	Male	0.39
Father	Female	0.46
Mother	Male	0.33
Mother	Female	0.31

The positive correlations indicate that if a parent is taller than average, then the child tends to be taller than average.

The Relationship Between Correlation and R^2

Given data on two variables, the sample correlation r is simply the square root of the R^2 value associated with the least squares line. The sign of the square root is the same sign as the slope of the least squares line. In our demand line example, the correlation between price and demand is $+\sqrt{0.87} = +0.93$.

Correlation and Regression to the Mean

If X is k standard deviations above average, the prediction from the least squares line used to predict Y from X will be kr standard deviations above average. (Below average values of X or Y are treated as negative.) *Since r is less than one in absolute value, this implies that the prediction for Y is closer to average than X. This is known as regression to the mean.* In the Galton data, for example, if the father was very tall (say, 2 standard deviations above average), we would predict the son to be 2 * (0.39) = 0.78 standard deviations taller than average. Thus, the son is predicted to be taller than average but not as tall as the father.

For another application, let Y = Number of games an NFL team wins this year and X = Number of games the team won last year. The average correlation between X and Y is 0.4, with the standard deviation of X and Y being near 2. An average team wins 8 games, so we would predict that a team that goes 12-4 in a season (2 standard deviations above average) would be predicted to win 8 + 2 * 2 * (0.4) = 9.6 games the following season. This regression to the mean is expected, because a 12-4 team probably had few injuries and peak performances, and during the next season, more injuries and less than peak performances are to be expected.

Correlation Need Not Imply Causation

It is well known from our knowledge of heredity that children inherit genes that influence their height. Therefore, the positive correlation between a parent's height and a child's height can be taken as some confirmation of genetics. In general, however, proving causation is very difficult. We refer the interested reader to Judea Pearl's excellent book *The Book of Why* (Basic Books, 2018) for an extensive discussion of causation.

To see why correlation need not imply causation, let X = Number of bars in a city and Y = Number of churches in a city. The correlation r between X and Y will certainly be near +1. Is this because bars "cause" churches? Of course not. The number of bars and churches in a city exhibits a strong positive correlation because a third unrelated variable, the size of the city, drives increases in both the number of bars and churches in a city.

We Are Not Living in a Linear World

As Madonna said, we are living in a material world, but not always in a linear world. A straight-line relationship between X and Y of the form Y = a + bX is a linear relationship. Recall that our assumption of a linear price demand relationship led to predictions of negative demand. Thus, as our demand line example shows, a linear relationship is often a poor representation of reality. In fact, economists rarely fit straight lines to data. More often they will fit a power curve relationship of the form $Y = A * X^b$. As you will soon see, the power b is the important number.

Taking the natural logarithm of both sides yields

$$LN(Y) = LN\ a + b * LN(X)$$

This equation implies a linear relationship between LN(X) and LN(Y) that can be estimated with the Trend Curve or SLOPE and INTERCEPT functions. To illustrate the idea, look at the file PowerDemand.xlsx. Figure 8.5 shows the product demand for different prices and a plot of demand as a function of price. Fitting a straight line would be foolish, so we use the LN function to take the natural logarithms of X and Y, and we see the relationship between LN(X) and LN(Y) is close to linear. Therefore, we fit a linear trendline to estimate B = -3.03.

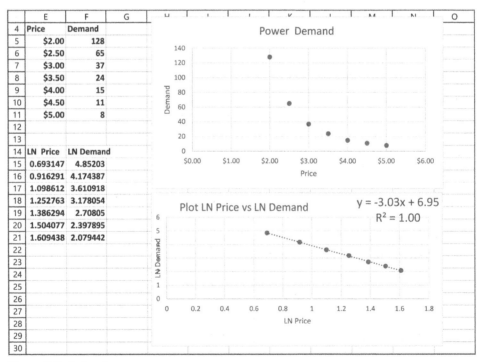

Figure 8.5: Estimating a power curve

The Concept of Elasticity

Economists love the power curve because it allows them to estimate *elasticities*. At any point on a demand curve, the price elasticity is the percentage increase in demand resulting from a 1% increase in price. For a demand curve modeled as a power curve, b represents the elasticity of demand. Since the elasticity is the same for each point on the curve, the power curve is often called a *constant elasticity demand curve*. For any price, a price increase of 1% will increase price by b%. For example, an elasticity of –3.03 means that for *any* price, a 1% increase in price results in a 3.03% decrease in demand.

Some actual product price elasticities are listed in Table 8.3. For example, we find that a 1% increase in wine price will decrease demand by 1%, whereas a 1% increase in the price of Coca-Cola will decrease demand by a much larger 3.8%.

Table 8.3: Product elasticities

PRODUCT	ELASTICITY
Wine	–1.0
Oil	–0.4
Coca-Cola	–3.8
Chicken	–0.5

In Chapter 9, "Intergenerational Mobility," you'll use your knowledge of elasticity and the power curve to understand how the important concept of *intergenerational income elasticity* is used to measure income mobility between generations.

Excel Calculations

In this section, we describe how to use Excel to chart a linear trendline, compute information about a least squares line, and calculate correlations.

Fitting a Trendline

To find the linear relationship between price and demand in the file Demand .xlsx, proceed as follows:

1. Select the data in the range E3:F19.
2. On the Insert tab, select the Insert Scatter button and choose the first option.

3. To obtain the trendline, select the data series, right-click the series, and choose Add Trendline.

4. Select the Linear option, and then select the Display Equation On Chart and Display R-squared Value On Chart check boxes to display the trendline, the trendline equation, and R^2 value.

Obtaining Properties of a Trendline

The following steps show how Excel functions can be used to compute important information about a least squares line:

1. In cell F1 of the file `Demand.xlsx`, we find the slope of the demand line with the formula `=SLOPE(F4:F19,E4:E19)`.

2. In cell F2 of the file `Demand.xlsx`, we find the intercept of the demand line with the formula `=INTERCEPT(F4:F19,E4:E19)`.

3. In cell I1 of the file `Demand.xlsx`, we find the standard error of the price trendline with the formula `=STEYX(F4:F19,E4:E19)`.

4. In cell E9 of the file `Dow.xlsx`, we find the R^2 value for predicting the closing Dow based on the previous day's close with the formula `=RSQ(C13:C2 526,B13:B2526)`.

Using New Datatypes to Find Company Betas

If you have Office 365, Excel enables you to recognize companies by name or stock ticker symbol and to write formulas that extract important information about the companies to your workbook. In cells B8:B14 of the `Betas.xlsx` workbook, we entered the stock ticker symbols or company names for seven companies. After selecting the range B8:B14, we selected Stocks from the Data Type group on the Data tab. Then, copying the formula `=B8.Beta` from B8 to B9:B14 returns each stock's beta to the range B8:B14. To update the betas to their current values, select Refresh from the Data tab.

Finding Correlations with the *CORREL* Function

In cell K9 of the workbook `Galton.xlsx`, we find the correlation between the father's height and the son's height with the following formula:

=CORREL(E2:E466,B2:B466)

Finding Correlations on a Subset of Data

Table 8.2 displayed the correlation between fathers or mothers with sons or daughters. The workbook Galton.xlsx and Figure 8.6 show how advanced Excel formulas were used for these computations. Here are the steps:

1. Select the cell range B1:H899, select Create From Selection, and then choose Names In Top Row. This names each column's data with the row 1 heading. For example, the cell range C2:C899 is assigned the name mother.

2. In cell J3, compute the correlation between fathers and male children by typing the formula

    =CORREL(IF(male=1,father,""),IF(male=1,height,""))

    and then pressing Ctrl+Shift+Enter. (Current versions of Office 365 allow you to simply press Enter.)
    This formula is an *array formula* that creates two arrays. The first array contains the father's height if the child is male and otherwise a blank. The second array contains the child's height if the child is male and otherwise a blank. Excel ignores blank cells in calculations, so this formula computes the correlation between the heights of fathers and male children. Similar formulas in cells J4:J6 are used to compute all other possible correlations.

	J	K	L	M	N	O	P	Q
3	0.391317	male with father		{=CORREL(IF(male=1,father,""),IF(male=1,height,""))}				
4	0.458761	female with father		{=CORREL(IF(male=0,father,""),IF(male=0,height,""))}				
5	0.334131	male with mother		{=CORREL(IF(male=1,mother,""),IF(male=1,height,""))}				
6	0.313698	female with mother		{=CORREL(IF(male=0,mother,""),IF(male=0,height,""))}				

Figure 8.6: Using array formulas to compute Galton correlations

CHAPTER
9

Intergenerational Mobility

From the moment I heard Billy Joel sing "It's nine o-clock on a Saturday," I fell in love with his songs. I particularly love his song "Allentown" and the following lyrics:

Every child has a pretty good shot
To get at least as far as their old man got
But something happened on the way to that place
They threw an American flag in our face.

The point is that the American Dream has been based on the belief that each future generation will have a better life than the previous generation. The brilliant Harvard economist Raj Chetty has shown this dream is no longer grounded in reality. As shown by Chetty (see Chart 4 on www.brookings.edu/ blog/social-mobility-memos/2018/01/11/raj-chetty-in-14-charts-big-findings-on-opportunity-and-mobility-we-should-know/), children born in 1940 had a 90% chance of earning more money (after adjusting for inflation) than their parents. After a steady decline, by 1980 the chance that a child's real income would exceed their parent's real income had dropped to 50%. This fact is an example of declining intergenerational mobility. *Intergenerational mobility (IM)* refers to how income and or social status changes for members of the same family between generations. In this chapter, we will discuss four techniques used to measure intergenerational mobility:

- Absolute intergenerational mobility
- Intergenerational elasticity (IGE)
- Rank-rank mobility
- Quintile studies of mobility

These techniques are tricky to explain and understand. Our goal is to help you understand what each technique measures and how scholars can cherry-pick between these measures to reverse-engineer a desired conclusion.

Absolute Intergenerational Mobility

As previously stated, one approach to intergenerational mobility is to look at the income in real terms of parents and children and analyze how the difference between parent and child incomes in the same family have changed as a function of the year of the child's birth. Raj Chetty et. al. (www.nber.org/papers/w22910.pdf) used U.S. Census and IRS data to track the incomes of members of the same family. We urge you to look at this paper, but here we summarize some of the important findings.

- As shown in Figure 9.1 and in the workbook MedianIncome.xlsx, children born in 1940 ended up making more than three times as much (measured by real median income) as children born in 1980. By 1980, children born had lower median income than their parents.
- The decrease in absolute mobility did not depend on your state of birth. In 1940 children born in every state had at least an 85% chance of exceeding their parent's real median income, whereas in all states except for South Dakota children born in 1980 had less than a 60% chance of exceeding their parents' real median income.

Intergenerational Elasticity

In Chapter 8, "Modeling Relationships Between Two Variables," we introduced the concept of price elasticity of demand. When studying IM, many economists attempt to measure the *intergenerational elasticity (IGE) coefficient*. Economists measure IGE by trying to predict the natural logarithm of a child's income from the natural logarithm of a parent's income. Most economists believe (see www.brookings.edu/blog/social-mobility-memos/2015/04/27/measuring-relative-mobility-part-1/) that the U.S. IGE is around 0.4. This implies that if Family 2 has a 20% higher income than Family 1, then we would predict the children of Family 2 to have a 20% * (0.4) = 8% higher income than the children of Family 1. Of course, a lower IGE estimate means a parent's income has less effect on a child's income and implies more IGE.

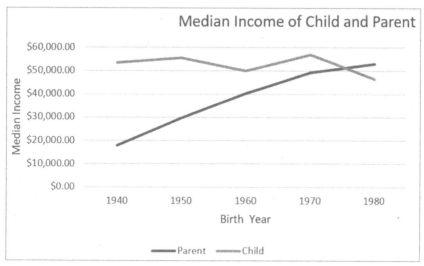

Figure 9.1: Median income for parent and child, birth year 1940–1980

Rank-Rank Mobility

To measure rank-rank mobility, we try to predict

- Y = the percentile rank of the child's income (measured relative to children born in the same year) from
- X = percentile rank of the parent's income (relative to people of the same age)

Raj Chetty, Nathaniel Hendren, Patrick Kline, and Emmanuel Saez (www.nber. org/papers/w19843.pdf) estimated the slope of the rank-rank mobility line to be 0.34, which implies that a 10% increase in a parent's percentile income rank is predicted to yield a 3.4% increase in a child's percentile income rank.

Comparing IGE and Rank-Rank Mobility

Based on the excellent discussion in part 1 of "Measuring Relative Mobility" (www. brookings.edu/blog/social-mobility-memos/2015/04/27/measuring-relative-mobility-part-1), we construct several examples to help the reader understand the differences between IGE and rank-rank mobility. The key point is that the degree of a nation's income inequality can complicate the interpretation of IGE and rank-rank mobility. Our work is shown in the workbook IGEvsRank.xlsx.

Case 1: An Unequal Immobile Society

In the worksheet Unequal Immobile, we made up Parent and Child incomes for 100 families. Fifty of the families are "poor," with incomes between $25,000 and $45,000. Fifty of the families are "rich," with incomes between $90,000 and $110,000. We ensured that each child of a poor family had an income that remained in the $25,000 to $45,000 range and every child of a rich family remained in the $90,000 to $110,000 range. Thus, we have an unequal, immobile society. We used Excel's RANK function (see the "Excel Calculations" section at the end of this chapter) to determine the percentile rank of each parent and child relative to their peers. After taking the natural logarithms of each parent and child's income, we used the trendline feature to estimate the IGE. We also estimated the rank-rank mobility slope with the trendline by predicting Child's rank from Parent's rank. Figure 9.2 shows the results of our analysis. We find IGE = 0.93 and rank-rank slope = 0.76.

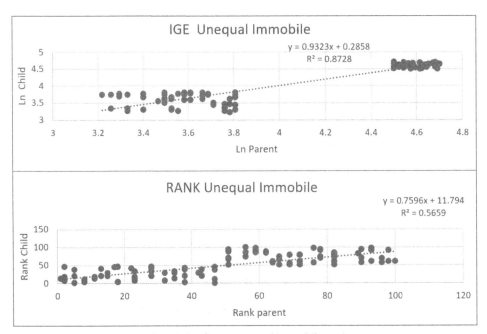

Figure 9.2: IGE and rank-rank mobility for an unequal immobile society

Case 2: An Equalizing Immobile Society

In the worksheet Equalizing Immobile, we assume the country attempted to reduce income inequality by shifting income from the rich to the poor. Every rich parent has a "less rich" child earning between $80,000 and $100,000. Every poor parent has a "less poor" child earning between $30,000 and $65,000. Figure 9.3 shows the charts used to calculate the IGE and rank-rank slope. Note the income transfer has improved income mobility as shown by the fact that the IGE has dropped from 0.93 to 0.45. Since no poor people make it to the "rich" level, the rank-rank slope remains virtually unchanged (from 0.76 to 0.75).

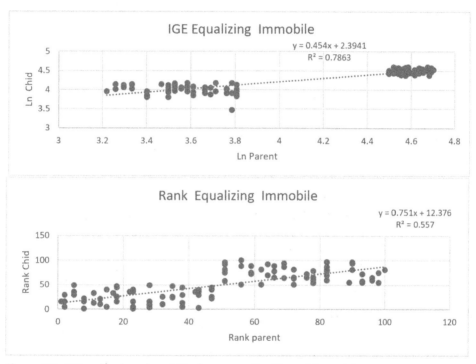

Figure 9.3: IGE and rank-rank mobility for an equalized immobile society

Case 3: An Unequal Mobile Society

In the worksheet Unequal Mobile, we consider a society in which there is a 30% chance that a poor parent's child becomes rich, and there is a 30% chance that a rich parent's child becomes poor. Therefore, our new society has a significant degree of intergenerational mobility. Unlike our Equalizing Immobile society, the government does not use transfer payments to reduce inequality. As shown in Figure 9.4, the IGE is now 0.61, and the rank-rank slope is 0.40.

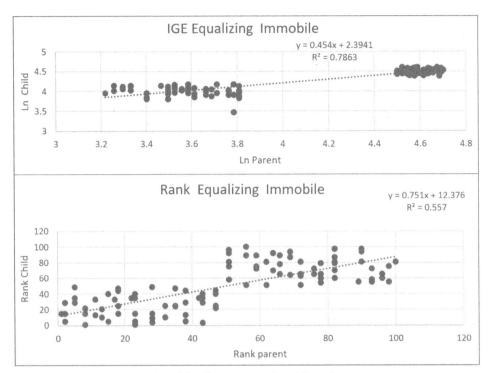

Figure 9.4: IGE and rank-rank mobility for an unequal mobile society

In summary, we see that IGE indicates more mobility for Case 2 than Case 3, whereas Rank-Rank slope indicates more mobility for Case 3, because many children change from rich to poor or poor to rich. These scenarios show that we must be careful when interpreting IGE and rank-rank mobility.

Measuring Mobility with Quintiles

Many people studying intergenerational mobility like to display a country's mobility using quintiles. For children born in the same year, we group the parents' income into five groups, each containing 20% of the parents:

- Parents whose income is in the bottom 20% (bottom quintile)
- Parents whose income ranks between the bottom 20% and bottom 40%
- Parents whose income ranks between the 40th and 60th percentile
- Parents whose income ranks between the 60th and 80th percentile
- Parents whose income is in the top 20% (top quintile)

Children born the same year also have their income ranked by quintile. The typical Intergenerational Mobility Quintile graph looks like Figure 9.5 (see www.brookings.edu/blog/social-mobility-memos/2015/04/28/measuring-relative-mobility-part-2/). We created our version of the chart using Excel's Stacked Column chart (see the file Quintile.xlsx and the "Excel Calculations" section).

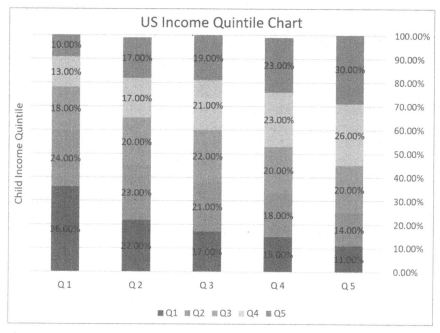

Figure 9.5: U.S. intergenerational mobility quintile chart

The Quintile chart makes it clear that if your parents' income was in the bottom quintile it is much harder to move up than if your parents' income is in the top quintile. More specifically, 36% of children whose parents' income is in the bottom quintile remain there, and only 10% make it to the top quintile. On the other hand, 30% of those whose parents are in top quintile remain there, whereas only 11% of those whose parents' incomes are in the top quintile end up in the bottom quintile.

While visually appealing, the quintile chart has problems:

▪ Much information is thrown away. For example, a child who moves from the 39th to the 41st percentile counts the same as a child who moved from the 21st to the 59th percentile.

▪ In countries (like the Scandinavian countries) with less income inequality than the United States, it takes a much smaller absolute change in income to move between quintiles. Thus, in Scandinavian countries, we should not be surprised that an average of only 27% of those in the bottom quintile remain there.

The Great Gatsby Curve

Many critics (see, for example, www.usatoday.com/story/life/books/2013/05/07/ why-the-great-gatsby-is-the-great-american-novel/2130161/) believe F. Scott Fitzgerald's *The Great Gatsby* is the best American novel. In the novel (spoiler alert!), Gatsby is the poster child for income mobility, rising from a bootlegger to the top of the Hamptons' society. In January 2012, the late Princeton economist Alan Krueger was the Head of President Obama's Economic Advisers and gave a famous speech (see cdn.americanprogress.org/wp-content/uploads/ events/2012/01/pdf/krueger.pdf) on income inequality.

On page 4 of his talk, Krueger introduced the "Great Gatsby Curve," stating that "Countries that have a high degree of inequality also tend to have less economic mobility across generations." Krueger plotted (see Figure 9.6 and file Gatsby.xlsx) on the x-axis the mid -1980s after-tax Gini index for several countries and on the y-axis the mid-1980s IGE for each country. From the graph, we find a strong positive correlation between income inequality and intergenerational mobility to equal $\sqrt{0.5926} = 0.77$. Of course, the name *Great Gatsby Curve* refers to the belief that the chart shows that most children born in the United States don't have the same opportunities as Gatsby to earn more than their parents.

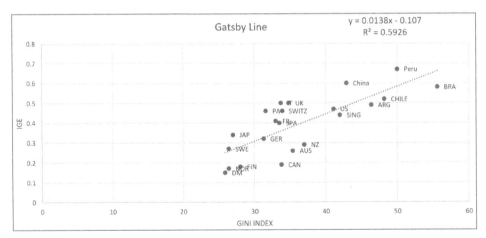

Figure 9.6: The Great Gatsby Curve

When referring to the curve, Krueger stated that "It is hard to look at these figures and not be concerned that rising inequality is jeopardizing our tradition of equality of opportunity." As you learned in Chapter 8, correlation need not imply causation, so I don't think it is reasonable to use this curve to conclude that income inequality reduces income mobility.

Prominent Harvard economist Gregory Mankiw criticized the Great Gatsby Curve on more technical grounds (see gregmankiw.blogspot.com/2013/07/some-observations-on-great-gatsby-curve.html). Mankiw perceptively observes that the single point for the United States is based on combining data from 50 states (plus the District of Columbia) that differ greatly in income inequality and average income. In contrast, there is a point on the chart for each European country. Mankiw argues that we should aggregate high-income inequality European countries (such as Italy) with low-income inequality European countries (like Denmark) and just have a single point for the European Union.

In the file CTMISS.xlsx, we try to explain the logic of Mankiw's criticism of the Great Gatsby Curve. We assume the United States consists of two states: Connecticut and Mississippi. As shown in Figure 9.7 and the workbook CTMISS. xlxs, each state has two families. The two families in Connecticut have incomes of $180,000 and $220,000, whereas the two families in Mississippi have incomes of $40,000 and $60,000. Each family in Connecticut has a child whose income is $200,000, and each family in Mississippi has a child whose income is $50,000. Taking logarithms of income values, we compute an IGE of 0 for each state.

▲	A	B	C	D	E	F	G	H	I
2			Connecticut				Mississippi		
3		Person	Parent	Child			Person	Parent	Child
4			1	$180,000.00	$200,000.00			1	$40,000.00	$50,000.00
5			2	$220,000.00	$200,000.00			2	$60,000.00	$50,000.00
6									
7		GINI		0.1			GINI		0.2
8			LN						
9		Person	Parent	Child			LN		
10			1	$12.10	$12.21			Person	Parent	Child
11			2	$12.30	$12.21			1	$10.60	$10.82
12								2	$11.00	$10.82
13		SLOPE		0			SLOPE		0
14			=SLOPE(D10:D11,C10:C11)						
15									
16		Person	Parent	Child					
17			1	$180,000.00	$200,000.00					
18			2	$220,000.00	$200,000.00					
19			3	$40,000.00	$50,000.00					
20			4	$60,000.00	$50,000.00					
21									
22		USA	LN						
23						GINI		LOWER	HIGHER	DIFFERENCE
24		Person	LN Parent	LN Child			1	$40,000.00	$60,000.00	$20,000.00
25			1	$12.10	$12.21			2	$40,000.00	$180,000.00	$140,000.00
26			2	$12.30	$12.21			3	$40,000.00	$220,000.00	$180,000.00
27			3	$10.60	$10.82			4	$60,000.00	$180,000.00	$120,000.00
28			4	$11.00	$10.82			5	$60,000.00	$220,000.00	$160,000.00
29								6	$180,000.00	$220,000.00	$40,000.00
30		SLOPE		0.94					
31			=SLOPE(D25:D28,C25:C28)			MEAN DIFFERENCE	$110,000.00		
32		MEAN	$125,000.00			TWICE MEAN	$250,000.00		
33						USA GINI	0.44		
34									

Figure 9.7: Mankiw's rebuttal to the Gatsby Curve

Economist Anthony Atkinson (`https://www.chartbookofeconomicinequality.com/economic-inequality/measures-of-economic-inequality/` came up with a simple method to compute a Gini index for a country with few inhabitants. You simply chose two people at random and average the difference in their incomes and divide the mean income by two. Using this method to compute the Gini index, we find the Gini index for Connecticut to equal (220,000 – 180,000) /(2 * 200,000) = 0.1 and the Gini index for Mississippi to equal 0.2. Now let's combine Connecticut and Mississippi to create our four-family USA. We find an IGE = 0.94, which indicates very little intergenerational mobility, and a Gini index of 0.44, which indicates a lot of income inequality. Thus, we see that aggregating all European countries might make it look like Europe has much more income inequality and less intergenerational mobility than the United States. It is certainly not clear from the chart where a single point for Europe would lie.

Of course, the rebuttal to Mankiw's rebuttal should be obvious: If we have states with income distributions like Connecticut and Mississippi, this proves that where you are born has a large effect on your adult income—and that certainly does not seem fair!

Excel Calculations

In this section, we show how the Excel RANK function is used to compute rank-rank mobility. Then we show how to use a stacked column chart to display intergenerational mobility. Finally, we discuss the formulas needed for our Connecticut-Mississippi example.

Ranking Numerical Values

In the worksheet Unequal Immobile of the workbook IGEvsRank.xlsx, we ranked the parent and child incomes by copying from H5:H104 the formula
=RANK(F5,F$5:F$104,0).

The last argument of 0 indicates that we are ranking items in descending order. A last argument of 1 would indicate that we are ranking items in ascending order.

Creating the Quintile Graph

The following steps create the stacked column chart to display intergenerational mobility:

1. Select the range D5:I10 in the workbook Quintile.xlsx.

2. Click the Insert Column or Bar Chart button on the Insert tab and then create a Stacked Column chart by selecting the second option (Stacked Column).

Rebutting the Great Gatsby Curve

In the workbook CTMISS.xlsx, we provided an example of Mankiw's criticism of the Great Gatsby Curve as follows:

1. We computed the Gini index for our combined 4-person U.S. in the cell range F24:I33 by looking at the six absolute differences in income for all possible pairs of people. We found the average difference equals $110,000. Since the average income for our 4-person U.S. was $125,000, the Gini index for the combined U.S. is $110,000 / (2 * $125,000) = 0.44.

2. In cell C30, we computed the IGE with the formula =SLOPE(D25:D28,C25:C28) to compute the slope of the least squares line with dependent variable LN(Child Income) and independent variable LN(Parents' Income).

CHAPTER 10

Is Anderson Elementary School a Bad School?

Every year, third-graders in the state of Indiana take a standardized test to measure their academic progress. The test name changes all the time, but in 2018, the test was called the ISTEP+ test and consisted of two sections: Math and ELA (English Language Arts). We obtained the fraction of students at every Indiana public school who passed both parts of the test from the Indiana Department of Education (DoE) website (www.doe.in.gov/accountability/ find-school-and-corporation-data-reports). We summarized these results in the file ISTEPTestsReg.xlsx. An average of 54% of all students taking the test passed both sections of the test. At Anderson Elementary School in Anderson, Indiana, only 36% of students passed both sections of the test. We take it as a given (although I don't think it is a good idea) that a school's quality can be entirely measured by how the students perform on standardized tests. The standard deviation of pass rates by school is 18%, so Anderson Elementary students performed nearly one standard deviation below average. At first glance, this indicates that Anderson Elementary is not getting the job done. However, we must ask if other factors exist besides school quality, such as family income, that might influence students' test performance.

How Can We Adjust for Family Income?

Consider two schools (1 and 2) that are entirely equal in their ability for preparing students for the ISTEP+ test. If School 1 students all had family incomes below the poverty level and all School 2 students had family incomes over $100,000, you might expect that School 2 students would perform better on standardized tests. The problem with testing this hypothesis is that we don't know the family income for the students. From the Indiana DOE website, we have the fraction of the students at each school who are on free or reduced-lunch programs. This seems a reasonable surrogate for the family income of a school's students. With this in mind, we define Y = Fraction of students at a school passing both parts of the ISTEP+ and X = Fraction of students at a school on free or reduced-price lunches, and try to fit the model Y = a + bX.

Estimating the Least Squares Line

Using the Excel functions INTERCEPT and SLOPE (discussed in Chapters 8 and 9), we found the least squares estimate for this relationship to be

$$Y = 0.84 - 0.59X$$

We find the correlation between X and Y to be −0.71. The slope of −0.59 indicates that an increase of 10% in the fraction of students in free or reduced-price programs appears to lower the pass rate by 5.9%. $R^2 = 0.51$ indicates that variation in free and reduced-lunch percentage explains over half the variation in test score performance.

In the worksheet named Better Than You Think, we used Excel's Filter capabilities (see the "Excel Calculations" section at the end of this chapter) to isolate all schools with a less than 40% pass rate on both parts of the test in which the school's performance was better than predicted by the least squares line. We find that Anderson Elementary had a 36% pass rate and that 96% of students are on free or reduced lunch. Then we predict a pass rate of 0.84 − 0.59 * (0.96) = 0.27. Therefore, the students performed 9% better than predicted, so I would strongly disagree with anyone who said Anderson Elementary School's low pass rate showed they were performing poorly.

Can We Compare Standardized Test Performance for Students in Different States?

Most states have different standardized tests. So, is it possible to compare test performance in Detroit, Michigan to student performance in Palo

Alto, California? Erin Fahle and Sean Reardon (journals.sagepub.com/doi/abs/10.3102/0013189X18759524) came up with a clever solution to this problem.

Each year a representative sample of students in each state take the National Assessment of Educational Progress (NAEP) test to measure ELA and math achievement. Based on this test, you can easily estimate the relative achievement of students in different states. For example, suppose Connecticut students score an average of 5% better than the national average on NAEP. Then a Connecticut school that scores 10% below the Connecticut average on Connecticut's state test is really only $10 - 5 = 5\%$ worse than the national average. The website cepa.stanford.edu/seda/overview gives a summary of educational performance throughout the nation. Fahle and Reardon found, for example, that Palo Alto, California students performed more than two standard deviations above average whereas Detroit, Michigan students performed more than two standard deviations below average.

Fahle and Reardon's landmark study is very readable and *incredibly important*. It is rare to find important papers that can easily be read by an intelligent non-expert! The authors analyzed performance at the school district rather than the school level. This allowed them to have detailed information on the students' socioeconomic status (SES) in each district. Fahle and Reardon found a 0.78 correlation between district SES status and district achievement. Recall that our simple study found a similar (0.71) correlation between free or reduced-price lunch performance and achievement.

Excel Calculations

In the worksheet named Better Than You Think, we used Excel's Filter capability to isolate schools with a pass rate less than 40% that performed better than predicted by the least squares line.

1. Select all the data (you can do this with the cursor in the data if you use the keystroke combination Ctrl+*). This approach would not work if we did not insert a blank row between our least squares line calculations and the data.

2. On the Data tab, select Filter. You now see drop-down arrows in the header row that allow you to filter the data based on multiple criteria.

3. From the drop-down in cell L4, choose Number Filters and then Less Than. Enter **0.40** to find all schools with a pass rate less than 40%.

4. From the drop-down in cell N4, choose Number Filters and then Greater Than. Enter **0** to find all schools that performed better than predicted by the least squares line.

The combination of our two filters isolates only those schools with a less than 40% pass rate that performed better than indicated by the least squares line.

CHAPTER 11

Value-Added Assessments of Teacher Effectiveness

In 2010, the *LA Times* published ratings of teacher effectiveness based on student test scores. The *Times* ratings were an early example of *value-added assessment* (*VAA*). As shown in `projects.latimes.com/value-added/teacher/rigoberto-ruelas/`, Rigoberto Ruelas was rated a very poor math teacher. His colleagues, however, rated him a great teacher. Soon after the *Times* published the ratings, Ruelas committed suicide. We will never know for sure if the low rating and suicide were related, but this tragedy caused many to question the validity and usefulness of value-added modeling for rating teacher effectiveness.

In this chapter, we will explore the following techniques used to evaluate teachers based on test scores:

- Simple gain score assessment
- Covariate adjustment assessment
- Layered assessment
- Cross-classified constant growth assessment

Our discussion is primarily based on Edward W. Wiley's excellent guide to VAA, *A Practitioner's Guide to Value-Added Assessment* (`nepc.colorado.edu/sites/default/files/Wiley _ APractitionersGuide.pdf`).

Simple Gain Score Assessment

Simple gain score assessment is based on relating the gain in a student's score to her teacher. An example is given in the worksheet Simple gain assessment of the workbook VAA.xlsx. Three fifth-grade teachers each have 30 students, and we are given each student's fourth- and fifth-grade test scores (using a percentile ranking from 1 to 100). Simple gain score assessment rates each teacher based on the average test score gain for their students. We used a PivotTable (see the "Excel Calculations" section at the end of this chapter) to obtain the results shown in Figure 11.1. We see that Teacher 1 earns the best score because Teacher 1's students improved by an average of 4.11% and that Teacher 3 earns the worst score because Teacher 3's students declined by an average of 2.39%.

Simple gain score assessment is easy to implement and explain, but it has many drawbacks:

- A teacher's assessment does not use data from previous years.

- Students are not randomly assigned to each teacher, so the characteristics of the students assigned to each teacher may be very different. For example, if there were only three disruptive students, and they were all assigned to Teacher 3, that might account for Teacher 3's poor performance.

- The assessment treats all 5-point gains, for example, as identical. It may be that an increase in score from 40 to 45 is different from an increase from 90 to 95.

- If all your incoming students have a score of 99, you have nowhere to go but down!

- Powerful parents (watch or read *Big Little Lies* or *Little Fires Everywhere!*) may successfully lobby for their children to be assigned to the teachers who are perceived the best. This may cause the data to overestimate the ability of the better teachers.

- If all three of our teachers in a school are good, then the "worst" of the three may really be an above-average teacher.

	J	K	L	M
6	Row Labels	Average of Change	Count of Teacher	Teacher Effect
7	1	8.57	30	4.11
8	2	2.73	30	-1.72
9	3	2.07	30	-2.39
10	(blank)			
11	Grand Total	4.46	90	

Figure 11.1: Example of simple gain score model

Covariate Adjustment Assessment

Simple gain score assessment does not allow for the effects of previous teachers to diminish over time. As Wiley points out, this omission can bias estimates of teacher effectiveness. For example, suppose a fourth-grade teacher would increase scores by 5 points on average. Also suppose the effect of a teacher diminishes at a rate of 20% per year. Suppose a student scores 80 in third grade, 85 in fourth grade, and 87 in fifth grade. Without accounting for the diminished effect of the fourth-grade teacher, we would incorrectly estimate the effect of the fifth-grade teacher as 87 − 85 = 2 points. In reality, the contribution of the fourth-grade teacher is now 0.80 * 5 = 4 points, so the fifth-grade teacher should be credited with a gain of 87 − 84 = 3 points.

In most implementations of covariate assessment, a student's gain in score is adjusted for demographic characteristics such as income, race, English as a second language, and school-level factors such as school crowding, and quality and quantity of support staff.

Covariate assessment has the disadvantage of being skewed by missing data (students may drop out or switch schools between fourth and fifth grade) and by ignoring a student's test scores from multiple previous years.

Layered Assessment Model

Versions of the Layered Assessment model are marketed by the statistical software firm SAS. It uses a student's test scores from multiple years but assumes teacher effects do not diminish. The most popular implementation of the layered model is the EVAAS (Education Value-Added Assessment System) model that originated in Tennessee. The EVAAS model does not adjust for student characteristics because its proponents believe that test scores incorporate a student's relevant demographic characteristics (sort of like the efficient market hypothesis postulates that the current price of a stock incorporates all information needed to predict the future price of the stock).

Cross-Classified Constant Growth Assessment

The cross-classified constant growth model assumes that each student makes progress (measured by their average change in test scores) at a constant rate during previous years.

Cross-classified constant growth assessment is illustrated in worksheet CC Constant Growth of the file VAA.xlsx. For each fifth-grade student, we are given

- The student's fifth-grade teacher (1, 2, or 3)
- The student's fourth-grade test score
- The average growth per year in the student's previous test scores
- The student's fifth-grade test score

Using a PivotTable (see Figure 11.2 and the "Excel Calculations" section), we found for each teacher the average change in test score from fourth to fifth grade. For example, Teacher 1's students improved by an average of 7.6 points. We also found the average for each teacher of their students' previous average growth rates over previous years. For example, we found that in previous years Teacher 1's students improved by an average of 5 points. Then we found the teacher-adjusted gains shown in Table 11.1. Note that Teacher 2 had the worst average improvement, but because Teacher 2's students had shown poor progress in the past, that teacher came out with the best rating. The average of the three adjusted gains was 2.06, so to adjust for this school's effect, we subtract 2.06 from each adjusted gain rating and find the final ratings shown in Table 11.2.

	K	L	M	N	O
4	Row Labels	Average of Score change	Average of Student Average change	Teacher Adjusted Gain	Teacher Effect
5	1	7.6		5	2.6	0.54
6	2	-1.1		-4	2.9	0.84
7	3	1.68		1	0.684211	-1.38

Figure 11.2: Cross-classified growth model

Table 11.1: Teacher adjusted gains

TEACHER	ADJUSTED GAINS
Teacher 1	7.6 – 5 = 2.6
Teacher 2	–1.1 – (–4) = 2.9
Teacher 3	1.68 – 1 = 0.68

Table 11.2: Final teacher ratings

TEACHER	FINAL RATING
Teacher 1	2.6 – 2.06 = 0,54
Teacher 2	2.9 – 2.06 = 0.84
Teacher 3	0.68 – 2.06 = –1.38

The classified growth assessment assumes a constant student growth rate and also assumes that previous teacher effects do not diminish. This may limit its usefulness. Also, the model does not include adjustments for possible changes in a student's demographic status that might change the student's growth trajectory.

Problems with VAA

The EVAAS model, the most commonly used VAA model, is complex and not easy to explain. Audrey Amrein-Beardsley and Tray Geiger present a devastating critique of EVAAS based on its implementation in Houston, Texas ("All Sizzle and No Steak: Value-Added Model Doesn't Add Value in Houston", *Phi Delta Kappan, Vol. 99 no. 2, September 2017, pages 53-59*).

- In 2011, EVAAS fired 221 teachers (partially based on their EVAAS evaluation).

- Five years later, Houston dropped EVAAS.

- During the years EVAAS was used, Houston students showed no improvement in test scores.

- A major problem in Houston was that teacher ratings were inconsistent from year to year. From one year to the next, more than 65% of all Houston teachers saw their ratings change by between two and four categories (for example, from highly ineffective to highly effective).

- In 2017, the Houston District Court agreed that Houston's teacher evaluation system (largely based on EVAAS) was seriously flawed (lawprofessors.typepad.com/education _ law/2017/08/federal-court-finds-texas-teacher-evaluation-system-is-a-house-of-cards-issuing-ruling-that-helps-it.html).

The lack of consistency in EVAAS ratings is probably due to the fact that VAA models indicate that teachers account for between 1% and 14% of student variation in test scores (amstat.tandfonline.com/doi/full/10.1080/2330443X.2014.956906#.XSPjBuhKguQ).

Since other factors contribute to most of the variability in test scores, it is hard to come up with models that all stakeholders will approve. For example, the NEPC (National Education Policy Center) used the same data as the *LA Times* and built their own VAA model (nepc.colorado.edu/publication/due-diligence). For more than half the teachers, the NEPC model disagreed with the *LA Times'* effectiveness rating.

A Columbia study (www0.gsb.columbia.edu/mygsb/faculty/research/pubfiles/11584/value-added.pdf) points out that correlations between year-to-year ratings of the same teacher range between 0.18 and 0.64. This degree of consistency does not seem to justify the use of EVAAS for high-stakes decisions such as teacher termination.

For another horror story, consider the classification of Pascale Mauclair as the worst teacher in New York City (www.ascd.org/publications/educational _ leadership/nov12/vol70/num03/Use _ Caution _ with _ Value-Added _ Measures. aspx). Her class consisted entirely of English as a second language students, and many of her students did not take the test used in the evaluation. Her rating was based on 11 students who entered her classroom during different parts of the year. Other teachers at her school report her as being an excellent teacher. I believe that if VAA is used, it must be combined with other metrics such as peer review to be useful in teacher evaluation.

Stanford professor Linda Darling-Hammond presents another devasting critique of VAA models (see edpolicy.stanford.edu/library/blog/573). She points out the following:

- When teachers are rated on quintiles (similar to the income quintiles discussed in Chapter 9, "Intergenerational Mobility"), ratings are very inconsistent from year to year. For example, 25%–45% of the teachers ranked in the bottom quintile one year move to the top quintile. Also, 25%–45% of the teachers in the top quintile one year move to the bottom quintile.

- Random assignment of students to teacher is a key component of accurate teacher ratings. To illustrate, if there were 50 students in a two-teacher school, you flip a coin for each student. Heads assigns a student to Teacher 1, and tails assigns a student to Teacher 2. Once a teacher has 25 students, then all other students are assigned to the other teacher. Random assignment ensures that on average each teacher has students near equal in ability and demographic characteristics. Unfortunately, random assignment is rare. In Houston, teachers with the most English language learners who were being transitioned into mainstream classrooms had the lowest ratings.

- Teachers of top students are less likely to show value-added because their students already have high scores.

How Much Is a Good Teacher Worth?

I believe an excellent K–12 teacher is worth much more to society than is indicated by their salary. Raj Chetty, John N. Friedman, and Jonah E. Rockoff agree. In their paper ("Measuring the Impacts of Teachers II: Teacher Value-Added and Student Outcomes in Adulthood," *American Economic Review*, Vol. 104, No. 9, September 2013, pages 2593-2632), Chetty, Friedman, and Rockoff appear to have come up with a (very complex) measure of teacher value-added that resolves problems with other VAA methods. The authors claim that a one-standard deviation improvement in value-added ability of a reading or math teacher in grades 4–8 reduces the probability that a female student gives birth while a teenager and also leads to a $4,600 increase in lifetime income (measured in today's dollars). Assuming 30 students per class, this implies that a teacher who is one standard deviation better than average in both math and reading would increase a student's lifetime earnings by 30 * $4,600 = $138,000 relative to the child's earnings if the teacher was average. Of course, this is far more than a teacher's annual salary.

Professor Dale Ballou of Vanderbilt wrote a clear, incisive review of Chetty and colleagues' study (see `nepc.colorado.edu/thinktank/review-long-term-impacts`). Ballou stated that the study's complex value-added measures are indeed superior to previous measures. Ballou concluded, however, that the improved later in life outcomes found by Chetty and colleagues might be due to a factor omitted from the study, such as the tendency of a family to emphasize the value of character and educational success. It is very possible that high value-added teachers have been assigned more students with "good parenting skills." Such parents may have successfully lobbied to get their children assigned to the better teachers. This nonrandom assignment (as measured by parenting skills) may have caused much of the observed better later in life outcomes.

Excel Calculations

In this section, we introduce you to Excel's powerful PivotTable tool, which allows you to "slice and dice" your data.

Creating the PivotTable for Simple Gain Score Assessment

The following steps show how to analyze the data used in our simple gain score adjustment example:

1. Select any cell in the range E4:H94 that contains the teacher and student data.

2. From the Insert tab, choose PivotTable and choose cell J6 in the current worksheet as the upper-left corner of the range where the PivotTable will be placed.

3. From the PivotTable Fields list, drag Teacher to the Rows and Values areas and Change to the Values area (above Teacher).

4. Select a cell in the range K7:K9, right-click and choose Summarize Values By, and choose Average.

5. Select a cell in the range L7:L9, right-click and choose Summarize Values By, and choose Count. This ensures that the PivotTable counts the number of students in each teacher's class.

Creating the PivotTable for Constant Growth Assessment

These steps show how to analyze the data used in our constant growth assessment example:

1. Select any cell in the range D3:H62.

2. From the Insert tab, choose PivotTable and choose cell K4 in the current worksheet as the upper-left corner of the range where the PivotTable will be placed.

3. From the PivotTable Fields list, drag the Student Average Change and Score Change fields to the Values area (with Score Change on top) and drag Teacher to the Rows area.

4. Select a cell in the range L4:L6, right-click and choose Summarize Values By, and choose Average.

5. Select a cell in the range M4:M6, right-click and choose Summarize Values By, and choose Average.

Berkeley, Buses, Cars, and Planes

You have to really be careful when you analyze data. In this chapter, we will use careful, logical thinking to resolve the following four famous paradoxes in data analysis and high school math:

- In 1973, a total of 35% of women applying to Berkeley's graduate school were admitted and 44% of men applying to Berkeley's graduate school were admitted (see `homepage.stat.uiowa.edu/~mbognar/1030/Bickel-Berkeley.pdf`). Does this discrepancy indicate that Berkeley admissions were biased against women?

- You take the bus to work every morning and the average time between buses is 60 minutes. With a quick calculation, you figure that on average if you arrive in the middle of a 60-minute interval, you should wait on average 30 minutes for a bus. It seems to you, however, that on average you wait much longer. What's going on?

- We drive from Bloomington, Indiana to Evansville, Indiana to visit my mother-in-law. In the morning, we drive the 80 miles at a speed of 80 miles per hour. In the evening, we drive back during rush hour and only average 40 miles per hour. Do we average 60 miles per hour for our trip?

- Your airline reports that the load factor—the average fraction of seats full on a flight—is 77.5%. As we all know, pre COVID-19 most flights were nearly completely full. How is this possible?

Simpson's Paradox and College Admissions

Simpson's paradox takes place when one type of behavior occurs in a total population (in the population of college students, women are less likely to be admitted than men). However, in subgroups of the population the behavior is reversed (*in every college major, women are more likely to be admitted than men!*). In the workbook `College.xlsx`, we use PivotTables and PivotCharts to explore Simpson's paradox. (See the "Excel Calculations" section at the end of this chapter for details.) For each of 1,000 applicants, we are given gender, major (1 or 2) applied for, and whether the person was admitted or rejected. Our data is fictitious, because our made-up data is easier to understand than the actual data.

First, we look at overall admission rate by gender (see Figure 12.1). We find that 42% of men were admitted but only 39.2% of women were admitted.

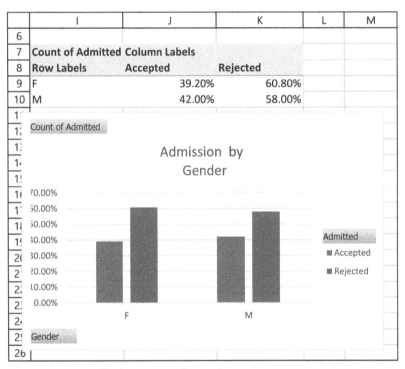

Figure 12.1: Overall admission rate by gender

Does this small difference in admission rates by gender indicate discrimination? In analytics, we always try to block out the effect of all variables that might influence the statistic of interest. Since different majors vary in selectivity, the applicant's major might influence their chance of admission. Therefore, in Figure 12.2, we use a PivotTable and PivotChart to calculate and display the admission percentage by gender for each major (Major 1 and Major 2). We find that in each major, a higher percentage of women are admitted: 12% to 10% in Major 1 and 80% to 50% in Major 2. Since in each major, women are accepted at a higher rate, why are women admitted at a lower rate overall? The only way this can happen is if a much larger percentage of women (relative to men) apply to the more selective major. As shown in Figure 12.3, this is exactly the situation. We find that 60% of the women apply to highly selective Major 1, whereas only 20% of the men apply to Major 1.

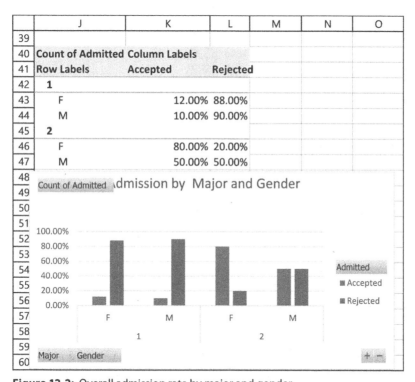

Figure 12.2: Overall admission rate by major and gender

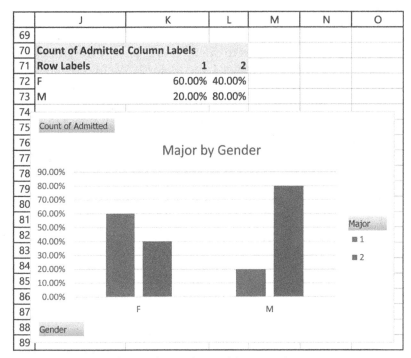

	J	K	L	M	N	O
69						
70	**Count of Admitted Column Labels**					
71	**Row Labels**	**1**	**2**			
72	F	60.00%	40.00%			
73	M	20.00%	80.00%			
74						
75	Count of Admitted					
76						
77						
78						
79						
80						
81						
82						
83						
84						
85						
86						
87						
88	Gender					
89						

Figure 12.3: Overall fraction by gender, applying to each major

The Waiting Time Paradox

There are many ways that the average time between buses can be 60 minutes, but let's suppose the time between buses is equally likely to be 30 or 90 minutes (which averages out to 60 minutes). Since there are as many 30-minute intervals as 90-minute intervals and a 90-minute interval covers three times as much time as a 30-minute interval, we are three times more likely to arrive during a 90-minute interval than during a 30-minute interval. If we arrive during a 90-minute interval on average, we will wait 45 minutes for a bus, and if we arrive during a 30-minute interval, we will on average wait 15 minutes for a bus. Therefore, the average waiting time is (3 / 4) * 45 + (1 / 4) * 15 = 37.5 minutes, which is longer than 30 minutes. It can be shown that unless buses always arrive *exactly 60 minutes apart*, then you will wait on average longer than 30 minutes.

When Is the Average of 40 and 80 Not 60?

I am driving 80 miles from Bloomington Indiana to Evansville Indiana and back. I drive 40 mph on my trip from Bloomington to Evansville and 80 mph on my return form Evansville. Why isn't my average speed 60 mph?

The key fact needed to understand this common question is the simple equation

Rate * Time = Distance or Time = Distance / Rate

If our trip is 80 miles each way, we spend 80 / 80 = 1 hour going one way and 80 / 40 = 2 hours the other way. Therefore, our average speed is 160 / 3 = 53.33 mph. The reason our average speed is less than (80 + 40) / 2 = 60 is because we spend more time traveling at the slower speed.

Why Pre COVID Were There Never Empty Seats on My Flight?

Let's suppose that the average percentage of seats full on all flights is 77.5%. Assume each plane has 100 seats. Then one way the "load factor" could be 77.5% would be if the airline ran four flights, three of which were 100% full and one that is 10% full. Then 310 people are on these flights, and you are equally likely to be any of these people. Three hundred people flying will be on a flight that is 100% full and only 10 people will be on a flight that is 10% full. Thus, on average a randomly chosen person will have (300 / 310) * 100 + (10 /310) * 10 = 97.1% of the seats full on her flight. This sad but true example explains why the flight attendant almost always says "We have a really full flight today!"

Excel Calculations

We now show how to use PivotTables to quickly resolve Simpson's paradox.

Determining Admission Rate by Gender

Use the following steps to determine the admission rate by gender:

1. Select any cell in the range C5:F1005, and from the Insert tab, select PivotTable. Choose cell I7 as the upper-left corner of your PivotTable range.

2. Drag Gender to the Rows area and drag Admitted to the Columns and Values areas. You now have a count of how many people of each gender are accepted or rejected.

3. Right-click in any of cells J9:K10 and then choose Show Values As % Of Row Total. You now see for each gender the fraction of applicants admitted.

4. Select any cell in the PivotTable, select PivotChart from the PivotTable Analyze tab (earlier versions of Excel may call it the Analyze or Options tab), and you obtain the chart shown in Figure 12.1.

Determining Admission Rate by Gender and Major

Use the following steps to determine the admission rate by gender and major:

1. Select any cell in the range C5:F1005 and from the Insert tab, select PivotTable. Choose cell J40 as the upper-left corner of your PivotTable range.

2. Drag Major and then Gender to the Rows area and drag Admitted to the Columns and Values areas. You now have for each major, a count of the number of people of each gender that are accepted or rejected.

3. Right-click in any of cells K43:L44 (or K46:L47) and then choose Show Values As % Of Row Total. You now see for each gender and major the fraction of applicants admitted.

4. Select any cell in the PivotTable, select PivotChart from the PivotTable Analyze tab (earlier versions of Excel may call it the Analyze or Options tab), and you obtain the chart shown in Figure 12.2.

Determining the Fraction of Each Gender Applying to Each Major

Use the following steps to determine the fraction of each gender applying to each major:

1. Select any cell in the range C5:F1005, and from the Insert tab, select PivotTable. Choose cell J70 as the upper-left corner of your PivotTable range.

2. Drag Gender to the Rows area and drag Major to the Columns and Values areas. Then right-click anywhere in the PivotTable and choose Summarize Values By and choose Count. For each major, you now have the number of people of each gender that are accepted or rejected.

3. Right-click in any of cells K72:L73 and then choose Show Values As % Of Row Total. You now see for each gender and major the fraction of applicants admitted.

4. Select any cell in the PivotTable, select PivotChart from the PivotTable Analyze tab (earlier versions of Excel may call it the Analyze or Options tab), and you obtain the chart shown in Figure 12.3.

CHAPTER 13

Is Carmelo Anthony a Hall of Famer?

The fantastic website Basketball-reference.com has a Hall of Fame Prediction tool (see `www.basketball-reference.com/leaders/hof _ prob.html`). The site gives Carmelo Anthony a 98% chance of making the Hall of Fame and Manu Ginóbili a mere 20% chance of making the Hall of Fame.

Entering the 2019–2020 season, Carmelo (Melo) Anthony had scored 25,551 points, ranking 19th on the all-time player list. LeBron James was the only active player ranking ahead of Melo. Melo did win three Olympic Gold Medals and an NCAA title, but I don't think his pro career merits election to the Springfield, Massachusetts Hall of Fame. As you will see, he did not have a great impact on his team winning games, and he took a lot of bad shots. Through the 2019 season, his teams won only three playoff series in 15 years. On average, NBA teams win 0.5 playoff series per year (15 series per year divided by 30 teams), so winning 0.2 playoff series per year is not great.

Basketball-reference.com's Hall of Fame tool gives Spurs legend Manu Ginóbili only a 20% chance of making the Hall of Fame. Manu scored only 14,043 (regular season) points in his career. I loved watching him play and loved Charles Barkley's comments on Ginóbili's take-no-prisoners style of play. (Listen to Charles on `www.youtube.com/watch?v=8SDMfiJfiyE`.) Manu's Spurs took four NBA titles. Manu also had a great international career, playing two years in Europe and leading Argentina to a second-place finish in the 2002 World Basketball Championships. I hope I can convince you that Manu's pro career deserves election to the Hall of Fame more than Melo's.

What Metric Defines Basketball Ability?

For many years, analysts tried to combine box score statistics into a single number that summarizes a player's abilities. Perhaps the most popular metric was John Hollinger's PER (player efficiency rating), which is still published on ESPN.com. PER assigns weights to each box score statistic with good things (like a steal) being assigned a positive weight and bad things (like a missed shot or turnover) being assigned a negative weight. On ESPN's great show *First Take*, Max Kellerman often refers to PER. Melo has a career PER of 20.3, and Manu has a virtually identical PER of 20.2; therefore, based on PER, Melo and Manu are basically equal.

PER has several problems:

- Since the box score includes few defensive statistics, PER does not capture the full impact of a player's defensive ability.

- If a player is a bad shooter (say, he makes 36% of his shots), then increasing the number of shots taken will increase a player's PER rating.

In 1999, the author and noted sports statistician Jeff Sagarin developed adjusted plus/minus (APM) (see `www.nytimes.com/2003/04/27/sports/pro-basketball-mavericks-new-math-may-be-an-added-edge.html`). The idea behind APM is that a good player helps move the score of the game in his team's favor when he is on the court, and when he is off the court, the score moves against his team.

To understand APM, we first need to understand the pure plus-minus measure (+/–). Pure +/– for a player is simply the points per 48 minutes a player's team outscores the opposing team when the player is on the court. For example, during the 2018–2019 season, Giannis Antetokounmpo of the Bucks led the league in +/– with 12.9. This means when Giannis was on the court, the Bucks outscored the opposing team by 12.9 points per 48 minutes. On the other hand, when Kevin Knox of the Knicks was on the court, the Knicks lost by a horrific 15.4 points per game. You cannot judge a player's ability by looking at pure +/–. To see why, suppose a player on the 2019 champion Raptors had a +/– of +1, and a player on the horrific Knicks had a +/– of +1. The Knicks player is much better because he made a poor team above average and the Raptors player must not be very good because he turned the best team into a near-average team.

Our contribution was realizing that a pure +/– needs to be adjusted for the other nine players on the court. After adjusting for the other nine players on the court, Jrue Holiday of the New Orleans Pelicans had an adjusted +/– of 18 points per game, even though the Pelicans only won by 5 points per game (PPG) when he was on the court. APM recognizes that you can do many things to help your team that don't show up in the box score.

Steve Ilardi and Jeremias Engelmann developed real plus-minus (RPM) for ESPN.com (see www.espn.com/nba/statistics/rpm/_/sort/RPM). RPM combines box score statistics and movement of the score margin when a player is on and off the court. In our discussion of Manu versus Melo, we will use RPM (publicly available) as a measure of player ability. RPM measures how many points per 100 possessions a player adds to his team's performance relative to an average NBA player. In the 2018–2019 season, Paul George of the Oklahoma City Thunder led with an RPM of +7.6 points per 100 possessions.

Wins Above Replacement Player (WARP)

Analytics professionals have recently fallen in love with trying to figure out a player's Wins Above Replacement Player (WARP). First proposed by baseball analyst Keith Woolner, WARP understands that players create ability by their ability (measured by RPM in basketball) but also for the minutes they play because most players are better than "a replacement player" who can be purchased at little cost. NBA replacement player level is an RPM near –3. I have reverse-engineered the ESPN WARP formula and some illustrations of how minutes played and RPM are converted to WARP, as shown in Table 13.1.

Table 13.1: WARP based on minutes and RPM

RPM	MINUTES PLAYED	WARP
3	800	3.1
2	1000	3.3
1	1200	3.1
0	2500	5
–1	2700	3.6
–2	2900	2

Note that if you play a lot of minutes and are an average player (RPM = 0), you create more wins than the first listed player who is an above average player who does not play many minutes. This version of WARP has the following desirable properties:

- Keeping minutes fixed, an increase in a player's RPM, increases his WARP.
- If a player's RPM is above –3.1 (basically a replacement-level player), then increasing his minutes played increases his WARP.

Manu, Melo, Dirk, and Dwayne

Most Hall of Fame voters will vote for a player if he exhibits dominant performance during his peak years. A perfect example is Sandy Koufax, who was an amazing pitcher for six years (1961–1966). In his first six years, Koufax generated only eight WARP. In his last six years, he averaged eight WARP per year! We arbitrarily will define the relative time frame for peak performance to be a player's best eight years. Table 13.2 shows Manu's and Melo's WARP for their best eight-year period. We also included information on Dwyane Wade and Dirk Nowitzki, both of whom are considered sure first-ballot Hall of Famers.

Table 13.2: WARP during peak years

PLAYER	YEARS	TOTAL WARP
Manu Ginóbili	2003–2004 to 2010–2011	84.2
Carmelo Anthony	2009–2010 to 2016–2017	66.9
Dwyane Wade	2006–2007 to 2013–2014	112.8
Dirk Nowitzki	2001–2002 to 2008–2009	147!

This data indicates that Manu has a better Hall of Fame case than Melo.

How Do 25,000 Points Lead to So Few Wins?

The natural question is, how could Melo have scored nearly twice as many points as Manu but generated fewer wins during their peak years? Our adjusted +/− numbers indicate that after adjusting for the other nine players on the court, Manu was around 2 points per 100 possessions better on defense than Melo during his peak years, and, despite scoring many fewer points, Manu was around 2 points better on offense than Melo.

A lot of why Manu shows up better in RPM than Melo is because Manu took better shots. It is now common knowledge that layups (0–3-feet shots) and three-pointers are good shots, and most other shots are much worse. During the 2018–2019 season (all stats that follow are from the priceless Basketball-reference.com site), players averaged 1.32 points per shot on 0–3-foot shots, 1.07 points on three-point shots, and only 0.74 points on other shots. Table 13.3 summarizes this data and Manu's and Melo's career points per shot based on shot location.

There are many important pieces of information contained in Table 13.3:

- Currently, NBA players are bad at mid-range shots.
- Melo was better than average on mid-range shots, *but he took way too many of these bad shots.*

Table 13.3: Shooting stats for 2018–2019 NBA, Manu and Melo

PLAYER	FRACTION OF 0–3-FT. SHOTS	PTS. PER SHOT ON 0–3-FT. SHOTS	FRACTION OF SHOTS THAT ARE 3S	POINTS PER SHOT ON 3S	FRACTION OF SHOTS FROM OTHER LOCATIONS	PTS. PER SHOT ON OTHER SHOTS	OVERALL PTS. PER SHOT
NBA 2018-2019	29%	1.32	36%	1.07	35%	**0.74!**	1.03
Manu	29%	1.24	40%	1.11	31%	0.80	1.05
Melo	31%	1.18	19%	0.99	**50%!**	0.80	0.95

■ Manu took a lot of three-pointers, even before three-pointers became fashionable, and averaged more points per shot on three-pointers than the current average NBA shooter.

NBA box scores still do not include charges taken, deflections, and other important statistics. With cameras in every NBA arena, I am sure future NBA analysts will come up with more and more key statistics that help us better understand what makes a great player. Some of the camera data is recorded on NBA.com (see stats.nba.com/players/hustle/). Here are examples from the 2018–2019 Regular Season data:

■ Paul George of the Thunder and Robert Covington of the Timberwolves led the league in deflections per game.

■ Paul George also led the league in loose balls recovered per game.

■ Eryan Ilyasova of the Bucks led the league in charges drawn per game.

■ Brook Lopez of the Bucks contested the most shots per game.

Was Derek Jeter a Great Fielder?

I'm not a Yankees fan, but like all baseball fans, I appreciated the greatness of Derek Jeter. He received 396 of 397 possible votes (only Yankee reliever Mariano Rivera was unanimous) in the 2020 Hall of Fame vote (the first year he was eligible). The Gold Glove is given each year in baseball to the best fielder at a given position. Jeter won the Gold Glove for shortstops five times: 2004–2006 and 2009–2010. (Only four shortstops won more Gold Gloves.) Unfortunately, these Gold Gloves were a miscarriage of justice, based primarily on a lack of understanding of what makes a good fielder (see grantland.com/features/ the-tragedy-derek-jeter-defense/). In this chapter, we will show that Jeter did not deserve his Gold Gloves. The moral of the chapter is that bad metrics can lead to improper evaluation of your employees.

Fielding Statistics: The First Hundred Years

The first Major League Baseball game was played in 1869. Until sabermetric genius Bill James came up with range factor in the 1970s, the most commonly used fielding statistic was fielding percentage, which is calculated by the formula Putouts + Assists divided by Putouts + Assists + Errors. Essentially, it is the fraction of balls that a fielder "handles" successfully. Table 14.1 shows Jeter's and the American league average (per Baseball-reference.com) fielding percentages during his Gold Glove years. For example, in 2009, Jeter successfully fielded

Table 14.1: Jeter and league average fielding percentages

YEAR	JETER'S FIELDING PERCENTAGE	LEAGUE AVERAGE
2004	.981	.972
2005	.979	.972
2006	.975	.970
2009	.986	.972
2010	.989	.973

98.6% of balls he handled, whereas the American league average was 97.2%. This is 14 more errors per 1,000 chances. Jeter averaged around 600 chances during his Gold Glove years, so he made around 8 fewer errors per year than an average shortstop.

In all five years that Jeter won the coveted Gold Glove, he successfully handled a higher percentage of balls than the average shortstop. Therefore, fielding percentage does not give any evidence that Jeter was a below average fielder. *The problem with fielding percentage is that it is not affected by balls a fielder does not get near. So, if a fielder has little mobility and just handles easy chances, then (all other things being equal), the fielder will raise his fielding percentage.* In the 1970s, baseball genius (and hopefully future Hall of Fame member!) Bill James came up with range factor, an incredibly simple but powerful improvement to fielding percentage. (Watch the great *60 Minutes* profile of James at `www.cbsnews.com/news/the-red-sox-stat-man-and-the-numbers-game/`.)

Range Factor

When Bill James came up with range factor, the only information we had for fielders were putouts (for a shortstop, usually a fly ball caught or stepping on second in a double play), assists (usually a successfully fielded ground ball on which the shortstop throws the ball to the first baseman and the ball arrives before the runner), and errors (a misplayed ball that could have been an assist or a putout). To measure the "range" of a fielder, James simply adds together Putouts + Assists per 9 innings and divides by the league average. Table 14.2 gives Jeter's range factors during his Gold Glove years. We find in 2010 that Jeter got to 14.1% fewer balls per 9 innings than an average shortstop. So, if there were 600 balls per year that an average shortstop would have fielded successfully, Jeter might have missed (0.141) * 600 = 84 balls that should have been outs! Of course, range factor does not estimate the difficulty of each chance and does not adjust for the fact that if Yankees pitchers struck out a lot of batters, he would have had fewer balls hit toward him.

Table 14.2: Jeter's range factors

YEAR	RANGE FACTOR
2004	.978
2005	1.03
2006	.922
2009	.894
2010	.859

It seems like the next step would be to watch every batted ball and estimate the chance that an average fielder would have successfully fielded the ball. This observation brings us to the next improvement in the evaluation of fielding.

The Fielding Bible: A Great Leap Forward

I believe that John Dewan—author of *The Fielding Bible* (ACTA Publications, 2020)—deserves the most credit for improving the evaluation of fielders. Beginning with the 2003 season, Dewan and his colleagues at Baseball Info Solutions watched videotape of every Major League Baseball play and determined how hard each ball was hit and into which "zone" of the field the ball was hit. Then they determined the chance (based on all plays during a season) that a ball hit at a particular speed to a zone would be successfully fielded. For example, they might find that 20% of all balls hit softly over second base are successfully fielded by shortstops. A shortstop who successfully fields such a ball has prevented 1 hit. An average fielder would have successfully fielded this ball 20% of the time, so our shortstop has prevented $1 - .2 = .8$ hits more than an average player. In this case, our shortstop receives a score of +.8 on the batted ball. If our shortstop fails to make the play, he has prevented $0 - .2 = -.2$ hits, and he receives a score of −.2 on the batted ball. Note that if our shortstop successfully fields 1 in 5 chances in this zone, his net score is $.8 - 4(.2) = 0$, as we would hope. If over the course of a season, a shortstop has a net score of −20, then he has effectively given up 20 more hits than an average fielder. A shortstop with a score of +30 has effectively prevented 30 more hits than an average fielder.

It turns out that a hit is roughly equivalent to 0.8 runs (see my *Mathletics*, Princeton University Press, 2012). Therefore, the extra hits given up can be converted to runs. There are versions of runs above or below average for a fielder. For example, Fangraphs.com publishes ultimate zone rating (UZR) and Baseball-Reference.com published runs above or below average. We can get lost in the weeds debating the merits of various versions of runs above or below average. Table 14.3 gives Jeter's runs above or below average for his Gold Glove seasons.

Table 14.3: Jeter's runs above or below average

YEAR	RUNS ABOVE OR BELOW AVERAGE
2004	5
2005	−5
2006	−4
2009	−1
2010	−7

In 2010, for example, Jeter's fielding was estimated to be 7 runs worse than an average shortstop. This hardly justifies (*Justified* is a great TV show!) his 2010 Gold Glove. According to this metric, only in 2004 was Jeter an above average shortstop.

Despite his below average fielding, Jeter certainly deserves to be in the Hall of Fame. For each player, the Baseball-reference.com calculates (based on a non-pitcher's hitting and fielding) wins above replacement (WAR). A player's WAR measures how many more wins than a "replacement player" (a player who ranks in the bottom 20% of ability) the player in question generates during a season. In 2019, Cody Bellinger of the Dodgers led the majors with 9.1 wins above replacement. Derek Jeter ranked 91st all-time in WAR (www.baseball-reference.com/leaders/WAR_career.shtml). This includes the fact that his fielding generated −9.4 WAR! Since there are 235 players in the Hall of Fame, Jeter deserves his membership—but probably did not deserve to be only one vote shy of a unanimous vote.

The Next Frontier

All Major League parks now have the Statcast system. The Statcast system uses radar and high-definition video to measure many interesting statistics (see en.wikipedia.org/wiki/Statcast). For example, for fielding, Statcast measures for each batted ball quantities such as

- Length of time from when the ball was hit until the fielder takes the first step. Wish we had this for Willie Mays's amazing 1954 catch (watch it on www.mlb.com/video/bb-moments-willie-mays-catch-c3218956).

- Time to make a pivot on a double play ball (real important for second basemen and shortstops).

- Maximum velocity of the ball on each throw.

Using Statcast data, the website `baseballsavant.mlb.com/outs_above_aver age?type=player&year=2018&min=q` measures outs above average (OAA) for a fielder based on the likelihood that an average fielder would successfully field the batted ball. Center fielder Lorenzo Cain of the Brewers led all major leaguers in 2018 with 22 outs above average.

"Drive for Show and Putt for Dough?"

I averaged 90 for nine holes in high school before somebody stole my clubs (probably the people I played with), and I retired from the sport. Like many other golfers and golf fans, I thought that putting was the most important part of the game. After all, you probably use your driver for 12–15 shots and your putter for 30–40 of your shots. Putting is easy to practice, so common sense would dictate that you should spend more time practicing putting than practicing driving or approach shots. In his great book *Every Shot Counts* (Avery, 2014), my good friend Mark Broadie of the Columbia School of Business debunked the "drive for show and putt for dough" myth.

Strokes Gained

Through the PGA's ShotLink System, Mark had access to 15 million shots by PGA golfers. Using clever yet easy-to-explain analysis, Mark developed many important insights that help us better understand what causes a golfer's success (or failure). As you will see, the key idea behind Mark's analysis is like John Dewan's approach to analyzing MLB fielders. In this chapter, we will provide an overview of Mark's brilliant insights and analyses.

Recall from Chapter 14, "Was Derek Jeter a Great Fielder?," that each fielding play either gains the defensive team a saved baserunner or costs the defensive team a baserunner. Similarly, in golf, each shot either gains strokes or loses strokes. For example, PGA golfers take an average of 1.54 shots to get your ball in the cup (often referred to as holing out) from 8 feet, so if the golfer makes an 8-foot putt, they have taken 0.54 shots better than expected to hole out, and their putting rating is rewarded with 0.54 strokes gained. If the golfer two-putts on the hole from 8 feet, they lost 2 – 1.54 = 0.46 strokes putting on that hole.

For another example, suppose on a 399-yard par 4 hole a golfer hits the shots shown in Table 15.1. The table gives the expected strokes to hole out before and after each shot, as well as the strokes gained on each shot.

Table 15.1: Example of strokes gained

BALL BEFORE SHOT	BALL AFTER SHOT	EXPECTED SHOTS NEEDED BEFORE SHOT	EXPECTED SHOTS NEEDED AFTER SHOT	STROKES GAINED ON SHOT
399 yards from hole	286 yards from hole	3.99	3.65	0.34 – 1 = –0.66
286 yards from hole	62 yards from hole in sand	3.65	3.15	0.5 – 1 = –0.50
62 yards from hole in sand	17 feet from hole	3.15	1.8	1.35 – 1 = +0.35
17 feet from hole	Made putt!	1.8	0	1.8 – 1 = +0.8

For example, before the tee shot, an average golfer would need 3.99 strokes to hole out. They spent one stroke on the tee shot to gain 3.99 – 3.65 = 0.34 strokes, so they gained 0.34 – 1 = –0.66 strokes on that hole.

The Myth Exposed

During the 2004–2012 period, Tiger Woods was the best golfer and gained 2.8 strokes per round. Mark broke this down as 0.6 strokes gained on driving, 1.3 shots gained on approach, 0.3 shots gained on the short game, and 0.6 shots per round gained on putting. Mark found that on average, Top 10 golfers gained 20% of their strokes on driving, *45% on approach shots*, 20% on the short game, and only 15% on putting. As Mark said at the 2014 M.I.T. Sloan Analytics Conference, "You don't drive for show and putt for dough. It's really the long game that matters."

CHAPTER 16

What's Wrong with the NFL QB Rating?

In Chapter 14, "Was Derek Jeter a Great Fielder?," you learned that fielding percentage was a poor metric for measuring fielding ability. In this chapter, you will see that the NFL's well-known quarterback rating (hereafter referred to as NFL QBR) is a severely flawed measure of a quarterback's passing ability. We will use the important analytics tool of *multiple regression* to better understand the computation of the NFL QBR. Then we will show that evaluating the effectiveness of an NFL play by the number of points (not yards) gained or lost due to a play is vital to understanding NFL football. Finally, we will discuss ESPN's sophisticated *Total Quarterback Rating* (often referred to as Total *QBR*).

NFL Quarterback Rating

The NFL quarterback rating has been used since 1973 to rate the passing ability of NFL quarterbacks. (For the details of the formula, see en.wikipedia.org/wiki/Passer _ rating). The formula, though complex, is based on four statistics:

- Completion percentage
- Yards gained per pass attempt
- TD pass percentage (fraction of pass attempts that are TDs)
- Interception percentage (fraction of passes that are interceptions)

A quarterback's passing rating will range between 0 and 158.3, and a higher rating is "thought" to be better. During every NFL game, each quarterback's QB rating is shown multiple times. As you will soon see, the QB rating system is seriously flawed. To better understand the NFL QBR system, you need to learn about *multiple linear regression*, which may be the tool most widely used by analytics professionals.

A Primer on Multiple Linear Regression

In Chapter 8, "Modeling Relationships Between Two Variables," we explored how to fit straight-line relationships of the form:

$$Y = A + BX$$

The idea is that once we know the independent variable X and know the "best" values of A and B, we can come up with a good prediction for the dependent variable Y. *Multiple linear regression* is used to come up with a prediction for Y based on more than one (say, n) independent variables X1, X2, . . . , Xn. The form of the assumed relationship is

$$(1)\, Y = B0 + B1 * X1 + B2 * X2 +, \ldots, + BnXn$$

B0 is the equation intercept and B1, B2, . . . , Bn are the regression coefficients. Why the name multiple linear regression?

- Equation (1) is linear because independent variables always appear alone and multiplied by a constant.
- Equation (1) is multiple because it involves more than one independent variable.
- "Regression" is simply the technical term used to indicate that you are predicting Y from a bunch of independent variables.

To introduce you to regression, let's use 2018 NFL quarterback statistics (see worksheet QB Data of the workbook QBRating.xlsx). This worksheet contains passing statistics for the 2018 season for the 40 quarterbacks with the most passing attempts. For each quarterback, we have included the following relevant information (see Figure 16.1):

- PCT = Completion percentage (multiplied by 100) (X1)
- YDS/A = Yards per passing attempt (X2)
- TD Rate = Fraction (multiplied by 100) of passing attempts resulting in a TD (X3)
- Interception Rate (Int Rate) = Fraction (multiplied by 100) of pass attempts resulting in an interception (X4)
- RATE = NFLQBR (Y)

For example, 2018 MVP Patrick Mahomes had the following statistics:

- PCT = X1 = 66
- YDS/A = X2 = 8.79
- TD Rate = X3 = 8.62
- Int Rate = X4 = 2.07
- RATE = 113.8

	A	B	C	D	E	F	G	H	I	J	K	L	M
1	RK	PLAYER	TEAM	ATT	PCT	YDS/A	TD Rate	Int Rate	TD	INT	RATE	Prediction	Error
2	1	Ben Roethlisberger, QE	PIT	675	67	7.6	5.037	2.370	34	16	96.5	96.50	0.00
3	2	Patrick Mahomes, QB	KC	580	66	8.79	8.621	2.069	50	12	113.8	113.83	-0.03
4	3	Matt Ryan, QB	ATL	608	69.4	8.1	5.757	1.151	35	7	108.1	108.08	0.02
5	4	Jared Goff, QB	LAR	561	64.9	8.36	5.704	2.139	32	12	101.1	101.11	-0.01
6	5	Andrew Luck, QB	IND	639	67.3	7.19	6.103	2.347	39	15	98.7	98.69	0.01
7	6	Aaron Rodgers, QB	GB	597	62.3	7.44	4.188	0.335	25	2	97.6	97.60	0.00
8	7	Tom Brady, QB	NE	570	65.8	7.64	5.088	1.930	29	11	97.7	97.68	0.02
9	8	Philip Rivers, QB	LAC	508	68.3	8.48	6.299	2.362	32	12	105.5	105.49	0.01
10	9	Eli Manning, QB	NYG	576	66	7.46	3.646	1.910	21	11	92.4	92.37	0.03
11	10	Kirk Cousins, QB	MIN	606	70.1	7.09	4.950	1.650	30	10	99.7	99.68	0.02
12	11	Deshaun Watson, QB	HOU	505	68.3	8.25	5.149	1.782	26	9	103.1	103.12	-0.02
13	12	Derek Carr, QB	OAK	553	68.9	7.32	3.436	1.808	19	10	93.9	93.92	-0.02
14	13	Drew Brees, QB	NO	489	74.4	8.16	6.544	1.022	32	5	115.7	115.66	0.04

Figure 16.1: 2018 NFL QB statistics

Using Excel's Data Analysis tool and the Regression option (see the "Excel Calculations" section), we can find the values of B0, B1, B2, B3, and B4 that make the prediction given by (1) best fit the data:

$$(2)\ \text{Predicted NFL QBR} = B0 + B1*(\text{PCT}) + B2*(\text{YDS}/\text{A})$$
$$+ B3*(\text{TD Rate}) + B4*(\text{Int Rate})$$

Excel chooses B0, and B1 through B4 to minimize the sum over all QBs of [Rating – (Predicted Rating from (2))]². The resulting Regression output is given in the worksheet named Results and is shown in Figure 16.2.

The following are the key outputs of the regression:

- The equation best-fitting QB rating is given in the Coefficients section of the output (A17:B21 in the Results worksheet). The equation best-fitting NFL QBR is

$$\text{NFL QBR} = 2.19 + 0.83*\text{PCT} + 4.16*(\text{YDS}/\text{A})$$
$$+ 3.34*\text{TD Rate} - 4.18*(\text{Int Rate})$$

- The P-value column (E17:E21) gives a number between 0 and 1 for each independent variable. A low P-value (usually considered less than 0.05) indicates that *after adjusting for the other independent variables,* any independent variable with a low P-value is useful in fitting or predicting Y. We find, for example, the P-value for TD Rate is 9E-73. The E-73 is an example of *scientific notation*—in this case, it means the P-value is 9 times 10^{-73}. To illustrate how scientific notation works, note that 3E05 represents the number 3 times $10^5 = 300,000$. And the number 3E-05 represents the number 3 times 10^{-5}. *The P-value is the chance that after adjusting for the other independent variables, the given independent variable does not help you better fit or predict Y.* E-73 is a very small number, so this P-value means there is virtually no chance that TD Rate does not help you predict QB rating. All other independent variables have very small P-values, which indicates that each independent variable is a significant predictor for QBR.

▪ The R Square in B5 of 0.99999 means that our equation explains 99.999% of the variation in QB. As Jack Nicholson would say, this is about "as good as it gets."

▪ The Standard Error of 0.03 in cell B7 is the analog of the standard error of regression discussed in Chapter 8. Ninety-five percent of our predictions should be accurate within 2 standard errors (0.06). Column L of Figure 16.1 gives each quarterback's predicted NFLQBR. For example, Mahomes's predicted NFLQBR and the error in the prediction are calculated as follows:

$$NFL\ QBR\ Prediction = 2.19 + 0.83*66 + 4.16*8.79 + 3.34*8.62 - 4.18*2.7 = 113.83$$

▪ Then the prediction error for Mahomes is

$$113.80 - 113.83 = -0.03$$

	A	B	C	D	E	F	G
1	SUMMARY OUTPUT						
2							
3	*Regression Statistics*						
4	Multiple R	0.999996505					
5	R Square	0.99999301					
6	Adjusted R Square	0.999992211					
7	Standard Error	0.030867903					
8	Observations	40					
9							
10	ANOVA						
11		*df*	*SS*	*MS*	*F*	*Significance F*	
12	Regression	4	4771.016401	1192.7541	1251804.985	1.11E-89	
13	Residual	35	0.033348959	0.000952827			
14	Total	39	4771.04975				
15							
16		*Coefficients*	*Standard Error*	*t Stat*	*P-value*	*Lower 95%*	*Upper 95%*
17	Intercept	2.189310785	0.088775015	24.66133962	1.03189E-23	2.0090879	2.369534
18	PCT	0.832542278	0.001506671	552.5706135	1.45739E-70	0.8294836	0.835601
19	YDS/A	4.164073574	0.010651711	390.9300054	2.6475E-65	4.1424495	4.185698
20	TD Rate	3.335041453	0.005224291	638.3721138	9.32767E-73	3.3244356	3.345647
21	Int Rate	-4.184470197	0.00632377	-661.704989	2.65552E-73	-4.1973081	-4.17163

Figure 16.2: NFL QB rating regression output

- As shown in column M of Figure 16.1, there are no outliers. The average QBR is around 92, and on average our predictions are off by only 0.02 (less than 1% of the average QBR), so we see that our fitted ratings are very accurate.

We can now interpret each independent variable's regression coefficient. Analytics professionals often use the phrase *ceteris paribus* to indicate that regression coefficients are interpreted with the caveat "all other things being equal." This means that a regression coefficient identifies the effect of an independent variable after adjusting for all other independent variables in the equation.

- Each 1% increase in completion percentage increases NFL QBR by 0.83.
- Each 1-yard increase in YDS/A increases NFLQBR by 4.16 points.
- Each 1% increase in TD Rate increases NFL QBR by 3.34.
- Each 1% increase in Interception Rate *decreases* NFL QBR by 4.18.

Problems with the NFL QBR

We now use a few carefully chosen examples to illustrate the problems with QBR:

- Consider two quarterbacks:
  - QB 1: 100 passes, 100 completions, 250 yards, 0 TD, 0 interceptions
  - QB 2: 100 passes, 50 completions, 850 yards, 0 TD, 0 interceptions

  QB 1 is consistent, but his completions for an average of 2.5 yards are not very helpful to the team. Despite his lower completion rate, QB 2 generates 3.4 times more yardage per pass attempt. Using equation (2), we can estimate each player's NFL QBR. Equation (2) predicts an NFL QBR of 95.9 for QB 1 and only 79.2 for QB 2. This does not jive with our intuitive view that QB 2 is the better QB.

- If Mahomes throws a 9-yard pass on 3rd down and 20 yards to go, he increases his completion rate and also his YDS/A; therefore, his NFL QBR would increase even though the pass failed to get the first down. *This suggests that each play should be assigned a point value. In this situation the pass would have a negative point value.* We will discuss points per play in the next section.

- The NFL QBR gives approximately an 80-yard bonus for a touchdown pass. To see this, consider a quarterback that throws 100 passes with 8 YDS/A. Pretend one of the QB's 8-yard passes that was not a TD became a TD. Then his ratings increase by 3.34 points. To generate this many points in NFL QBR, his YDS/A must increase by 3.34 / 4.16 = 0.80. On 100 passes this requires 80 more passing yards. Such a trade-off hardly seems reasonable.

- The NFL QBR ignores sacks, fumbles, and quarterback rushing plays.

Also, how much better is an NFL QB rating of 90 than an NFL QB rating of 80? Who knows? You will soon see that points per play is much easier to interpret and much more meaningful than NFL QBR.

The Importance of Points per Play

To see why we need a concept of points per play, suppose a team has the ball on the 50-yard line, and it is 3rd down and 3 yards to go. If a rushing play gains 3 yards, it was a good play. If the situation was 3rd down and 9 yards to go at midfield and 3 yards were gained, the play was a bad play. Fantasy football and NFL official statistics would count these two plays as being equally effective, which is nonsense.

In 1971, Cincinnati Bengals Quarterback Virgil Carter and his thesis adviser at Northwestern, Robert Machol (*Operations Research*, 1971, pages 541–544) came up with the germ of the ideas needed to evaluate points per play. Carter and Machol looked at all 1st down and 10 yards–to-go plays from the 1969 season. Then they tracked the next game score and figured out the average number of points by which the team with the ball outscored the opponent. For example, they found when a team had 1st and 10 on their own 25-yard line, they outscored their opponent by an average of 0.25 points, and when a team had 1st and 10 from the opponent's 25-yard line, they outscored their opponent by an average of 3.68 points. Thus, we can say the "value" of having the ball 1st and 10 on your own 25 is 0.25 points and the value of having the ball 1st and 10 on the other team's 25 is 3.68 points. Therefore, a 50-yard pass play from your own 25 would generate 3.68 – 0.25 = 3.43 points.

Carter and Machol did not estimate point values for any situation other than 1st and 10. During 1983 in an unpublished paper, the author, along with noted *USA* sports statistician and my colleague the late, great Victor Cabot (his daughter Megan wrote *The Princess Diaries*) found values for all downs, yards to go, and yard line situations. Many versions of these values now exist, and there is no consensus on the correct values. *The important point is that the points added by a play is the value of the situation after the play – the value of the situation before the play.*

The wonderful website `Pro-football-reference.com` (PFR) gives point values for every play. The workbook `Superbowl19.xlsx` shows PFR's point values for each play. A few representative samples are given in Table 16.1.

As shown in Figure 16.3 and the worksheet Points Per Play in the workbook `QBRating.xlsx`, PFR has evaluated average points per play on passing attempts for each team during the 2018 season.

Table 16.1: Examples of points gained

DOWN	YARDS TO GO	YARD LINE	PLAY RESULT	POINTS ADDED
1	10	Own 48	19-yard gain	1.25
1	10	Own 37	3-yard gain	−0.14
2	8	Own 29	Incomplete pass	−0.7
2	3	Opp 31	29-yard gain	3.29
2	10	Opp 27	Interception 27 yards down the field	−2.85
1	10	Opp 45	Sacked for a 9-yard loss	−1.76
3	5	Opp 40	Incomplete pass	−1.42
1	10	Opp 49	3-yard gain	−0.13
1	10	Opp 49	4-yard gain	0.00

	D	I	J
3	Tm	Points per play	QBR Rank
4	Kansas City Chiefs	0.44	2
5	New Orleans Saints	0.40	1
6	New England Patriots	0.33	10
7	Los Angeles Chargers	0.31	5
8	Los Angeles Rams	0.29	7
9	Atlanta Falcons	0.27	4
10	Seattle Seahawks	0.24	3
11	Tampa Bay Buccaneers	0.24	16
12	Pittsburgh Steelers	0.23	13
13	Indianapolis Colts	0.22	9
14	Philadelphia Eagles	0.20	14
15	Houston Texans	0.19	6
16	Chicago Bears	0.18	15
17	Carolina Panthers	0.13	17
18	New York Giants	0.12	20
19	Cincinnati Bengals	0.11	25
20	Dallas Cowboys	0.11	12
21	Detroit Lions	0.11	23
22	San Francisco 49ers	0.11	24
23	Baltimore Ravens	0.10	27
24	Green Bay Packers	0.10	11
25	Minnesota Vikings	0.08	8

Figure 16.3: Expected points per passing attempt

For the most part, the team rankings by NFL QB rating and points per passing attempt yield consistent rankings, but there are several notable exceptions. The Patriots rank only 10th in NFL QB rating but rank third in points per passing attempt. This is to be expected, because Tom Brady is great when the game is on the line. The Vikings rank 8th on NFL QB rating but a poor 22nd on points per passing attempt. This means that in many key situations, Vikings passes failed to get the needed yardage.

We can also evaluate plays based on how a play changes the chance of a team winning a game. See "Evaluating NFL Plays: Expected Points Adjusted for Schedule," by Pelechrinis Konstantinos, Wayne Winston, Jeff Sagarin, and Vic Cabot, for the details (`dtai.cs.kuleuven.be/events/MLSA18/papers/pelechrinis_mlsa18.pdf`).

I predict that by 2023, NFL telecasts will routinely show points per play for a team's rushing and passing offense and defense, and the NFL QB rating will not be shown.

ESPN's Total Quarterback Rating

ESPN's Total Quarterback Rating (Total QBR) does a great job of isolating a quarterback's contribution to a team's success. The worksheet ESPN QBR (see Figure 16.4) of the workbook `QBRating.xlsx` gives Total QBRs for the 2018 season.

QBR begins with the expected points per play involving a QB (pass attempts, sacks, fumbles, rush attempts, and penalties) and then tries to allocate the expected points per play between the QB, receiver, and offensive line. For example, the receiver influences the credit given to the QB through yards gained after the catch and dropped passes. More weight is given to plays in clutch situations than plays that occur during garbage time. QBR is calibrated so the QBR is an estimate of the fraction of games a team would win with their QB if the rest of the team was average. Therefore, QBR should average to 50, and a QBR of 75 corresponds to a Pro Bowl-level quarterback. It's not surprising that Patrick Mahomes and Drew Brees rank #1 and #2 in QBR, respectively, but Bears QB Mitch Trubisky's #3 ranking may surprise you, because his NFL QB rank is #17. Trubisky's surprisingly high ranking may be due to the Bears not having great receivers.

	D	E	F
3	RK	PLAYER	TOTAL QB
4	1	Patrick Mahomes, KC	81.8
5	2	Drew Brees, NO	80.8
6	3	Mitchell Trubisky, CHI	73
7	4	Ben Roethlisberger, PIT	71.7
8	5	Andrew Luck, IND	71.7
9	6	Tom Brady, NE	70.5
10	7	Philip Rivers, LAC	70
11	8	Jameis Winston, TB	68.3
12	9	Matt Ryan, ATL	67.9
13	10	Jared Goff, LAR	65.9
14	11	Russell Wilson, SEA	65.6
15	12	Carson Wentz, PHI	64.3
16	13	Deshaun Watson, HOU	64.1
17	14	Kirk Cousins, MIN	61.9
18	15	Andy Dalton, CIN	61.8

Figure 16.4: 2018 ESPN QBR ratings

Excel Calculations

Here we describe how to run a multiple regression and then create predictions from it.

Running a Multiple Regression

Before running a multiple regression, you must first enable the Data Analysis add-in:

1. Select Options from the File tab.
2. Choose Add-Ins, select Excel Add-ins from the Manage drop-down list, and click Go.
3. Select the Analysis ToolPak (not the VBA) option and click OK. On the Data tab, you should now see Data Analysis on the right side of the ribbon.

To run the regression shown in Figure 16.2, proceed as follows.

1. Select Data Analysis from the Data tab and then choose Regression.
2. For Input Y Range, enter the QB ratings (range K1:K41), including the label in K1.

3. For Input X Range, enter the values of the four independent variables X1–X4 by entering the range E1:H41.

4. Select Labels (because our data has labels in the first row).

5. Select Residuals so that Excel returns for each observation the prediction as well as the error = actual NFLQBR – predicted NFLQBR.

6. Click OK to yield the regression output shown in Figure 16.2.

Creating Predictions from a Multiple Regression

The Excel TREND function provides a powerful (although tricky) method for creating predictions from a multiple regression. You don't even need the multiple regression coefficients! The TREND function is an array function. See Chapter 91 of my *Microsoft Excel 2019 Data Analysis and Business Modeling* (Microsoft Press, 2019). To use an array function, you need to first select the range where the results of the array function will go, and then type the formula and use the keystroke combination Ctrl+Shift+Enter. In newer versions of Office 365, you simply need to press Enter. To create the predictions from equation (2), we begin by selecting the range L2:L41. In cell L2, type the formula

= TREND(K2:K41,E2:H41,E2:H41).

After using the keystroke combination Ctrl+Shift+Enter, we obtain the predictions from (2) shown in L2:L41. Note that you can use the TREND function even if you do not know the regression equation (2)!

CHAPTER 17

Some Sports Have All the Luck

Most of us think our sports teams are cursed with bad luck. Certainly Franco Harris's "immaculate reception" (watch it here /www.youtube.com/ watch?v=dHIXFKrrUhA) was a lucky play for the Steelers and unlucky for the Raiders. In this chapter, we investigate a controversial topic: Among the NFL, MLB, NBA, NHL, Men's Olympic Basketball, Premier League Soccer, and the Premier Lacrosse League, which leagues have plays that involve the most skill (or least luck)?

Skill vs. Luck: The Key Idea

Senior Database Architect of Stats for MLB Advanced Media analyst Tom Tango was the first person to approach this knotty problem (see www.wired.com/2012/11/ luck-and-skill-untangled-qa-with-michael-mauboussin/). Michael Mauboussin brought more attention to this issue in his book *The Success Equation* (HBR Press, 2012). The basic idea presented by Tango and Mauboussin is embodied in the following equation:

$$\text{Outcome} = \text{Skill} + \text{Luck}$$

Most investigators have defined outcome as the fraction of games a team wins in a season (see, for example, (statsbylopez.github.io/NESSIS2017 _ files/ NESSIS _ 2017.html).

I prefer to try to understand the fraction of a sport's outcome that is luck by looking at the result of every game during a season. The data I use for each sport is the margin of victory in each game and two teams playing in the game. Then I use multiple regression (see Chapter 16, "What's Wrong with the NFL QB Rating?") to evaluate the relative skill level for each team. For example, for the 2016 Men's Olympic Basketball competition, the USA men's team was 22 points better than an average team, and China was 25 points worse than an average team. Therefore, based on skill level, we would predict the USA to beat China by 25 – (–22) = 47 points. (USA won by 57 points.)

To estimate the fraction of each sport that is "skill," we proceed as follows:

1. Use simple linear regression to determine the relative skill level or rating of each team (in points, goals, or baseball runs).

2. Predict the actual game margin from the "skill prediction," which equals Team 1 rating – Team 2 rating.

3. Compute actual margin by which Team 1 defeats Team 2.

4. Use a linear regression (Actual Margin = A + B * Predicted Margin) to predict the Actual Margin from the Predicted Margin.

5. Find the R^2 for this least squares line.

Then $1 – R^2$ is the fraction of the sport's results due to luck, and R^2 is the fraction of the sport's results due to skill.

Essentially, the main idea of the Outcome = Skill + Luck equation is that after you adjust for the skill level of the opposing teams, what's left is luck. For example, in the NFL every year, you look at actual game margin – Vegas Point spread, and you get a standard deviation of around 14 points. This randomness about the Vegas line we attribute to luck. Figure 17.1 and Figure 17.2 (see also the file `SkillSample.xlsx`) show simple examples of our approach.

In Figure 17.1, we see that the teams (see ratings in C4:C7) are very evenly matched but that, relative to the team skill differences, there is a lot of uncertainty about the game margin. Our skill estimate in cell G17 is 0.3%, and our luck estimate is 1 – 0.03 = 99.7%.

In Figure 17.2, we see that the teams (see ratings in C4:C7) are not evenly matched and that, relative to the team skill differences in game outcomes, there is little uncertainty about the game margin. Our skill estimate in cell G17 is 94.7%, and our luck estimate is a mere 1 – 0.947 = 5.3%.

	B	C	D	E	F	G	H
1							
2							
3	Team			Team 1	Team 2	Margin	Forecast
4	1	-1		1	2	-9	0.00
5	2	-1		1	3	3	-0.75
6	3	-0.25		1	4	-6	-3.25
7	4	2.25		2	3	-4	-0.75
8		0		2	4	-12	-3.25
9				3	4	-4	-2.50
10				1	2	-1	0.00
11				1	3	4	-0.75
12				1	4	1	-3.25
13				2	3	-5	-0.75
14				2	4	3	-3.25
15				3	4	0	-2.50
16						skill	
17						0.003584	

Figure 17.1: A lot of luck

	B	C	D	E	F	G	H
1							
2							
3	Team	Rating		Team 1	Team 2	Margin	Forecast
4	1	-14.125		1	2	-8	-7.375
5	2	-6.75		1	3	-13	-12.75
6	3	-1.375		1	4	-39	-36.375
7	4	22.25		2	3	-2	-5.375
8		0		2	4	-24	-29
9				3	4	-23	-23.625
10				1	2	-7	-7.375
11				1	3	-10	-12.75
12				1	4	-36	-36.375
13				2	3	-10	-5.375
14				2	4	-33	-29
15				3	4	-23	-23.625
16						skill	
17						0.947205	

Figure 17.2: Not much luck

The Results

Table 17.1 gives our estimates of skill and luck for a variety of sports.

Table 17.1: Skill vs. luck

SPORT	LUCK	SKILL
Baseball (MLB)	92%	8%
Hockey (NHL)	92%	8%
NBA	79%	21%
Lacrosse (PLL)	76%	24%
Soccer (Premier League)	75%	25%
NFL	67%	33%
Men's Olympic Basketball	45%	55%
Women's Olympic Basketball	15%	85%

These results indicate that baseball and hockey have the most luck. The problem with my analysis of baseball was that I predicted the outcome of each game based on each team's overall offensive and defensive (avoiding giving up runs) abilities and did not factor in the quality of each team's starting pitcher. In baseball, the starting pitcher has a large effect on runs given up. If I had Las Vegas lines (which incorporate the ability of the starting pitchers) that predicted run differential in each game, I am confident that my luck estimate for baseball would be reduced.

It is interesting that in Olympic Basketball, skill is more important than in the NBA. This is because in around 80% of Olympic games, one team is at least 5 points better than their opponent, whereas in the NBA one team is at least 5 points better than their opponent around half of the time. It is also interesting to note that in the NBA and Men's Olympic Basketball, our predictions were off by an average of 10 points, whereas in the Women's Olympics our predictions were off by an average of only 6 points.

CHAPTER 18

Gerrymandering

During 2018 and 2019, approval of Congress was around 19% (`www.statista`
`.com/statistics/207579/public-approval-rating-of-the-us-congress/`). To
put American's view of Congress in perspective, we note that in 2017, polygamy
had 17% approval (`news.gallup.com/opinion/polling-matters/214601/`
`moral-acceptance-polygamy-record-high-why.aspx`).

Yet, as shown in Table 18.1, the fraction of House incumbents winning reelection
each year averages well over 90% (`www.thoughtco.com/do-congressmen-ever-`
`lose-re-election-3367511`).

Table 18.1: Fraction of incumbent House members winning reelection

YEAR	FRACTION INCUMBENTS REELECTED
2008	94%
2010	85%
2012	90%
2014	95%
2016	97%
2018	91%

How can we reconcile America's disapproval of Congress with the virtually automatic incumbent reelection rate? The answer is that in 37 of 43 states with more than one member of the House, the state legislatures set the House district boundaries. In our partisan nation, Republican-controlled state legislatures set district boundaries that meet legal constraints and are likely to elect the most Republicans, whereas Democratic-controlled state legislatures set district boundaries that are likely to elect the most Democrats. Congressional districts are set after each census, so in most states the current districts were set by the state legislatures elected in 2010. *Gerrymandering* is the name given to the process of setting district boundaries to give the party in power a partisan advantage. Gerrymandering is named after Governor Elbridge Gerry of Massachusetts. In 1812, Gerry signed a bill that created a district that looked like a salamander!

In June 2019, the Supreme Court of the United States (SCOTUS) decision *Rucho v. Common Cause* (`casetext.com/case/rucho-v-common-cause-2`), a bitterly divided court decided 5-4 that federal courts cannot decide whether a state's districts exhibit extreme gerrymandering that violates the constitution. For all practical purposes, this means that federal courts cannot overturn districts set by state legislatures. This decision is probably one of the most important SCOTUS decisions ever because it will drastically affect the laws passed in the future by Congress. For a detailed discussion of gerrymandering, we recommend David Daley's *Ratf**ked: Why Your Vote Doesn't Count* (Liveright, 2016).

In this chapter, we will discuss how gerrymandering is accomplished and look at how hundreds of mathematicians worked on developing models that try to objectively define gerrymandering (see `sites.duke.edu/quantifying-gerrymandering/`).

A Stylized Example

In the 1960s, *the Baker v. Carr* (1962) (`supreme.justia.com/cases/federal/us/369/186/`) and *Reynolds v. Sims* (1964) (`caselaw.findlaw.com/us-supreme-court/377/533.html`) SCOTUS decisions effectively made the phrase "one man, one vote" the law of the land. Invoking the Equal Protection Clause of the 14th Amendment to the Constitution (passed in 1868 after the Civil War), the Court ruled that state legislatures need to set districts that have roughly the same number of people, and the districts need to be redrawn every 10 years after each census. In the Voting Act of 1965 (passed as part of President Lyndon B. Johnson's Great Society Program), Congress made it illegal to set districts that deliberately reduce the voting power of a protected minority. In the 2017 5-3 ruling *Cooper v. Harris*, SCOTUS ruled that North Carolina's 1st and 12th Districts were "packed" with black voters. This diluted the power of black voters by reducing the number of congressional districts in which their votes matter. Figure 18.1 shows North Carolina's 12th district, which closely followed the I-85 corridor between Charlotte and Greensboro. The shape was narrowed to exclude white voters living near I-85, ensuring a black majority in the district. As you will see later, courts often look at a lack of compactness as an indication of gerrymandering, and that is where the mathematicians enter the fray.

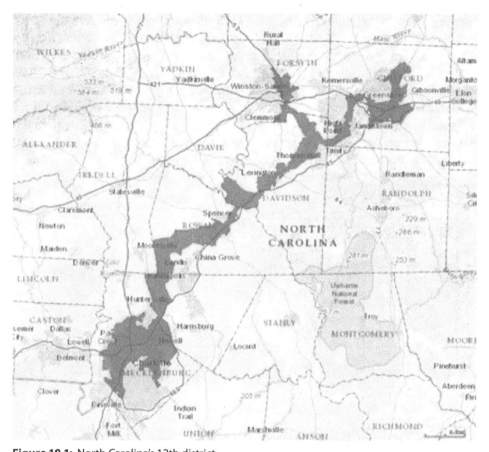

Figure 18.1: North Carolina's 12th district
Source: www.govtrack.us/congress/members/NC/12

The worksheet CALCS of the file `Gerrymander.xlsx` contains information on the fictional state of Gerryberry consisting of 15 counties that have eight congressional districts. Figure 18.2 shows the number of Democrats and Republicans in each county. Suppose that each district must have between 140 and 260 voters and the Democrats want to win the most districts. Note that only 51% (827 / 1630) of the voters are Democrats, so it is reasonable to expect a 4-4 split in the districts. If each county must be assigned to a single district, can the Democrats do better? As shown in Figure 18.3, the assignment of counties to districts shown in Figure 18.2 gives the Democrats 75% (six out of eight) of the districts. This simple example shows that partisan drawing of districts can enable a party to win a much higher percentage of available seats than their actual vote implies that they deserve.

In our made-up data, we used Excel to sift through all possible district-ing schemes. Recently it has become fairly simple (see www.theatlantic.com/politics/archive/2017/10/gerrymandering-technology-redmap-2020/543888/) to use census data to sift through many possible districting maps and generate legal maps for a state that maximize the expected number of seats the party in power will win. In *Dune*, author Frank Herbert wrote, "He who controls the spice controls the universe." If he were still alive, Herbert might have said, "The party that controls the state legislatures controls the United States." The Republicans realized this and put a lot of money into the 2010 state legislature races. This enabled them to not only set congressional district boundaries for the next 10 years, but also to set the state legislature boundaries for the next 10 years. Former Attorney General Eric Holder now heads a Democratic initiative National Democratic Redistricting Committee whose goal is to take back control of state legislatures (democraticredistricting.com/about/).

	A	B	C	D
2	District	Counties	GOP	DEM
3	2	1	80	34
4	5	2	43	61
5	3	3	40	44
6	4	4	20	24
7	7	5	40	114
8	1	6	40	64
9	8	7	70	34
10	2	8	50	44
11	6	9	70	54
12	1	10	70	64
13	8	11	80	45
14	5	12	40	50
15	4	13	50	60
16	3	14	60	65
17	6	15	50	70
18			803	827

Figure 18.2: Fifteen voter distribution in Gerryberry

	F	G	H	I
2	District	GOP	DEM	Winner
3	1	110	128	DEM
4	2	130	78	GOP
5	3	100	109	DEM
6	4	70	84	DEM
7	5	83	111	DEM
8	6	120	124	DEM
9	7	40	114	DEM
10	8	150	79	GOP
11		803	827	

Figure 18.3: Democrats win six seats in Gerryberry

The 2019 Supreme Court decision on gerrymandering basically boiled down to whether the court thought that the North Carolina district map (drawn by Republicans) and/or the Maryland district map (drawn by Democrats) was unconstitutional. Due to space limitations, we restrict our discussion to the North Carolina districts. In 2010, the Democrats won 7 of 13 House seats. After the 2010 census, the Republicans redrew the districts in 2011. In 2014, the Republicans got 55% of the statewide vote yet won 10 of 13 seats. Figure 18.4 shows the district boundaries drawn by the Republicans in 2011. You can see that Districts 1 and 12 have crazy shapes that are not "compact." (We will discuss compactness later in the chapter.)

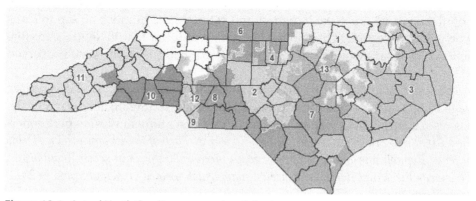

Figure 18.4: Actual North Carolina congressional districts

Professor Jowei Chen of the University of Michigan used simulation (which we will discuss later in the chapter) to come up with the map shown in Figure 18.5 (campaignlegal.org/sites/default/files/2018-07/Supp%20Chen%20Dec%20July%20 11%202018 _ 0.pdf). The Federal District Court ruled that this map was far superior to the Republican map. I don't think that you need to know much math to believe that Dr. Chen's map has "more natural" districts than the Republican map.

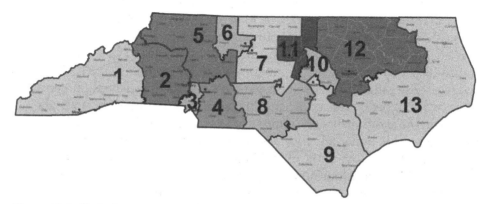

Figure 18.5: Math alternative to North Carolina congressional district boundaries

Source: roseinstitute.org/wp-content/uploads/2016/05/Expert-Report-of-Jowei-Chen.pdf

The Mathematics of Gerrymandering

We would love to have a mathematical formula that courts could plug into and determine whether a state's districts exhibit excessive gerrymandering. Unfortunately, the holy grail of gerrymandering does not exist. The basic ideas behind the math of gerrymandering are well explained in `sinews.siam.org/ Details-Page/detecting-gerrymandering-with-mathematics`.

Mathematicians have applied the following process in their attempts to measure gerrymandering. A computer is programmed to generate thousands of maps that score well on four criteria. (We will come back to the criteria later in this chapter.) For each generated map, you "play out" the election based on the population of voters in each district and estimate the number of Republicans who will win election to the House. If it is very unlikely that 10 Republicans (the actual 2014 result) would win in the generated maps, then the state is deemed to have excessive gerrymandering.

In Elena Kagan's blistering dissent to the *Rucho v. Common Cause* decision (see page 19 of Kagan's dissent here: `www.supremecourt.gov/opinions/18pdf/18-422 _ 9oll.pdf`), Justice Kagan points out that one mathematical expert generated 3,000 reasonable maps for North Carolina. *Each of these maps produced nine or fewer Republicans and 77% of these maps produced only six or seven Republicans. This made the actual Republican-drawn map, which yielded 10 Republicans in 2014, seem like an outlier.*

In the majority's defense, however, there are many ways (most involving complex math) to draw reasonable maps, and it is hard to determine whether a court could pick out a single procedure for drawing them. In the rest of this section, we will introduce the basic mathematics behind drawing a lot of "reasonable" maps.

Generating Random Maps

For our Gerryberry example, we give a simple way to generate random maps. As shown in Figure 18.6 and the worksheet MAPS of the workbook `Gerrymander.xlsx`, we begin with the assignment of counties to districts, as shown in Figure 18.3.

We begin in row 18 with the assignment of counties to districts given in Figure 18.2. Then we randomly generate a pair of integers between 1 and 15 and use those randomly chosen integers to swap the district assignments for those two counties. For example, our first set of random integers is 9 and 6, so we switch the assignments of County 9 to District 6 and County 6 to District 1. After the swap, County 9 is now assigned to District 1, and County 6 is now assigned to District 6, with the other 13 counties keeping their previous assignment. Row 19 contains our new assignment. We continue in this fashion, and after generating a lot of maps, we discard those maps that contain any districts with fewer than 140 or more than 260 voters. This left us with 486 maps. In the worksheet CALCS, we calculated for each of the 486 maps the number of districts in which the Democrats won at least six districts, which was the number the Democrats won with our gerrymandered map. We found Democrats won at least six districts in only 19 of the 486 randomly generated maps (3.9%). This indicates that our gerrymandered map is extreme.

	G	H	I	J	K	L	M	N	O	P	Q	R	S	T	U	V	W
19	Swap1	Swap2	2	5	3	4	7	1	8	2	6	1	8	5	4	3	6
20	9	6	2	5	3	4	7	6	8	2	1	1	8	5	4	3	6
21	13	14	2	5	3	4	7	6	8	2	1	1	8	5	3	4	6
22	5	5	2	5	3	4	7	6	8	2	1	1	8	5	3	4	6
23	13	1	3	5	3	4	7	6	8	2	1	1	8	5	2	4	6
24	11	14	3	5	3	4	7	6	8	2	1	1	4	5	2	8	6
25	2	4	3	4	3	5	7	6	8	2	1	1	4	5	2	8	6
26	9	13	3	4	3	5	7	6	8	2	2	1	4	5	1	8	6
27	15	6	3	4	3	5	7	6	8	2	2	1	4	5	1	8	6
28	8	12	3	4	3	5	7	6	8	5	2	1	4	2	1	8	6
29	12	1	2	4	3	5	7	6	8	5	2	1	4	3	1	8	6
30	14	13	2	4	3	5	7	6	8	5	2	1	4	3	8	1	6
31	5	13	2	4	3	5	8	6	8	5	2	1	4	3	7	1	6
32	6	13	2	4	3	5	8	7	8	5	2	1	4	3	6	1	6

Figure 18.6: Generating random maps

Not All Randomly Generated Maps Are Equally Good

When the experts choose among their randomly generated maps, each map does not have the same chance of being chosen. The chance that a map is chosen depends on how well the map meets the following four criteria:

- Compactness
- Population equality across districts
- Minimal splitting of counties
- Racial gerrymandering constraints

Compactness

There are many ways to measure the compactness of a district. A high degree of compactness is desirable because it usually implies that the residents of the district live close to each other and are more likely to have common opinions on key issues. In most cases, a larger value for the ratio of a (district's area)/(district's perimeter) indicates that a district is more compact. For example, a long thin district, such as North Carolina District 12, will have a lot of perimeter and little area and will have a small ratio. Of course, this criterion can be rendered less valid when nature intervenes in the form of irregular coastlines (look at a map of Alaska), rivers, and state boundaries. As a matter of fact, on the basis of compactness, the *Washington Post* (see www.washingtonpost. com/news/wonk/wp/2014/05/15/americas-most-gerrymandered-congressional-districts/?utm_term=.6ace4ddbea22) declared our old friend North Carolina District 12 the nation's most gerrymandered district.

We now describe three measures of compactness (see workbook Gerrymanderindex.xlsx and Figure 18.7). The three measures of compactness are based on the famous *Isoperimetric theorem* of geometry, which states that with a given perimeter, the shape that encloses the maximum area is a circle. For our example, we let the cell range F3:G4 represent District 9 and H6:H13 represent District 12. We assume each cell represents a 1 mile–by–1 mile square. Note that the area of District 9 is 2 * 2 = 4 and the perimeter of District 9 is 4 * 2 = 8. For District 12, the area is 8 * 1 and the perimeter is 8 + 8 + 1 + 1 = 18.

	F	G	H	I	J	K
1				Reock	Area Circumscibed circle	Area District
2	District 9			District 9	6.28	0.64
3	x	x		District 12	38.48	0.21
4	x	x				small bad
5			District 12			
6			x			
7			x			
8			x			
9			x			
10			x			
11			x			
12			x			
13			x			
14						
15						
16			Schwartzberg		large bad	
17	District	District Perimeter	District Area	Radius of Circle Same Area	Perimeter of Circle Same Area	Gerrymander Index
18	9	8	4	1.13	7.09	1.13
19	12	18	8	1.60	10.03	1.80
20	small bad	Polsby Popper				
21	District	District Perimeter	District Area	Radius circle with same perimeter	Area of Circle with same perimeter	Gerrymander Index
22	9.00	8.00	4.00	1.27	5.09	0.79
23	12.00	18.00	8.00	2.86	25.78	0.31

Figure 18.7: Three measures of compactness

Schwartzberg Measure

$$(\text{District Perimeter}) / (\text{Perimeter of Circle with same area as district})$$

The Isoperimetric theorem implies that the Schwartzberg measure is always at least 1. A larger value indicates a less compact district. For District 9, the radius r of a circle with the same area is found by solving $\pi r^2 = 4$ or $r = \sqrt{4/\pi} = 1.13$. The perimeter of this circle is $2\pi * (1.13) = 7.09$. Therefore, District 9 has a Schwartzberg measure of $8 / 7.09 = 1.13$. In a similar fashion, we find District 12 has a larger Schwartzberg measure of 1.8. This indicates that District 12 is less compact than District 9.

Polsby–Popper Measure

$$(\text{Area of District}) / (\text{Area of Circle with same perimeter as district})$$

A smaller Polsby-Popper measure indicates less compactness. The Polsby–Popper measure is always less than or equal to 1. For District 9, we find the radius r of a circle with the same perimeter of the district by solving $2\pi r = 8$ or $r = 1.27$. The area of this circle is $\pi * 1.27^2 = 5.09$. Then the Polsby–Popper measure is $4 / 5.09 = 0.79$. We find that District 12, as expected, has a smaller Polsby–Popper measure of 0.31.

Reock Measure

$$(\text{District Area}) / (\text{Area of smallest circle circumscribing the district})$$

A smaller Reock measure indicates less compactness, because a more spread-out district will need a circumscribed circle with a relatively large radius. For District 9, the length of the radius of the circumscribed circle equals the length of the diagonal of a 1×1 square, or $\sqrt{2}$. The area of this circle is $\pi * \sqrt{2}^2 = 6.28$. Then the Reock measure for District 9 is $4/6.28 = 0.64$. As expected, District 12 has a smaller Reock measure of 0.21, indicating that District 12 is less compact.

If over all districts one map has less compactness than another map and all other criteria being equal, the map with less compactness has less chance of being chosen.

Population Equality Across Districts

Suppose North Carolina has 13 million people. With 13 districts, the principle of one person, one vote, should reward an assignment of voters that comes as close as possible to allocating one million people to each district. One method to accomplish this goal is shown in Figure 18.8 (see worksheet Equal Pop of the workbook `GerrymanderIndex.xlsx`). For each district, you compute

$$[(\text{Number of voters in District}) / (\text{Ideal Number}) - 1]^2$$

and total this across all districts and take the square root of the sum. As shown in Figure 18.8, Map 1 is off by 10% in 12 of 13 districts, whereas Map 2 is off by 20% in 12 of 13 districts. We find that Map 2 scores twice as badly as Map 1 on population equality, and this disparity would reduce the chance of Map 2 being chosen.

	D	E	F	G	H	I	J
3				Penalty 1	Penalty 2		
4				0.35	0.69		
5	District	Map 1	Map 2	Contribution Map 1	Contribution Map 2		
6	1	0.9	0.8	0.01	0.04	=(E6-1)^2	=(F6-1)^2
7	2	1.1	1.2	0.01	0.04	=(E7-1)^2	=(F7-1)^2
8	3	0.9	0.8	0.01	0.04	=(E8-1)^2	=(F8-1)^2
9	4	1.1	1.2	0.01	0.04	=(E9-1)^2	=(F9-1)^2
10	5	0.9	0.8	0.01	0.04	=(E10-1)^2	=(F10-1)^2
11	6	1.1	1.2	0.01	0.04	=(E11-1)^2	=(F11-1)^2
12	7	0.9	0.8	0.01	0.04	=(E12-1)^2	=(F12-1)^2
13	8	1.1	1.2	0.01	0.04	=(E13-1)^2	=(F13-1)^2
14	9	0.9	0.8	0.01	0.04	=(E14-1)^2	=(F14-1)^2
15	10	1.1	1.2	0.01	0.04	=(E15-1)^2	=(F15-1)^2
16	11	0.9	0.8	0.01	0.04	=(E16-1)^2	=(F16-1)^2
17	12	1.1	1.2	0.01	0.04	=(E17-1)^2	=(F17-1)^2
18	13	1	1	0	0	=(E18-1)^2	=(F18-1)^2

Figure 18.8: Population equality

Minimal Splitting of Counties

It is considered undesirable to split counties. In North Carolina, both Wake (Raleigh) and Mecklenburg (Charlotte) counties must be split because they have more than 1/13 of North Carolina's population. More unnecessary county splits reduce the chance that a map is chosen. Also, a 50%–50% population split between two counties is considered worse than the extreme of a 95%–5% split.

Racial Gerrymandering Constraints

African Americans make up 20% of North Carolina's population, so the 1965 Voting Rights Act is interpreted as implying that in any districting plan, African Americans should be able to elect representatives from at least .2 * 13 = 2.6 districts, which is rounded down to two districts. A complex formula involving the percentage of African Americans in the two districts with the highest percentage of African Americans is used to penalize maps that have a small likelihood of African Americans having a significant chance to control the election of two representatives.

The 3,000 maps referred to by Justice Kagan in her dissent were generated by a process that incorporated these constraints. For example, if Map 1 scored better on compactness and population equality, had no unnecessary county splits, and satisfied the racial gerrymandering constraints, and Map 2 was much less compact, scored worse on population equality, split several counties, and failed to meet the racial gerrymandering constraints, then in the selection process used to generate 3,000 maps, Map 2 would have a much smaller chance of being chosen than Map 1.

As we all know actions have consequences. Americans need to realize that due to pervasive gerrymandering, their votes for state legislature elections during a census year largely determine the character of the House of Representatives for the next 10 years. Hopefully this chapter has helped the reader understand the complexities that underlie the setting of Congressional district boundaries.

Evidence-Based Medicine

The great American statistician W. Edwards Deming (1900–1993) once said, "In God we trust; all others need data." Evidence-based medicine (EBM) attempts to use data from well-designed research studies to help health-care professionals make better medical decisions. In this chapter, we will describe three examples of EBM:

- James Lind's 18th-century discovery that citrus fruits would cure scurvy
- Britain's 1946 randomized controlled clinical trial that showed streptomycin was effective against tuberculosis
- The late-20th-century controversy over whether hormone replacement improved menopausal women's health

James Lind and Scurvy: The Birth of Evidence-Based Medicine

During the 17th and 18th century, England and other European nations embarked on many long sailing expeditions (including circumnavigating the globe). Many sailors tragically died of scurvy. On one 1740–1744 around-the-world trip, over half the sailors died of scurvy. Scurvy had many painful symptoms, including bleeding gums, bruising, and swollen joints. Death often occurred from infection, bleeding, or heart failure.

In 1754, Scottish surgeon James Lind (1716–1794), chose 12 sailors on the *HMS Salisbury* with scurvy whom he believed were comparable in their health (or lack thereof) and age. He divided the 12 sailors into six groups of two sailors. The six groups were given the following treatments daily:

- Group 1: Cider
- Group 2: Oil of vitriol
- Group 3: Vinegar
- Group 4: Seawater
- Group 5: *Oranges and lemons*
- Group 6: Garlic, radish, balsam, and myrrh

In six days, the two sailors given citrus fruits (Group 5) were better and none of the other 10 sailors had improved.

It took a while, but in 1770, famed Captain James Cook fed sailors on his circumnavigation voyage lemons, limes, and oranges, and his crew experienced only one fatality. By 1795, lemon juice was given to most British sailors, and scurvy became a rare occurrence. Many British historians believe lemons were a huge factor in Lord Nelson's great 1805 victory over Napoleon Bonaparte at Trafalgar.

A key to Lind's work was controlling (to the best of his ability) his "clinical trial" so that the only variable that differed between the six groups of sailors was the treatment. Lind chose sailors with similar age and symptoms, kept them in the same part of the ship, and kept the rest of their diets the same.

As you will soon see, the gold standard of EBM is the *randomized controlled clinical trial*, in which people are randomly assigned to several groups. Each group receives a different clinical intervention. As a control, one of the groups often receives a placebo. The randomized assignment of people to different interventions assures us that the only difference in the resulting health of participants is due to the different clinical interventions. Based on the scurvy trial, Lind is often considered the originator of EBM.

We note that recently scholars have questioned whether Lind actually conducted the clinical trial on the *HMS Salisbury* (see "Sailors' Scurvy before and after James Lind—A Reassessment," *Nutrition Reviews*, 2009, vol. 67, no. 6, pp. 315–332). We will assume, however, that the trial was conducted as stated by most sources.

Can we create a simple mathematical model to assess the strength of the evidence Lind found for citrus fruits curing scurvy? Let's start with the hypothesis that all six treatments had the same chance (an unknown value) of curing scurvy. We know two of 12 sailors were cured. Given our hypothesis, what is the chance that both cured sailors would be the two who were fed citrus fruits? There are (12 * 11) / 2 = 66 ways to choose two sailors out of 12. This follows because the first sailor can be one of 12 and the next sailor one of 11. We divide by 2, because choosing, for example, Sailor 1 and then Sailor 2 is the same combination as choosing Sailor 2 and then Sailor 1. Under the assumption that each of the six treatments is equally effective and knowing two sailors were cured, there is only a (small!) 1/66 chance that both the cured sailors would be the sailors who were given citrus fruits.

If you're interested in the history of evidence-based medicine, check out the beautifully illustrated website `www.jameslindlibrary.org`.

The Randomized Streptomycin Tuberculosis Trial

In the early 1900s, tuberculosis was the leading cause of death in young European and North American adults. Penicillin was discovered in 1928, and was effective in curing many diseases but was not effective in curing tuberculosis. In the 1940s, a new antibiotic, streptomycin, was developed, and British professor of medical statistics Austin Bradford Hill of the British Medical Research Council (MRC) set up a randomized clinical trial to determine whether streptomycin was effective in curing acute tuberculosis (see J. Crofton, "The MRC Randomized Trial of Streptomycin and Its Legacy: A View from the Clinical Front Line," *Journal of the Royal Society of Medicine,* vol. 99, no. 10, Oct. 2006, pages 531–534). In 1946, all patients between the ages of 15 and 30 who had acute tuberculosis were enrolled in the study. By essentially flipping a coin, patients were assigned to one of two groups. Group 1 received the standard treatment, bed rest, whereas Group 2 received bed rest *and streptomycin.* The patients enrolled in the study were similar demographically and clinically, so it seems reasonable to attribute differences in outcomes to the presence of streptomycin. After 6 months, there were 4 deaths among 55 patients in the streptomycin group and 15 deaths among the 52 patients in the bed rest group. As shown in the "Excel Calculations" section, if we assume that bed rest + streptomycin was no better than bed rest, then there were only 3 chances in 1,000 that streptomycin would have performed as well as it did.

You may be thinking that it was unethical to withhold streptomycin from many sick patients. Due to the expense and difficulty in manufacturing streptomycin, the drug was in limited supply, so the hope was that the trials would prove the drug to be effective and that more resources would be allocated to producing it.

Many patients were resistant or allergic to streptomycin, and it was soon found that a combination of streptomycin with the drug para-aminosalicylic acid (PAS) was much more effective in curing tuberculosis.

Besides leading to a cure for tuberculosis, the MRC study was important because Crofton and other participants spoke in many countries about how to conduct randomized controlled clinical trials. As stated by Roy Porter (*The*

Greatest Benefit to Mankind, pages 529–530, Norton, 1997), the randomized controlled clinical trial is the "gold standard for all such studies." Certainly, the MRC study paved the way for an explosion in the number of randomized controlled clinical trials.

Excel Calculations

Recall that 4 in 55 TB patients receiving streptomycin died in 6 months and 15 in 52 patients on bed rest died in 6 months. How can we evaluate the significance of this difference in death rates?

In the file `Tbtrials.xlsx`, we answer this question. We assume patients 1–55 are the patients receiving streptomycin and patients 56–107 are the patients receiving bed rest. We then "shuffle" the 19 patients who died and give each of them the same chance to be patient 1–107. Finally, we find that given the assumption that the death rate with or without streptomycin is identical, there are around 3 chances in 1,000 that 4 or fewer deaths would have occurred in the streptomycin group. The following summarizes the procedure (see Figures 19.1 and 19.2):

1. Generate 107 random numbers that are equally likely to be between 0 and 1 by copying from F8 to F9:F114 the formula `=RAND()`.

	E	F	G	H	I
4	4 deaths in 55 Streptomycin				
5	15 in 52 bed rest in 6 months				
6					
7	Patient	rand	Assigned		
8	1	0.279707	72	=RAND()	=RANK(F8,$F$8:$F$114,0)
9	2	0.722071	31		
10	3	0.179711	83		
11	4	0.273717	73		
12	5	0.870129	17		
13	6	0.894211	13		
14	7	0.93839	8		
15	8	0.538057	48		
16	9	0.053497	96		
17	10	0.478809	57		
18	11	0.800995	23		
19	12	0.850276	18		
20	13	0.87759	15		
21	14	0.668439	37		
22	15	0.209617	80		
23	16	0.619262	40		
24	17	0.102793	91		

Figure 19.1: Shuffling the 19 deaths among the streptomycin and bed rest groups

Chapter 19 ▪ Evidence-Based Medicine   147

	K	L	M	N	O	P	Q	R
3								
4		Assign the 19 deaths randomly to 1-107						
5		chance						
6		Deaths in 1st 55<=4						
7								
8		=COUNTIF(O11:O10010,"<=4")/10000				0.0032		
9		how many deaths in 1st 55 patients						
10		11			11		3 chances in 1000	
11				1	8			
12	=COUNTIF(G8:G62,"<=19")			2	9			
13				3	10			
14				4	10			
15				5	11			
16				6	12			
17				7	7			
18				8	10			

Figure 19.2: Counting times <= 4 deaths in streptomycin group

2. Copying from G8 to G9:G114 the formula =RANK(F8,$F$8:$F$114,0) "shuffles" the integers 1–107 in the cell range G8:G114. This formula assigns a 1 in column G to the patient having the largest random number in column F, a 2 in column G to the patient having the second-largest random number in column F, and so on. Numbers 1–19 in column G correspond to patients who died.

3. To "simulate" the number of deaths among patients 1–55, we simply use the formula =COUNTIF(G8:G62,"<=19") in cell L10 to count the number of integers 1–19 that occur in G8:G62. In effect, this COUNTIF formula counts the number of simulated deaths in the streptomycin group.

4. Next, we play out this procedure 10,000 times to estimate the chance (assuming no benefit from streptomycin) that 4 or fewer deaths would occur for the 55 patients given streptomycin. To begin, enter a **1** in cell N11 and with the cursor in cell N11, go the Home tab, and from the Editing group, select Fill and then Series. Then choose Series In Columns and specify a Stop value of 10,000. You now have entered the integers 1–10,000 in Column N.

5. In cell O10, simply copy the number of deaths in the streptomycin group with the formula =L10.

6. Next we use Excel's powerful data table feature to "play out" 10,000 times the number of deaths in the streptomycin group. Select the range N10:O10010.

7. From the What-If Analysis command on the Data tab, choose Data Table. *Leave the Row input cell blank* and choose any blank cell as the Column input cell. Excel puts a 1 in the blank cell and recomputes the data table output cell (our formula in O10), and then places a 2 in the selected blank

cell and recomputes the formula in O10, and so on. *Each time Excel puts an integer 1–10,000 in a blank cell, our `=RAND()` functions recalculate*, and we obtain an "iteration" recording the number of the 19 deaths occurring in the streptomycin group.

8. In cell P8 we used the formula `=COUNTIF(O11:O10010,"<=4")/10000` to count the fraction of our 10,000 iterations resulted in 4 or fewer deaths in the streptomycin group. We found 4 or fewer deaths occurred around 0.3% of the time. Since this small probability was based on the assumption that streptomycin did not reduce mortality, it leads us to question our assumption that streptomycin is not effective in combating tuberculosis.

Hormone Replacement: Good or Bad?

During the 1980s and 1990s, many studies were published that purported to show that giving hormone replacement to menopausal women reduced cardio-vascular disease in women by around 50%. These studies were summarized in Elizabeth Barrett-Connor and Trudy Bush, "Estrogen and Coronary Heart Disease in Women," *Journal of the American Medical Association*, 1991, vol. 265, no. 14, pages 1861–1867. These studies were *observational studies* that noted the reduction in the incidence of cardiovascular disease in menopausal women who used estrogen and progestin. There is no evidence that the women observed in these studies were like the general population. Even the authors of the afore-mentioned paper noted that the women observed using hormone replacement were more likely to be white, higher income, and more highly educated. These factors alone would certainly reduce the risk of cardiovascular disease.

What was needed, of course, was a randomized controlled clinical trial in which menopausal women were equally likely to be prescribed a placebo or hormone replacement. In 2002, the Women's Health Initiative reported the results of such a study that involved 161,809 women (Writing Group for the Women's Health Initiative Investigation, "Risks and Benefits of Estrogen Plus Progestin in Healthy Menopausal Women," *Journal of the American Medical Association*, vol. 288, no. 3, 2002, pages 321–333). The authors found the demographic characteristics of the women receiving a placebo and hormone replacement to be virtually identical. Therefore, any difference in health outcomes could be attributed to the hormone replacement. After five years the authors found that the women receiving hormone replacement had the following outcomes (relative to the women receiving the placebo):

- A 29% increase in cardiac heart disease events
- A 41% increase in strokes
- A doubling of venous thromboembolisms

- A 26% increase in breast cancer
- A 34% decrease in hip fractures

The results of this randomized trial appeared to show that hormone replacement has substantial adverse effects on women's health and that randomized trials can totally contradict an observational study in which the observed groups may differ significantly in health and demographic characteristics.

The 2002 study is not the end of the story, however. A 2017 update published in the Women's Health Initiative Randomized Trial Group ("Menopausal Hormone Therapy and Long-Term All-Cause and Cause-Specific Mortality," *Journal of the American Medical Association*, vol. 308, no. 10, 2017, pages 927–938) updated the 2002 study by continuing the randomized trial through 2014. A total of 27,347 postmenopausal U.S. women ages 50–79 participated in the study. A total of 16,608 women with a uterus were randomized to receive either a placebo or estrogen + progesterone (the CEE + MPA group), and 10,739 with a hysterectomy were randomized between a placebo or estrogen (CEE).

As expected in a large-sized randomized trial, in each cohort there was no significant difference between the placebo and hormone replacement groups on any demographic, income, and health characteristics. The authors found that CEE + MPA or just CPE hormone replacement resulted in the same overall mortality, cancer mortality, and cardiovascular mortality as the mortality in the placebo group.

With regard to breast cancer mortality, the authors' best estimate was that for women with a uterus CEE + MPA increased breast cancer mortality as compared to the placebo group by 44%, but for women with a hysterectomy CEE decreased breast cancer mortality compared to the placebo group by 45%. Who knows what future research will show!

How Do We Compare Hospitals?

If you or a loved one is sick, you want the best care available. Many ratings of hospitals are available. In "Rating the Raters" (see www.medscape.com/viewarticle/917243), medical experts evaluated the four major hospital rating systems:

- CMS (Centers for Medicare & Medicaid Services)
- Healthgrades
- *U.S. News & World Report*
- Leapfrog

"Rating the Raters" (RTR) found severe flaws in all four rating systems, and only *U.S. News & World Report* received a B grade. In this chapter, we give a brief summary of how "Rating the Raters" arrived at their ratings. See www.usnews.com/static/documents/health/best-hospitals/BHPC _ Methodology _ 2018-19.pdf for a detailed description of the *U.S. News & World Report* rating methodology.

Ratings Criteria

When rating hospitals (or colleges and universities, business schools, medical schools, etc.), you need to identify criteria you feel are important measures of quality. RTR identified six criteria used to evaluate hospital quality–rating systems:

- Potential for misclassification of hospital performance
- Importance/impact
- Scientific acceptability
- Iterative improvement
- Transparency
- Usability

Potential for Misclassification of Hospital Performance

All four rating systems include patient safety indicators (PSIs) as one measure of hospital quality. As an example of a PSI, consider PSI12, the risk of postoperative venous thromboembolism (VTE) in postsurgery recovery. As explained in `journals.lww.com/annalsofsurgery/fulltext/2015/03000/Postoperative_Venous_Thromboembolism_Outcomes.6.aspx`, hospitals that do more diagnostic imaging tend to perform worse on PSI12, even though their patients are not actually suffering a higher fraction of postoperative VTEs. Like PSI12, other PSIs can fail to correspond to better quality and can lead to a ranking system that misclassifies hospitals.

All four rating systems get most of their data from Medicare (CMS). Most of this data is for patients 60 years or older, so how do we know if the performance indicated by Medicare data applies to younger patients?

Medicare penalizes hospitals if they have a higher-than-average rate of patient readmissions within 30 days. Ratings services use a higher 30-day readmission rate as one indicator of poorer hospital quality. As pointed out by Jerry Muller in his excellent book *The Tyranny of Metrics* (pages 120–123, Princeton University Press, 2018), many hospitals gamed the system by sending patients who needed readmission as inpatients to the ER and classified them as *outpatients* on "observational status." Such observational admissions to the ER increased 96% after Medicare began penalizing hospitals for 30-day readmissions! Just like some PSIs, 30-day readmission rates are not always accurate measures of hospital quality. Also, the 30-day readmission rule could easily be gamed by readmitting (to their detriment) patients 31 days after discharge, when they should have been admitted sooner. This is an example of Goodhart's law, which states that "When a measure becomes a target, it ceases to be a good measure" (see `en.wikipedia.org/wiki/Goodhart%27s_law`).

As pointed out in RTR, much of the data used by the raters is self-reported by the hospital. This creates a huge incentive for hospitals to falsify the data. RTR therefore suggests that self-reported hospital data should be subject to audit.

Importance/Impact

RTR believes that a rating system must have features that resonate with patients and providers. For example, a patient needing a procedure such as colon cancer surgery should be able to easily evaluate the performance of all hospitals in their area on colon cancer surgery. RTR is a bit vague on importance/impact, but RTR rewarded CMS for its large size (all people on Medicare) but penalized them for failing to rate hospitals on many elective procedures.

Scientific Acceptability

It is crucial that measures of quality such as mortality rate need to be risk adjusted based on the hospital's patient mix. For example, as explained on pages 18–19 of `media.beam.usnews.com/8c/7b/6e1535d141bb9329e23413577d99/190709-bh-methodology-report-2019.pdf`, *U.S. News & World Report* adjusted measures such as mortality rate for a procedure based on such factors as

- Age at admission
- Sex
- Year of admission (hospital quality tends to improve over time)
- Income level
- Comorbidities: adjust mortality rates based on other patient illnesses. For example, a patient with diabetes and a history of heart attack(s) is probably less likely to survive colon cancer.

For a simple example of risk adjustment, let's compare the performance on open heart surgery for two hospitals: Emergency Room (ER) and Chicago Hope (CH). The file `Hospital.xlsx` contains, for 403 patients, the hospital where the surgery took place, whether the patient lived or died, and whether the patient was a high- or low-risk patient. Using PivotTables (see the "Excel Calculations" section at the end of the chapter), we can first look at the overall survival rate for each hospital. As shown in Figure 20.1, the overall survival rate at the two hospitals is virtually identical. When we compare the survival rate at the two hospitals for each risk class, however, a different picture emerges. For high-risk patients, 80% survive at ER, compared to only 68% at Chicago Hope. For low-risk patients, 93% survive at ER, compared to only 85% at Chicago Hope. *After adjusting for risk, this shows that ER is the better hospital for each type of patient.* As shown in Figure 20.1, ER sees 160 high-risk patients and Chicago Hope only 22.

Chicago Hope also sees many more low-risk patients than ER. This accounts for Chicago Hope having a higher overall survival rate. (Remember Simpson's paradox that we discussed in Chapter 12, "Berkeley, Buses, Cars, and Planes.")

	I	J	K	L	M	N	O	P	Q
6	Row Labels	⏷ Die	Live						
7	CH		16.75% 83.25%						
8	ER		17.50% 82.50%						
9									
10									
11									
12	Count of Outcome	Column Labels ⏷				Count of Outcome	Column l ⏷		
13	Row Labels	⏷ Die	Live	Grand Total		Row Labels	⏷ Die	Live	Grand Tot
14	⊟High		21.43% 78.57%	100.00%		⊟High	39	143	182
15	CH		31.82% 68.18%	100.00%		CH	7	15	22
16	ER		20.00% 80.00%	100.00%		ER	32	128	160
17	⊟Low		13.57% 86.43%	100.00%		⊟Low	30	191	221
18	CH		14.92% 85.08%	100.00%		CH	27	154	181
19	ER		7.50% 92.50%	100.00%		ER	3	37	40
20	Grand Total		17.12% 82.88%	100.00%		Grand Total	69	334	403

Figure 20.1: ER is better than CH

Iterative Improvement

This criterion simply refers to the rating system's ability to incorporate feedback and use this feedback to create a loop that leads to continuous improvement of the rating system.

Transparency

To be transparent, a rating of hospitals must make its methodology clear. The rating system must also use publicly available data so that the results can be reproduced.

Usability

It is important that a rating system be easy for patients to use. For example, a patient living in Bloomington, Indiana contemplating hip or knee replacement can quickly find information on hip and knee complications with the Hospital Compare Tool (see www.medicare.gov/hospitalcompare/profile.html#vwgrph= 1&profTab=3&ID=150051&loc=47401&lat=39.0793558&lng=-86.438974&name=IU%20

`HEALTH%20BLOOMINGTON%20HOSPITAL&Distn=9.7` and Figure 20.2). As shown in Figure 20.2, Bloomington Hospital rated as No Different Than The National Rate for all categories shown. Hospitals can also be rated on different statistics as Better Than The National Rate or Worse Than The National Rate.

	IU HEALTH BLOOMINGTON HOSPITAL	NATIONAL RESULT
Rate of complications for hip/knee replacement patients	No Different Than the National Rate	2.5%
Serious complications (From PSI ⓘ)	No Different Than the National Value	1.00
Deaths among patients with serious treatable complications after surgery (From PSI ⓘ)	No Different Than the National Rate	163.01

Figure 20.2: Bloomington, IN hospital performance on hip and knee replacements

Medicare Hospital Compare (see `www.medicare.gov/hospitalcompare/search.html?`) also rates each hospital as a 1–5-star hospital by computing a weighted average (see Figure 20.3 and `www.medicare.gov/hospitalcompare/Data/Hospital-overall-ratings-calculation.html`) of the hospital's performance in the seven areas shown in Table 20.1.

Table 20.1: Medicare weightings for star ratings

MEASURE CATEGORY	WEIGHT
Mortality	22%
Safety of Care	22%
Readmission	22%
Patient Experience	22%
Effectiveness of Care	4%
Timeliness of Care	4%
Efficient Use of Medical Imaging	4%

Above the national average is better for all categories.	
Category	**National Average Comparison**
	IU HEALTH BLOOMINGTON HOSPITAL
Mortality	Same as the national average
Safety of Care	Above the national average
Readmission	Above the national average
Patient Experience	Below the national average
Effectiveness of Care	Same as the national average
Timeliness of Care	Same as the national average
Efficient use of Medical Imaging	Above the national average

Figure 20.3: Bloomington, IN hospital ratings

The distribution of star ratings is shown in Table 20.2.

Table 20.2: Distribution of Medicare.gov star ratings

RATING	FRACTION OF HOSPITALS WITH THIS RATING
5 stars	6%
4 stars	24%
3 stars	28%
2 stars	17%
1 star	6%
No rating	19%

Conclusion

It is incredibly important to have accurate ratings of hospitals for different procedures. As pointed out on page 18 of RTR, no "A" level ratings exist, and current ratings need to be interpreted cautiously. As pointed out in *The Tyranny of Metrics* (page 122), risk adjustment is very difficult, and hospitals that serve a sicker, lower-income patient base are most likely to be penalized in rating systems.

You would think that after a metric becomes an important component of hospital ratings, hospitals would improve on that metric. Wrong again! Again, as pointed out in *The Tyranny of Metrics* (pages 115–116), since Medicare began reporting mortality rates, there has been no improvement in mortality rates.

There are many success stories in using metrics to improve health care. Consider the insertion of central lines. Central lines are tubes used to give patients needed medicines, but they often lead to infections. Following a checklist of five simple procedures (see page 109, *The Tyranny of Metrics*) when implanting a "central line" reduced infections by 66%!

Hopefully, better hospital ratings and better care are on the way!

Excel Calculations

The overall death rates at ER and Chicago Hope can be compared as follows:

1. Open `Hospital.xlsx`, click anywhere in the data (cell range E3:G406), and then select PivotTable from the Insert tab.

2. In the PivotTable Fields pane, drag Hospital to the Rows area and Outcome to the Columns and Values areas.

3. Right-click any number in the PivotTable and select the % Of Row Total option from Show Values As. You now can see the percentage survival rate at each hospital.

4. Move your cursor to a blank area of the worksheet, press Alt+D+P, and then choose Another PivotTable Report Or PivotChart Report.

5. Select the only available PivotTable. The PivotTable Fields pane reappears.

6. Drag Risk Category and then Hospital to the Rows area and Outcome to the Columns and Values areas.

7. Change the display to % Of Row Total.

You now see that ER has superior outcomes for both high- and low-risk patients.

CHAPTER 21

What Is the Worst Health Care Problem in My Country?

The well-known author Augusten Burroughs is credited with saying, "When you have your health, you have everything." Until the 1990s, there was no way to compare the health of different areas of the world and no way to measure how much a given health problem (heart disease, low back pain, etc.) reduced a nation's health. Largely due to the amazing efforts of Dr. Alan Murray (see Jeremy Smith, *Epic Measures,* Harper, 2015), we can now compare the "healthiness" of different countries and understand how different maladies affect the health of a country. If you want to understand how health in the world is measured and how different "unhealthiness" is in different regions of the world, please read "Disability-Adjusted Life Years (DALYs) for 291 Diseases and Injuries in 21 Regions, 1990–2010: A Systematic Analysis for the Global Burden of Disease Study 2010" (Christopher Murray et al., *The Lancet,* vol. 380, December 2012, pages 2197–2223). We will often refer to this article using the abbreviation DALY2012.

Disability-Adjusted Life Years

Murray's key metric is Disability-Adjusted Life Year (DALY). DALY is the sum of years of life lost due to early death (YLL) and years lost due to disability (YLD).

YLL are computed based on the average life expectancy in the country with the longest life expectancy. (Japan ranks #1; the United States ranks #31!) Japanese women have a life expectancy of 87 years. If a woman dies of cancer at age 75, then cancer causes 87 − 75 = 12 YLL. The average life expectancy of a Japanese man is 81 years, so a man who dies in a car accident at age 25 suffers 81 − 25 = 56 YLL.

Years lost to disability (YLD) is much trickier. Consider a person who suffers schizophrenia for 10 years. To determine the YLD, we need a weighting of the "health" lost due to each year a person lives with schizophrenia. (Later in the chapter, we will address the method used to determine disability weights for different diseases.) The weight the experts give to a year of schizophrenia is 0.53 years lost to disability. Then a person suffering for 10 years with schizophrenia lost 10 * (0.53) = 5.3 years to disability. Table 21.1 gives the weights used in 2010 by the World Health Organization (WHO).

Table 21.1: 2010 Disability Weights

CONDITION	DISABILITY WEIGHT
Schizophrenia	0.53
Blindness due to glaucoma	0.60
Alzheimer's	0.67
Deafness	0.23
HIV not on antiretroviral therapy (ART)	0.51
HIV on ART	0.17
Back Pain	0.06

```
www.who.int/healthinfo/global_burden_disease/GBD2004_
DisabilityWeights.pdf?ua=1
```

If you're interested, you may want to spend some time with a DALY calculator (`daly.cbra.be/?main=daly`), which allows you to input information about a person's health and compute their contribution to a nation's DALY.

Determination of Disability Weights

Determination of disability weights is a controversial issue. When Murray first proposed DALY, disability weights were determined by health care professionals. Beginning in 2010, disability weights were determined by surveys of the general public (see `www.researchgate.net/publication/258264019_Common_ values_in_assessing_health_outcomes_from_disease_and_injury_ disability_weights_measurement_study_for_the_Global_Burden_ of_Disease_Study_2010_Appendix`). Inhabitants of Bangladesh, Tanzania,

Indonesia, Peru, and the United States were randomly chosen for the survey as representative of the world's cultural, language, and socioeconomic diversity. Participants in the survey were asked two types of questions related to paired comparisons and paired equivalences.

Paired Comparisons

Participants were asked to *pairwise compare* for up to 15 pairs which of two (out of 220) health "states" was more serious. For example, a participant might be asked which condition is more severe:

- Condition 1: A right-handed person breaks their arm and has their arm in a cast for six weeks and then recovers.

- Condition 2: A person breaks their foot and has their foot in a cast for six weeks and then recovers.

Using some advanced math, paired comparisons can be used to rank the severity of these health states. Since we know which health states are associated with a disease, this information can be used to rank the relative severity of diseases.

Paired Equivalences

Participants were also asked questions such as the following fill-in-the-blank statement. The blank should be filled in with the number that makes the two programs equal in health benefit.

Consider two health programs: Program 1 will prevent 1,000 people from getting an illness that causes rapid death. Program 2 will cause ____ people (choices given were 1,500, 2,000, 3,000, and 10,000) who will have lifelong angina to be immediately cured.

For obvious reasons, this type of question is called a *paired equivalence*. Suppose a participant answers 3,000 to this question. Let DWA = This person's view of the disability weight for mild angina. If EL = A given person's expected remaining lifetime, then Program 1 saves 1000 * EL lost years of life and saves 3000 (EL * DWA) disability years. Our participant's answer implies that she believes

$$1000 * EL = 3000 * EL * DWA, \text{ or } DWA = 1 / 3$$

Aggregating the information from the paired comparisons and paired equivalences, disability weights based on public opinion were utilized in DALY2012 to computed DYL. Before we discuss the important information on world health contained in DALY2012, we need to explore two technical issues that Murray and company addressed in DALY2012.

To Age Weight or Discount, That Is the Question

Before computing DALY, we must address two more technical issues:

- **Age weighting:** Should each year of a person's life receive the same weight? For example, should dying at 79 instead of 80 accrue the same benefit in DALY as dying at 29 instead of 30 or dying at 9 instead of 10?

- **Discounting:** When companies value present and future cash flows, they usually discount future cash flows by the *weighted average cost of capital (WACC)*. For example, a WACC of 10% (a typical value) means that a cash flow received 1 year from now is equivalent to a cash flow of $1/1.10$ now; a cash flow two years from now is equivalent to a cash flow of $1/1.10^2$ two years from now; and so forth.

We now briefly discuss how age weighting and discounting were conducted prior to 2010. Since 2010, age weighting and discounting considerations have been eliminated.

Age Weighting

Prior to 2010, the weight W assigned to a year of life lost or a year of disability (relative to an average value of 1) was given by

$$W = 0.1658 * Y * e^{-0.04Y}$$

where Y is the person's age when the year of life or year lost to disability occurs. Figure 21.1 graphs this function. Figure 21.1 shows that a year of life for very young and very old people is given little value relative to people who are between 20 and 50 years old. The weighting is based primarily on how economic productivity depends on age. The constant 0.1658 was chosen to make the average weight equal to 1. Beginning in 2010, age weighting was dropped (in effect W = 1 for any age).

Discounting

Before 2010, future years of life lost or disability were discounted at 3% per year. Thus, a year of life lost five years from now was valued $1/1.03^5$ times as important as a year of life lost now. According to www.who.int/healthinfo/statistics/GlobalDALYmethods _ 2000 _ 2011.pdf, discounting of DALYs was used to be consistent with the usual practice of discounting the cost of health care initiatives.

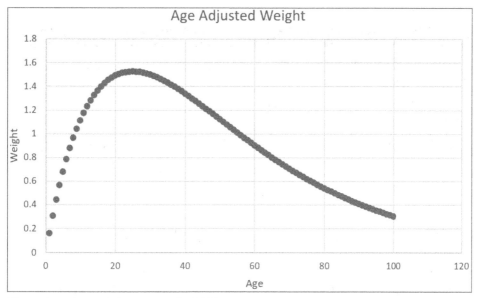

Figure 21.1: Age weighting curve for DALY

For a detailed discussion of the pros and cons of "social discounting," refer to `https://digitalcommons.law.yale.edu/cgi/viewcontent.cgi?article=1577&context=ylpr`, which discusses how potential future effects of climate change should be discounted.

Again, we note that current computation of DALYs ignores age weighting and discounting.

In Chapter 48, "How can we Improve K-12 Education?", we provide a more extensive discussion of discounting.

Key Facts About World Health

Now that we understand the basics of DALYs, we can summarize some of the key insights about world health contained in DALY2012.

In 2010, there were 361 DALYs per 1,000 people. A breakdown of the percentage of DALYs due to major causes is shown in Table 21.2.

Table 21.2: Percentage of 2010 DALYs by Major Cause

CAUSE	PERCENTAGE OF DALYS
Cardiovascular and circulatory diseases	12%
Injuries (such as car accidents)	11%
Neonatal disorders	8%
Cancer	8%

Continues

Table 21-2 (*continued*)

CAUSE	PERCENTAGE OF DALYS
Mental and behavioral health disorders	7%
Chronic respiratory disorders	5%
Musculoskeletal disorders (such as back pain)	7%
Diabetes and kidney disorders	5%
Lower respiratory infections	5%
Chronic respiratory diseases	5%
HIV	3%
Malaria	3%

Source: Murray et al. 2012

Figure 21.2, from the University of Washington's Institute for Health Metrics and Evaluation (IHME) website, gives the 2004 breakdown of DALY by region, broken down by YLL and YLD. This figure makes it clear that Africa's YLL per 1000 people was much higher than any other region.

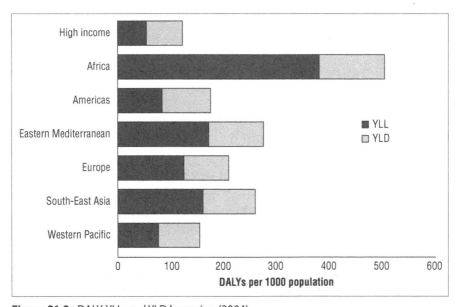

Figure 21.2: DALY, YLL, and YLD by region (2004)

Source: https://vizhub.healthdata.org/gbd-compare/

The causes of DALYs differ greatly by region. For example, heart disease is ranked first in High Income North America and all of Europe but ranks no higher than 14th in any part of Sub-Saharan Africa. On the other hand, HIV/ AIDS is ranked in the top five in all regions of Sub-Saharan Africa but ranks 37th in High Income North America. Tragically, interpersonal violence was the leading cause of DALY in Central Latin America.

The IHME website allows you to create thousands of visualizations that compare the causes of DALY, YLL, and YLD in many locations. For example, Figure 21.3 from the IHME website shows a visualization (in a treemap or mosaic chart) of the percentage of DALYs during 2017, due to each cause in El Salvador. You can see that in El Salvador, violence is the leading cause of DALYs. It is no wonder that many people want to leave El Salvador.

I hope you will spend hours exploring these amazing visualizations and gain a better picture of the causes of DALYs in different areas of the world.

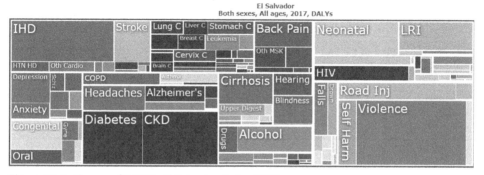

Figure 21.3: Causes of DALY in El Salvador during 2017

Part

II

What Will Happen?

In This Part

Does a Mutual Fund's Past Performance Predict Future Performance?

In many aspects of life, we hope that we can use past performance to gain insight into future performance. Sometimes past performance does not help us accurately predict future performance. For example:

- On October 19, 2019, the last place football team in the Big Ten West division (Illinois) upset undefeated Wisconsin (24-23). The oddsmakers predicted Wisconsin to win the game by 31 points.

- In November 2007, Barack Obama was given only an 8% chance of winning the 2008 presidential election (see understandinguncertainty.org/node/222), and the rest is history.

- In late 2007, the International Monetary Fund (IMF) predicted 4.75% world economic growth in 2008 (www.imf.org/en/News/Articles/2015/09/28/04/53/sores1017b). As we know, the worst recession since 1929 began in 2008.

- In 2000, New England Patriot QB Tom Brady was selected 199th in the NFL draft. I don't think any of the 198 players drafted before Brady had a better career than Brady. According to Pro-Football-Reference.com's measure of career success (Career Approximate Value) (www.pro-football-reference.com/leaders/av_career.htm), nobody in NFL history had a better career!

- In 1980, the prestigious consulting firm McKinsey predicted that by the year 2000, the United States would have 900,000 mobile phone subscribers (see `digital-stats.blogspot.com/2014/07/mckinsey-company-projected-that-there.html`). In 2000, there were actually 109 million mobile phone subscribers.

In this chapter, we will explore the question of whether Morningstar's well-known and well-respected mutual fund ratings are helpful in predicting future mutual fund performance. We begin by providing some background on mutual funds.

Mutual Fund Basics

Mutual funds raise money from investors and then invest the money in available vehicles such as stocks (U.S. and international), bonds, real estate, and commodities. In 2018, U.S.-based mutual funds invested $17.71 trillion (see `www.statista.com/topics/1441/mutual-funds/`). In an *actively managed investment fund*, the fund's management team decides how to invest the fund's money. In 2017, actively managed funds charged an average annual fee of 0.78% of invested funds. In a *passively managed fund*, investments are chosen automatically to match an index. VFIAX (The Vanguard 500 Index Fund) is an example of a passively managed fund that attempts to track the Standard and Poor's Index. In September 2019, VFIAX had $491 billion invested. VFIAX charged an annual fee of 0.14%.

Morningstar Ratings

You can find a list of mutual fund ticker symbols at `eoddata.com/stocklist/USMF.htm`. If you type a mutual fund ticker symbol into your favorite search engine, you can quickly navigate to the Morningstar page that gives information on the selected fund. As an example, we chose MGIAX (MFS International Intrinsic Value A fund). This fund's Morningstar page can be found at `www.morningstar.com/funds/xnas/mgiax/quote`. We accessed this page on October 21, 2019.

Morningstar classifies funds into categories so that they can compare funds in the same category (see `morningstardirect.morningstar.com/clientcomm/Morningstar_Categories_US_April_2016.pdf` for a list of Morningstar categories). We see that MGIAX is a U.S. Fund Foreign Large Growth. Figure 22.1 shows the information that appeared on October 21, 2019, on the MGIAX Morningstar page.

From Figure 22.1, we see the following:

- There were 439 funds in MGIAX's category.
- In 2009, the 74 percentile means that 74% of all funds performed better, and in 2018, the 6 percentile means only 6% of funds were ranked better.

▲	E	F	G	H	I	J	K	L	M	N	O
16	Total Return %	2009	2010	2011	2012	2013	2014	2015	2016	2017	2018
17	Fund	24.64	9.13	-1.96	15.81	27.35	1.28	6.48	3.93	26.83	-9.22
18	+/- Category	-13.38	-5.65	10.35	-1.89	8.76	5.2	5.53	6.07	-4.05	4.86
19	+/- Index	-14.03	-5.33	12.25	-0.86	11.86	3.93	7.73	3.8	-5.18	5.21
20	Quartile	4	2	1	4	1	1	1	1	2	1
21	Percentile Rank	74	29	3	62	5	4	2	18	31	6
22	# of Funds in Cat.	266	261	251	250	278	341	361	363	399	439

Figure 22-1: Morningstar data on MGIAX fund

- In each year, a quartile rating is assigned based on 1 = Top 25%, 2 = 26th percentile to 50th percentile, 3 = 51st percentile to 75th percentile, 4 = 76th percentile to 100th percentile. Therefore, a lower quartile rating indicates better performance.

- In 2018, MGIAX had a return of –9.22%. This was 4.86% better than the average fund in the same category and 5.21% better than the Market Index.

Risk-Adjusting Fund Returns

Morningstar gives the top 10% of funds in a category five stars, the next 22.5% four stars, the next 35% three stars, the next 22.5% two stars, and the bottom 10% one star. Before assigning star ratings to funds, Morningstar adjusts each fund's monthly returns for risk. To see why risk adjustment is necessary, consider the following two fictitious funds:

- Fund 1: Every year this fund has a return of 5% on invested capital.

- Fund 2: In odd-numbered years, this fund returns 80%; in even-numbered years, it returns –50%.

Fund 2 averages returning 15% a year (the average of 0.80 and –0.50), whereas Fund 1 clearly returns an average of 5% per year. Every two years, however, $1 invested in Fund 2 will turn into $1 * (1.8) * (.5) = 90 cents, so in the long run, your initial investment in Fund 2 will disappear while your initial investment in Fund 1 will continue to grow! Basically, Fund 2's high risk or volatility eventually negates the advantage of a larger mean return.

We now discuss several measures that Morningstar looks at when they risk-adjust fund returns. To illustrate the computation of these measures, we will use annual returns for the time period 1990–2018 for the Renaissance Medallion Fund (RMF), which is widely considered to have been the most successful investment fund (see www.bloomberg.com/news/articles/2016-11-21/how-renaissance-s-medallion-fund-became-finance-s-blackest-box). Our work is in the worksheet Renaissance of the workbook Chapter22.xlsx. Some of the data we will use is shown in Figure 22.2.

	A	B	C	D	E	F	G	H	I
1					Mean Returns	0.171915	0.088861		
2				Year	REN Return	Stocks	T Bills	Excess REN	Excess Stocks
3				1990	56.00%	-0.0306	0.0624	49.76%	-9.30%
4				1991	39.40%	0.3023	0.15	24.40%	-15.23%
5	Beta	-0.56	=SLOPE(E3:E31,F3:F31)	1992	34.00%	0.0749	0.0936	24.64%	1.87%
6	Alpha	0.36	=INTERCEPT(H3:H31,I3:I31)	1993	39.10%	0.0997	0.1421	24.89%	4.24%
7	Rsq	0.19	=RSQ(E3:E31,F3:F31)	1994	70.10%	0.0133	-0.0804	78.14%	-9.37%
8	Correlation	-0.44	=CORREL(E3:E31,F3:F31)	1995	38.30%	0.372	0.2348	14.82%	-13.72%
9				1996	31.50%	0.2268	0.0143	30.07%	-21.25%
10	mean REN return	0.41	=AVERAGE(E3:E31)	1997	21.20%	0.331	0.0994	11.26%	-23.16%
11	mean tbill return	0.06	=AVERAGE(G3:G31)	1998	41.50%	0.2834	0.1492	26.58%	-13.42%
12	standard deviation	0.22	=STDEV(E3:E31)	1999	24.50%	0.2089	-0.0825	32.75%	-29.14%
13	sharpe	1.60	=(B10-B11)/B12	2000	98.50%	-0.0903	0.1666	81.84%	25.69%

Figure 22-2: Data on Renaissance Medallion Fund 2000–2018

We will discuss the following five statistics:

■ Standard deviation

■ Sortino ratio

■ Beta

■ R-Squared vs. Standard Index

■ Alpha

Standard Deviation

In Chapter 1, "Preliminaries," we discussed the concept of standard deviation as a summary measure of spread about the mean. As shown in Figure 22.2, the standard deviation of the annual 1990–2018 RMF Returns was 22%. For comparison, the standard deviation of the annual returns on stocks during the same period was 17%, and the annual standard deviation of the annual return on 90-day T-bills was 9%. Just looking at standard deviations, you would conclude that the RMF was much riskier than stocks or T-bills. Most of Renaissance's risk, however, is upside risk, which is good, not bad. When we discuss the Sortino ratio, you will see that after properly measuring only downside risk, the RMF has very little risk!

Sortino Ratio

In our discussion of the Madoff fraud in Chapter 5, "How Did Bernie Madoff Keep His Fund Going?," we defined the Sharpe ratio for an investment as

(Average Annual Return – Risk Free Return) / (Standard Deviation of AnnualReturn)

The problem with the Sharpe ratio is that the standard deviation equally weights upside and downside risk, and only downside risk is bad. To compute the Sortino ratio, we need to define a target return for our investments. Let's set an optimistic target of a 20% annual return. Next, for each year, we compute the downside risk for that year to equal 0 if the investment return exceeds 20%, and as a 0.20 investment return if the investment return is less than 20%. For example, an annual return of 15% incurs a downside risk of 5%, whereas an annual return of 22% incurs no downside risk. Then the Sortino ratio for an investment is given by

(Average Annual Return) – (Target Annual Return) / (Average Downside Risk)

Essentially, the Sortino ratio measures the return in excess of a target per unit of downside risk, so clearly a larger Sortino ratio is better than a smaller ratio. In the worksheet Sortino, we computed the Sortino ratio for RMF, Stock, and T-bill returns during the period 1990–2018. As shown in Figure 22.3, we used an IF formula to compute the downside risks for each year and investment in columns G–I. For example, in cell G5 the formula =IF(D5<target,target-D5,0) compares the 1990 RMF return to 20% and returns 0 because the 1990 return exceeded 20%. In cell H5, the formula =IF(E5<target,target-E5,0) shown in Figure 22.3 returns 23.06%, because the 1990 stock return of –3.1% was 23.1% below our 20% target annual return.

In cells G3:I3, we compute the average annual downside risk for each investment, and in D3:F3, we compute the average annual return on each investment. Finally, in cells D1:F1, we compute each investment's Sortino ratio. For example, Stocks have a Sortino ratio of (0.1065 – 0.20) / 0.1213 = –0.77. RMF has a Sortino ratio of 37.90, and T-bills have a Sortino ratio of –0.99.

	C	D	E	F	G	H	I	J	K	L
1	Sortino	37.9042	-0.771	-0.991						
2	Average Downside Risk	0.00561	0.1213	0.14						
3	mean	41.28%	10.65%	6.15%	0.56%	12.13%	13.97%			
4	Year	REN Return	Stocks	T Bills	REN Down	Stock Down	T Bills Down			
5		1990 56.00%	-0.031	0.062	0.00%	23.06%	13.76%	=IF(D5<target,target-D5,0)		
6		1991 39.40%	0.3023	0.15	0.00%	0.00%	5.00%			
7		1992 34.00%	0.0749	0.094	0.00%	12.51%	10.64%			
8		1993 39.10%	0.0997	0.142	0.00%	10.03%	5.79%			
9		1994 70.10%	0.0133	-0.08	0.00%	18.67%	28.04%			
10		1995 38.30%	0.372	0.235	0.00%	0.00%	0.00%			
11		1996 31.50%	0.2268	0.014	0.00%	0.00%	18.57%			
12		1997 21.20%	0.331	0.099	0.00%	0.00%	10.06%			

Figure 22-3: Computation of the Sortino ratio

Beta

If we define Y = Return on an investment during a time period (usually a month) and X = Return on the market index during the time period, then the beta of an investment is the slope of the least squares line. Basically, the *beta* of a stock measures the sensitivity of the stock's return to market movements. For example, a beta of 2 means a 1% increase in the market return results on average in a 2% increase in the return on the investment, and a beta of 0.5 means that a 1% increase in the market return results on average in only a 0.5% increase in the investment's return. Of course, the market has a beta of 1. As shown in cell B5 of Figure 22.2, the formula =SLOPE(E3:E31,F3:F31) shows that RMF had a negative beta of –0.56 (based on annual returns). This means that a 1% increase in the market would, on average, hurt the Renaissance Medallion Fund. This is because Renaissance is a *hedge fund* that tries to reduce its sensitivity to market movements. Hedge funds will be discussed further in Chapter 51, "How do Hedge Funds Work?."

By the way, if you have Office 365 (recently changed to Microsoft 365), it is easy to find the beta for any company. As shown in the worksheet Beta (see Figure 22.4), we typed **Microsoft** in cell F5, **IBM** in cell F6, and the ticker symbol (**LUV**) for Southwest Airlines in cell F7. After selecting the range F5:F7, we went to the Data tab and selected Stocks. Then, copying the formula =F5.Beta from G5 to G6:G7 returns the beta (as of October 22, 2019) for each stock. You can see Southwest (with a beta of 1.48) is most sensitive to market movements. If you select F5:F7 and choose Refresh All from the Data tab, then your betas will automatically update.

	F	G	H
5	🏛 Microsoft Corp (XNAS:MSFT)	1.23	=F5.Beta
6	🏛 International Business Machines Corp (XNYS:IBM)	1.36	=F6.Beta
7	🏛 Southwest Airlines Co (XNYS:LUV)	1.48	=F7.Beta

Figure 22-4: Obtaining stock betas with Office 365

R-Squared vs. Standard Index

Actively managed mutual funds charge a higher expense ratio than passively managed funds that follow an index. Therefore, investors are interested in how closely fund returns are explained by the market. After all, if the fund simply follows the market, then why pay the higher fees? Morningstar looks at the percentage variation in excess (over the T-bill rate) fund returns explained by excess returns in a market index. If we consider Stocks as the market index, then as shown in cell B7 of Figure 22.2 we can use Excel's RSQ function in the formula =RSQ(F3:F31,G3:G31) to find that changes in the market index explain only 19% of RMF's annual returns. As shown in cell B8, the Renaissance annual returns have a –0.44 correlation with annual stock returns. If you square the correlation between two variables, you get the R^2 value (note that $-0.44^2 = 0.19$). These calculations show that changes in the market have little effect on RMF returns.

Alpha

Talk to anyone who works in investments, and they will tell you one of their goals is to maximize *alpha*. Essentially, the alpha of an investment is the excess average return (over the 90-day T-bill return) after adjusting for the investment's beta. To find RMF's alpha, simply find the intercept for the least squares line using Y = annual return on RMF – annual return on 90-day T-bills and X = annual return on the stock market – annual return on 90-day T-bills. As shown in Figure 22.2, in cell B6 we compute RMF's alpha with the formula

$$=INTERCEPT(H3:H31,I3:I31)$$

RMF's alpha of 0.36 means that after adjusting for RMF's beta, over a nearly 30-year time period, RMF has an annual return that is 36% better than expected. To put this in perspective, at the end of 2018, the mutual fund with the best three-year alpha was AQR Style Premia Alternative with an alpha of 10.68%, less than one-third the alpha of RMF over nearly 30 years (see `www.financial-planning.com/slideshow/highest-alpha-which-funds-generate-additional-value`)!

How Well Do Morningstar Star Ratings Predict a Fund's Future Performance?

We would hope that a Morningstar 5-star rating would usually be indicative of excellent future performance and a Morningstar one-star rating would be indicative of future poor performance. In October 2017, the *Wall Street Journal* studied the predictive power of Morningstar fund ratings (see `www.wsj.com/articles/the-morningstar-mirage-1508946687`). Table 22.1 shows the average rating after 10 years for funds given 1–5 stars. This table assumes that merged funds are dropped from the analysis.

Table 22-1: Ten-year average Morningstar ratings

RATING	AVERAGE RATING 10 YEARS LATER
5 stars	3.1
4 stars	2.9
3 stars	2.6
2 stars	2.3
1 star	1.9

`www.wsj.com/articles/the-morningstar-mirage-1508946687`

Thus, we see that after 10 years, a highly rated 5-star fund becomes on average a 3-star fund, and a poorly rated 1-star fund becomes on average a 2-star fund. This appears to be a classic example of *regression toward the mean*. Basically, when applied to a measure (such as a fund's star rating) that varies over time, regression toward the mean states that an extreme value (for example, a 5-star Morningstar rating) for a measurement will tend to be closer to average when measured later.

A detailed description of the methodology used in the study can be found here: www.wsj.com/articles/how-the-wall-street-journal-did-its-analysis-of-morningstar-ratings-1508947039?tesla=y.

Figure 22.5 (see the worksheet 3 Years Stars) shows for each rating of a fund the chances that in three years the fund will have 1–5 stars, be merged, or be liquidated. This figure shows that in three years 27% of 5-star funds become 1- or 2-star funds. Also, in three years, 14% of one-star funds become 4- or 5-star funds. The figure does show, however, that three years hence, one-star funds are much more likely than 5-star funds to be merged or liquidated (34% to 5%).

	D	E	F	G	H	I	J	K	L
1									
2									
3				Rating in Three Years					
4			5	4	3	2	1	Merged	Liquidated
5		5	14.00%	25.00%	29.00%	17.00%	10.00%	3.00%	2.00%
6		4	9.00%	23.00%	34.00%	17.00%	8.00%	5.00%	4.00%
7	Current	3	6.00%	17.00%	33.00%	22.00%	7.00%	9.00%	6.00%
8	Star Rating	2	4.00%	12.00%	25.00%	24.00%	11.00%	15.00%	9.00%
9		1	5.00%	9.00%	17.00%	20.00%	15.00%	20.00%	14.00%

Figure 22-5: Morningstar ratings in 3 years

Despite the lack of predictive power, Morningstar ratings have a huge influence on investors' behavior. Over each three-year period, the *Wall Street Journal* classified funds on two dimensions:

- The average star rating over the three-year period
- The star rating the fund deserved based on their performance during the three-year period

For each possible combination of these quantities, Figure 22.6 (see the worksheet Outflows) shows the fraction of funds that experienced a net outflow during the three-year period.

For example, we find that 77% of funds with an average 1-star rating during three years and an ending 5-star rating experienced a net outflow of funds. This shows that investors' behavior during the three-year period was influenced more by the fund's low average star rating than the fund's actual performance during the three years.

	D	E	F	G	H	I	J	K
					Rating at end of Three Years			
6								
7				1	2	3	4	5
8			1	85%	81%	78%	78%	77%
9	Average Rating		2	83%	79%	73%	69%	60%
10	Over Three Years		3	76%	71%	62%	56%	48%
11			4	61%	54%	47%	41%	34%
12			5	45%	38%	31%	27%	20%

Figure 22-6:

The Effect of Expense Ratio on Long-Term Performance

As we previously noted, actively managed funds charge a higher percentage of funds invested than do passively managed funds. Consider an investor who at the beginning of each month for 30 years invests $500 with a mutual fund that yields a 10% annual return each year (before charging for expenses). Figure 22.7 (see the worksheet Expense Ratio) shows the dependence of ending cash on the annual expense ratio. For example, with a 0.10% annual expense ratio (similar to Vanguard), the ending cash position is $1,019,653.69, whereas with a 1.5% annual

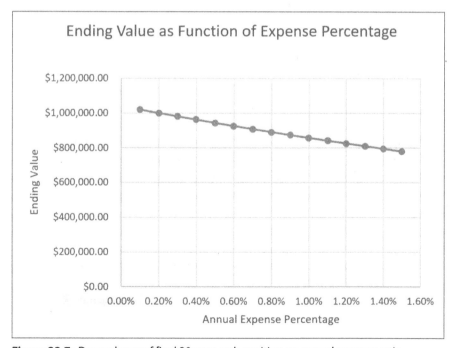

Figure 22-7: Dependence of final 30-year cash position on annual expense ratio

expense ratio, the ending cash position is $779,175.04. In the "Excel Calculation" section, we show how Excel's great FV (Future Value) function was used to create the chart shown in Figure 22.7.

Excel Calculations

The Excel FV function, which has the syntax FV(rate,nper,pmt,[pv],[type]), can be used to determine the final cash position resulting from equal, regularly spaced cash inflows. The arguments of the FV function are as follows:

- rate = The return rate per period
- nper = The number of periods
- pmt = The size of cash inflow during each period (use a minus sign)
- pv = An optional argument that represents (with a minus sign) the amount of cash on hand
- type = An optional argument, where 0 = cash flows occurring at the end of each period, and 1 = cash flows occurring at the beginning of each period

To use the FV function to evaluate the effect of a mutual fund's expense ratio on the final cash position, we need to compute the effective (after adjusting for the expense ratio) monthly rate of return on our investments. Let R = effective monthly rate and ER = Annual expense ratio. Then $(\$1) * (1 + R)^{12} = (1 + 0.10 - ER)$.

Solving for R, we find that $R = (1 + 0.10 - ER)^{1/12} - 1$. For example, with a 1% annual expense ratio, we find that the effective monthly rate is $(1.09)^{1/12} - 1 = 0.72\%$.

The worksheet Expense Ratio (see Figure 22.8) shows how we computed the ending cash position for expense ratios between 0.1% and 1.5% when $500 was deposited at the beginning of each of 360 months. Column F contains the key formulas used to compute our ending cash position. For example, the formula =FV(H18,360,-500,0,1) in cell F18 computes our ending cash position if we earn a 0.72% return per month and invest $500 at the beginning of each month for 360 months.

We note that if a passively managed fund charges 0.10% per year and an actively managed fund charges 1.5% per year, then the active management needs to add 1.4% to the mean annual return in order to justify its higher expense fee.

	E	F	G	H	I	J	K
			Adjusted Annual	Adjusted Monthly			
8	Annual Expense Fee	Ending Value	Return	Return			
9	0.10%	$1,019,653.69	9.90%	0.007897747	=FV(H9,360,-500,0,1)	=0.1-E9	=(1+G9)^(1/12)-1
10	0.20%	$1,000,071.19	9.80%	0.00782129	=FV(H10,360,-500,0,1)	=0.1-E10	=(1+G10)^(1/12)-1
11	0.30%	$980,890.33	9.70%	0.007744769	=FV(H11,360,-500,0,1)	=0.1-E11	=(1+G11)^(1/12)-1
12	0.40%	$962,102.77	9.60%	0.007668183	=FV(H12,360,-500,0,1)	=0.1-E12	=(1+G12)^(1/12)-1
13	0.50%	$943,700.32	9.50%	0.007591534	=FV(H13,360,-500,0,1)	=0.1-E13	=(1+G13)^(1/12)-1
14	0.60%	$925,674.99	9.40%	0.007514821	=FV(H14,360,-500,0,1)	=0.1-E14	=(1+G14)^(1/12)-1
15	0.70%	$908,018.92	9.30%	0.007438043	=FV(H15,360,-500,0,1)	=0.1-E15	=(1+G15)^(1/12)-1
16	0.80%	$890,724.44	9.20%	0.007361201	=FV(H16,360,-500,0,1)	=0.1-E16	=(1+G16)^(1/12)-1
17	0.90%	$873,784.03	9.10%	0.007284295	=FV(H17,360,-500,0,1)	=0.1-E17	=(1+G17)^(1/12)-1
18	1.00%	$857,190.32	9.00%	0.007207323	=FV(H18,360,-500,0,1)	=0.1-E18	=(1+G18)^(1/12)-1
19	1.10%	$840,936.10	8.90%	0.007130287	=FV(H19,360,-500,0,1)	=0.1-E19	=(1+G19)^(1/12)-1
20	1.20%	$825,014.31	8.80%	0.007053186	=FV(H20,360,-500,0,1)	=0.1-E20	=(1+G20)^(1/12)-1
21	1.30%	$809,418.03	8.70%	0.006976021	=FV(H21,360,-500,0,1)	=0.1-E21	=(1+G21)^(1/12)-1
22	1.40%	$794,140.48	8.60%	0.00689879	=FV(H22,360,-500,0,1)	=0.1-E22	=(1+G22)^(1/12)-1
23	1.50%	$779,175.04	8.50%	0.006821493	=FV(H23,360,-500,0,1)	=0.1-E23	=(1+G23)^(1/12)-1

Figure 22-8: Fraction of funds experiencing a net outflow during a three-year period

Is Vegas Good at Picking NFL Games?

A 2017 Gallup poll (news.gallup.com/poll/4735/sports.aspx) indicated that for 37% of Americans, NFL football was the favorite sport to watch, with basketball, at 11%, a distant second. Betting on sports has been legal in Nevada since 1949, and in England since 1961. In May 2018, the Supreme Court ruled in the 6-3 *Murphy v. National Collegiate Athletic Association* decision that individual states could set up their own framework to conduct legalized sports gambling. In this chapter, we will explain how the most common NFL bets work and show that Las Vegas is fantastic at predicting the outcome of NFL games. Our discussion also applies to betting on NBA games as well as NCAA football and basketball.

How NFL Betting Works

Most betting on the NFL involves three types of bets:

- Point spread bets
- Totals bets
- Money line bets

We use the 2019 Rams versus Patriots Super Bowl to illustrate how these bets work.

Point Spread Bets

For each game, Vegas forecasts a margin of victory. In the 2019 Rams versus Patriots Super Bowl, the Patriots were a 2.5-point favorite. Let's consider $10 as our unit bet. If you bet $10 on the Rams, you win the spread bet and $10 if the Rams lost by 2 points or less (or won), and you lose the spread bet and $11 if the Rams lost by 3 points or more. In a similar fashion, a $10 spread bet on the Patriots would win and pay $10 if the Patriots won by 3 points or more and lose the spread bet and $11 if the Patriots won by 2 points or less or lost. The Patriots won by 10 points (13-3), so the Patriot bettor would have won $10 on the game, and the Rams bettor would have lost $11 on the game. Note that if Vegas has half the money bet on either side, they can't lose, because (assuming all bets are for $10) half the bettors win $10 and the other half would lose $11.

With the recent legalization of gambling in Indiana, let's help a typical Hoosier bettor understand how good they need to be at betting against the spread to make betting profitable. To answer this question, we need to understand the concept of *expected value of a discrete random variable*. Recall that a discrete random variable can assume a finite number of values. Then we find the expected value of a discrete random variable X by summing over all possible values of the random variable:

$$(\text{the probability that } X = x) * x$$

Essentially, the expected value of a random variable is the average value you would expect if you repeated many times the situation (or experiment) generating the random variable.

Let's suppose our bettor has a probability P of winning each bet. Then the bettor's expected profit on each spread bet is

$$P * 10 + (1 - P) * (-11) = 21P - 11$$

The bet's expected profit of $21P - 11$ is positive if, and only if, P is greater than $11 / 21 = .524$. *Thus, to make money betting, yon need to win more than 52.4% of your bets.* As you will soon see, this is not easy!

If you only pick 50% against the spread (we will see it is really hard to do much better), what is the "house edge" or the percentage a bettor will lose per dollar bet? On a $10 bet, we assume the bettor is risking $.5 * \$10 + .5 * \$11 = \$10.50$. The bettor will have an expected profit per $10 bet of $.5 * (\$10) + .5 * (-\$11) = -\$0.50$. Thus, the bettor loses on average $\$0.50 / \$10.50 = 4.8\%$.

Totals Bets

Vegas also predicts the total number of points scored in an NFL game. For example, for the 2019 Super Bowl, Vegas set the "Totals" line at 56 points.

A bettor can bet either "over" or "under" the totals line. If you bet $10 on the over, you win $10 if 57 or more points are scored in the game and lose $11 if 55 or fewer points are scored in the game. If 56 points are scored, then the bet is a push, and no money changes hands. If you bet $10 on the under, you win $10 if 55 or fewer points are scored in the game and lose $11 if 57 or more points are scored in the game. If 56 points are scored, then the bet is a push, and no money changes hands. As with point spread bets, Vegas can't lose if half the money comes in on each side. For a bettor who picks 50% against the total line, the house edge is again 4.8%. Later in the chapter, you will see that Vegas is very good at setting totals lines.

Money Line Bets

Some bettors simply want to bet on who wins the game. For bets on who wins or loses an NFL game, Vegas sets a *money line*. For the 2019 Super Bowl, the money line on the Patriots was −150 and on the Rams +130. This means that to win $100 for a Patriots win, you need to risk $150, and to win $130 for a Rams win, you need to risk $100.

When will a given money line bet be profitable? Let P = the actual (but unknown) probability that the Patriots will win the game. Then the money line bet on the Patriots will have a positive expected profit if

$$100 * P - 150 * (1 - P) > 0 \text{ or } 250 * P > 150 \text{ or } P > 0.6$$

The money line bet on the Rams will have a positive expected profit if

$$130 * (1 - P) - 100 * P > 0 \text{ or } 130 > 230 * P \text{ or } P < 13 / 23 = 0.565$$

Since Vegas wants bettors to have negative expected profit, Vegas must think the Patriots' chance of winning the game is between 56.5% and 60%. It seems reasonable to infer that Vegas's opinion was that the Patriots' chance of winning the game was the average of 0.565 and 0.60, which equals 58.3%.

As you will see later in the chapter, mean the margin of victory for the favorite in an NFL game is close to the point spread, and the actual margin closely follows a normal random variable (see Chapter 1, "Preliminaries") with a standard deviation near 12.7 points. Then, using the Excel NORM.DIST function (see Chapter 1), we can use the point spread (see the file Patsrams.xlsx and Figure 23.1) to estimate the chance that the Patriots would win the game as the sum of

- The chance the Patriots win by .5 points or more.
- Half of the chance that the Pats win by between .5 and −5 points. This corresponds to the game being tied after 60 minutes and the Pats winning in overtime.

⬚	F	G	H	I	J	K	L	M
5	Mean	2.5						
6	Standard Deviation	12.7						
7	Chance Pats by >=.5	0.562567	=1-NORM.DIST(0.5,Mean,Standard__Deviation,TRUE)					
8	Chance Pats win in OT	0.015401	=0.5*(NORM.DIST(0.5,Mean,Standard__Deviation,TRUE)-NORM.DIST(-0.5,Mean,Standard__Deviation,TRUE))					
9	Total Chance Pats Win	0.577968	=G7+G8					

Figure 23-1: Using a normal random variable to estimate the chance the Patriots win the Super Bowl

This yields a 57.8% chance of the Patriots winning, which is very consistent with the money line.

Bias and Accuracy

Almost every organization forecasts future quantities of interest. For example, a drug company might forecast projected demand next year for a given drug and profit generated from that drug. A museum might project their fundraising for each of the next three years. Forecasts should be evaluated on two attributes: *bias* and *accuracy*.

Measuring Forecast Bias

Forecasts are biased on the high side if on average the forecast is larger than the actual values. Forecasts are biased on the low side if on average the forecasts are smaller than the actual value. When teaching a modeling class at a leading Fortune 500 corporation to the finance department, I asked the class if marketing forecasts of product sales were biased high or low. A corporate controller said marketing forecasts were too high. I asked how he corrected for this, and he replied (tongue in cheek, I hope) that finance always divided marketing forecasts by 10! The worksheet Bias and Accuracy (see Figure 23.2) of the Patsrams. xlsx workbook gives a simple illustration of two different measures of forecast bias. You are given monthly unit sales of a product during a four-month period.

To determine *additive bias*, we compute for each observation the forecast error = Actual value − Predicted value. Months 1 and 4 have an error of +10, meaning we under-forecasted demand, and Months 2 and 4 have an error of −10, meaning we over-forecasted demand. To compute additive bias, we simply average the forecast errors. In this case, the additive bias of 0 indicates that our forecasts are unbiased. Later in the chapter, you will see that Vegas predictions for the point spread, totals, and probability of winning a game exhibit very little additive bias.

When the data being forecasted grows over time (like corporate revenues), it is usually better to measure bias by averaging the percentage error for each period. For example, as shown in Figure 23.2, the percentage error for Month 1

	C	D	E	F	G	H	I
1							
2	Month	Actual	Forecast	Error	Percentage Error	Absolute Error	Absolute Percentage Error
3		1	50	40	10	20.00%	10	20.00%
4		2	80	90	-10	-12.50%	10	12.50%
5		3	90	100	-10	-11.11%	10	11.11%
6		4	100	90	10	10.00%	10	10.00%
7								
8				=D3-E3	=(D3-E3)/D3	=ABS(F3)	=ABS(G3)
9	MAD		10	=AVERAGE(H3:H6)			
10	MAPE		13.40%	=AVERAGE(I3:I6)			
11							
12	Additive Bias		0	=AVERAGE(F3:F6)			
13	Average %age Bias		1.60%	=AVERAGE(G3:G6)			

Figure 23-2: Example of forecast accuracy and bias

is (50 − 40) / 50 = 20% and the percentage error for Month 2 is (80 − 90) / 80 = −12.5%. Averaging these percentage errors yields a second measure of bias, *average percentage bias*. As shown in Figure 23.2, the average percentage bias is 1.6%, indicating that by this measure we slightly under-forecasted demand.

Measuring Forecast Accuracy

The most common measure of forecast accuracy is the mean absolute deviation (MAD). The MAD is simply the average of the absolute value of the forecast errors. In our example, our forecasts were off by 10 each month, so MAD = 10.

When the quantity being forecast (like revenues) grows over time, analytics professionals usually measure forecast accuracy using the mean absolute percentage error (MAPE), which is the average of the absolute value of the percentage errors. For our example, the MAPE = 13.40%, which means our forecasts are off by an average of 13.4%.

Vegas Forecasts Are Unbiased

The great site ThePredictionTracker.com tabulates Vegas predictions for every NFL game as well as the Vegas forecasts. The site also tabulates the predictions made by many algorithmic-based rating systems. If Vegas forecasts were biased, bettors would take Vegas to the cleaners. For example, if for all games where the home team was favored by at least 10 points, home teams won by an average of 5 points less per game than Vegas predicted, then bettors could profit by betting in these games on the visiting team.

	A	B	C	D	E	F	G	H	I
1	Home	Road	line	rscore	hscore	home margin	error		Mean Bias
2	Arizona	Washington	2	24	6	-18	-20		0.156367041
3	Baltimore	Buffalo	7.5	3	47	44	36.5		=AVERAGE(G2:G1069)
4	Carolina	Dallas	3	8	16	8	5		Std Dev of Errors
5	Cleveland	Pittsburgh	-3.5	21	21	0	3.5		12.70586382
6	Denver	Seattle	3	24	27	3	0		=STDEV(G2:G1069)
7	Detroit	N.Y. Jets	7	48	17	-31	-38		Std Error of Mean Errors
8	Green Bay	Chicago	7	23	24	1	-6		0.388793119
9	Indianapoli	Cincinnati	2	34	23	-11	-13		=I5/SQRT(COUNT(G2:G1069))
10	LA Charger	Kansas City	3.5	38	28	-10	-13.5		Z Score
11	Miami	Tennessee	0	20	27	7	7		0.402185722
12	Minnesota	San Francisco	6	16	24	8	2		=I2/I8

Figure 23-3: Calculation of NFL forecast bias in predicting game margins

The file `TheLine.xlsx` (see Figure 23.3) contains for all 2015–2018 NFL games the betting line (the number of points by which the home team was favored) and the score of each game. In Column F we computed the number of points by which the home team won each game (a negative number indicates the home team lost), and in Column G, we computed the Vegas error (line) – (home margin). For example, for the first game, the home team won by 6 – 24 = –18 points, and Vegas predicted the home team would win by 2 points. The error (computed in cell G2) was –18 – 2 = –20 because the home team performed 20 points worse than the line predicted. In cell I2 we computed the mean bias by averaging the errors in Column G. We find that, on average, home teams performed a mere 0.16 points better than the line predictions.

The question, of course, is whether this is a significant bias. Mathematically, we define a random variable X that equals the bias occurring for a randomly chosen NFL game. The question is whether it is reasonable to conclude that the mean of $X = 0$. This is our *null hypothesis*, and like a defendant in a trial, the null hypothesis is "innocent" until proven guilty. In both situations, we want to require a lot of proof before discarding the null hypothesis or the defendant's innocence. To disprove that the mean bias is different from 0, we need to determine if the observed mean bias of 0.16 is more than two standard deviations different from 0. The standard deviation of an average of many observed errors turns out to be close to

(the sample standard deviation of the observed errors) / sqrt (Number of observed errors)

The standard deviation of the mean errors is called the standard error of the mean errors and is computed in cell I8 as 12.7 / sqrt (1068) = 0.39.

Finally, to compute how inconsistent our observed errors are with our null hypothesis, we compute in cell I11 a *Z-score*, which equals the number of standard errors by which our observed mean error differs from the hypothesized mean error of 0:

$$Z - \text{score} = (0.156 - 0) / 0.39 = 0.40$$

This indicates that a mean error of 0.156 is very consistent with the null hypothesis that the mean error in Vegas predictions on margin of victory equals 0.

To provide stronger evidence that Vegas predictions on the margin of victory in an NFL game are unbiased, we grouped the Vegas predictions in three-point buckets and used a PivotTable (see Figure 23.4) to compute the mean error for each point bucket and a Z-score based on the mean bias in each bucket.

	K	L	M	N	O
7					
8	Row Labels	Average of error	How Many Games	Std Error	Z Score
9	-14--11	-3.166666667	6	5.187147	-0.610483
10	-11--8	-2.37037037	27	2.445245	-0.96938
11	-8--5	-1.414285714	70	1.518641	-0.931284
12	-5--2	1.368556701	194	0.912228	1.500236
13	-2-1	-0.195652174	92	1.324678	-0.147698
14	1-4	0.035447761	268	0.776134	0.045672
15	4-7	0.065445026	191	0.919364	0.071185
16	7-10	0.142335766	137	1.085535	0.13112
17	10-13	0.590909091	44	1.915481	0.308491
18	13-16	1.705882353	34	2.179038	0.78286
19	16-19	-4.8	5	5.682235	-0.844738
20	Grand Total	0.156367041	1068		

Figure 23-4: Analysis of Vegas bias as a function of point spread

For example, in the 268 games in which the home team was favored by between 1 and 3.5 points (4 points is included in 4–7 points), the average bias was 0.035 points and the standard error of the average bias as 12.7 / sqrt (268) = 0.78. Then the Z-score for this data is 0.035 / 0.78 = 0.045. None of the Z-scores in Figure 24.4 is close to 2, so again we have convincing evidence that Vegas point spreads forecasts exhibit no significant bias.

We note that the procedure we used to show that Vegas point spreads exhibit no significant bias is often used by statisticians to test whether a null hypothesis is true. The procedure is summarized as follows:

1. Define a null hypothesis.
2. Collect data that will be examined to determine if the data is consistent with the null hypothesis.

3. Use the data to compute a Z-score (or other test statistic) computed from the observed data to measure the consistency of the data with the null hypothesis. If the Z-score is between –2 and +2, accept the null hypothesis; otherwise, reject the null hypothesis.

Totals Predictions and Money Line Predictions Are Unbiased

In the file NFLResearch.xlsx, we examine whether Vegas predictions for totals and probabilities implied by the money line are unbiased. In the Data worksheet, we computed for 1,068 NFL games played during the 2015–2018 seasons the error for predicting the total points scored in each game. For example, if Vegas predicted 55 points and 60 points were scored, the error is 60 – 55 = 5, and if only 50 points were scored, the error is 50 – 55 = –5.

We found the mean average bias was an amazing –0.09. The standard deviation of the errors was 13.42. Following our analysis of the point spread bias, we find the Z-score for testing the null hypothesis that mean totals bias = 0 is

$$-0.09 / (13.42 / \text{sqrt} (1068)) = -0.20$$

This small Z-score is very consistent with the hypothesis that the mean bias in Vegas total predictions equals 0.

In the MoneyLineResults worksheet, we tested the null hypothesis that mean bias in predicting the chance of winning a game = 0. We had money lines for 1,057 games. As described for the 2019 Super Bowl, we used the money lines for each game to determine an implied probability of the favorite winning the game. Then we treated a win by the favorite as an outcome of 1, a loss by the favorite as an outcome of 0, and a tie as an outcome of 0.5. Suppose the money line implies a 60% chance for the favorite winning. Then, if the favorite wins, the error is 1 – 0.6 = 0.4; if the underdog wins, the error is 0 – 0.6 = –0.6; and if the game ends in a tie, the error is 0.5 – 0.6 = –0.1. The mean of all errors is –0.75%, and the standard deviation of our errors was 0.46. Then the Z-score for this bias is –0.53, which is again very consistent with the null hypothesis that the money line–implied probabilities do a great job of estimating, on average, the chance of the favorite winning an NFL game.

NFL Accuracy: The Line vs. the Computers

Using the data from ThePredictionTracker.com, we found that during the 2015–2018 seasons, the opening line predicted the winners of 65% of all games and that the opening line point spreads were off by an average of 9.77 points per game. We then used ThePredictionTracker.com to tabulate the results from 37 computer prediction algorithms. These 37 algorithms predicted on average 63% winners, beat the spread an average of 51% of the time, and were off by an average of 10.33 points per game. No computer algorithm predicted more than 66% winners. Also, *no computer algorithm beat the spread more than 52% of the time.* Recall that you need to beat the spread 52.4% of the time to break even betting! *No computer algorithm beat the line's MAD of 9.77.*

A System Works Until It Doesn't

In William Poundstone's excellent book *Rock Breaks Scissors* (Little Brown, 2014, page 194), he points out that during the 2001–2008 seasons, betting on home underdogs to beat the point spread would have won 57.7% of all bets. This system would have been highly profitable during those seasons. Any betting system needs to be profitable, however, on games that are out of sample. In the worksheet Home Dog of the workbook TheLine.xlsx, we found that during the 2014–2018 seasons, home underdogs covered the point spread only 50.7% of the time, which is not profitable. The home underdog strategy illustrates an important fact: given a set of sports results, it is not that hard to cherry-pick the data and create a profitable gambling system. When tested on new data, however, most systems fall apart.

CHAPTER
24

Will My New Hires Be Good Employees?

The quality of an organization's employees is critical to the success of the organization. In this chapter, we will examine how various attributes of potential hires can be used to help predict an employee's job performance. Our discussion is primarily based on Frank L. Schmidt's 2016 paper, *The Validity and Utility of Selection Methods in Personnel Psychology: Practical and Theoretical Implications of 100 Years of Research Findings* (`https://testingtalent.com/wp-content/uploads/2017/04/2016-100-Yrs-Working-Paper-on-Selection-Methods-Schmit-Mar-17.pdf`). This paper is a *meta-analysis* that combines the results from many studies on the subject. The reader who is interested in exploring the details of meta-analysis should read *Introduction to Meta-Analysis,* by Michael Borenstein, Larry V. Hedges, Julian P. T. Higgins, and Hannah R. Rothstein (Wiley, 2009).

For a simple example of meta-analysis, suppose previous treatments for a cancer have resulted in a 10% survival rate. Five hospitals gave a new treatment to 100 patients, and at each hospital, 13 of 100 patients survive. Is the new treatment significantly better than previous treatments? If we look at any one hospital, you can show that if the new treatment had a 10% survival rate, then there would be a 19% chance that 13 or more patients would survive at a single hospital (see the "Excel Calculations" section and workbook `MetaAnalysis.xlsx`). We combine the results from all five hospitals; then if the new treatment had only a 10% survival rate, the chance that at least 65 of 500 patients would survive is only 2%, and we can conclude that the new treatment is significantly better than the old treatment.

What Data Do We Need to Determine Attributes That Best Predict Employee Performance?

The first question is, what metric do we use to measure an employee's job performance? Most of the studies referenced by Schmidt use supervisor ratings as a measure of job performance. Some use job rank (such as the rank of military personnel).

The next question is, what attributes might be useful for predicting employee performance? Schmidt found 31 attributes that had been considered. Most turned out to have little predictive power. In this chapter, we will restrict our attention to seven attributes:

- General mental ability (GMA) tests
- Integrity tests
- Employee interviews
- Reference checks
- Biographical data
- Personality- and ability-based emotional intelligence
- College grade point average (GPA)

As you will soon see, GMA is by far the most useful tool for predicting employee performance. We now give a brief description of these attributes.

GMA Tests

The idea of a g factor that can measure intelligence goes back to 1904 when British psychologist Charles Spearman first proposed the concept of a general intelligence that could be measured. Most of us have encountered the g factor through taking an IQ test. The term IQ (intelligence quotient) was coined in 1912 by German psychologist William Stern. Many researchers have made use of the U.S. government's huge database of GMA scores based primarily on two tests:

The General Aptitude Test Battery (GATB)   See www.nap.edu/read/1338/chapter/6#93 for a great summary and discussion of the GATB test. This test is available to high schools, labor unions, and state governments for use in vocational counseling. Following are some examples of the type of questions asked on the GATB:

- Question 1: What is 502 times 3? (Answer: 1506)
- Question 2: Which two words have the same meaning: happy, sad, glad, tall? (Answer: happy and glad)

- Question 3: If there are two quarts of gasoline in a one-gallon can, how full is the container? (Answer: 50%)

The Army General Classification Test (AGCT) and the Armed Services Vocational Aptitude Battery (ASVAB) Test   These tests are used to determine suitability for enlistment and suitability for different job classifications, such as an aviation technician or Special Forces candidate.

Integrity Tests

Tests of integrity predict whether a potential employee will engage in undesirable behavior, such as drug use, stealing, sabotage, fighting, or falsified absenteeism.

Employee Interviews

Schmidt evaluated the predictive value of structured and unstructured in-person interviews, and structured phone interviews. You will soon see that after adjusting for a potential hire's GMA, interviews are not very useful.

Reference Checks

Employers often check references. In the 1970s and '80s, former employees could sue employers who gave out negative information. Of course, this possibility would impact the veracity of the references. By 2000, thirty-six states had passed laws exempting former employers from legal liability due to unfavorable references. As you will see, after adjusting for GMA, reference checks are not that useful.

Biographical Data

Biodata includes data on extracurricular activities, hobbies, nature of family upbringing, and so forth. Again, you will see that after adjusting for GMA, biographical data has little value for predicting job performance.

Emotional Intelligence

According to the Oxford Dictionary, *emotional intelligence* is "the capacity to be aware of, control, and express one's emotions, and to handle interpersonal relationships judiciously and empathetically." The concept of emotional intelligence became popular after the publication in 1995 of Daniel Goleman's book *Emotional Intelligence: Why It Can Matter More than IQ* (Bantam Books). In their meta-analysis of job performance studies, Schmidt considered the effect of two types of emotional intelligence (personality-based measures and ability-based measures) on job performance.

Personality-based measures of emotional intelligence are described here: onlinelibrary.wiley.com/doi/10.1111/j.1468-5884.2011.00502.x

The authors describe four aspects of personality-based emotional intelligence:

- **Temperament:** This includes attributes such as degree of introversion or extroversion and susceptibility to moodiness or anxiety.

- **Information processing:** This includes the ability to respond to facial expressions or other external emotional cues.

- **Emotion regulation:** This includes stability in how you view your own abilities and the development of strategies to manage your emotions.

- **Emotional knowledge and skills:** This involves the ability to recognize situations in context and react in an acceptable fashion.

Ability-based measures of emotional intelligence are explained in "Measuring Emotional Intelligence with the MSCEIT V.2.0," by J.D. Mayer, P. Salovey, D. R. Caruso, and G. Sitarenios (*Emotion*, vol. 3, no. 1, 2003, pages 97–105). The authors' test evaluates a person's ability to perceive, understand, and manage emotions. Their test also measures an individual's ability to use emotions to communicate feelings and improve cognitive processes.

Before researching the determinants of job performance, I was sure emotional intelligence would be a useful predictor of job performance. As you will see, after adjusting for GMA, it turns out (surprisingly) that emotional intelligence has little predictive value.

GPA

This is only for college graduates and represents a student's undergraduate or graduate school grade point average.

The Range Restriction Problem

Consider trying to determine how GMA affects job performance. Suppose a company uses a GMA test where scores range between 200 and 800 as the sole criterion for hiring, and they only hire applicants who score at least 500. You might think you could evaluate the influence of GMA on job performance by looking at the correlation between employees' GMA and their job performance. *The problem is that this approach ignores the data on applicants who were not hired.* If the GMA test had some predictive value, applicants who scored below 500 on the GMA most likely would have, if hired, had a worse job performance in aggregate than the hired applicants. To illustrate the idea, look at the file

RestrictedRange.xlsx (see Figure 24.1). Suppose in the past that applicants with scores in the 400–500 range had been hired. The file contains GMA scores and job performance ratings for 790 fictitious job applicants. We assume everyone who scored over 500 was hired. Figure 24.1 shows the average job performance rating for each 50-point GMA range. The figure makes it clear that there is a large decline in average performance for applicants with an under-500 GMA score. Of course, a researcher would not know this if they started collecting data after the 500-point cutoff was instituted. Using the Excel CORREL function, we found a 0.45 correlation between GMA score and job rating for applicants with a GMA of at least 500. *When we include data on past hires with GMA scores less than 500, the correlation increases substantially to 0.84.*

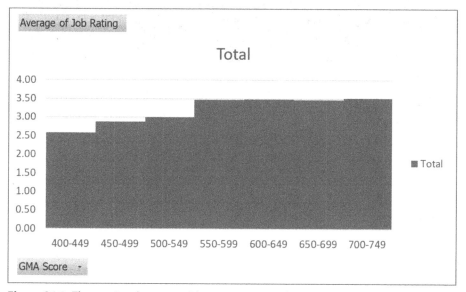

Figure 24.1: The restricted range problem

This example illustrates the *range restriction problem*. When a sample has a restricted range of scores (in our example, at least 500), the correlation between the scores and an output measure (such as job performance) will understate the correlation that would be found if all scores were included. John E. Hunter, Frank L. Schmidt, and Huy Le ("Implications of Direct and Indirect Range Restriction for Meta-Analysis Methods and Findings," *Journal of Applied Psychology,* vol. 91, 2006, pages 594–612) developed a method (beyond the scope of this chapter) to correct for the range restriction problem. Schmidt incorporated the correction to the range restriction problem in his meta-analysis. We now describe his results.

Besides GMA, Not Much Affects Job Performance

Table I (see page 65) of Schmidt's paper combines the data from many research studies to estimate the correlation between 31 selection procedures and job performance. The table also gives the gain in correlation (versus using just GMA to predict job performance) when other attributes are used with GMA to predict job performance. We show the relevant data in Table 24.1.

Table 24.1: Correlation between selection procedures and job performance

SELECTION PROCEDURE	CORRELATION TO JOB PERFORMANCE	GAIN IN CORRELATION RESULTING WHEN SELECTION PROCEDURE IS ADDED TO A REGRESSION INCLUDING GMA
GMA test	.65	Not relevant
Integrity test	.46	.13
Structured in-person interview	.58	.12
Unstructured in-person interview	.58	.09
Structured phone interview	.46	.09
Reference checks	.26	.08
Biographical data	.35	.06
Personality-based EI	.32	.05
Ability-based EI	.23	.004
College GPA	.34	.009

Source: https://testingtalent.com/wp-content/uploads/2017/04/2016-100-Yrs-Working-Paper-on-Selection-Methods-Schmit-Mar-17.pdf

For example, the correlation between GMA and job performance is 0.65. This correlation is 0.74 for professional and managerial jobs and only 0.39 for unskilled jobs. Also, the correlation between integrity test results and job performance is 0.46, but after including an employee's GMA, integrity test results add .13 to correlation. More specifically, Schmidt found that if you predict job performance using both GMA and integrity of the employee, your predictions have a 0.78 correlation with the employee's job performance.

The big shocker is the fact that once you know an employee's GMA, then knowledge of their emotional intelligence (EI) does not help you predict the employee's job performance. Best-selling author and Wharton Professor Adam Grant has a great post (`www.linkedin.com/pulse/20140930125543-69244073-emotional-intelligence-is-overrated/`) on this issue. Grant, along with Dana Barnes of Optimize Hire Grant, gave hundreds of salespeople tests of emotional intelligence and GMA. Grant and Barnes measured the annual revenue generated by the salespeople and found that GMA had more than five times the predictive value of emotional intelligence. Grant mentions two possible reasons why, once you know GMA, EI fails to add significant value in predicting job performance:

- Perhaps current tests of EI fail to measure EI accurately. Better tests of emotional intelligence are needed.

- EI is strongly correlated with GMA, so once you know a person's GMA, EI adds little predictive power.

In the last paragraph of his paper, Schmidt points out that many firms have suboptimal hiring processes because they overemphasize attributes such as EI and (believe it or not) graphology or handwriting analysis. Graphology has a miniscule .02 correlation with job performance and, after knowing a person's GMA, adds no predictive value. Despite this fact, companies in Israel, France, and other countries (see `www.sofeminine.co.uk/career/graphology-handwriting-analysis-s564037.html`) often incorporate handwriting analysis as an important factor in the hiring process.

Excel Calculations

In our cancer meta-analysis example, assume that the new treatment is no better than previous treatments. Then each patient has a 10% chance of survival and a 90% chance of not surviving. Each patient is a *Bernoulli trial* that can result in success (survival) or failure (death). Probabilities involving repeated and independent Bernoulli trials with the same probability of success can be computed with the *binomial random variable*. The `Binom.dist.range` function, with the syntax `Binom.DIST.RANGE(n, p, Lower, Upper)`, computes the chance in n trials with probability p of success on each trial of observing between lower and upper successes inclusive. As shown in Figure 24.2, if we assume the new treatment is no better than the old treatment, if we look at a single hospital, the formula `=BINOM.DIST.RANGE(100,0.1,G4,100)` shows there is a 19.8% chance that at least 13 patients survive at a single hospital. When we combine in a meta-analysis the results from all five hospitals, the formula `=BINOM.DIST.RANGE(500,0.1,G9,500)` shows that if the new treatment were no better than the old treatments, there would only be

	F	G	H	I	J	K	L	M
3		Better	Not Better					
4		13	87	0.198179	=BINOM.DIST.RANGE(100,0.1,G4,100)			
5		13	87					
6		13	87					
7		13	87					
8		13	87					
9	Total	65	435	0.017972	=BINOM.DIST.RANGE(500,0.1,G9,500)			

Figure 24.2: Cancer example of meta-analysis

a 1.8% chance that at least 65 patients would have survived. Given this small probability, it seems reasonable to conclude that the new treatment is better.

Of course, when combining the results from different hospitals we need to make sure that the patients have similar symptoms to the patients in the current study and the patients with the 10% survival rate. In most meta-analysis research, tricky issues need to be resolved before studies are combined. Again, for a detailed discussion of meta-analysis, check out *Introduction to Meta-Analysis*.

CHAPTER 25

Should I Go to State U or Princeton?

In April of his senior year at Riverdale High, Archie Andrews has been accepted to both Princeton and State U. He knows Princeton is #1 in the 2020 U.S. News College rankings and State U is #57 (Penn State was #57). Being smart, Archie has found that 10 years after graduation, Princeton grads make a lot more money than State U grads. Archie's parents don't have a lot of money, so he is not sure what to do. The late Princeton economics professor Alan Krueger and mathematician Stacy Dale of Mathematica Policy Research conducted some brilliant research that might help Archie make an informed decision. (See /www.theatlantic.com/business/archive/2017/04/what-is-an-elite-college-really-worth/521577/ for a summary of the research, and you can find the research paper at www.nber.org/papers/w17159). Krueger and Dale found that after adjusting for the superior quality (as measured by SAT scores) of students at more selective schools, the more selective schools do not add significant value. In this chapter, we will analyze a fictitious data set that will help you understand the essence of the Dale-Krueger research. We will use Princeton to represent more selective schools and Penn State to represent less selective schools.

According to the 2020 U.S. News Best Colleges Report, the 25th–75th percentile range for the average of a Princeton student's SAT math and verbal scores is 720–785 and the 25th-75th percentile range for Penn State is 580–680. If you want to understand whether Princeton adds more value to students than State U, it would be nice if you could "block out" the effect of Princeton's superior SAT scores. *Krueger and Dale's brilliant insight was to study students who were admitted to both Princeton and Penn State. Since they were accepted to Princeton, they probably have high SAT scores. Looking at the difference in the average earnings of the students in this group who attended Princeton and Penn State, we have blocked out the difference in student quality (assuming SAT is a measure of student quality), and the observed difference in average salaries is a good measure of the financial value added by Princeton compared to Penn State.* The authors found that this difference is not significantly different than 0. Thus, if Archie cares only about future earnings, Penn State is probably a better deal.

Let's now walk through an analysis of our fictitious data set. Of course, the lower cost of the less selective college tilts the decision toward the less selective school.

Analyzing Princeton vs. Penn State

Archie got an A+ in Advanced Placement (AP) Statistics, so he is anxious to analyze the data in the file `Princeton.xlsx`. This file contains the following (fictitious) information about 20,000 college applicants:

- The average of each student's math and verbal SAT scores

- The student's annual earnings 10 years after graduation

- Whether the student was accepted at Princeton, Penn State, or both schools (1 = acceptance and 0 = non-acceptance)

- The school the student attended

Figure 25.1 shows a sample of the data. We see, for example, that Student #1 was accepted by Penn State and Princeton and attended Princeton. The average of her math and verbal SAT scores was 564, and 10 years after graduation, her annual salary was $142,000. Many of the students were accepted to at least one of these schools.

Luckily for Archie, his AP Stats class covered PivotTables. (See the "Excel Calculations" section for a description of how to create the relevant PivotTables.) Archie began his analysis of the data by calculating the average salary 10 years after graduation from Princeton or Penn State (see Figure 25.2). Archie also calculated the average SAT score of each school's graduates. As shown in Figure 25.2, Princeton graduates averaged making nearly $24,000 more per year than Penn State graduates. Princeton graduates also averaged SAT scores 43 points higher than Penn State graduates.

Archie now makes a key observation: maybe the Princeton grads make more money because they have more innate ability, not because Princeton adds more value. To test this idea, Archie decides to look at the average SAT scores and salaries of students who were admitted to *both* Penn State and Princeton.

	B	C	D	E	F	G	H
				Princeton			School
2	Student	SAT	Earnings	in	PSU in	In both	attended
3	1	564	$142,000	1	1	1	Princeton
4	2	646	$123,000	0	0	0	none
5	3	783	$155,500	0	0	0	none
6	4	642	$91,000	0	1	0	PSU
7	5	536	$26,000	0	0	0	none
8	6	728	$128,000	0	0	0	none
9	7	559	$25,500	0	1	0	PSU
10	8	654	$133,000	0	0	0	none
11	9	518	$71,000	0	1	0	PSU
12	10	736	$198,000	1	1	1	Princeton
13	11	588	$142,000	0	1	0	PSU
14	12	763	$223,500	0	0	0	none
15	13	535	$91,500	0	1	0	PSU

Figure 25.1: Data on Princeton and Penn State graduates

	K	L	M
10	Row Labels	Average of Earnings	Average of SAT
11	Princeton	$152,822.16	699.36
12	PSU	$128,957.55	656.19

Figure 25.2: Average salaries and SAT scores of PSU and Princeton graduates

He creates a PivotTable that calculates the average salary and SAT scores for students who were accepted to both schools and attended Penn State or Princeton (see Figure 25.3). Archie finds that the average SAT score for the students attending each school are virtually identical, and the Penn State grads earn a slightly higher salary than the Princeton grads. The students admitted to both schools are, therefore, similar in overall ability, but Princeton added slightly less value to these students than Penn State! This simple analysis indicates that the higher salaries of Princeton grads are mainly due to superior input, not to added value.

	K	L	M	N
			School	
16	Row Labels	Average of Earnings	attended	Average of SAT
17	⊟1			
18	Princeton	$152,822.16	2103	699.36
19	PSU	$154,194.19	878	691.52

Figure 25.3: Average salaries and SAT scores of students accepted to PSU and Princeton by school attended

Of course, our example simplifies the sophisticated analysis in the Dale-Krueger paper, but the main point is that when you adjust for the quality of student input, the financial return from attending a more selective school is not significantly different from 0. Dale-Krueger did find, however, that more selective schools do add significant value to black and Hispanic students and students whose parents were not college graduates.

Excel Calculations

To create the PivotTable that summarizes average salary and SAT score for students attending both schools (see Figure 25.2), we dragged School Attended to the Rows area and Earnings and SAT scores to the Values area. Then, after right-clicking Summarize Values By, we changed the Summary from Sum to Average. Finally, we clicked the drop-down arrow shown in the upper-left cell of the PivotTable and deselected None, so data from the students who attended neither school does not show in the PivotTable.

To create the PivotTable that summarizes information for students admitted to both schools (see Figure 25.3), we dragged In Both (a 1 means student was admitted to both schools and a 0 means the student was not admitted to both schools) and School Attended to the Rows area and SAT, Earnings, and School Attended to the Values area. Then, after right-clicking the SAT and Earnings columns, we chose Summarize Values By and changed Sum to Average. Then we clicked the drop-down arrow by Row Labels and selected 1 and deselected 0. This ensures that all calculations shown only use data on students accepted to both schools.

Will My Favorite Sports Team Be Great Next Year?

In 2015, the NFL Arizona Cardinals had a great season. They won 13 of 16 games and lost in the NFC championship game. Fans probably had high hopes for the 2016 season. Unfortunately for Cardinals fans, in 2016, the Cardinals fell back to earth and had a mediocre 7-8-1 season. This decline from excellence is not unusual. The eight teams that won at least 12 of 16 games in 2016 or 2017 averaged only 9.5 wins the next year. On the other hand, the six teams that won 4 or fewer games in 2016 or 2017 averaged winning 5.9 games the next season. The moral is that a good team is likely to be better than average next year but not as good as last year, and a bad team is likely to be worse than average next year but not as bad as they were last year. This is a notable example of *regression to the mean*.

Francis Galton and Regression to the Mean

Francis Galton (1822–1911) was a brilliant Englishman who made important contributions to many fields, including statistics, meteorology, psychology, and geography. Galton is credited with creating the concept of correlation and regression. Galton also coined the phrase "nature versus nurture." Galton collected the following data for 898 children (see the file `Galton.xlsx`):

- Height of the mother and father
- Height of the child

Recall from Chapter 8, "Modeling Relationships Between Two Variables," that the correlation between two data sets is always between –1 and +1. Galton observed that mothers and fathers who were taller than average had children who were taller than average but not as tall as their parents. Galton also observed that mothers and fathers who were shorter than average had children who were shorter than average but not as short as their parents.

The correlations between parents' and child's heights found by Galton are shown in Figure 26.1. The "Excel Calculations" section later in this chapter shows how we computed these correlations.

	J	K	L	M	N	O	P
2	Correlation	Parent and Child					
3	0.39	male with father	{=CORREL(IF(male=1,father,""),IF(male=1,height,""))}				
4	0.46	female with father	{=CORREL(IF(male=0,father,""),IF(male=0,height,""))}				
5	0.33	male with mother	{=CORREL(IF(male=1,mother,""),IF(male=1,height,""))}				
6	0.31	female with mother	{=CORREL(IF(male=0,mother,""),IF(male=0,height,""))}				

Figure 26.1: Galton's correlations

For example, Galton found the correlation between a father's height and a female child was 0.46.

To formally explain the idea of regression to the mean, suppose you try to predict a dependent variable Y (daughter's height) from an independent variable X (father's height). If r = correlation between X and Y and X is k standard deviations above average, then our best prediction for Y will be k * r standard deviations above Y's average. *Since r is between –1 and +1, we know that our prediction for Y is closer to average than X.* The fact that a prediction for a variable such as next year's wins will be closer to average than last year's wins explains the regression of team performance towards 8 wins in the NFL and 41 wins in the NBA.

Galton's father-daughter correlation of 0.46 implies that for a father, 2 standard deviations taller than average (around 74 inches tall), we would predict the daughter's height to be 2 * 0.46 = 0.92 standard deviations above average. The average height of the daughters is 64.1 inches and the standard deviation of the daughter's height is 2.4 inches, so for a father whose height is two standard deviations taller than average we predict the daughter's height to be 64.1 + .92 * (2.4) = 66.3 inches.

Regression to the Mean in the NFL and the NBA

The file `TeamStandings.xlsx` contains the number of games won by each NFL team during the 2016–2018 seasons and for each NBA team the number of games won during the 2016–2017 and 2017–2018 seasons and the number of games won during the next season. For the NFL, we counted a tie as half a win. Using Excel trendlines (see the "Excel Calculations" section), we found the least squares line (and the associated correlation) that relates last year's team wins to next year's wins (see Figures 26.2 and 26.3).

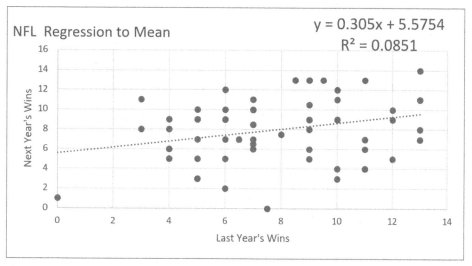

Figure 26.2: NFL regression to the mean

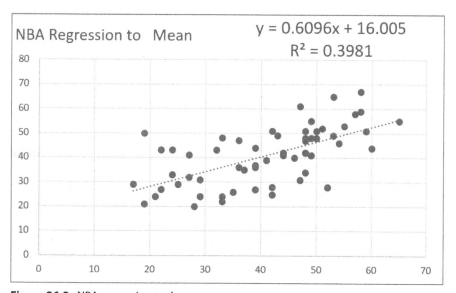

Figure 26.3: NBA regression to the mean

For the NFL, our predicted wins (out of 16 games) next year based on last year's wins is

$$\text{Next Year's Wins} = 5.57 + 0.305 * (\text{Last Year's Wins})$$

For example, a team that was 12-4 last year is predicted to win 5.57 + 0.305 * (12) = 9.6 games next year. The correlation between last year's wins and next year's wins is $\sqrt{0.085} = 0.29$.

For the NBA, our predicted wins (out of 82 games) next year based on last year's wins is

$$\text{Next Year's Wins} = 16.005 + 0.6096 * (\text{Last Year's Wins})$$

For example, an NBA team that went 60-22 last year is predicted to win 16.005 + 0.6096*(60) = 52 games. The correlation between last year's wins and next year's wins is much higher than the correlation we found in the NFL: $\sqrt{0.3981} = 0.63$.

Why is the correlation between last year's and next year's wins much stronger in the NBA than the NFL? Here are some possible reasons:

- NFL teams that win their division play a tougher schedule next year than teams that came in last in their division.

- I don't know of a definitive study, but I believe the NFL draft is more of an equalizer than the NBA draft. Ignoring trades, teams draft in inverse order to their won-lost record. This means that teams performing worse in a given year have better opportunities to improve their team. In the NFL draft each team gets 7 picks, and in the NBA draft team gets two picks. I know of no studies that analyze which draft better promotes team parity, but in a survey of my Twitter followers (many of whom are experts in sports analytics), 57% of the respondents opined that the NFL draft contributes more to league parity than the NBA draft. This is consistent with the fact that NFL team performance tends to regress more to the mean than NFL performance.

- The NBA is more of a star-driven league than the NBA. If a top NBA team can keep their two stars, then they are likely to have continued success. In the NFL, it is vitally important to keep a star QB (surely the most important position in professional sports), but unless you keep a good offensive line, even a star QB will have limited success. Thus, it seems easier to keep the key pieces of talent intact in the NBA than in the NFL.

- During the 2017–2018 season, NBA teams lost about 20% of their salary dollars to injury (see `instreetclothes.com/2018/06/22/reviewing-injury-totals-2017-18-nba-regular-season/`). `FootballOutsiders.com` estimated that during the 2018 NFL season, teams lost about 22% of games played due to injury (see `www.footballoutsiders.com/stat-analysis/2019/`

2018-adjusted-games-lost-part-ii). If we assume injuries are due to (bad) luck, then injuries would contribute slightly more toward regression to the mean in the NFL than in the NBA.

Excel Calculations

In this section, we discuss how we calculated the correlations between parents and children in the Galton data. Then we show how we found the least squares lines predicting next year's NFL and NBA wins from last season's wins.

Computing Galton's Correlations

In the file Galton.xlsx, we used an advanced Excel feature, array formulas, to compute the correlation between parents' and children's heights. For example, in cell J3, we used the following array formula to compute the correlation between the heights of fathers and sons:

```
{=CORREL(IF(male=1,father,""),IF(male=1,height,""))}
```

The curly brackets indicate that the formula is an array formula. This means that instead of pressing the Enter key to enter the formula, you need to press the Ctrl+Shift+Enter key combination. This formula checks every row of data and determines if Male = 1 (indicating child is a boy). This formula creates two arrays. If Male = 1, the formula the row in the first array contains the father's height, and the other contains the son's height. In other rows, the two arrays each contain blanks. Then the formula computes the correlation on these two arrays. (Blanks are ignored.) The other three correlations are computed in a similar fashion.

Analyzing NFL and NBA Regression to the Mean

To create Figure 26.2, proceed as follows:

1. Select the range C13:D77 in the worksheet NFL of the file TeamStandings. xlsx.
2. Select Scatter Chart from the Insert tab.
3. Select all the points, right-click a point, and then select Add Trendline.
4. Select the Linear option from the Format Trendline pane, and then select the Display Equation On Chart and Display R-Squared Value On Chart options.

You now see the least squares line that best predicts next year's wins from last year's wins as well as the equation of the least squares line and the percentage of variation in next year's wins explained by last year's wins.

How Did Central Bankers Fail to Predict the 2008 Recession?

If you read Michael Lewis's great book (or saw the movie) *The Big Short* (Norton, 2011), you know that many investors predicted the severe 2008 recession that was primarily caused by a bubble in housing prices. The Government Accounting Office (GAO) estimated that the 2008 financial crisis cost the U.S. economy *$22 trillion*, or more than $60,000 per person (see www.huffpost.com/entry/financial-crisis-cost-gao_n_2687553). Incredibly, Federal Reserve Chair Ben Bernanke and Treasury Secretary Henry Paulson did not see this economic train wreck coming. On February 14, 2008, the two told the Senate Banking Committee that they predicted for 2008 1.8% growth in the U.S. GNP. The President's Council of Economic Advisers was more optimistic, predicting 2.7% GNP growth for 2008 (see money.cnn.com/2008/02/14/news/economy/bernanke_paulson/index.htm).

Lehmann Brothers filed for bankruptcy on September 15, 2008, and the economy's deep descent accelerated. Incredibly, as stated on page 6 of the Fed's minutes from a September 16, 2008 meeting (see www.federalreserve.gov/monetarypolicy/files/fomcminutes20080916.pdf), the Fed stated, "The staff continued to expect that real GDP would advance slowly in the fourth quarter of 2008, and at a faster rate in 2009."

In this chapter, we will discuss three data-driven techniques that would have predicted a severe economic downturn:

- The yield curve was inverted (see www.nytimes.com/2019/11/08/business/yield-curve-recession-indicator.html). Starting in August 2006, the rate earned on 10-year bonds was less than the rate on 90-day Treasury bills.

- Economist Claudia Sahm found that if the average of the unemployment rate for the last three months is at least 0.50 percentage points above the lowest unemployment rate during the last 12 months (see `www.brookings.edu/blog/up-front/2019/06/06/how-will-we-know-when-a-recession-is-coming/`), then the economy is already in recession. The official declaration by the U.S. government that the economy was in recession came in December 2008, while the unemployment indicator indicated a recession in January 2008.

- Applying the simple ideas of statistical process control (SPC) to the monthly change in the U.S. ratio of housing price changes to rent changes showed in February 2006 that housing prices were starting to decline.

The Inverted Yield Curve

When people borrow money for 10 years, they usually pay a higher rate of interest than when they borrow for a short term (such as 90 days). After all, if a lender is tying up their money for a longer period, they deserve more compensation. When the 90-day T-bill rate is greater than the 10-year bond rate, the yield curve is said to be *inverted*. Since recessions usually result in lower interest rates, it is reasonable to assume that an inverted yield curve is a sign that investors expect lower interest rates and/or a reduction in economic growth, which implies that a recession is coming. In the file `Inverted.xlsx`, we downloaded from the Federal Reserve Bank of St. Louis site (`fred.stlouisfed.org`) the daily 10-year and 90-day T-bill rates for the period 1962–2019. In Column B, we computed the spread = 10-year rate − 90-day T-bill rate. We used conditional formatting (see the "Excel Calculations" section) to highlight all days on which the spread was less than 0. Table 27.1 summarizes the months in which an inverted yield curve occurred and the month during which the ensuing recession began. Note that an inverted yield curve preceded each recession.

Note that the inverted yield curve in August 2006 presaged the Great Recession.

Table 27.1: Inverted yield curve signaling a recession

MONTH YIELD CURVE INVERTS	MONTH RECESSION BEGINS
June 1973	November 1973
November 1979	January 1980
November 1980	July 1981
June 1989	July 1990
August 2000	March 2001
August 2006	December 2007

Dates recessions began from `Wikipedia.com`

The Sahm Rule: Early Warning Signal for Recession

As we saw in 2008, the federal government often doesn't recognize a recession until much of the damage has been done. Economist Claudia Sahm of the Brookings Institute came up with a simple and brilliant test to determine if the economy is in recession (see page 21 of `www.hamiltonproject.org/assets/files/Sahm_web_20190506.pdf`). If the average of the unemployment rate for the last three months is at least 0.50 percentage points above the lowest unemployment rate during the last 12 months, then the economy is already in recession. Sahm proposed that when this test is met, the government should begin automatic stimulus payments to mitigate the recession. In Column C of the file `Sahm.xlsx`, we computed the average unemployment rate for the last three months – smallest unemployment rate during the last 12 months. According to the Sahm rule, when this number first is at least 0.5%, a recession has begun. Table 27.2 shows that since 1970, the Sahm rule has a *perfect* record of spotting recessions *and always predicted a recession before the government announced a recession*. Conditional formatting was used to highlight months in which the Sahm criteria were satisfied.

Table 27.2: Comparison of Sahm predictions to actual start date of recessions

SAHM PREDICTION	DATE GOVERNMENT ANNOUNCED RECESSION	RECESSION START DATE
March 1974	No public announcement	November 1973
February 1980	June 1980	January 1980
November 1981	January 1982	July 1981
September 1990	April 1991	July 1990
June 2001	July 2003	March 2001
January 2008	December 2008	December 2007

Control Charts and the Housing Price/Rent Ratio

Control charts were developed during the 1920s by Walter Shewhart (1891-1967) of Bell Labs. Since then, countless organizations have used control charts to determine if a manufacturing or business process is stable or in control. An in-control process exhibits "normal" variation. Shewhart's brilliant idea was finding an easy way to determine if a process has changed.

The process we will analyze is the *change* in the monthly ratio of the Housing Price Index (January 2000 = 100) to the Rental Price Index (1982–1984 = 100). From the wonderful FRED site, we extracted the monthly housing price and rental price indexes for the period 1987–2019. Our analysis is in the workbook `HousingNew.xlsx`.

The workbook `HousingNew.xlsx` contains the monthly housing price index and monthly rent price index (1982–1984 = 100). A subset of the data is shown in Figure 27.1. During the period 1987–2019, the correlation between monthly U.S. rents and housing prices was 0.93, indicating that housing prices and rents tend to move up and down together.

	A	B	C	D	E
10	Frequency: Monthly				
11	observation_date	CSUSHPINSA	Rent	Housing/Rent	Change
12	1987-01-01	63.75500000000000	121.3	0.525597692	
13	1987-02-01	64.15500000000000	121.7	0.527156943	0.16%
14	1987-03-01	64.49000000000000	121.8	0.529474548	0.23%
15	1987-04-01	64.99500000000000	122	0.532745902	0.33%
16	1987-05-01	65.56900000000000	122.3	0.536132461	0.34%
17	1987-06-01	66.23800000000000	122.3	0.541602617	0.55%
18	1987-07-01	66.80200000000000	123	0.543105691	0.15%
19	1987-08-01	67.28300000000000	123.8	0.543481422	0.04%
20	1987-09-01	67.63700000000000	124.4	0.543705788	0.02%
21	1987-10-01	67.91600000000000	124.8	0.544198718	0.05%
22	1987-11-01	68.10700000000000	124.8	0.545729167	0.15%
23	1987-12-01	68.35900000000000	125.6	0.544259554	-0.15%
24	1988-01-01	68.59800000000000	126	0.544428571	0.02%
25	1988-02-01	68.93100000000000	126.3	0.545771971	0.13%
26	1988-03-01	69.33800000000000	126.4	0.548560127	0.28%
27	1988-04-01	69.80000000000000	126.6	0.551342812	0.28%
28	1988-05-01	70.41900000000000	126.9	0.554917258	0.36%

Figure 27.1: 1987 Housing and rent indices

Control charts plot in time order observations from a process and try to spot changes in the process. For each month, we will compute the ratio of housing prices to rents and analyze the *change* in this ratio. For example, in January 1987, the ratio of the housing index to the rent index (we will abbreviate this ratio as HRR) was 63.76/121 = 0.5256. In February 1987, HRR increased to 64.16/122 = 0.5272. Therefore, in February 1987, as shown in cell E13, HRR increased by 0.5272 – 0.5256 = 0.16%. If housing prices and rents were moving together, then HRR should remain unchanged. To show this, let H = Housing index in a month and R = Rent index in the same month. Then HRR = H/R. If H and R both increase during the next month by 1%, then HRR becomes 1.01H/1.01R = H/R, which is the same as last month. Thus, if housing prices are increasing faster than rents, then the change in HRR will tend to be positive, whereas if housing prices are increasing at a rate slower than rents, the change in HRR will tend to be negative.

We can now describe how we determine when the monthly HRR time series is "out of control." We start our analysis in the row for January 1989.

We begin in the cell range E36:E402 by computing each month's change in the HRR. This is the "process" that we will examine to determine if the process is in control (not changing) or out of control (undergoing a change). Next in F36:G402, we compute (based on all prior months) the average HRR (called

XBAR) and the standard deviation (called S) of the HRR. The average HRR is the "center line" for the control chart.

Shewhart classifies all observations within 3S of XBAR into one of six zones:

- Upper Zone A: Between XBAR+2S and XBAR+3S
- Lower Zone A: Between XBAR-3S and XBAR-2S
- Upper Zone B: Between XBAR+S and XBAR+2S
- Lower Zone B: Between XBAR-2S and XBAR-S
- Upper Zone C: Between XBAR and XBAR+S
- Lower Zone C: Between XBAR-S and XBAR

Shewhart's tests for a process mean changing (or the process mean being out of control) is based on the assumption that observations follow a normal random variable, and if the process mean does not shift, then most points will be near the center line. More precisely, around 68% of the points will be within S of the centerline, around 95% of the points within 2S of the centerline, and around 99.7% of the points within 3S of the centerline. Based on this assumption, Shewhart classified a process as out of control if any of the tests shown in Table 27.3 are satisfied. The table gives the probability of each test being met if the process mean has not shifted as well as the conclusion that is indicated if the test criteria are satisfied.

Table 27.3: Tests for out-of-control process

TEST CRITERIA	PROBABILITY	CONCLUSION
More than 3S above center line	0.00135	Process mean has increased
More than 3S below center line	0.00135	Process mean has decreased
At least 2 of last 3 points in Upper Zone A or beyond	0.001354	Process mean has increased
At least 2 of last 3 points in Lower Zone A or below	0.001354	Process mean has decreased
At least 4 of last 5 points in Upper Zone B or beyond	0.002766	Process mean has increased
At least 4 of last 5 points in Lower Zone B or below	0.002766	Process mean has decreased
Last 7 points above center line	0.007813	Process mean has increased
Last 7 points below center line	0.007813	Process mean has decreased

To apply control charts to the HRR process, we used conditional formatting (see the "Excel Calculations" section) to highlight in gray each month in which the HRR indicates the process mean has increased and to highlight in red each month the process mean has decreased. To begin, we compute beginning in January 1989, a Z-score for each month's HRR. The Z-score for an observation tells us for each observation the number of standard deviations by which the standard deviation differs from its average. For example, in January 1989, the mean and standard deviation of the previous HRR's are both 0.16 (coincidence). The January 1989 HRR is 0.08, so the January 1989 Z-score is $(0.08 - 0.16) / 0.16 = -0.5$.

Beginning in June 2002 (see Figure 27.2), we see many months that meet a test that indicates that the process mean has increased, indicating that housing prices are increasing relative to rents much quicker than their historical pattern indicates. For example:

- June 2002 indicates an increase in the process mean because 2 of the last 3 months are in Upper Zone A or beyond.

- July 2002 indicates an increase in the process mean because 2 of the last 3 months are in Upper Zone A or beyond.

- August 2002 indicates an increase in the process mean because the last 5 months are all in Upper Zone B or beyond.

- September 2002 indicates an increase in the process mean because the last 5 months are all in Upper Zone B or beyond.

- October 2002 indicates an increase in the process mean because the last 7 months are all above the centerline.

	A	F	G	H
34	1988-11-01			
35	1988-12-01	Zscore	Mean	Sigma
191	2001-12-01	-1.79	0.17%	0.19%
192	2002-01-01	-0.78	0.17%	0.20%
193	2002-02-01	-0.64	0.16%	0.20%
194	2002-03-01	1.09	0.15%	0.20%
195	2002-04-01	2.20	0.14%	0.19%
196	2002-05-01	2.92	0.14%	0.19%
197	2002-06-01	2.18	0.15%	0.21%
198	2002-07-01	1.50	0.17%	0.24%
199	2002-08-01	0.87	0.18%	0.25%
200	2002-09-01	0.12	0.20%	0.25%
201	2002-10-01	-0.28	0.20%	0.25%
202	2002-11-01	-0.69	0.20%	0.25%
203	2002-12-01	-0.44	0.20%	0.25%

Figure 27.2: June–October 2002 HRR indicating a housing price bubble

As former Fed Chair William McChesney Martin said in 1955, "The Fed should act like a chaperone who has ordered the punch bowl removed just when the party was really warming up." In 2002, the Fed evidently did not take the punch bowl away, because by the end of 2005, twelve more months indicate an increase in the HRR mean.

Our control also shows the housing bubble beginning to deflate in February 2006. Starting in February 2006, *27 consecutive months* indicate a decrease in the HRR process mean.

The Fed prides itself on having complex econometric (another word for very sophisticated regression models) models that can give the Fed some idea of where the economy is going. In this chapter, we have shown three relatively simplistic analytic models, which indicated that trouble was brewing well before the Great Recession of 2008. If the Fed had realized sooner that an economic winter was coming, perhaps 9 million people would not have lost their homes, and some of the $22 trillion in losses to the U.S. economy could have been avoided.

Excel Calculations

Conditional formatting allows you to format a cell based on the contents of a cell. In this section, we show how we highlighted months in which the yield curve was inverted, months where the Sahm recession test was met, and months that indicated an increase or decrease in the mean HRR. To use Excel's conditional formatting capabilities, you begin by selecting the data you want formatted and then go to the Home tab and select Conditional Formatting. Then, as we now discuss, you can create the desired conditional format.

Highlighting Months Where the Yield Curve Is Inverted

For days in the period 1962–2019 in the workbook Inverted.xlsx, the cell range B12:B15100 contains the 10-Year Rate – 90-Day T-Bill Rate. We want to highlight each negative spread. After selecting the cell range B12:B15100, on the Home tab, we selected Conditional Formatting, Highlight Cells Rules, and Less Than, and entered **0** and red fill. Now every negative spread is highlighted.

Highlighting Months Where the Sahm Criteria Is Satisfied

In the file Sahm.xlsx, the cell range C264:C873 contains, for months in the period 1969–2019, the Average Unemployment Rate for the last 3 months – Lowest Unemployment Rate in the last 12 months. We want to highlight all values in this range that are at least 0.5. To begin, select the range C264:C873 and choose Conditional Formatting from the Home tab. Then choose Highlight Cells Rules, select Greater Than, enter **.499**, and select a red font. Now every value satisfying the Sahm criteria is highlighted.

Highlighting Out-of-Control HRR Values

Recall that there are eight criteria that can cause us to mark an HRR value as Out of Control (refer to Table 27.3). To check whether an HRR value for the years 1989–2019 in the range F36:F402 in the workbook `Housingnew.xlsx` meets any of the criteria, we proceed as follows:

1. Select the cell range F36:F402.

2. Choose Conditional Formatting from the Home tab, select New Rule, and then select the Use A Formula option.

3. Now for each criterion, we enter a formula that when copied down from F36 (Excel does the copying automatically) is true in exactly the cells we wished to be formatted. We also enter the desired format (gray fill for criteria that indicate an increase in the process mean, and red font for criteria that indicate a decrease in the process mean). You can see the formulas used to create the eight formats by selecting any cell in the range F36:F402 and choosing Manage Rules from the Conditional Formatting menu. Figures 27.3 and 27.4 show examples of our conditional formatting formulas.

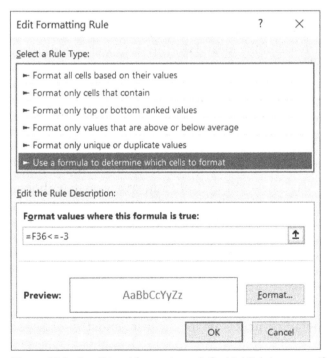

Figure 27.3: Conditional formatting rule for highlighting a row if more than 3S above center line of HRR values

For example, the formula `F36>=3` will highlight a cell in gray fill any HRR Z-score that is greater than or equal to 3.

The formula `=COUNTIF(F32:F36,"<=-1")>=4` will highlight an HRR Z-score in red font if at least 4 of the last 5 HRR Z-scores are less than or equal to –1.

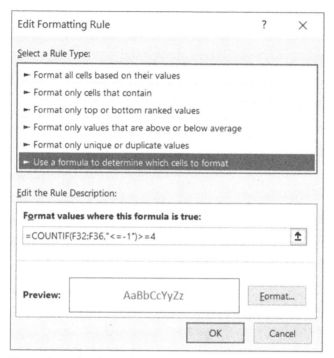

Figure 27.4: Conditional formatting rule highlighting a row if at least 4 of last 5 months are at least **S** below center line of HRR values

Creating conditional formats based on a formula allows you to use any Excel formula, no matter how complex, to control the creation of your formats. This gives an Excel guru the power to create many useful formats based on complex criteria.

CHAPTER 28

How Does Target Know
If You're Pregnant?

My beautiful wife Vivian, loves Target. She goes at least once a week and spends over $5,000 a year at Target. She knows where everything is, goes early in the morning when the store is not crowded, and every other week she comes home with a very cute outfit. I am sure Target has a reasonable estimate of Vivian's *customer lifetime value (CLV)*. (For more discussion of CLV, which is the value in today's dollars of the profit Vivian generates, see Chapter 19 of *Marketing Analytics*, Winston, 2014, Wiley.) Target knows that once a shopper like Vivian chooses Target over competitors like Walmart, Costco, or Kohls, Target probably has them as a loyal customer for a long, long time. Enticing customers to choose Target as their go-to store is crucial to growing Target's bottom line.

An opportune time to make someone a loyal customer is during a woman's (especially first) pregnancy. If Target convinces the woman that Target is on target for them, then the customer will generate profits for many years based on purchases for her growing family. A 2012 *New York Times* article (see www. nytimes.com/2012/02/19/magazine/shopping-habits.html?mtrref=www.google. com&gwh=1DADCD60FE8964BBA7D4ACAE5977C697&gwt=pay&assetType=REGIWALL) by Charles Duhigg, author of the bestseller *The Power of Habit* (Random House, 2012), describes the methods used by Target to identify women who were likely in the second trimester of their pregnancies. In this chapter, we describe Target's approach and the unexpected challenges they encountered.

What Available Data Can Be Used to Identify Pregnant Women?

From Target credit cards and other sources, Target can obtain the purchase history (items purchased and date of purchase) for many customers. From baby shower registries, Target has access to the projected due date for many pregnant women. Led by Target statistician Andrew Pole, Target's data science team put together the due dates of pregnant women and their recent purchase history. Working backward from the projected due date, Target's analysts found that pregnant women tended to purchase lots of vitamin and mineral supplements during the first 20 weeks of their pregnancy. During the second trimester, pregnant women tended to buy lots of unscented lotions (chemicals might harm the baby) and lots of cotton balls. (Cotton balls can be used to remove makeup without using potentially harmful chemicals.) Based on a woman's past purchase history, Target assigned a score based on the recent purchase history of 25 products that predicted the likelihood that a woman is pregnant. Later in this chapter, we present a simplified example that illustrates the method used to create a pregnancy score.

If a woman's score indicated that she is likely in her second trimester, then Target sent out coupons for products such as unscented lotions, cotton balls, cribs, baby clothes, and diapers. Of course, Target hoped that these coupons would increase the chance that the woman (and her family) would become long-term loyal Target customers.

Problems Arise

One day, the father of a teenager in suburban Minneapolis opened mail addressed to his teenage daughter and found Target coupons for baby clothes and cribs. He was furious and complained to a store manager. He felt that Target was trying to incentivize his daughter to get pregnant. Later the father found out his daughter was actually pregnant and apologized to the store manager. Still, this story was not a great look for Target.

Sending a Target customer coupons exclusively targeted to products that appeal to pregnant women could be construed as spying on the women. To mitigate this issue, Target mixed coupons for products that would not overly appeal to pregnant women (wineglasses, cleaning products, and lawn mowers, for example) with the coupons for baby-related products. As Duhigg points out, this trick would increase the chance the woman will visit the store and turn her into a loyal Target customer.

An Example of a Pregnancy Prediction Score

When trying to predict a binary dependent variable (one that can assume only two values), the data analyst cannot use ordinary regression. (See Chapter 17 of Winston [2014] for more details.) Often, *logistic regression* is used to derive from the values of one or more independent variables a *probability* for each outcome. Some examples are shown in Table 28.1.

Table 28.1: Examples of logistic regression

DEPENDENT VARIABLE	INDEPENDENT VARIABLES
Field goal is good or no good	Distance of field goal attempt
Customer subscribes or does not subscribe to *Vogue*	Age, gender, income, where person lives
Firm goes bankrupt or does not go bankrupt in the next year	Financial ratios such as current assets/current liabilities
Person has heart attack or does not in next year	Age, gender, body mass index (BMI), blood sugar level, cholesterol, blood pressure, alcohol use, smoking
Woman of childbearing age is pregnant or not pregnant	Age and recent product purchases

Target needed logistic regression, because on any random date, they want to predict the probability that a woman is in her second trimester of pregnancy. The worksheet Logit of the workbook `Target.xlsx` contains a simplified (fictitious) example in which we attempt to determine an equation that estimates the probability a woman is in her second trimester based on the number of bottles of unscented lotion purchased during each of the last three months. We assume that Target has chosen a random date (say 1/1/2021) as the date used to calibrate the data. From baby shower registries, they extracted to rows 4–4189 data on 4,186 women who were in their second trimester of pregnancy on January 1, 2021. The file also contains data on 4,814 women of childbearing age who Target believed were not in their second trimester on January 1, 2021. A subset of the data is shown in Figure 28.1. For each woman, the following data is available:

- Column H indicates whether the woman is in the second trimester of pregnancy (1 = second trimester, 0 = not in second trimester). For women in the second trimester, Column M gives the woman's estimated due date.

- We assume that there are at most two dates in the three months prior to January 1, 2021, on which a woman bought unscented lotions. Columns E–G give the number of bottles of unscented lotion bought by each woman during these three months.

From Figure 28.1, we see that the first woman in row 4 was in her second trimester, and due on May 28, 2021. In November 2020, she bought four bottles of lotion and bought none during October and December.

	E	F	G	H	I	J	K	L	M
1	date	1/1/2021							
2	10.00		11.00	12.00					
3	oct	nov	dec	pregnant	buy1	amt1	buy2	amt2	duedate
4	0	4	0	1	11	1	11	3	5/28/2021
5	0	6	0	1	11	4	11	2	5/15/2021
6	0	0	2	1	12	2	12	0	4/15/2021
7	4	0	0	1	11	0	10	4	6/20/2021
8	0	0	3	1	12	3	12	0	5/24/2021
1194	0	0	8	1	12	4	12	4	5/13/2021
1195	0	5	4	1	12	4	11	5	4/7/2021
1196	0	0	4	1	12	2	12	2	6/7/2021
1197	0	0	0	1	11	0	11	0	5/28/2021
1198	0	3	3	1	12	3	11	3	5/15/2021
1199	0	10	0	1	11	6	11	4	6/15/2021
1200	3	0	0	1	10	3	10	0	6/16/2021

Figure 28.1: Subset of fictitious Target data set

If we wanted to use ordinary multiple linear regression to use the number of bottles of unscented lotion bought in each of the last three months to predict a probability that each woman was in the second trimester, we might want to find coefficients B0, B1, B2, and B3 that enable the equation:

$$(1)\, B0 + B1 * \big((\text{October bottles}) + B2 * (\text{November bottles}) + B3 * (\text{December bottles})\big)$$

to best predict Column H and use the result of equation (1) as an estimate for the probability that the woman is in the second trimester of pregnancy. There are many problems with this approach, as described in Chapter 17 of Winston (2014). One obvious problem is that the prediction from (1) might be negative or greater than 1, which means the prediction cannot be used as a probability.

The logistic regression solution to predicting a binary dependent variable is to define

$$\text{Score} = B0 + B1 * \big((\text{Oct. bottles}) + B2 * (\text{Nov. bottles}) + B3 * (\text{Dec. bottles})\big)$$

and estimate the probability that a woman is in the second trimester of pregnancy by the *logistic equation* $e^{\text{Score}} / \big(1 + e^{\text{Score}}\big)$. Note that the logistic equation will always yield a probability between 0 and 1.

Using the technique of maximum likelihood, discussed in Chapter 17 of Winston (2014), we found that

$$\text{Score} = -3.71 + 1.05 * (\text{October bottles}) + 1.16 * (\text{November bottles}) +$$
$$1.13 * (\text{December bottles})$$

This "Score" is an example of the pregnancy score referred to in Duhigg (2012).

The worksheet analysis shows the estimated probability (see Figure 28.2) based on the logistic equation that each woman is in the second trimester of pregnancy. For example, the second woman whose data is recorded, in row 5, bought 6 bottles of unscented lotion in November 2020, and we would estimate the chance she is pregnant as $e^{-3.71+6*1.16} / (1 + e^{-3.71+6*1.16}) = 0.963$.

	E	F	G	H	I	J	K	L
1	date	1/1/2021					const	-3.711206
2	1.05		1.16	1.13				
3	oct	nov		dec	pregnant	duedate	Score	Chance	Likelihood
4	0	4	0		1	5/28/2021	0.9	0.72	0.718356
5	0	6	0		1	5/15/2021	3.3	0.96	0.963034
6	0	0	2		1	4/15/2021	-1.4	0.19	0.190082
7	4	0	0		1	6/20/2021	0.5	0.62	0.623571
8	0	0	3		1	5/24/2021	-0.3	0.42	0.421013
9	1	0	0		1	5/24/2021	-2.7	0.07	0.065545
10	0	4	0		1	6/17/2021	0.9	0.72	0.718356
11	0	0	5		1	6/8/2021	1.9	0.87	0.874694
12	6	0	0		1	4/9/2021	2.6	0.93	0.931675

Figure 28.2: Logistic prediction of women being in second trimester of pregnancy

The PivotTable shown in Figure 28.3 shows the accuracy of the logistic predictions.

	O	P	Q	R
7	Count of pregnant	Column Labels		
8	Row Labels	0	1	Grand Total
9	0-0.1	95.97%	4.03%	100.00%
10	0.1-0.2	76.29%	23.71%	100.00%
11	0.3-0.4	75.07%	24.93%	100.00%
12	0.4-0.5	66.03%	33.97%	100.00%
13	0.6-0.7	26.36%	73.64%	100.00%
14	0.7-0.8	19.74%	80.26%	100.00%
15	0.8-0.9	13.71%	86.29%	100.00%
16	0.9-1	1.99%	98.01%	100.00%
17	Grand Total	53.49%	46.51%	100.00%

Figure 28.3: The chance a woman is in second trimester of pregnancy given logistic prediction

We find, for example, that when the logistic prediction of second trimester is between 90% and 100%, 98% of the women were indeed in the second trimester of pregnancy. Based on this data set, if Target sent coupons for pregnancy- and infant-related products to women with a prediction of second semester pregnancy of at least 0.9, they can be confident that very few of these coupons would go to women not in their second trimester of pregnancy. Of course, Target's analysis was much more complex in part because it involved purchases of 125 different products. Also, Target's analysis might have involved techniques more sophisticated than logistic regression.

How Does Netflix Recommend Movies and TV Shows?

We have so many choices in today's world. What book should we read next? What movie should we rent? What hot new song should we download to our smart phone? *Collaborative filtering* is the buzzword for methods used to "filter" choices using the collective intelligence of other people's product choices. The web has made it easy to store the purchasing history and preferences of consumers. The question is how to use this data to recommend products to you that you will like but didn't know you wanted. If you ever streamed a movie from a Netflix recommendation, bought a book from an Amazon.com recommendation, or downloaded a song from iTunes from a GENIUS recommendation, you have utilized a result generated by a collaborative filtering algorithm.

In this chapter, we use simple examples to illustrate the key concepts used in collaborative filtering. We will discuss *user-based* and *item-based collaborative filtering algorithms*. To illustrate the difference between these two methods, suppose we have not seen the movie *Bohemian Rhapsody* and want to know if we would like it. In user-based collaborative filtering, we look for moviegoers whose rating of movies we have seen is most like ours. After giving a heavier weighting to the most similar moviegoers who have seen *Bohemian Rhapsody*, we can use their ratings to generate an estimate of how well we would like *Bohemian Rhapsody*. In item-based collaborative filtering (first used by Amazon.com), we would first determine how similar all the movies we have seen are to *Bohemian Rhapsody*. Then we create an estimated rating for *Bohemian Rhapsody* by giving more weight to our ratings for the movies most similar to *Bohemian Rhapsody*.

User-Based Collaborative Filtering

Badrul Sarwar, George Karypis, Joseph Konstan, and John Riedl ("Item-Based Collaborative Filtering Recommendation Algorithms," *Transactions of the Hong Kong ACM*, 2001, pages 1–11) contains a detailed discussion of user-based collaborative filtering. We will utilize the following simple example to illustrate how user-based collaborative filtering works. Suppose seven people (Lana, George, Manuel, Charles, Noel, James, and Theresa) have each rated on a 1–5 scale a subset of six movies (*Sixth Sense, Sully, Still Alice, Superman, DodgeBall,* and *Parasite*). Figure 29.1 (see the file `FinalUserBased.xlsx`) shows the ratings each person gave to some of the listed movies.

	B	C	D	E	F	G	H	I	J
7			Sixth Sense	Sully	Still Alice	Superman	Dodge Ball	Parasite	Mean
8		Lana	2.5	3.5	3	3.5		2.5	3.00
9		George	3	3.5	1.5	5		3.5	3	3.25
10		Manuel	2.5	3		3.5			4	3.25
11		Charles		3.5	3	4		2.5	4.5	3.50
12		Noel	3	4	2	3		2	3	2.83
13		James	3	4		5		3.5	3	3.70
14		Theresa		4.5		4		1		3.17
15			1	2	3	4		5	6	
16	Person1	Lana	2.5	3.5	3	3.5		2.5	0	
17	Person2	Theresa	0	4.5	0	4		1	0	
18		Lana	_	3.5 _		3.5		2.5 _		
19		Theresa	_	4.5 _		4		1 _		
20										
21		Correlation	Lana Theresa		0.99 =CORREL(D18:I18,D19:I19)				

Figure 29.1: Movie ratings

Let's suppose we want to predict Theresa's rating for the tearjerker *Still Alice*, which she has not seen. To generate a reasonable member-based forecast for Theresa's rating for *Still Alice* we will proceed as follows:

1. Establish Theresa's average rating of all movies she has seen.

2. Identify the people whose ratings on movies seen by Theresa are most like Theresa's ratings.

3. Use the ratings of each person who has seen *Still Alice* to adjust Theresa's average rating. The more similar the person's other ratings are to Theresa's, the more weight we give their ratings.

Evaluating User Similarity

Many measures are used to evaluate the similarity of user ratings. (See Robert Blattberg, *Database Marketing*, Springer, 2008, pages 356–358 for an excellent discussion of similarity measures.) We will define the similarity between two users to equal the correlation between their ratings on all movies seen by both people. Recall that if two people's ratings have a correlation near +1, then if one person rates a movie higher than average, it is more likely that the other person will rate the movie higher than average, and if one person rates a movie lower than average, then it is more likely that the other person rates the movie lower than average. On the other hand, if two people's ratings have a correlation near –1, then if one person rates a movie higher than average, it is more likely that the other person will rate the movie lower than average, and if one person rates a movie lower than average, then it is more likely that the other person rates the movie higher than average.

The Excel CORREL function can be used to determine the correlation between two data sets. For example, rows 18 and 19 give the rating for the movies seen by *both* Lana and Theresa. In cell E21, the CORREL function is used to show that their ratings are strongly (0.99) correlated. This means that Lana and Theresa appear to have similar views on the quality of movies they both rated. Figure 29.2 shows for each pair of movie viewers the correlation between their ratings. The construction of this table required some advanced Excel manipulations; see page 395 of my book *Marketing Analytics* (Wiley, 2014).

▲	H	I	J	K	L	M	N	O
22	Correlations							
23	0.99124071 Lana		George	Manuel	Charl Noel		James	Theresa
24	Lana	1.00	0.40	0.87	0.94	0.60	0.85	0.99
25	George	0.40	1.00	0.20	0.31	0.41	0.96	0.38
26	Manuel	0.87	0.20	1.00	1.00	-0.26	0.13	-1.00
27	Charles	0.94	0.31	1.00	1.00	0.57	0.03	0.89
28	Noel	0.60	0.41	-0.26	0.57	1.00	0.21	0.92
29	James	0.85	0.96	0.13	0.03	0.21	1.00	0.66
30	Theresa	0.99	0.38	-1.00	0.89	0.92	0.66	1.00

Figure 29.2: User similarities

Estimating Theresa's Rating for *Still Alice*

Now we will use the following formula to estimate Theresa's rating for *Still Alice*. All summations are over moviegoers who have seen *Still Alice*.

$$(1)\ \text{Estimate of Theresa's Rating for } \textit{Still Alice} = \left(\text{Theresa's Mean Rating}\right) +$$

$$\frac{\sum_{\text{other moviegoers}} \left(\textit{similarity of moviegoer to Theresa}\right) * \left(\begin{array}{l}\textit{Moviegoer's rating for Still Alice} \\ - \textit{Moviegoer's average rating}\end{array}\right)}{\sum_{\text{all Moviegoers}} \left|\textit{Moviegoers Similarity to Theresa}\right|}$$

To generate our estimate of Theresa's rating for *Still Alice*, we start with Theresa's average rating of all movies and utilize the following types of moviegoers to increase our estimate of Theresa's rating for *Still Alice*:

- People who have a positive similarity to Theresa and like *Still Alice* more than their average movie
- People who have a negative similarity to Theresa and like *Still Alice* less than their average movie

We utilize the following types of moviegoers to decrease our estimate of Theresa's rating for *Still Alice*:

- People who have a positive similarity to Theresa and like *Still Alice* less than their average movie
- People who have a negative similarity to Theresa and like *Still Alice* more than their average movie

The denominator of equation (1) ensures the sum of the absolute value of the weights given to each moviegoer add to 1. As shown in Figure 29.3, our estimate of Theresa's rating for *Still Alice* is computed as follows:

$$3.17 + \frac{.99(3-3) + .38(1.5-3.25) + .89(3-3.5) + .92(2-2.83)}{.99 + .38 + .89 + .92} = 2.58$$

George, Charles, and Noel all saw *Still Alice* and gave the movie a lower rating than the average rating they gave all movies. Also, George, Charles, and Noel had a positive similarity to Theresa. Therefore, each of these people reduces our prediction for Theresa's rating of *Still Alice*.

⊿	H	I	J	N	O	P	Q	R	S
33	Predict rating for	Person	Mean		Mean	Similarity	Movie Rating	Adjustment	Correlation
34	Still Alice	Theresa	3.17	Lana	3.00	0.99	3.00	0.00	0.99
35				George	3.25	0.38	1.50	-1.75	0.38
36				Manuel	3.25	-1.00	0.00	0.00	0.00
37				Charles	3.50	0.89	3.00	-0.50	0.89
38				Noel	2.83	0.92	2.00	-0.83	0.92
39				James	3.70	0.66	0.00	0.00	0.00
40				Theresa	3.17	1.00	0.00	0.00	0.00
41									
42				Total Adjustment	-0.59				
43				Final Rating	2.58				
44									

Figure 29.3: Estimating Theresa's user-based rating for *Still Alice*

Item-Based Filtering

Let's again assume that we want to estimate Theresa's rating for *Still Alice*. To apply *item-based filtering* in this situation, we look at each movie Theresa has seen and proceed as follows:

1. For each movie that Theresa has seen, we use the correlation of the user ratings to the ratings for *Still Alice* to determine the similarity of these movies to the unseen movie (*Still Alice*).

2. Use equation (2) to estimate Theresa's rating for *Still Alice*:

$$(2)\ \text{Theresa's Estimated Rating for } \textit{Still Alice} = \left(\text{Theresa's Average Rating}\right) +$$

$$\frac{\sum_{\textit{movies Theresa has seen}} \left(\textit{Correlation of movie to Still Alice}\right) * \left(\begin{array}{c} \textit{Theresa's rating for movie} \\ - \textit{Theresa's average rating} \end{array}\right)}{\sum_{\textit{movies Theresa has seen}} |\textit{Correlation of movie to Still Alice}|}$$

Analogously to equation (1), equation (2) gives more weight to the movies Theresa has seen that are more similar (in the sense of absolute correlation) to *Still Alice*. For movies whose ratings are positively correlated to *Still Alice's* rating, we increase our estimate if Theresa rated the movie above her average. For movies whose ratings are positively correlated to *Still Alice's* rating, we decrease our estimate if Theresa rated the movie below her average. The file FinalItem-Based.xlsx contains our calculations of an estimate of Theresa's rating for *Still Alice* (see Figure 29.4 and Figure 29.5). The details of the Excel steps are tedious, and again we refer you to Chapter 17 of *Marketing Analytics* for the details. Figure 29.4 gives the correlations between the ratings for each pair of movies.

	N	O	P	Q	R	S	T
21	-0.485661864 Sixth Sense	Sully		Still Alice	Superman	Dodge Ball	Parasite
22	Sixth Sense	1.00	0.76	-0.94		0.49	0.33	-1.00
23	Sully	0.76	1.00	-0.33		0.16	-0.07	-0.63
24	Still Alice	-0.94	-0.33	1.00		-0.42	-0.49	0.94
25	Superman	0.49	0.16	-0.42		1.00	0.98	-0.30
26	Dodge Ball	0.33	-0.07	-0.49		0.98	1.00	-0.33
27	Parasite	-1.00	-0.63	0.94		-0.30	-0.33	1.00

Figure 29.4: Item correlations

Using the information in Figures 29.4 and 29.5, we calculate based on equation (2) an estimate of Theresa's rating of *Still Alice* as

$$(2)\ 3.17 + \frac{\left(4.5 - 3.17\right)*.33 + \left(4 - 3.17\right)*\left(-.42\right) + \left(1 - 3.17\right)*\left(-.49\right)}{.33 + .42 + .49} = 3.37$$

⬚	B	C	D	E	F	G	H
25			Person Mean				
26	Person	Theresa	3.17				
27	Movie	Still Alice					
28				Rating	Similarity	Movie Rating-Mean	Abs Similarity
29			1 Sixth Sense	0	0.00	0.00	0.00
30			2 Sully	4.5	-0.33	1.33	0.33
31			3 Still Alice	0	0.00	0.00	0.00
32			4 Superman	4	-0.42	0.83	0.42
33			5 Dodge Ball	1	-0.49	-2.17	0.49
34			6 Parasite	0	0.00	0.00	0.00
35							
36		Adjustment	0.21	=SUMPRODUCT(G29:G34,F29:F34)/SUM(H29:H34)			
37		Final rating estimate	3.37	=D26+D36			

Figure 29.5: Calculation of estimate for Theresa's item-based rating of *Still Alice*

The item-based method we discuss is described in Sarwar, Karypis, Konstan, and Riedl 2001. Companies such as Amazon.com with many customers prefer the item-based approach to the user-based approach because the item-based matrix of correlations is more stable over time than the user-based matrix of correlations and therefore needs to be updated less frequently.

The Netflix Competition

Perhaps the best-known example of collaborative filtering was the Netflix Prize competition, which began in October 2006. Netflix made public over 100 million movie ratings (the Training Set). A total of 1.4 million ratings, the Test Set, were withheld from the competitors. The accuracy of a forecasting algorithm was measured by root mean squared error (RMSE). Letting N = Number of ratings in the Testing Set, RMSE is defined as

$$\text{RMSE} = \sqrt{\sum_{all\ ratings\ in\ Test\ Set} \frac{\left(actual\ rating - predicted\ rating\right)^2}{N}}$$

Netflix's own algorithm had an RMSE of 0.9514. Netflix offered a $1 million prize to the first entry that beat this RMSE by at least 10%. In June 2009, the BellKor Pragmatic Chaos team became the first team to improve RMSE by 10%. BellKor won by submitting their entry only 20 minutes before the second-place team! The prize-winning recommendation system was actually a combination of over 100 algorithms. If you're interested, check out the discussion of the Netflix Prize in Chapter 4 of Mung Chiang's excellent book *Networked Life* (2012).

How Netflix Chooses Shows

Netflix debuted the hit show *House of Cards* in 2013 (and thus began my experience with streaming). Since then, streaming through sites such as Netflix, Amazon Prime, Disney+, Hulu, etc., has accelerated to the point that in 2018, nearly 60% of American households have joined the streaming revolution (see www.cnbc.com/2018/03/29/nearly-60-percent-of-americans-are-streaming-and-most-with-netflix-cnbc-survey.html).

Netflix committed $100 million to *House of Cards*, and they were confident the show would be a hit. As explained in www.salon.com/2013/02/01/how_netflix_is_turning_viewers_into_puppets, Netflix learned by looking at the viewing records of subscribers that there was a lot of overlap between Netflix subscribers who liked director David Fincher's movies (such as *The Social Network*), Kevin Spacey movies (such as *American Beauty*), and the British *House of Cards* show. Based on this information, Netflix was confident that a remake of the British *House of Cards* show starring Spacey and directed by Fincher would have a guaranteed audience. The hope was that word of mouth on the show from these core viewers would result in many viewers. The first week that the final season (Season 6, without Kevin Spacey) came out, 2,875,000 subscribers viewed Episode 1 on TV sets. When *House of Cards* debuted in 2013, Netflix's stock price was $25. In 2019, Netflix's stock price peaked at $421! I am sure that the ushering in of binge-watching by *House of Cards* was the leading cause of this amazing increase in Netflix's stock price. As an example, in summer 2019, some 64 million member households watched Season 3 of *Stranger Things* during the first four weeks it was available for streaming. In 2020, 64 million households streamed *Tiger King* (https://variety.com/2020/tv/news/netflix-tiger-king-love-is-blind-viewing-64-million-1234586272/) during the first 30 days the series was available on Netflix.

Can We Predict Heart Attacks
in Real Time?

One out of four deaths in the United States is caused by heart attacks (see www.cdc.gov/heartdisease/facts.htm). Are we near the time when your smartwatch will sense that you are high risk for a heart attack and text you to go to the hospital before the heart attack occurs? Unfortunately, as of April 2020, we are not close to realizing this goal. In this chapter, we will discuss the Apple Heart Study, which is (hopefully) a first step toward accurate prediction of the likelihood that a participant will suffer a heart attack (if not treated) in the near future.

Smartwatches such as the Apple Watch have an optical heart sensor that can continuously monitor a user's heart rate and heart rate variability (see med.stanford.edu/news/all-news/2019/11/through-apple-heart-study--stanford-medicine-researchers-show-we.html). Every several hours, the watch creates a plot (a tachogram) that shows the time between heartbeats. Beginning with WatchOS 5.1.2, the owner of the watch can sign up for the Apple Heart Study and receive a notice of potential arrhythmia (irregular heartbeat) if five of the last six tachograms indicate an irregular heartbeat. Atrial fibrillation and atrial flutter (AF) are two types of irregular heartbeats. The presence of AF increases the risk of a stroke 500%, and it is estimated that 700,000 people have AF and don't know it. With these facts in mind, Apple and Stanford University cooperated in the Apple Heart Study, which attempts to send early warning messages to participants who were likely to have AF. The study (see med.stanford.edu/news/all-news/2019/03/apple-heart-study-demonstrates-ability-of-wearable-technology.html) enrolled over 400,000 participants. As Professor Venk Murthy of the University of Michigan points out (see the tweet sequence from March 2019 at `twitter.com/venkmurthy/status/1106956668439617537?s=20`), the study has not been an unabashed success. To understand Professor Murthy's brilliant analysis, we need to discuss some important terms in the analytics of medicine: posterior probability, sensitivity, specificity, and the receiver operating characteristic (ROC) curve.

Posterior Probability

Suppose a test for a disease can have two results: positive (+) and negative (–). We assume that after observing a positive test result on a randomly chosen person, a doctor believes it is more likely the patient has the disease, and after observing a negative test result, the doctor believes it is less likely the patient has the disease. We are interested in the *posterior probability* (here, posterior means after) that after observing the test result, the patient has the disease. To illustrate the concept of posterior probability, let's assume 1% of the population has a disease, and we have a test that is 95% accurate. That is, for 95% of the people with the disease, the test yields a positive result, and for 95% of the people who do not have the disease, the test indicates the person does not have the disease. Given a person tests positive, what is the posterior probability that the person has the disease?

To answer this question, let's look at 10,000 people governed by the given probabilities. Table 30.1 (called a 2 × 2 contingency table) shows how things shake out.

Table 30.1: 2 × 2 Contingency table for hypothetical disease test

HEALTH STATUS	TEST POSITIVE (+)	TEST NEGATIVE (–)
Has disease	10,000 * .01 *.95 = 95	10,000 * .01 * .05 = 5
Healthy	10,000 * .99 * .05 = 495	10,000 * .99 * .95 = 9405

If we define P(Has disease|+ Test) to equal the posterior probability that a person receiving a positive test result has the disease, we find the answer to be 95 / (95 + 495) = 16.1%. Even though the test is 95% accurate, a positive test result increases the chance a randomly chosen person has the disease from 1% to only 16.1%. This is because most people don't have the disease, so even a very accurate test will result in many false positives (in this case, 495 false positives). Our simple example illustrates *Bayes's theorem*, which is the basis for the fast-growing field of Bayesian statistics. When Bayesians try to estimate a probability, they combine their prior view of the world with observed data. For a great history of Bayesian statistics, we recommend Sharon Bertsch McGrayne's *The Theory That Would Not Die* (Yale University Press, 2011).

Sensitivity and Specificity

When evaluating a medical test for a disease, it is important to know the fraction of the people who have the disease that test positive. This is known as the *sensitivity* of the test. From Table 30.1, we find that, as expected, of the 100 people with the disease, 95 people test positive. Therefore, the test's sensitivity is 95 / (95 + 5) = 95%.

We are also interested in the fraction of people who do not have the disease and test negative. This is known as the *specificity* of the test. From Table 30.1, we find that of the 9,500 healthy people, 9,405 test negative, so the test's specificity is 9405 / (9405 + 495) = 95%.

From a test's 2 × 2 contingency table, we can compute sensitivity and specificity from the following formulas:

$$\text{Sensitivity} = \frac{\textit{Number with disease who test positive} \left(+\right)}{\textit{Number who are sick}}$$

$$\text{Specificity} = \frac{\textit{Number healthy who test negative} \left(-\right)}{\textit{Number who are healthy}}$$

The question, of course, is what defines a positive or negative test result. For example, on the PSA test for prostate cancer, a score of at least 4 is usually defined to be a positive test result. As you will see, there is a trade-off between sensitivity and specificity, so you can't always get what you want. Increasing the cutoff that defines a positive PSA result decreases the sensitivity (you will miss more people who have prostate cancer) but increases specificity (you will have fewer false positives). The trade-off between sensitivity and specificity is usually summarized with the test's ROC curve.

ROC Curve

For any test, the *receiver operating characteristic (ROC) curve* summarizes the trade-off between sensitivity and specificity. For different cutoffs, defining a positive (+) and negative (−) test result, we plot on the x-axis 1 − specificity = probability that a negative test result will be viewed as a false positive, and on the y-axis, we plot the sensitivity.

Figure 30.1 shows three hypothetical ROC curves. The maximum possible area under the ROC is 1, and the larger the area under the curve, the better the test. The diagonal line shown in Figure 30.1 has area 0.5 under the line and represents a worthless test. For example, the point (0.6, 0.6) on the line represents a test where 60% of the people who test positive have the disease, and 60% of the people who test negative also have the disease. According to Eric Topol's excellent book *Deep Medicine* (Basic Books, 2019), an area of 0.7–0.8 under the ROC is good, and an area of 0.8–0.9 under the ROC is excellent. In Figure 30.1, the top curve has area 0.82 under it, and the other curve has area 0.71 under it. Suppose you randomly choose a person with the disease and a healthy person. It can be shown that the area under the ROC is the probability that the diseased person has a more abnormal test score than the healthy person.

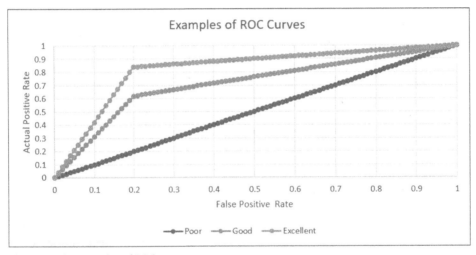

Figure 30.1: Examples of ROC curves

Figure 30.2 shows an ROC curve for the PSA test constructed from data discussed in Robert Riffenburgh's outstanding book *Statistics in Medicine* (3rd edition, Academic Press, 2012). The file ROC.xlsx contains the data, and Figure 30.3 shows a subset of the data.

For example, if a PSA of at least 7 is considered a positive test result, then 51 out of 95 people classified as sick were actually sick, so the cutoff of 7 yields a Sensitivity = 51 / 95 = 0.54. A total of 148 out of 206 people classified healthy were actually healthy, so the cutoff of 7 yields Specificity = 148 / 206 = 0.72 and 1 − Specificity = 0.28. Thus, the point (0.28, 0.54) is on the ROC curve. The cutoff chosen by the medical profession depends on the ratio of the cost of classifying someone as sick who is healthy to the false positive cost of classifying someone who is healthy as sick.

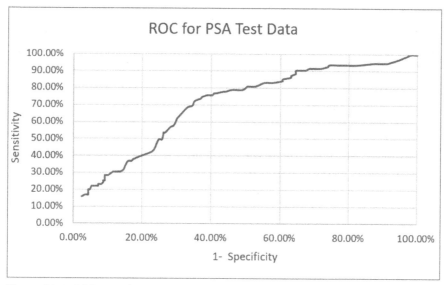

Figure 30.2: ROC curve for PSA test

	D	E	F	G	H	I	J	K
		called sick and actually healthy	called healthy and actually sick	called sick and actually sick	called healthy and actually healthy			
4	cutoff	healthy	sick	sick	healthy	sens	spec	1-spec
15	1	184	5	90	22	0.95	0.11	0.89
25	2	152	7	88	54	0.93	0.26	0.74
35	3	137	9	86	69	0.91	0.33	0.67
45	4	130	13	82	76	0.86	0.37	0.63
55	5	95	20	75	111	0.79	0.54	0.46
65	6	76	25	70	130	0.74	0.63	0.37
75	7	58	41	54	148	0.57	0.72	0.28

Figure 30.3: Subset of PSA data

Back to the Apple Heart Study

Armed with our brief foray into medical statistics, we are now ready to return to Murthy's analysis of the Apple Heart Study. In November 2019, Apple and Perez et al. ("Large-Scale Assessment of a Smartwatch to Identify Atrial Fibrillation," *New England Journal of Medicine*, November 14, 2019, vol. 381, pages 1901–1919) reported preliminary results from the heart study but provided little analysis of the results. Apple did admit the study's "accuracy is still far short of more traditional and currently used monitoring techniques. This is just a glimpse of the future, but we have a ways to go" (see `www.acc.org/latest-in-cardiology/articles/2019/03/08/15/32/sat-9am-apple-heart-study-acc-2019`). Murthy used Apple's test results to discuss the usefulness of the study (see `twitter.com/venkmurthy/status/1106956668439617537?s=20`).

We now summarize Murthy's analysis:

- 419,297 people participated in the study.

- 2,162 participants (0.52%) received a notification of an irregular pulse.

- 450 of these 2,162 participants sent back ECG patches that were analyzed to determine if AFib was present.

- AFib was found on 153 (34%) of the people who sent back their ECG patches (an average of 13 days later).

- Murthy points out that 450 − 153 = 297 of these people did not have AFib.

- Murthy now attempts to fill in the 2 × 2 contingency table that is like Table 30.1. We now know that

(1) 297 = False Positives + (Non-AFib people who test negative)

- 86 of the 450 people with irregular pulse notifications were also wearing an ECG patch; 72 of them had AFib, and 14 did not. This implies that there were 14 false positives. Now (1) tells us that there were 283 Non-AFib people who tested negative.

We now know all numbers in the 2 × 2 contingency table shown in Table 30.2, except for the AFib Test Negative cell. Since there are a total of 450 people, we can determine that the number of people with AFib testing Negative = 450 − 283 − 14 − 72 = 81.

Table 30.2: 2 × 2 Contingency table for Apple Heart Study

DISEASE STATUS	TEST POSITIVE (+)	TEST NEGATIVE (−)
Have AFIB	72	81
Do not have AFIB	14	283

`twitter.com/venkmurthy/status/1106956668439617537?s=20`

We can now determine the sensitivity, specificity, and posterior probability of having AFIB, given that a positive test result has been observed:

- Sensitivity = 72 / (72 + 81) = 47%

- Specificity = 283 / (283 + 14) = 95%

- P(AFib|+ Test Result) = 72 / (72 + 14) = 84%

To help us put the sensitivity and specificity of the Apple Heart study in perspective, Table 30.3 shows the sensitivity and specificity for three important medical tests.

Table 30.3: Examples of sensitivity and specificity

DISEASE	SENSITIVITY	SPECIFICITY
PSA test for prostate cancer[1]	67%–80%	60%–70%
Blood sugar test for diabetes[2]	64%	75%
Mammogram to detect breast cancer in women under 40[3]	77%	87%

[1] emedicine.medscape.com/article/457394-overview
[2] www.ncbi.nlm.nih.gov/pubmed/17337498
[3] emedicine.medscape.com/article/1945498-overview

We see that the Apple AFib test has a very low sensitivity (as I often do) relevant to the other listed tests. Therefore, a lot of improvement is needed.

AliveCor and KardiaBand

In March 2018, the Cleveland Clinic reported that the KardiaBand marketed by AliveCor could detect AFib with 90% sensitivity and 93% specificity (see www.alivecor.com/press/press_release/cleveland-clinic-study-affirms-accurate-detection-of-atrial-fibrillation/). In August 2019, AliveCor pulled the KardiaBand off the market (see www.medpagetoday.com/blogs/skeptical-cardiologist/81850).

AliveCor stated, "This was due to changes beyond our control in the Apple Watch operating system, which caused SmartRhythm to perform below our quality standards" (see alivecor.zendesk.com/hc/en-us/articles/360025110774-Why-was-SmartRhythm-discontinued-).

Is Proactive Policing Effective?

Police react to crimes as they are reported, but they also have developed strategies (often referred to as *proactive policing*) that attempt to prevent, rather than react to, crimes. In this chapter, we will discuss evidence concerning the effectiveness (or lack thereof) of the following proactive policing procedures.

- **Hot spots policing**—Assigning more police resources to known high-crime areas.

- **Predictive policing**—Using methods such as regression to predict crime for a given time and place and allocating resources based on the predicted level of crime.

- **CCTV** (Closed Circuit TV)—The use of cameras to monitor high-crime areas.

- **Stop and frisk**—Police stop and search a person when they believe there is a "reasonable suspicion" (see SCOTUS 1968 decision *Terry v. Ohio*) that the person has committed a crime or is about to commit a crime. Stop and frisk is often referred to as SQF (stop, question, and frisk).

- **Broken windows**—Based on the belief that social disorder causes crime, police increase the number of arrests for misdemeanors such as broken windows.

Much of our discussion is drawn from *Proactive Policing* (National Academy of Sciences, Engineering, and Medicine, 2018).

Hot Spots Policing

It seems reasonable that assigning more police resources to "hot spots" or high-crime areas might significantly reduce crime. In Chapter 19, "Evidence-Based Medicine," we illustrated how randomized control trials (RCTs) have been used to determine if drug treatments are effective. Lawrence Sherman and David Weisburd ("General Deterrent Effects of Police Patrol in Crime 'Hot Spots': A Randomized, Controlled Trial," *Justice Quarterly*, vol. 12, no. 4, 1995, pages 625–648) applied the RCT methodology in Minneapolis to show that hot spot policing can significantly reduce crime.

Based on the crime rate during a baseline year, the authors identified 110 different high-crime areas in Minneapolis as hot spots. Using a method similar to that described in Chapter 19's "Excel Calculations" section, the 110 areas were randomly classified into one of two groups: Treatment or Control. Those areas classified as Treatment received approximately two to three times more police patrol presence than the Control group during the year following the baseline year. The randomization "blocks out" the differences between the hot spots assigned to the Treatment and Control groups. Then the authors recorded for each of the 110 areas the percentage change in crime for the year following the baseline year relative to the baseline year. If the average change in the crime rate in the Treatment group is a significantly smaller number than the average change in the crime rate in the Control group, then the authors could conclude that the increased resources allocated to the Control group of locations significantly reduced crime.

Figure 31.1 and the file `Hotspots.xlsx` show a subset (fictitious data) of the change in the crime rate in each of the 110 hot spots. For example, in the first location receiving more police patrol resources, crime decreased by 2.25%, and in the first location not receiving additional police resources, crime decreased by 0.82%. As shown in Figure 31.1, the Treatment locations experienced an average 6% decrease in crime, whereas the Control locations experienced an average 1% decrease in crime. The question is whether this difference is statistically significant. We want to use the results of the RCT to decide between the following two hypotheses:

▪ Null Hypothesis: Mean Change in Crime in Treatment Group – Mean Change in Crime in Control Group >= 0

▪ Alternative Hypothesis: Mean Change in Crime in Treatment Group – Mean Change in Crime in Control Group < 0

As shown in this chapter's "Excel Calculations" section, a Two-Sample Z-Test yields a P-value shown in cell I12 (again see Figure 31.1) of 0.005. *This means that if the mean change in crime in the Treatment group equaled the Mean change in crime in the Control group, then there is only a 0.5% chance (see P-value in cell I12) that we would observe a difference smaller than −.06 − (−.01) = −5% in the mean change in crime in the Treatment and Control groups.* This small probability (usually a P-value < = .05 is used as the cutoff for rejecting a null hypothesis) indicates that the null hypothesis should be rejected and we should conclude that the Treatment group experienced a significantly larger decline in crime than the Control group.

	D	E	F	G	H	I	J
3	Location	Treatment	Control				
4	1	-2.25%	-0.82%		z-Test: Two Sample for Means		
5	2	1.39%	-8.04%				
6	3	-9.54%	-11.34%			Treatment	Control
7	4	5.47%	12.50%		Mean	-0.06	-0.01
8	5	-0.06%	-27.74%		Known Variance	0.01	0.01
9	6	9.50%	-5.07%		Observations	55.00	55.00
10	7	-5.55%	-1.89%		Hypothesized Mean Dif	0.00	
11	8	-15.70%	-2.92%		z	-2.56	
12	9	-7.17%	6.21%		P(Z<=z) one-tail	0.005	
13	10	-12.91%	2.68%		z Critical one-tail	1.64	
14	11	3.63%	-2.01%		P(Z<=z) two-tail	0.01	
15	12	-24.93%	-10.91%		z Critical two-tail	1.96	
16	13	-14.20%	-20.20%				

Figure 31.1: Hot spots changes in crime rate

An inquiring mind might speculate that increasing police resources allocated to a hot spot might simply displace crime from the heavily policed hot spot to a neighboring location. Sherman and Weisburd showed that crime displacement did not occur (see page 124 of *Proactive Policing*).

Predictive Policing

Many cities partner with vendors (see Jennifer Bachner's report at www.businessofgovernment.org/sites/default/files/Management%20 Predictive%20Policing.pdf for an explanation of IBM's approach) to build predictive analytic models (often using multiple linear regression) that are used to predict at any time the parts of the city where crimes are most likely to occur. Then additional resources are allocated to the areas where the likelihood of crime is the largest. The independent variables used to predict the incidence of crime include the following:

- Type of likely crime sites (such as shopping malls) in the area.
- Easy escape routes (such as public transportation) for criminals.
- Indications (bars, adult retail stores, etc.) that criminals may be nearby.
- Day of the week and time of day.

- Payday schedule.
- Phases of the moon. (There is a reason the word *lunatic* is used; more crimes are committed during a full moon—see `www.google.com/search?q=full+moon+more+crimes&rlz=1C1CHBD _ enUS733US733&oq=full+moon+more+crimes&aqs=chrome..69i57j0.6029j0j4&sourceid=chrome&ie=UTF-8`.)

As an example of the implementation of predictive policing, Bachner's report points to Santa Cruz, California. The Santa Cruz Program highlights fifteen 150 × 150-meter squares that have the highest predicted crime rates. Officers are briefed on these locations and encouraged to spend extra time patrolling these areas.

As pointed out on page 132 of *Proactive Policing*, there is insufficient evidence that predictive policing is effective. Most studies involve vendors who market predictive policing algorithms and are not conducted by impartial scholars. Also, it is difficult to differentiate between hot spot and predictive policing.

CCTV

B. C. Welsh and D. P. Farrington ("Effects of Closed Circuit Television Surveillance on Crime," *American Political Science Review*, vol 587 no. 1, April 2003, pages 110-135) conducted a meta-analysis of RCTs in which CCTV was added to a high-crime area and found that CCTV had a significant effect on reducing crime and was most effective in reducing vehicle crime in car parks. Eric L. Pizza, Joel Caplan, Leslie W. Kennedy, and Andrew M. Gilchrist ("The Effects of Merging Proactive CCTV Monitoring with Directed Police Control: A Randomized Controlled Trial," *Journal of Experimental Criminology*, vol. 11, no. 1, 2015, pages 43–69) examined an RCT in Newark, New Jersey in which the Treatment group had trained operators monitor the CCTV and immediately contact a patrol car when the operator identified a suspicious occurrence. The Control group reported suspicious incidents to patrol cars via a computer dispatch system. The authors found a 40%–49% reduction in violent crime in the Treatment group, which had a P-value of less than 10%.

Stop and Frisk

Stop and frisk involves detaining and stopping a person who officers believe has committed a crime or is about to commit a crime. During the years 2003–2013, New York City Police made over 100,000 stops per year. Stop and frisk has been extremely controversial. During his time as mayor of New York City (NYC), Mayor Bloomberg defended stop and frisk (see `www.washingtonpost.com/opinions/michael-bloomberg-stop-and-frisk-keeps-new-york-safe/2013/08/18/`

8d4cd8c4-06cf-11e3-9259-e2aafe5a5f84 _ story.html), but after entering the 2020 Democratic presidential race, Bloomberg apologized for stop and frisk due to its disproportionate impact on blacks and Hispanics (www.nbcnews.com/news/ nbcblk/bloomberg-apologizes-stop-frisk-police-practice-n1084756).

Studies of the impact of stop and frisk on crime (see pages 148–151 of *Proactive Policing*) have yielded mixed results. Ideally, RCTs would have been conducted in NYC to estimate the effectiveness of SQF, but I could not find any such studies. Without RCTs, it is difficult to determine if a reduction in crime is due to SQF or other factors, such as changes in a city's age demographics (young males commit most crimes) or improvements in a city's overall socioeconomic status.

In Philadelphia, a RCT by Ratcliffe et al. ("The Philadelphia Foot Patrol Experiment: A Randomized Controlled Trial of Police Patrol Effectiveness in Violent Crime Hotspots," *Criminology* Vol. 49, No. 3 (2011): 795–831) implemented SQF in 60 crime hot spots and after controlling for other variables found a 23% reduction in crime.

A vitally important issue is determining whether blacks and Hispanics are treated unfairly by SQF. African American Harvard Professor Roland Fryer ("An Empirical Analysis of Racial Differences in Police Use of Force," *Journal of Political Economy*, Vol. 127, No. 3, 2019, pages 1210–1261) has done the definitive research on this matter. Fryer analyzed 5 million NYC SQF incidents from the years 2003–2013.

Fifty-six percent of the SQF incidents analyzed by Fryer involved blacks, and blacks made up 25.5% of the civilian population. Critics of SQF often use this discrepancy as evidence for the disparate impact of SQF on blacks. A back-of-the-envelope analysis would calculate that blacks are involved in 56 / 25.5 = 2.2 times as many stops as their population would indicate. Non-blacks are involved in 44 / 74.5 = 0.59 times as many stops as their population would indicate. Thus, a crude estimate of the disparate impact of SQF on blacks would be 2.1 / 0.58 = 3.62, where a number greater than 1 indicates a disparate impact on blacks. More formally, we might define Disparate Impact on Blacks (as compared to whites) by

$$DI = \frac{(\%\text{age of black SQF}) / (\%\text{age blacks in pop})}{(\%\text{age of white SQF}) / (\%\text{age whites in pop})}$$

Fryer points out (see page 1227) that on a per capita basis, blacks are involved in more law violating behavior than whites. For example, in 2016 (www1.nyc .gov/assets/nypd/downloads/pdf/analysis _ and _ planning/year-end-2016- enforcement-report.pdf), blacks were involved in 71% of recorded gun violence incidents, and whites were involved in 2% of all shootings. With this in mind, Fryer conducted a precinct by precinct analysis on 77 precincts using regression to estimate the disparate impact of SQF on blacks when the percentage of blacks in the population varied based on unlawful behavior (see page 1227 and Table 1 of Fryer). The results are shown in Table 31.1.

Table 31.1: Disparate impact of SQF on blacks based on different population definitions

POPULATION DEFINITION	DISPARATE IMPACT MEASURE
%age Civilian 18–34-year-old males, blacks and whites	4.23
%age of 10 felonies and misdemeanors committed by blacks and whites	1.43
% of 6 most serious felonies committed by blacks and whites	1.03
% of robberies committed by blacks and whites	0.55

Fryer 2019, Table1

For example, if we consider the population of blacks and whites to equal the number of the six most serious felonies committed by each group, blacks suffer 3% more disparate impact than whites. Surprisingly, if we consider the population of blacks and whites to equal the number of robberies committed by blacks and whites, then per person blacks are stopped 45% less often than whites.

Fryer also utilized logistic regression (see Chapters 28 and 54 for further discussion of logistic regression) to estimate (after adjusting for many variables such as whether the officer was in uniform, civilian behavior, whether the stop was in a high-crime area or during a high-crime time) how much more or less likely a black would be arrested than a white. Fryer found that after adjusting for these variables, blacks were 8% more likely to be arrested after an SQF stop. This indicates that given the current decision-making process used to determine stops, a marginal stop of a black would be more productive (in terms of arrests) than a marginal stop of a white. On the other hand, after adjusting for the same independent variables, an SQF of a black was 22% less likely to yield contraband or a weapon than a stop of a white. This indicates that given the current decision-making process used to determine stops, a marginal stop of a black would be less productive (in terms of finding contraband or a weapon) than a marginal stop of a white and is indicative of bias against blacks.

Broken Windows

The broken windows theory purports that if the government reduces social disorder, then more serious crimes will be greatly reduced. One approach to reducing social disorder is to more strictly enforce serious crimes such as subway fare evasion, public urination, and writing of graffiti in subways, then more serious crimes will be greatly reduced. Beginning in 1993, Mayor Rudy Giuliani of NYC began enforcing the broken window theory and NYC did experience a large reduction in crime. For example, violent crime decreased by 56% in NYC during the 1990s compared to 28% in the nation as a whole (see www.nber.org/digest/jan03/w9061.html).

Another approach to reducing social disorder in an area is to improve the physical characteristics of an area through activities such as cleaning up vacant lots, improving trash collection, and reducing the number of abandoned buildings.

Despite the large crime reduction in 1990s NYC, a large body of research (see pages 163–168 of *Proactive Policing*) maintains that the 70% increase in misdemeanor arrests during the 1990s was not a major cause of the substantial crime decline in NYC. Factors such as the 35% increase in the size of the NYC police force, a large drop in the unemployment rate, the 1990s economics boom, and a large drop in the number of 18–34-year-olds surely contributed to the large drop in crime.

On the other hand, place-based approaches to reducing social disorder, such as improving the quality and quantity of affordable housing, *do* cause a significant reduction in crime (see Matthew Freedman and Emily Greene Owens, "Low-Income Housing Development and Crime," *Journal of Urban Economics*, vol. 70, no. 2, 2011, pages 115–131).

Excel Calculations

Using the percentage reduction in crime in 55 (fictitious) Treatment and Control groups in the file Hotspots.xlsx, we want to choose between the following hypotheses:

- Null Hypothesis: Mean Change in Crime in Treatment Group – Mean Change in Crime in Control Group >= 0

- Alternative Hypothesis: Mean Change in Crime in Treatment Group – Mean Change in Crime in Control Group < 0

Since there are at least 30 locations in each group and crime reductions in each location are assumed independent, the Central Limit Theorem implies that the sample mean change in each group will be normally distributed. If we assume the sample standard deviation of the percentage crime change in each group equals the actual standard deviation of the percentage crime change in each group, we may utilize the z-Test: Two Sample for Means tool to test our two hypotheses. The sample standard deviation of the percentage change in the Treatment group is 0.89%, and the sample standard deviation of the percentage change in the Control group is 1.27%.

To conduct our hypothesis test, we proceed as follows:

1. From the Data tab, select the Data Analysis Add-In and choose z-Test: Two Sample For Means.

2. Fill in the dialog box, as shown in Figure 31.2. Note that we entered the sample variance for each group as the assumed population variance.

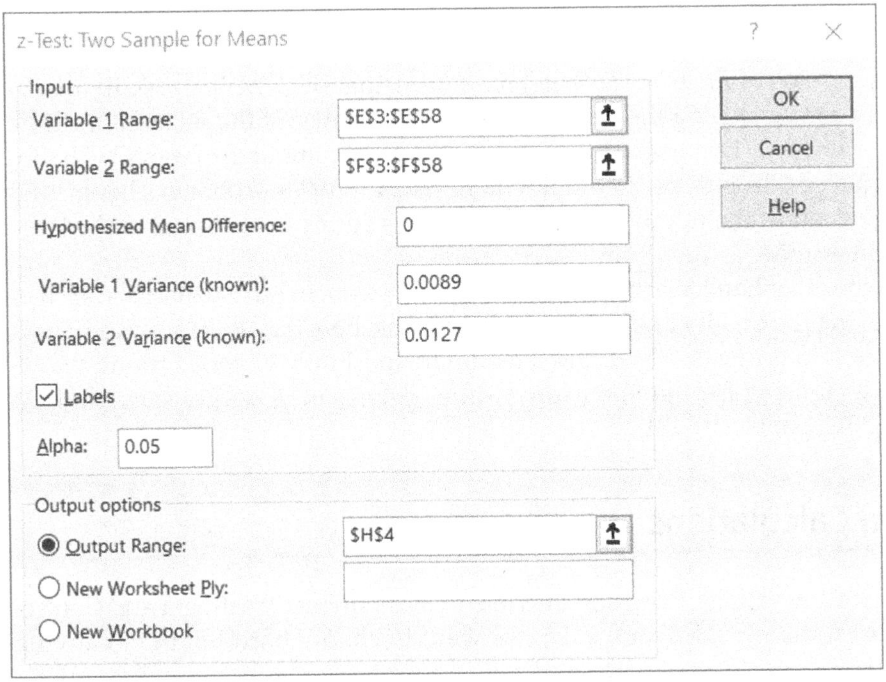

Figure 31.2: Dialog box for two-sample z-Test

Since we are only interested in testing for a difference in means in a single direction, we report a P-value of 0.005, which tells us that if the Null hypothesis is true, there is at most one chance in 200 that we would observe the Treatment group locations experiencing an average percentage change in crime at least 5% better than the Control group locations. The fact that this probability is so small leads us to reject the Null hypothesis and accept the Alternative hypothesis that the mean percentage change in crime in the Treatment locations is less than (more negative) than the mean percentage change in crime in the Control locations.

Guess How Many Are Coming to Dinner?

Small businesses need accurate forecasts of how many customers will show up every day. This helps them plan (using queueing theory discussed in Chapter 45, "The Waiting is the Hardest Part") their daily staffing needs. In this chapter, we use 4.5 years (June 2001 through the end of 2005) of daily customer counts at a branch of a national restaurant chain to develop a simple model that can be used to forecast daily supper customer counts. We will predict the daily customer count using equation (1). Our work is in the file Dinner.xlsx.

$$(1) \text{ Daily Customer Count} = \text{Constant} + \text{Day \#*}(\text{Daily Trend}) +$$

$$(\text{Day of the Week Effect}) + (\text{Week of the Year Effect}) +$$

$$(\text{Adjustment Due to Special Day})$$

For example, suppose we want to predict the number of customers on Super Bowl Sunday, February 3, 2002. As we will see, this is the least busy day of the year for the restaurant. For this day:

- Day # = 219 (February 3, 2002 is the 219th day in the data set).
- Day of Week = Sunday.
- Week of the Year = 32. The restaurant classified Thursday, June 28, 2001 as the first week of the year. They wanted to avoid partial weeks, so in 2002, Thursday June 27 was the first day of the year; in 2003, Thursday

June 26 was the first day of the year; in 2004, Thursday July 1 was the first day of the year; and in 2005, Thursday June 30 was the first day of the year. This classification results in 2003 having 53 weeks. February 3, 2002 is in the 32nd week of 2001.

■ Special Day Adjustment will equal the adjustment for Super Bowl Sunday.

The parameters needed to predict the customer count for Super Bowl Sunday 2002 (see the worksheet ALL IN) are shown in Table 32.1. The rest of the chapter will be devoted to showing you how we obtained these parameters.

Table 32.1: Parameters needed to predict Super Bowl Sunday customer count

PARAMETER	VALUE
Constant	430.52
Daily Trend	−0.0380
Day of the Week Effect	−1.23
Week of the Year Effect	−5.30
Super Sunday Effect	−213.86

Given these parameters, our predicted customer count for Super Bowl Sunday is calculated as

$$430.52 + 219 * (−0.0380) − 1.23 − 5.3 − 213.86 = 202$$

Actually, 229 customers showed up, so our error was 229 − 202 = 27, which indicates 27 more customers showed up than our forecast indicated. We now explain how we found the parameters that make equation (1) best fit the actual customer counts. The Excel Solver makes the determination of the best parameter values a snap!

Which Parameters Must Be Estimated?

Our simple model requires that 71 parameters be estimated. Our model could be set up as a multiple linear regression in which the parameters are coefficients for each of the 71 independent variables, but Excel can only estimate regressions with up to 15 independent variables. The needed parameters are as follows. Our work is in the worksheet ALL IN of the workbook `Dinner.xlsx`. Figure 32.1 shows our final parameter estimates:

■ A constant that is used to "anchor" our forecasts. This parameter is in cell AB10.

	Y	Z	AA	AB	AC	AD
1						
2			weekday	1.3E-14	week	2.4E-10
3			1	-121.6	1	-3.7395
4	MAD base		2	-100.61	2	-27.046
5		112	3	-71.254	3	21.3909
6			4	-42.475	4	-15.665
7	MAD		5	142.598	5	-12.686
8		43	6	194.573	6	7.151
9			7	-1.2271	7	-18.755
10			constant	430.523	8	-5.6612
11					9	-34.91
12					10	-47.181
13	trend				11	-33.551
14		-0.037903682			12	-32.057
15					13	-34.992
16	Special				14	-17.384
17	Fourth of July	-165.5			15	-25.89
18	New Years	-32.404			16	14.3347
19	Valentine's	367.824			17	-32.614
20	Mother' s day	346.043			18	-21.331
21	New Year's Eve	270.286			19	-19.744
22	Halloween	-128.75			20	-10.425
23	Super bowl	-213.86			21	13.0899
24	Christmas Eve	172.465			22	-4.8853
25	Labor Day	134.151			23	-3.0518
26					24	39.098
27					25	44.7919
28					26	98.1347

Figure 32.1: Estimates of dinner forecast parameters

▪ A parameter for how many more or fewer people than average show up on each of the seven days of the week. We will find, for example, that on Saturday, 194.6 more people come than on an average day. We will constrain the average of the weekday parameters to equal 0. Then a negative parameter indicates that the day of the week is less busy than average, and a positive factor indicates that the day of the week is busier than average. These parameters are in cells AB3:AB9.

▪ A parameter for how many more or fewer people than average show up during each of the 53 weeks of the year. As with the day of the week, we constrain the average of these 53 parameters to equal 0. Then a negative parameter indicates that the week of the year is less busy than average, whereas a positive parameter indicates that the week of the year is busier than average. We find that the effect of week 26 (the week involving Christmas and New Year's) is by far the busiest, with 98 more customers than average coming during that week. The week of the year parameters are in cells AD3:AD55.

▪ A parameter for each of the holidays or special days that affect customer counts are in cells Z17:Z25. We find, for example, that Mother's Day adds 346 customers and that Super Bowl Sunday reduces customer count by 214 customers.

■ A parameter for the daily trend. Our trend estimate of –0.0379 in cell Y14 implies that each day, the average number of customers decreases by nearly 0.04 customers.

All these parameter values are ceteris paribus, which means they are our best estimates after adjusting for all other independent variables.

The Data

Figure 32.2 (many columns have been hidden) shows our underlying data and forecasts:

■ Column I has the daily customer counts. For example, on June 28, 2001, a total of 402 customers came to dinner.

■ Column H has the day of the week and the week of the year. June 28, 2001 was a Thursday during the restaurant's first week of the year.

■ Columns D–G contain the month, day of the month, day of the week, and week of the year, respectively.

■ Column C contains the year.

■ Column B contains the entire date.

■ Column A contains the day number, with June 28, 2001 as day 1, June 29, 2001 as day 2, and so on.

■ Using equation (1) in column S gives our forecast for the day's customer count. For example, cell S3 gives our forecast of 384.

	A	B	C	D	E	F	G	H	I	S	T	U	V	W
					Day	Day		Day	Cust count				Abs Forecast	Abs Base
2	Day	Date	Year	Month	Month	week	Week	Week	dinner	Forecast	Error	Sq Error	error	error
3	1	6/28/2001	2001	6	28	4	1	Thr01	402	384	18	314	18	1
4	2	6/29/2001	2001	6	29	5	1	Fri01	573	569	4	14	4	172
5	3	6/30/2001	2001	6	30	6	1	Sat01	564	621	-57	3277	57	163
6	4	7/1/2001	2001	7	1	7	1	Sun01	403	425	-22	502	22	2
7	5	7/2/2001	2001	7	2	1	1	Mon01	275	305	-30	899	30	126
8	6	7/3/2001	2001	7	3	2	1	Tue01	356	326	30	903	30	45
9	7	7/4/2001	2001	7	4	3	1	Wed01	248	190	58	3391	58	153
10	8	7/5/2001	2001	7	5	4	2	Thr02	271	361	-90	8046	90	130
11	9	7/6/2001	2001	7	6	5	2	Fri02	569	546	23	541	23	168
12	10	7/7/2001	2001	7	7	6	2	Sat02	542	598	-56	3099	56	141
13	11	7/8/2001	2001	7	8	7	2	Sun02	363	402	-39	1508	39	38
14	12	7/9/2001	2001	7	9	1	2	Mon02	326	281	45	1987	45	75
15	13	7/10/2001	2001	7	10	2	2	Tue02	313	302	11	113	11	88
16	14	7/11/2001	2001	7	11	3	2	Wed02	403	332	71	5085	71	2
17	15	7/12/2001	2001	7	12	4	3	Thr03	378	409	-31	953	31	23
18	16	7/13/2001	2001	7	13	5	3	Fri03	513	594	-81	6546	81	112

Figure 32.2: Dinner data and forecasts

- Columns J–R (hidden) have mostly zeroes, with ones whenever the given special day occurs. For example, cell J9 = 1, because row 9 represents the 4th of July, 2001.

- Column T gives each day's error = actual customers – forecast. For example, on June 28, 2001, a total of 18 more people than forecasted showed up and on June 30, 2001, a total of 57 fewer people than expected showed up.

- Column V contains the absolute value of each day's forecast errors.

- Column W contains the absolute daily error if our forecast is simply the daily average of 401.1 customers.

The Results

As explained in the "Excel Calculations" section later in this chapter, the parameters shown in Figure 32.1 were calculated to minimize the sum of the squared forecast errors. In cell I1, we compute the R^2 value associated with predicting our actual daily customer count from our forecasts. From the R^2 value shown in cell I1, we find that equation (1) explains 82% of the daily variation in customer count, with 18% of the daily variation unexplained by our model.

In cell Y5, we find that if we simply forecast each day's customer count to equal the daily average (401.11), then our daily forecast is off by a daily average of 112 customers (almost 28% of our daily average). In cell Y8, we calculated the average of our daily absolute errors based on our forecasts from equation (1). Our average daily absolute error (MAD, or mean absolute deviation) has been reduced to only 43 customers (around 11% of our daily average). The standard deviation of our forecast errors is 57.3, and we would expect 95% of our forecasts to be accurate within 2 * 57.3 = 114.6.

From our parameter estimates in Figure 32.1, we glean the following quick insights:

- Each year, the average number of customers is decreasing by 0.0379 * 365 = 14 customers per year.

- On a typical Saturday, we predict nearly 600 customers, while on a typical Monday, we predict only 280 customers.

- Week 26 of the year (involving Christmas and New Year's) has double the effect of any other week of the year.

- Mother's Day and Valentine's Day nearly double the predicted number of customers. On Valentine's Day, we would expect more than four times as many customers as Super Bowl Sunday. I'd bet the numbers are nearly reversed for your local pizza joint!

Which Factor Really Matters?

A quick way to see the relative importance of the four factors (trend, day of the week, week of the year, special days) incorporated in equation (1) is to eliminate one factor at a time and look at how our R^2 (the percentage of variation in actual customer count explained by our forecast) and MAD change. Table 32.2 summarizes these results. This table makes it clear that the day of the Week is the key driver of our forecasts. Although omitting special days reduces our R^2 by only 5%, the special day parameters have a huge influence on our forecasts for those special days.

Table 32.2: Factors that most affect our forecasts

WORKSHEET AND FACTOR REMOVED	R^2	MAD
No Trend	0.81	45
Day of Week	0.13	105
No Week of Year	0.79	46.8
No Special Days	0.76	47.1

Excel Calculations

An *optimization model* allows you to determine the best way to accomplish a goal subject to constraints. In this section, we explain how we develop an optimization model using the Excel Solver to determine the values of our parameters that minimize the sum of the squared forecast errors. We square forecast errors because if we simply add up errors, then positive and negative errors would cancel out.

An optimization model consists of three parts: objective or target cell, changing variable cells, and constraints.

Objective (or Target Cell)

You must have an *objective* (often referred to as a *target cell*) that you want to maximize or minimize. In our model, the objective is to minimize the sum of the squared daily forecast errors.

Changing Variable Cells

In any optimization problem, there are cells (called *changing variable cells*) that a decision maker can change to optimize (in this case, minimize) the objective cell. In our forecast model, our parameters are as follows:

- The trend parameter (1 changing cell)
- The constant (1 changing cell)
- The day of the week parameters (7 changing cells)
- The week of the year parameters (53 changing cells)
- The special day factors (9 changing cells)

Constraints

Constraints are restrictions on the changing cells. In most optimization models, the changing cells are restricted to be non-negative. In our model, parameters (such as the Super Bowl Sunday Parameter) can be negative. Our model has simply two constraints:

- Average day of the week factor = 0
- Average week of the year factor = 0

These constraints enable us to easily identify days with many or few customers and identify weeks of the year with many or few customers.

Our model is in the worksheet ALL IN of the workbook `Dinner.xlsx`. We now outline the steps needed to estimate our parameters:

1. Copying from S3 to S4:S1560 the formula

    ```
    =constant+trend*A3+VLOOKUP(G3,week,2)+VLOOKUP(F3,weekday,2)
    +$Z$17*J3+$Z$18*K3+$Z
          $19*L3+M3*$Z$20+N3*$Z$21+O3*$Z$22+P3*$Z$23+Q3*$Z$24+R3
    *$Z$25
    ```

    computes a forecast for each day based on equation (1).

    - Our forecast starts with the constant.
    - The trend term picks up the effect of the trend on each day's forecast.
    - `VLOOKUP(G3,week,2)` looks up the week of the year effect.
    - `VLOOKUP(F3,weekday,2)` looks up the day of the week effect.
    - The other terms pick up a day's special day effect when that day occurs. Recall that Columns J–R contain a 1 whenever a day is a special day and 0 otherwise.

2. Copying from T3 to T4:T1560 the formula `=I3-S3` computes the error in each day's forecast.

3. Copying from U3 to U4:U1560, the formula `=T3^2` computes each day's squared error.

4. Cell U1 computes our objective, the sum of squared errors, with the formula `=SUM(U3:U1560)`.

5. Copying from V3 to V4:V1560, the formula =ABS(T3) computes the absolute error for each day's forecast.

6. Copying from W3 to W4:W1560, the formula =ABS(I3-$X$8) computes each day's absolute error if we forecasted each day's customer count as the overall average.

7. For any set of parameter values, the formula =RSQ(S3:S1560,I3:I1560) in cell I1 computes the fraction of variation in daily customer count explained by our forecasts.

8. The formula =AVERAGE(V3:V1560) in cell Y8 computes the MAD by averaging our daily absolute errors.

9. The formula =AVERAGE(W3:W1560) in cell Y5 computes the MAD if our daily forecast always equals the average customer count.

10. The formula =STDEV(T3:T1560) in cell X3 computes the standard deviation of our forecast errors.

11. The Excel Solver performs optimization. If you see Solver on the right-hand side of the Data tab, then you do not need to add it. Otherwise, from the File tab on the ribbon, choose Options ➪ Add-ins. After clicking Go, check the Solver Add-in and click OK. You should now see Solver on the right-hand side of the Data tab.

12. Go to the Data tab, select Solver, and fill in the Solver dialog box as shown in Figure 32.3.

   ▪ The objective is to minimize the sum of squared errors in cell U1. Make sure you select Minimize.

   ▪ Separated by commas, select the Trend, Constant, Special Days, Day Of Week, and Week Of Year parameters as changing cells.

   ▪ Add the constraints $AD$2 = 0 and $AB$2 = 0 to ensure that the average of the week of year and average of the day of week parameters are equal to 0.

   ▪ Since our changing cells can be negative, uncheck the Make Unconstrained Variables Non-Negative check box.

   ▪ Our objective squares errors, which makes our objective a nonlinear function of our changing cells. Therefore, select the GRG Nonlinear Solver Method. After clicking Solve, you will find the parameter values shown in Figure 32.1, which minimize the sum of squared errors. These values give us the "best" forecast based on equation (1).

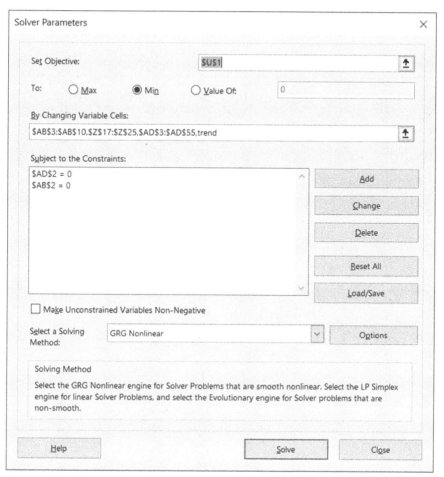

Figure 32.3: Solver settings for forecast model

13. In the other worksheets, we individually eliminated each of the factors one by one to see how each factor impacted forecast accuracy. For example, in the worksheet Day of Week, we added the constraint $AB$3:$AB$9 = 0 to ensure that the day of week parameters all equal 0. Note that eliminating the day of week parameters reduces our R^2 from 81% to 13%.

Can Prediction Markets Predict the Future?

The only thing that is certain about the future is that it is uncertain. Some questions about the future we might want to answer include the following:

- What is the chance the Democrats win the next U.S. presidential election?

- For a manufacturing company, estimate the mean and standard deviation of the number of units sold for each product during the next month? Accurate predictions of future sales of each product will help us cut inventory costs and reduce shortages.

- What is the chance the Patriots win the next Super Bowl?

In this chapter, we will explore how *prediction markets* can aggregate information from many people and turn that information into surprisingly accurate information about the future. The term *wisdom of crowds* (popularized by James Surowiecki in his book *The Wisdom of Crowds*, Doubleday, 2004) is often used to refer to the fact that a sensible aggregation of information from many people usually outperforms purported experts in answering a question or forecasting the uncertain outcome of a future event.

Examples of Trade Contracts

In prediction markets, participants buy and sell contracts, the payoff of which is tied to the outcome of a future event. Then the price of each contract gives us an estimate about an uncertain quantity, such as the probability of an event occurring or the mean or median of the uncertain quantity. Using the outcome of the 2016 U.K. Brexit referendum for illustration purposes, Table 33.1 shows three examples of commonly traded contracts. (See Justin Wolfers and Eric Zitzewitz's survey paper on prediction markets, www.nber.org/papers/w12083 .pdf, for a great introduction to prediction markets.) In what follows, we explain why binary options, index futures, and spread betting provide reasonable estimates of the probability of an event occurring, the mean of an uncertain quantity, and the median of an uncertain quantity, respectively.

Table 33.1: Examples of prediction market contracts

TYPE OF CONTRACT	EXAMPLE	PARAMETER ESTIMATED
Binary Option	Contract pays $1 if Brexit wins and costs $P1.	P1 estimates chance Brexit wins.
Index Future	Contract pays $1 for each percentage point of vote received by Brexit and costs $P2. For example, if Brexit receives 55% of the vote, then contract pays $55.	P2 estimates the expected percentage of the vote received by Brexit.
Spread Betting	Contract costs $1 and for some value V* pays $2 if Brexit received at least a percentage V* of the vote, and $0 otherwise.	V* estimates the median of the vote Brexit will receive. That is, there is a 50% chance that Brexit will receive at least a share V* of the vote.

Let V be the random variable representing the actual share of the vote received by Brexit. Then define

- PROB = Probability Brexit wins (V > 50)
- E(V) = Expected percentage of votes received by Brexit
- MEDIAN = Median of V, that is Prob (V >= Median = 0.5)

We now show that each of the three contracts described in Table 33.1 provides a plausible estimate of the desired parameter. The profit from each contract is a random variable. In each case the expected profit from the contract (see Chapter 23 for a discussion of how to compute the expected profit of a random variable) turns out to equal 0, which implies that each contract is fair.

P1 Estimates Prob

With probability PROB the Binary Option pays \$1, and with probability 1-PROB the binary option pays \$0. Therefore, the expected profit from the binary option will equal 0 if

$$\text{PROB} * (1 - P) + (1 - \text{PROB}) * (-P) = 0$$

Solving for PROB, we find that PROB = P, so if the price of the binary contract equals the true probability of Brexit winning, then the binary contract is a fair bet.

P2 Estimates Mean Brexit Vote

Let v_i = probability that Brexit receives i% of the vote. Then the Index Option will yield an expected profit of 0 if

$$\sum_{i=0}^{i=100} i v_i - \text{P2} = 0$$

which is true if P2 equals the expected share of the vote received by Brexit.

V* Estimates the Median of Brexit Vote

The Median Spread Bet described in Table 33.1 will yield an expected profit of 0 for the value of V* satisfying

$$(2 - 1) * \text{Prob}(V >= V^*) + (-1) * \text{Prob}(V < V^*) = 0$$

This equation will only be satisfied if Prob(V >= V*) = Prob(V < V*) = 0.5, or V* equals the median of V.

Prediction Market Trading Mechanisms

Pages 14–18 of Stefan Luckner et al. (*Prediction Markets*, Gabler Verlag, Berlin, 2011) describes many trading mechanisms utilized in prediction markets. We now give an example of the *double auction (DA) trading mechanism*, which is the most common trading mechanism used in the financial and prediction markets.

Let's reconsider the Brexit Binary Option and suppose it is currently selling for \$0.55 and all participants own some options that pay out \$1 if Brexit wins and \$0 when Brexit loses. A *very simplified* example is now used to illustrate how trading might work. Suppose 11 people are interested in trading today, and for each integer v between 53 and 63 inclusive, there is one person who feels that

Brexit has a v% chance of passing, and each person is interested in buying or selling at most one binary option. Suppose the people (labeled by their perceived view of Brexit's percentage chance of passing) arrive in the following order: Person63, Person53, Person62, Person54, Person61, Person55, Person 60, Person56, Person59, Person57, Person58. Each person makes their perceived view of Brexit known to the trader.

In our simple example, the organization running the market (often called a market maker) will pair off potential traders based on the current price and perceived valuations. Trading will proceed as follows:

1. Person63 will buy a Brexit binary option from Person53 at the current price of $0.55. Based on their Brexit views, both people are getting a satisfactory deal.

2. Person62 will buy a Brexit binary option from Person54 at the current price of $0.55. Based on their Brexit views, both people are getting a satisfactory deal.

3. Person61 will buy a Brexit binary option from Person55 at the current price of $0.55. Based on their Brexit views, both people are getting a satisfactory deal.

4. When Person60 and Person56 arrive, Person56 does not want to sell at the current price of $0.55. Therefore, the market maker can raise the price to $0.56. Then Person56 will be willing to sell a Brexit binary option to Person60.

5. When Person59 and Person57 arrive, the market maker needs to increase the price to $0.57 to facilitate a trade.

6. Finally, when Person58 arrives, they need to wait for another person who values the contract at less than or equal to $0.58. For example, if a person valuing the contract at $57.50 arrives, any market price between $57.50 and $58.00 will clear the orders.

Observe that on average the 11 traders entering the market give Brexit a 58% chance of winning. Since 0.58 > 0.55, the market maker must increase the price of the binary option to ensure that the maximum number of trades are executed.

Accuracy of Prediction Markets and Wisdom of Crowds

There are many situations in which prediction markets or simple aggregation of individuals' opinions outperform other methods used to estimate quantities or predict outcomes of future events:

▪ On the U.S. version of the British show *Who Wants to Be a Millionaire*, a contestant who is unsure of an answer can "phone an expert" or ask the studio audience for guidance. Experts know the answer 65% of the time, whereas the studio audience gets the correct answer an amazing 92% of the time (see page 62 of Donald Thompson's fascinating book *Oracles* [HBR Press, 2012]).

▪ The Hollywood Stock Exchange (HSX) (see www.hsx.com) gives you $2 million to use in trading in a prediction market that predicts movie revenues and Oscar winners. I could not find details on the accuracy of the HSX Movie predictions, but many studios (see page 37 of *Oracles*) purchase the HSX Movie predictions. For the years 2009–2011, HSX correctly predicted 83% of Oscar winners. For these years, HSX outperformed trade papers such as *Variety* and the *Hollywood Reporter* (see page 39 of *Oracles*).

▪ Best Buy (see Chapter 8 of *Oracles*) asked 190 employees to predict February gift card sales. Best Buy's normal forecasting process was off by 5%, whereas the average of the 190 employee forecasts was off by only 1%.

▪ Iowa Electronic Markets (IEM, at iemweb.biz.uiowa.edu) is probably the best-known prediction market. IEM uses prediction markets, like public opinion polls, to predict the outcome of elections. In 451 of 596 elections, the IEM prediction was more accurate than the major U.S. election polls (see blog.gnosis.pm/the-power-of-prediction-markets-fedea0b71244).

▪ Hewlett Packard (HP) used prediction markets to predict printer sales for eight different products (see authors.library.caltech.edu/44358/1/wp1131.pdf). For six of the eight forecasts, the prediction markets were more accurate than HP's official forecasts. For another test of the power of prediction markets, the authors created a distribution for product sales based on the forecasts associated with the most recent 50% of trades. If more (less) than half these trades were higher than the official forecast, then HP assumed that actual sales would exceed (be less than) the official forecast. By this standard, the prediction market forecasts were 8 for 8!

Despite these successes, we note that prediction markets failed to predict the victories of Brexit and Trump in 2016. In the next chapter, we will discuss how political polls fared in these elections.

Prediction markets can be used to predict many things, and in the future, we expect to see many more applications to predicting the future.

The ABCs of Polling

In the 2016 U.S. presidential election, 216 million people were of voting age, and 55% of them voted for president (www.electproject.org/2016g). As we all know, Donald Trump was elected (based on the Electoral College), but he lost the popular vote to Hillary Clinton by 1.9%. Of the major polls, only the *LA Times*/USC Poll picked Trump to win the popular vote. An unweighted average of the major 2016 polls computed by Real Clear Politics (www.realclearpolitics .com/epolls/2016/president/us/general_election_trump_vs_clinton-5491.html) had Clinton winning by an average of 3.2%, well within the margin of error (a concept that we will discuss later in the chapter). Where the polls fell down in 2016 was predicting the presidential election outcome in states, particularly Midwestern states (www.washingtonpost.com/politics/were-the-polls-way-off-in-2016-a-new-report-offers-a-mixed-answer/2017/05/04/a80440a0-30d6-11e7-9534-00e4656c22aa_story.html). In this chapter, we attempt to give the reader a basic understanding of the issues involved in polling, and review some of polling's greatest failures.

Why Are 1,112 People Enough to Represent U.S. Voters?

For now, let's assume that *every* person of voting age votes, and in all elections, a Democrat runs against a Republican. A pollster wants to predict the fraction of the Republican vote in three different elections:

- A mayoral election in a city with 20,000 people of voting age
- A state gubernatorial election in a state with 10 million people of voting age
- A presidential election with 250 million people of voting age

Suppose you want to predict the GOP percentage of the vote and believe that with 95% probability, your poll result is within 3% of the *actual* GOP percentage. It is an amazing fact that despite the different number of people eligible to vote in each of these three hypothetical elections, for each election, sampling 1,112 people will be enough. *We assume that each person of voting age has the same chance of being included in our sample.*

Define:

- PBAR = Fraction of *sampled* voters who support the GOP
- N = Number of voters sampled
- P = *Actual* fraction of people of voting age supporting the GOP

Each time a pollster samples N voters, they can get a different value of PBAR. It turns out that if the sample size is at most 10% of the number of people of voting age, then for at least 95% of our samples of size N, the *actual* fraction P of people of voting age supporting the GOP will be between

$$PBAR - 2\sqrt{1/4N} \text{ and } PBAR + 2\sqrt{1/4N}.$$

In our simplified situation, $2\sqrt{1/4N}$ is the *sampling margin of error*.

A little algebra (a dangerous thing) shows that for N = 1,111, the sampling margin of error is 3%. The file Polls.xlsx (see also Figure 34.1) illustrates this idea. Using Excel's =RAND() function in Column C, we generate 1,111 independent numbers equally likely to assume any value between 0 and 1.

The formulas in Column B ensure that the sampled person is a Republican if the random number is less than or equal to 0.5 or a Democrat if the random number is greater than 0.5. Thus, we are sampling from an infinite number of voters who are equally likely to vote Republican or Democratic. Cell G7 records the fraction of sampled voters who vote Republican. Hitting F9 recalculates all the RAND() functions and also performs the sampling of 1,111 voters 10,000 times. Finally, cell E13 records the fractions of our samples for which the fraction of GOP voters is between 47% and 53%. Of course, this is also the fraction of the time our sample estimate of the fraction of GOP voters in the population is within 3% of the true percentage of GOP voters (50%).

As shown in Figure 34.1, we found that 95.29% of our samples estimated the percentage of GOP voters (as expected) within the margin of error (3%) of the true percentage.

	A	B	C	D	E	F	G	H
1								
2								
3	Person	Party	Rand					
4	1	blue	0.819					
5	2	blue	0.822					
6	3	red	0.041				Red	Blue
7	4	red	0.179				50.77%	49.23%
8	5	blue	0.886		D4 formula			
9	6	red	0.496		=IF(C4<=0.5,"red","blue")			
10	7	blue	0.719		Fraction for GOP			
11	8	blue	0.779		=COUNTIF(Party,G6)/1111			
					Between 47% and			
12	9	red	0.455		53%			
13	10	blue	0.545		95.15%			
14	11	red	0.273		=COUNTIFS(J7:J10006,">=.47",J7:J10006,"<=.53")/1000			
15	12	red	0.336					

Figure 34.1: Illustrating a political poll

Why Doesn't a Larger Population Require a Larger Sample Size?

At first blush, it seems incorrect to assert that sampling 1,111 voters will have the same margin of error in a presidential race and a mayoral race in a city with 200,000 people of voting age. The best explanation of this idea I have seen comes from Anthony Salvanto's (head of CBS Polling) excellent book *Where Did You Get This Number?* (Simon & Schuster, 2018). Suppose you are making 40 gallons of lentil soup in a single pot to feed 640 hungry college students (40 gallons = 640 cups). The 40 gallons of soup contain 30,720 teaspoons of soup. If you want to make sure the whole batch of soup is of high quality, you can randomly choose from the soup container 1,011 teaspoons of soup and determine if each teaspoon is of high quality. If your 1,011 teaspoons are spread throughout the 40-gallon container, you should have a pretty good idea of the quality of the entire 40 gallons of soup. Now assume you are making your soup for 6,400 soldiers at an Army base. You need to make 400 gallons of soup, but it seems reasonable that we do not need to taste more than 1,011 teaspoons. Basically, if your sample is large enough, you will get a pretty good idea of what the population is like.

In a similar fashion, sampling less than 2,000 randomly chosen voters can give you a good idea of the fraction of voters who prefer each candidate for a town with a population of 50,000 or a country with 300 million people.

So, What Can Go Wrong?

We now look at several examples where polling gave unsatisfactory results. By explaining why polling failed in these examples, we will gain an understanding of what is required to create a successful poll.

Landon Does Not Beat Roosevelt

In the 1936 presidential election, Democratic President Franklin Delano Roosevelt ran against Kansas Republican Alf Landon. This election occurred in the midst of the Great Depression. *The Literary Digest* weekly magazine mailed out 10 million ballots and, based on the 2.4 million returned ballots, predicted Landon would win in a landslide and receive 57% of the popular vote. FDR actually received 61% of the vote and won 46 of 48 states. (Landon only won Maine and Vermont. See news.google .com/newspapers?id=fkYbAAAAIBAJ&sjid=IU8EAAAAIBAJ&pg=2555,806060&dq= literary-digest&hl=en.)

How could a much larger sample result in such a poor prediction? The 10 million ballots sent out by the *Digest* were sent out to subscribers, telephone owners, and automobile owners. During the Great Depression, few of the "Forgotten Men (and Women!)" who supported FDR would receive these ballots, so the *Digest's* 2.3 million returned ballots were in no way representative of the electorate. Within two years *The Literary Digest* was out of business.

As pointed out by Maurice Bryson ("The *Literary Digest* Poll: Making of a Statistical Myth," *Journal of the American Statistical Association*, vol. 30, no. 4, 1976, pages 184–185), the *Literary Digest* was a victim of *response bias*. Only 23% of ballots were returned. In retrospect, it seems clear that anti-Roosevelt voters (who were probably higher-income voters) were much more likely to return ballots than pro-Roosevelt voters.

Interestingly enough, even though political polling was in its infancy, the Gallup Poll predicted, based on 50,000 responses, that FDR would get 56% of the vote, which was close to FDR's actual 61% (www.amsi.org.au/ESA_Senior_Years/ SeniorTopic4/4b/4b_2content_4.html).

Dewey Does Not Beat Truman

If you ever took a U.S. history course, you surely saw a picture of Harry Truman proudly holding the November 5, 1948 *Chicago Tribune's* headline "Dewey Defeats Truman" (en.wikipedia.org/wiki/Dewey_Defeats_Truman). The famed Gallup Poll predicted Dewey would win by 6%. Truman beat Dewey by 4.5%, so Gallup was off by 10.5%, well outside the desired margin of error.

Three reasons are commonly given for Gallup's failure:

- Gallup stopped polling two weeks before the election and likely missed a late surge toward Truman.

- Gallup used *quota sampling* (see `explorable.com/quota-sampling`). In quota sampling, the pollster attempts to ensure that the sampled individuals mirror the voting population. For example, if 12% of the electorate are rural African Americans, then each interviewer is given a quota that ensures that in the total sample, the sampled potential voters would be 12% rural African Americans. As long as each interviewer finds individuals that match their quota, then it is up to them who should be interviewed. Clearly such a method does not give each person of voting age the same chance of being chosen for the sample.

- A good poll needs to accurately estimate the chance that each sampled voter will actually vote, and then weight the voter's choice by their estimated chance of voting. In 1948, such methods did not exist.

Sanders Does Not Beat Clinton

In presidential primary elections, voter turnout is much lower than in the November general election. For example, in the hotly contested 2016 primaries, only 29% of registered voters voted in primaries (see `www.electproject.org/2016g`), whereas 59% of registered voters voted in the general election (see `www.pewresearch`
`.org/fact-tank/2016/06/10/turnout-was-high-in-the-2016-primary-season-but-`
`just-short-of-2008-record/`). This makes it clear that to predict the outcome of a primary election accurately, a pollster's model must create a sample that mirrors the voters who will vote in the primary, not a sample that mirrors the population of eligible voters. The 2016 Democratic Michigan primary provides a textbook example of a situation in which the potential voters sampled by a poll were not representative of the actual voters who went to the polls (`www`
`.washingtonpost.com/news/the-fix/wp/2016/03/09/why-were-the-polls-in-`
`michigan-so-far-off/`). Bernie Sanders defeated Hillary Clinton by 1.5% in the primary. Before the primary, the Mitchell/Fox2 poll predicted that Clinton would win by 61% to Sanders's 34%. To identify potential voters in the 2016 primary, the polls went back to the 2008 Democratic primary. (In 2012, Obama was running for a second term, so the primary was of no significance.) But in 2008, Obama did not file paperwork to run in Michigan, so Clinton ran against an uncommitted slate. This greatly reduced turnout in the 2008 primary and made the 2008 primary electorate of little use in predicting the outcome of the 2016 primary. About 75% of the voters sampled in the Mitchell/Fox2 poll were over 50, but only 55% of the actual voters were over 50. Since Sanders was much stronger with younger voters, this discrepancy was a key factor in the Mitchell/Fox2 poll's inaccuracy.

How Did the Pollsters Miss Trump's Rust Belt Triumph?

Trump surprised the pollsters with his narrow wins (by less than a total of 100,000 votes) in the Rust Belt states of Pennsylvania, Michigan, and Wisconsin. Here are several reasons why the pollsters missed on calling Trump's surprising Rust Belt victories.

- Trump beat Clinton 67% to 29% among noncollege whites (www.pewresearch .org/fact-tank/2016/11/09/behind-trumps-victory-divisions-by-race-gender-education/). In Rust Belt state Pennsylvania, turnout of noncollege whites significantly increased (www.americanprogress.org/issues/ democracy/reports/2017/11/01/441926/voter-trends-in-2016/). In Pennsylvania, for example, noncollege white turnout increased by 4.3%. Since turnout models must be based on past data, there was no way for the pollsters to predict this increase in noncollege white turnout. African American turnout, a group that favored Clinton, also dropped in 2016.

- Many pollsters reach voters by dialing randomly selected phone numbers. Noncollege whites are less likely to answer the phone than other voting groups (www.npr.org/2016/11/14/502014643/4-possible-reasons-the-polls-got-it-so-wrong-this-year), so this fact probably caused Trump's strongest supporters to be underrepresented in many polls.

- Even in 2016, it was difficult for pollsters to capture a late surge for a candidate. In key states, late deciders broke for Trump (www.washingtonpost .com/news/the-fix/wp/2016/11/17/how-america-decided-at-the-very-last-moment-to-elect-donald-trump/). In Pennsylvania, Trump won late deciders by 17%. In Michigan, Trump won late deciders by 11%, and in Wisconsin, Trump won late deciders by 29%. Most state polls were completed between three and seven days before the election. If you adjust these polls for the late deciders, then the polls would have nailed Trump's Rust Belt surprise.

How Did the Pollsters Miss the 2016 UK Brexit Victory?

In June 2016, the United Kingdom voted to leave the European Union. Brexit won by 4%, whereas the average of polls indicated that "Remain" would win by 1%. This 5% error is outside the 3% margin of error associated with polls, so what went wrong? According to *The Telegraph* (www.telegraph.co.uk/news/2016/06/24/ eu-referendum-how-right-or-wrong-were-the-polls/), the following problems might have distorted the poll results:

- The turnout of 72% was much higher than pollsters anticipated, and the pollsters' modeling of turnout was less accurate than anticipated. Older voters (60% who supported Brexit; see lordashcroftpolls.com/2019/03/

a-reminder-of-how-britain-voted-in-the-eu-referendum-and-why/) turned out at a higher rate than expected, whereas younger voters who mostly (73%) opposed Brexit turned out at a lower rate than expected.

- Phone polls were less accurate than online polls. Phone polls are known to have a bigger problem reaching low-education voters, and these voters were more likely to support Brexit.

- There were many late deciding voters (24%, according to `lordashcroftpolls` `.com/2019/03/a-reminder-of-how-britain-voted-in-the-eu-referendum-` `and-why/`), and possibly because the Brexit vote had no historical precedent, pollsters had trouble modeling the final vote of the late deciders.

Rating Polls

FiveThirtyEight.com rates polls (`projects.fivethirtyeight.com/pollster-` `ratings/`). In the file `PollsterStatsFull.xlsx`, we downloaded the ratings on January 2, 2020. For an explanation of the rating methodology, see `fivethir-` `tyeight.com/features/how-fivethirtyeight-calculates-pollster-ratings/`. Without diving into the weeds, two key factors in the FiveThirtyEight.com ratings are *simple plus minus* and *bias*. For example, the Monmouth Poll has a simple +/– of –1.9%, which means after adjusting for sample size, types of races polled, and other factors, the Monmouth Poll performed an average of 1.9% better than expected. (This is good.) On average, the Monmouth Poll is biased 1.3% in favor of the Democrats, which means that on average Democrats performed 1.3% better than Monmouth predicted. Overall, Monmouth received the highest rating (A+). On the other hand, the Rasmussen Poll had a simple +/– of +0.3% and an average Republican bias of 1.5%, which led to a C+ rating. The online Survey Monkey Poll received a D–, due to a 5.1% Democratic bias and a simple +/– of 2.3%.

How Did Buzzfeed Make the Dress Go Viral?

On February 26, 2015, Buzzfeed (`https://knowyourmeme.com/memes/the-dress-what-color-is-this-dress`) created a post that showed a dress that appeared to some people as black and blue (33%) and to other people as white and gold (67%). Through Tumblr, Twitter, Facebook, and other social media, "The Dress" rapidly spread, and by March 1, 2015, the original Buzzfeed post had over 37 million views. How does a site like Buzzfeed quickly identify that a post will go viral? A key metric used by Buzzfeed and other social media sites is

$$\text{Social Lift} = 1 + \frac{Number\ of\ Social\ Views}{Number\ of\ Seed\ Views}$$

As an example, suppose that a Buzzfeed post is clicked on the Buzzfeed site 100,000 times and that the post is clicked 50,000 times on social media sites. Then the post has a social lift of 1 + 50,000 / 100,000 = 1.5.

Only Buzzfeed knows the social lift for each of their posts, but according to my daughter, Jennifer Winston, who was working at Buzzfeed when the dress went viral, highly viral posts have a social lift of 20 or more. Whenever Buzzfeed posts a quiz or story, Buzzfeed employees are monitoring minute by minute the social lift. If a post has a high social lift, then Buzzfeed employees spring into action. The first few minutes after the initial posting of "The Dress" article are described on FiveThirtyEight's podcast (`fivethirtyeight.com/features/podcast-how-buzzfeed-made-thedress-go-viral/`). Buzzfeed social media manager Samir Mezrahi was working the afternoon of February 26, 2015, and heard employees engaged in vigorous arguments about the color of the dress. He tweeted it out from @Buzzfeed, and the likes and retweets were off the charts. Once a post does well on Twitter, Buzzfeed often posts it to Facebook. Mezrahi first posted the dress as a photo and saw that the engagement from that post was lower (based on the Twitter response) than expected. Then Mezrahi posted a link to the original Buzzfeed article—and the rest is history.

Measuring Instagram Engagement

In March 2020, Instagram had more than 1 billion users (`www.omnicoreagency.com/instagram-statistics/`). On an average day, more than 500 million people use Instagram. If you post to Instagram, how can you tell if your post has done well? The usual measure is *engagement*. The engagement of an Instagram post is (Likes + Comments) / Followers. An engagement rate above 6% is considered very high (see `https://www.plannthat.com/calculate-engagement-rate-on-instagram/#:~:text=Facebook%20%26%20Twitter%20attract%200.5%25%20%E2%80%93,you%20to%20much%20bigger%20opportunities`. As an example, my daughter (follow her at @Jenerous!) has 187,000 followers, and a post she put up after the 2020 Screen Actors Guild Awards (at that time she had 112,000 followers) received 8,790 likes and 3,005 comments for an engagement of (8,790 +3,005) / 112,000 = 10%.

Tweets Do Not Always Go Viral Immediately

Unlike "The Dress," many tweets take a while to go viral. As an example, on September 24, 2015, my daughter, Jen Winston, "won the Internet" (see `www.dailykos.com/stories/2019/9/25/1887905/-Woman-turns-the-tables-on-Trump-and-thereby-wins-today-s-internet`). Her tweet, "What were you wearing?" eventually got 39,500 retweets and 153,200 likes, but unlike "The Dress," the tweet did not quickly explode. After one day, the tweet had about 15,000 likes, but within a week, the tweet had nearly 150,000 likes. The tweet is still gaining likes. When actor Mark Ruffalo liked the tweet, many likes quickly appeared. This illustrates how people with lots of followers can really help a tweet spread.

Many experts in social media have studied factors that can make a tweet have more success. For example (see `blog.hootsuite.com/twitter-statistics/`), it appears that adding video to a tweet will multiply engagement (retweets, comments, and likes) tenfold. Also, adding a hashtag (#) to a tweet will double engagement.

Do the First Few Days Predict the Future of a Meme?

In 1976, noted scientist and atheist Richard Dawkins wrote an influential book titled *The Selfish Gene*. In the book, Dawkins defined a meme to be a "self-replicating unit of transmission." In the June 1993 issue of *Wired Magazine,* journalist Mike Godwin proposed the term *Internet meme* to refer to ideas that spread in a viral fashion through the Internet. Now everyone drops the word "Internet" and refers to images or posts that spread widely through the Internet as "memes." With their proprietary metrics, Buzzfeed knew almost instantly that "The Dress" would go viral. I scoured the Internet in vain, looking for a methodology that allows you to predict, a few days after a post first went viral, how many searches the post would generate in the first 30 days. Christian Bauckhage (see "Insight into Internet Memes," *Proceedings of the Fifth International Conference on Weblogs and Social Media,* 2011, accessed at `https://www.semanticscholar.org/paper/Insights-into-Internet-Memes-Bauckhage/eaeecfe9501e96b78b6c6fc073d0822c9c0c7b13`) developed a model that would fit (after searches had died down) the number of monthly Google searches. However, what you really want is a model that, in real-time would tell you after knowing perhaps three days of Google searches how many total searches will ensue. Recent research by Xiaojia Guo, Kenneth C. Lichtendahl, and Yael Grushka-Cockayne (see "An Exponential Smoothing Model with a Life Cycle Trend" at `papers.ssrn.com/sol3/papers.cfm?abstract_id=2805244`) appears to make progress on this important problem. Unfortunately, their analysis uses an advanced methodology that is beyond the scope of this book.

In an attempt to look for a pattern in how Google searches for memes progress over time, I looked at 18 Internet memes (see Figure 35.1 and the workbook `Memes.xlsx`). From Google Trends, I found the day with the most Google searches (a value of 100 on Google Trends). Then, I computed the total relative number of searches for that day and the next 29 days by adding up the Google Trend indices for those 30 days. Finally, I computed the fraction of the searches for those 30 days that occurred during the first three and four days. Note that the two memes that got the highest percentage of their searches in the first three or four days ("The Dress" and "Grumpy Cat") were posted by Buzzfeed. I think this indicates Buzzfeed's great ability to "spread the word" quickly. Note that "Gangnam Style" and "Bye Felicia" did not have a larger percentage of their 30-day searches in the first three or four days. If you go to Google Trends, you will see that both these memes had many searches after 30 days, whereas "The Dress" burned out rather quickly. I guess Buzzfeed subscribes to Neil Young's view that "it's better to burn out than fade away."

	N	O	P	Q	R
5	Meme	3 days	4 days	ratio	total
6	The Dress	64.10%	68.91%	1.075	312
7	Metoo	61.59%	65.23%	1.05914	302
8	Grumpy Cat	76.92%	80.54%	1.047059	221
9	Old Spice	31.48%	38.40%	1.220096	664
10	Imma let you finish	33.58%	40.26%	1.199134	688
11	Delete your account	52.26%	57.42%	1.098765	465
12	Old Town Road	31.48%	38.40%	1.220096	664
13	Honey Badger	35.43%	40.68%	1.148148	381
14	Dabbing	31.48%	38.40%	1.220096	664
15	Hater's gonna say its fake	39.54%	39.54%	1	306
16	Bye Felicia	15.54%	19.89%	1.279863	1885
17	Gangnam Style	15.67%	18.53%	1.182609	1468
18	Nyan Cat	11.35%	14.49%	1.276596	2070
19	Dancing Baby	38.46%	44.90%	1.167347	637
20	Keyboard Cat	17.25%	20.58%	1.193237	1200
21	Pepe the Frog	44.58%	49.37%	1.107345	397
22	Nigerian Prince	36.19%	40.46%	1.118227	561
23	Troll Face	16.09%	17.60%	1.093897	1324

Figure 35.1: Searches for Internet memes during the first three and four days the memes went viral

Predicting *Game of Thrones* TV Ratings

Hollywood moguls who underwrite TV shows and movies would love to be able to predict the TV show's ratings or a movie's revenues. It seems reasonable that the number of people searching the Internet for information on the show or movie in advance of its release should correlate well with the number of viewers of the TV show or the number of people paying to see the movie. Fortunately, Google Trends allows you to easily download into Excel information about the frequency of searches for any search term. In this chapter, we will show you how to use Google Trends and close the chapter by using Google Trends data to forecast the ratings of the premiere episode for multiple seasons of *Game of Thrones* (GOT).

What Does Google Trends Tell Us?

If you are interested in the search history for a particular term, you can go to Google Trends (`trends.google.com/trends/`) and type in one (or more) search terms and get the relative number of searches for that term for any time range going back to 2004. You can choose the desired location for the searches. (We chose the United States.) Choosing Custom Time Range From The Past 12 Months drop-down-list allows you to select any desired time range. If you choose a time range containing at most 90 days, then you can download a comma-separated value file (a file with a .csv extension) which contains a *daily* query index. When you open a .csv file, you may then save it as an Excel file. For a given region, the query index is based on the query share, which is the total number of queries for the search term in that region divided by the total number of queries in that region for the relevant time period. Google Trends scales the query index so that the maximum query share is scaled to 100. Using the Compare feature, you can add more search terms and overlay the results.

To illustrate Google Trends output, on April 24, 2020, we entered as search terms the singer Taylor Swift and former *Suits* star Meghan Markle. Markle married Prince Harry on May 19, 2018. The resulting chart for the last five years is shown in Figure 36.1. Note that Markle had more searches only during the time periods of December 3-9, 2017 (her engagement was announced on November 27, 2017) and May 6-26, 2018 (the royal wedding was May 19, 2018). Clicking the down arrow shown in Figure 36.1 downloads a comma-separated value file containing the data used to generate the chart.

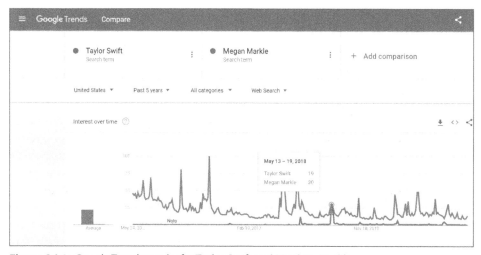

Figure 36.1: Google Trends results for Taylor Swift and Meghan Markle

Predicting the Present with Google Trends

Governments release economic statistics for a month, quarter, or year several weeks after the time period ends. An investment analyst whose job is to predict future stock prices for auto stocks would have an edge on competitors if at the end of a month, they had the best prediction model to estimate actual vehicle sales before the government released the actual figures. Hyunyoung Choi and noted economist Hal Varian (see "Predicting the Present with Google Trends," *Economic Record*, vol. 88, June 2012, pages 2–9) show how to use search results to develop improved forecasts of monthly U.S. motor vehicle sales (see `fred. stlouisfed.org/series/RSMVPD` for the data). Choi and Varian used data for the period January 2004 through June 2011.

Define

$$Y_t = \text{Sales during month t}$$

Choi and Varian begin by trying to predict LN Y_t by using LN(Y_{t-1}) and LN(Y_{t-12}) as independent variables. They found that the P-values for both independent variables were less than 1 in 10,000 and found the best-fitting equation

$$LN(Y_t) = 0.67266 + 0.64342 * LN(Y_{t-1}) + 0.29565 * LN(Y_{t-12})$$

to have an R^2 of 71.85%.

The authors found that incorporating as independent variables the Google Trends Index available at the end of each month for the search terms Trucks and SUVs and Automotive Insurance enables you to create improved predictions for Y_t. The best-fitting equation using these four independent variables is

$$LN(Y_t) = -0.45798 + 0.61947 * LN(Y_{t-1}) + 0.42865 * LN(Y_{t-12}) + 1.05721 *$$

$$(\text{Truck and SUV Query Index during Month t}) - 0.52966 *$$

$$(\text{Automotive Insurance Query Index during Month t})$$

This equation increases the R^2 to 81.79% and, more importantly, reduces the standard error of the estimate by 17.5%.

For obvious reasons, Choi and Varian call this use of Google Trends data *nowcasting*.

Using Google Trends to Forecast *GOT* Ratings

The HBO show *Game of Thrones* (*GOT*) was not my cup of tea, but during its run from 2010–2019, the show dominated Monday watercooler conversation. The series finale was the most watched HBO show ever. In this section, we use Google Trends data on *GOT* searches to predict the U.S. ratings for the first episode of Seasons 3–8. The worksheet Monthly Searches in the `AllThrones.xlsx` workbook contains the monthly query indices for each month during the time period January 2011 through April 2019. April 2019 (the first month of *GOT*'s final season) had a query index of 100, which indicates that April 2019 had the largest query index for any month. In the worksheet Daily Searches, we individually downloaded the daily query indices for the 90 days preceding the first episode of Seasons 3–8 of *GOT*. Note that each of these searches will contain a query index of 100 for the day during the downloaded period with the most searches. We cannot use Google Trends to determine the *actual number* of searches on each day, but we will show how to determine the relative number of searches for the 30 days before each season premiere. Then we will try to predict the number of viewers for the premiere episode from our relative number of searches.

To illustrate our approach, note that Season 6 of *GOT* premiered on April 24, 2016. The Google Trends Index for March 2016 was 13, and for April 2016, it was 37. The 30 days before April 24 are April 1–23 and March 25–31. From our daily data, we found that 26.4% of March *GOT* searches were March 25–31 and 53.6% of April *GOT* searches were April 1–23. Therefore, we can create a relative index for *GOT* searches in the 30 days before the Season 6 premiere as 0.536 * 37 + 0.264 * 13 = 23.24. The data for Seasons 3–8 of GOT is summarized in Figure 36.2.

	K	L	M	N	O	P
3	Premiere Date	Year	Sum query index 30 days before	Prediction	Premiere Rating (millions)	
4	3/31/2013	2013	16.05	4.16358	4.37	
5	4/6/2014	2014	21.55	7.13908	6.64	
6	4/12/2015	2015	21.39		8	Easter April 5!
7	4/24/2016	2016	23.24	7.907557	7.94	
8	7/16/2017	2017	28.21	9.770313	10.11	
9	4/14/2019	2019	39.84	11.81254	11.76	

Figure 36.2: *GOT* web searches and ratings

We would like to use the 30-day query indices in Column M to predict the ratings of each season's premiere (in Column N). Note that the 2015 searches were smaller than the 2014 searches, but the 2015 premiere rating was much larger than the 2014 premiere rating. This would seem to indicate that increased searches do not predict larger ratings. Note, however, that in 2015 Easter was on April 5, seven days before the GOT premiere aired. Easter surely generated many searches, and since Google Trend's query index is based on all searches during the relevant time period, the March 2015 and April 2015 query indices for *GOT* are deflated by the increased searches for Easter. Also, many Americans would have paid more attention to Easter than *GOT*, and this would have also reduced the query indices for the month before the premiere. For this reason, we will omit the 2015 data point from our subsequent analysis. Using the Excel trend curve feature (see the "Excel Calculations" section), we found the quadratic formula that best fit the remaining five data points (see Figure 36.3).

As shown in Figure 36.3, the following equation does a great job of predicting *GOT* ratings, with our average absolute error being around 3%:

$$\text{Predicted Premiere Rating} = 0.012 * \left(\text{Searches}^2\right) + 0.9922 * \text{Searches} - 8.6685$$

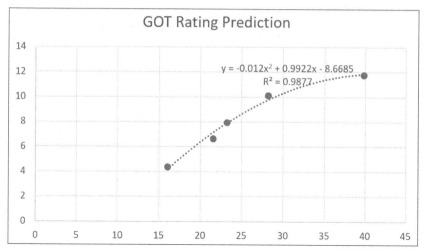

Figure 36.3: Prediction equation for *GOT* ratings based on web searches

Other researchers have used, with great success, the number of tweets prior to a movie's release to predict a movie's opening weekend box office (see www.fastcompany.com/1604125/twitter-predicts-box-office-sales-better-prediction-market-updated). We expect in the future that web searches and social media data will be used more frequently to predict quantities of interest such as product sales.

Excel Calculations

To use the Excel trend curve to predict *GOT* ratings, proceed as follows:

1. Delete the 2015 data point and then select the remaining data in the range T13:U17 of the worksheet Monthly Searches.

2. Select the Scatter chart icon from the Insert tab and choose the first option.

3. Select the data in the chart, right-click a data point, select Add Trendline, chose the Polynomial (2) option, and then select the Display Equation On Chart and Display R-squared Value On Chart checkboxes.

The resulting trend curve is shown in Figure 36.3.

Part

III

Why Did It Happened?

In This Part

Does Smoking Cause Lung Cancer?

I am sure everyone reading this book believes that smoking causes lung cancer. Doctors and statisticians followed a long and winding road before this conclusion became generally accepted. As late as 1960, only one third of all U.S. doctors believed that smoking caused lung cancer (see `www.ncbi.nlm.nih.gov/pubmed/22345227`). In this chapter, we will show you how the world became convinced that smoking causes lung cancer.

Correlation and Causation Redux

As first discussed in Chapter 8, "Modeling Relationships Between Two Variables," two quantitative variables, X and Y, have a correlation that is always between –1 and +1. *Correlation* measures the strength of the linear relationship between X and Y. A correlation near +1 tells us that when X is larger (smaller) than average, Y tends to be larger (smaller) than average. A correlation near –1 tells us that when X is larger (smaller) than average, then Y tends to be smaller (larger) than average. Many people believe that a correlation near +1 or –1 implies a *causal* relationship between X and Y. This is often untrue. The website `www.tylervigen.com/spurious-correlations` contains many examples of highly correlated variables for which there is surely no cause effect relationship. For example, between 2000 and 2009, there is a 0.9926 correlation between the divorce rate in Maine and per capita consumption of margarine! Sometimes a third variable can explain a correlation. For example, if we let X = number of bars in a city and Y = number of churches in a city, X and Y will have a correlation very near +1, because large cities have lots of bars and lots of churches and small cities have few bars and few churches. This correlation is driven by the size of the cities, not by any causal relationship between bars and churches.

The Key Evidence

Recall that we met Austin Bradford Hill in our Chapter 19, "Evidence-Based Medicine," discussion of streptomycin. The pioneering paper by Richard Doll and Bradford Hill ("Lung Cancer and Other Causes of Death in Relation to Smoking," *British Medical Journal*, vol. 5001, November 10, 1956, pages 1071–1081) began to make the case that smoking causes lung cancer. In 1951, Doll and Hill sent questionnaires to 59,600 British physicians asking the doctors their sex, age, amount of tobacco smoked, method of smoking, and whether they had continued to smoke or quit smoking. Male physicians submitted 34,494 responses. (Few of the women smoked.) The authors painstakingly tracked down the cause of death for every doctor dying during the next 53 months. Of the approximately 6,000 male nonsmokers, only one died of lung cancer, and of the approximately 28,000 male smokers, 83 died of lung cancer (see Gilbert Welch's *Less Medicine, More Health*, Beacon Press, 2015, page 7). Using the resampling approach discussed in Chapter 19, we find that if nonsmokers and smokers die of lung cancer at the same rate, then there is less than one chance in 10,000 that at least 83 of the observed lung cancer deaths would occur among smokers. This appears to be pretty strong evidence that smokers die of lung cancer at a higher rate than nonsmokers. Putting it another way, the likelihood that a smoker died of lung cancer was 83 / 28,000 and the likelihood that a nonsmoker died of lung cancer was 1 / 6,000. This implies that a smoker was $\dfrac{83 / 28,000}{1 / 6000} = 17.8$ times as likely to die of lung cancer as a nonsmoker. The factor 17.8 is the *relative risk* of lung cancer for smokers relative to nonsmokers.

Doll and Hill marshaled more evidence to support the case that smoking causes lung cancer:

- Per 1,000 person-years (for men aged at least 35), the death rate for nonsmokers was 0.07, and the death rate for smokers was 0.90.

- Per 1,000 person-years for light smokers (1–14 cigarettes per day), the lung cancer death rate was 0.47; for medium smokers (15–24 cigarettes per day), the lung cancer death rate was 0.86; for heavy smokers (at least 25 cigarettes per day), the death rate was 1.66!

In short, the more a man smoked, the more likely it was the man would die of lung cancer.

Could Air Pollution Have Caused Lung Cancer?

Since air pollution increased post–World War II with growing population and industrial production, some public health experts felt that air pollution might be a significant cause of lung cancer. Doll and Hill examined this possibility ("A Study of the Aetiology of Carcinoma of the Lung," *British Medical Journal,* vol. 2 no. 4797, 1952, pages 1271–1286). During the period January 1950–February 1952, British lung cancer patients under 75 were interviewed and asked about their smoking habits, place of residence, and social status. Doll and Hill found that living in a rural area (presumably having less air pollution than an urban area) was not associated with a significantly decreased risk of lung cancer. They also found that living near a gasworks (and inhaling fumes from the gasworks) did not increase lung cancer risk. Finally, they also found that the type of heating (gas, coal, electric, radiator, or other) was not associated with an increased risk of lung cancer. Together these results seem to imply that the quality of the air you breath was not a significant contributor to the incidence of lung cancer.

The Cigarette Companies Hit Back

Sharon Milberger et al. (see "Tobacco Manufacturers' Defence Against Plaintiffs' Claims of Cancer Causation: Throwing Mud at the Wall and Hoping Some of It Will Stick," *Tobacco Control,* 2006; 15 (Suppl IV): iv17–iv26) found that in 21 of 34 cases where plaintiffs sued tobacco companies for damages due to lung cancer deaths, the cigarette companies used the defense that the statistical association of smoking with lung cancer does not imply causation. Note that the gold standard of randomized controlled clinical trials (RCTs) explored in Chapter 19 cannot be applied to study the smoking and lung cancer link. You cannot flip a coin and tell half of men to smoke and the other half not to smoke. The impossibility of using RCTs allows deniers of causality to argue that there is some unknown difference between smokers and nonsmokers that causes lung cancer. The most notable defender of this view was the great British statistician (and smoker) Ronald Fisher. According to the great statistician Bradley Efron (see "R. A. Fisher in the 21st Century," *Statistical Science,* vol. 13, no. 2, 1998, pages 95–122), Fisher was the greatest statistician of the 20th century. In a 1958 letter to the prestigious journal *Nature,* Fisher stated that genetic factors (perhaps a "smoking gene"?) partially determined the likelihood that a person would smoke. He found that 24% of identical twins had different smoking habits, whereas 51% of fraternal twins had different smoking habits. Since fraternal twins have genetic differences and identical twins do not, Fisher concluded that a person's genetic makeup influenced their smoking choices. Fisher used this association between genetic makeup and smoking choice to conjecture that there might be a gene that predisposed people to smoke, and the same gene might make people more susceptible to lung cancer. If this were the case, then perhaps cigarettes are not an important cause of lung cancer.

The brilliant American statistician Jerome Cornfield (1912–1979) destroyed Fisher's argument (see Cornfield et al., "Smoking and Lung Cancer: Recent Evidence and a Discussion of Some Questions," *Journal of the National Cancer Institute*, 1959, vol. 22, pages 173–203).

To understand Cornfield's argument, let

- E = An observable effect (lung cancer)
- A = An observed factor (smoking) that has no effect on lung cancer
- B = An unobservable factor (a lung cancer gene?) that is positively associated with smoking
- R = Relative risk of smokers getting lung cancer compared to nonsmokers; Doll and Hill found R = 17.85

Cornfield proved an inequality (see a proof in the "Excel Calculations" section) that implies that the fraction of smokers having the unobservable factor must be at least R (again here 17.85!) times as large as the fraction of nonsmokers having the unobservable factor. It seems absurd to believe that smokers are 18 times as likely as nonsmokers to have an undiscovered lung cancer gene. Fisher never responded to Cornfield's argument.

We close by noting that proving causality is extremely difficult. If you want to learn more about causality, check out the excellent book *The Book of Why* (Judea Pearl and Dana Mackenzie, Basic Books, 2018).

Excel Calculations

In what follows, we give a proof of Cornfield's inequality.
Define

$$P(E \mid B) = r1, P(E \mid \text{Not } B) = r2. \text{ Since B is proposed to cause E}, r1 > r2.$$

$$P(B \mid A) = p1 \text{ and } P(B \mid \text{Not } A) = p2. \text{ Since A and B are assumed}$$
$$\text{to be positively associated}, p1 > p2.$$

Then:

$$P(E \mid A) = p1r1 + (1 - p1)r2 \text{ and } P(E \mid \text{Not } A) = p2r1 + (1 - p2)r2$$

Let R = Relative Risk of Lung Cancer for smokers relative to nonsmokers. Then:

$$R = \frac{p1r1 + (1 - p1)r2}{p2r1 + (1 - p2)r2}$$

Since p1 > p2 and r1 > r2, it follows that R > 1.

$$\text{Now } (1) \left(\frac{p1}{p2} \right) - R = \frac{p1p2r1 + p1r2*(1 - p2) - p1p2r1 - p2r2*(1 - p1)}{p2*(p2r1 + (1 - p2)r2)}$$

The numerator of (1) will be positive if

$$(2)\, p1 * r2 * (1 - p2) > p2 * r2 * (1 - p1)$$

Since p1 > p2, we know that (1 – p2) > (1– p1), so equation (2) is true, and the numerator of (1) is positive.

This means that p1 / p2 is greater than R. But p1 / p2 is the ratio of the fraction of smokers who have the lung cancer gene to the fraction of nonsmokers who have the lung cancer gene. Based on Doll and Hill's data, R = 17.75. This implies p1 / p2 > 17.75, which is unreasonable.

Why Are the Houston Rockets a Good Basketball Team?

In 2000, my former student Mark Cuban hired noted sports statistician Jeff Sagarin and me (see `twitter.com/jeopardy/status/1083830913077788672?lang=en`) to analyze Dallas Mavericks players and lineups. According to Mark, we were the first NBA data scientists. Today, every NBA team has an analytics department (see `www .nbastuffer.com/analytics101/nba-teams-that-have-analytics-department/`). Teams are pretty quiet about what their analytics departments work on, but to the casual fan probably the most visible impact of analytics departments is the huge increase in three-point attempts since 2000. As shown in Figure 38.1 (see the workbook `3PtShooting.xlsx`), three-point attempts have more than doubled since 2000. In fact, during the 2017–2018 season, more than half of the Houston Rockets' field goal attempts were three-pointers. As you can see, three-point shooting percentage has not changed much since 2000, so increased accuracy did not cause the increase in the number of three-point attempts.

In this chapter, we will show how middle school math explains the rise of the three-pointer and why the Houston Rockets have consistently been a top 5 NBA team.

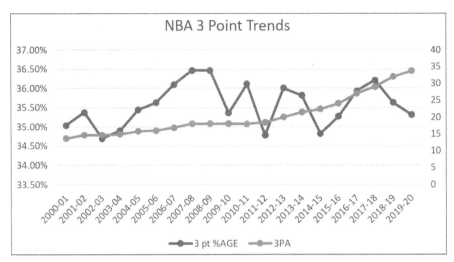

Figure 38.1: Trends in NBA 3-point shooting

NBA Shooting Math 101

In many NBA ads, NBA players tell you "It's a make or miss league." It's not as catchy, but the players should probably say, "It's a point per shot league." During the 2017–2018 and 2018–2019 seasons, the Houston Rockets won more regular season games (118) than any NBA team. We will ignore the fact that they flamed out in the playoffs (they missed 27 straight three-pointers in their 2018 Game 7 loss to the Golden State Warriors). Most fans consider the Rockets an offensive juggernaut. The Rockets are terrific on offense, but it is not because they are a great shooting team; *it's because they take great shots.*

Of course, skills besides shooting offense and defense matter in basketball. In his book *Basketball on Paper: Rules and Tools for Performance Analysis* (Potomac Books, 2004), Dean Oliver, now a Washington Wizards assistant coach in charge of analytics, came up with four factors that explain a basketball team's performance:

- EFG Factor = Effective Field Goal Percentage (EFG) for a Team's Offense – Effective Field Goal Percentage for a Team's Opponents
  EFG is simply Points Scored on Shots / (2 * Shots). For example, consider a team that makes 40 baskets in 100 attempts, and 10 of the baskets are three-pointers. They scored 90 points, so their EFG = 90 / 200 = 45%. This is reasonable because without the three-pointers, the team shot 40% and the 10 made three-pointers add 10 points, which is the same as making five more two-pointers.

- Rebounding Differential = Offensive Rebounding Percentage for Team – Offensive Rebounding Percentage for Opponents

- Turnover Differential = Turnovers per 100 Possessions by Opponents – Turnovers per 100 Possessions by Team

- Free Throws Made Differential = (Free Throws Made by Team) / (Team Field Goal Attempts) – (Free Throws Made by Opponent) / (Opponent's Team Field Goal Attempts)

The EFG factor is by far the most important, accounting for 40% of variation in team performance (see `www.basketball-reference.com/about/factors.html`).

The great site `Basketball-reference.com` gives for every team and every NBA player the following information about their shooting:

- Fraction of shots taken from five distances: 0–3 feet, 3–10 feet, 10–16 feet, 16 feet to three-point land, and three-pointers

- For each of these shot locations, the percentage of shots made

Figure 38.2 (see the worksheet 5 teams in the workbook `RocketsShooting.xlsx`) summarizes this data for the 2017–2018 Bulls, Warriors, Rockets, Raptors, and Wizards. Cells M38:Q38 of the worksheet Shooting 17_18 gives league average data for the 2017–2018 season. *The key fact to note is that 0–3-foot shots yield on average 2 * (.658) = 1.32 points per shot and three-pointers yield on average 3 * (.362) = 1.09 points per shot. Any other shot between three feet and three-point land yields only around 2 * (.4) = .8 points per shot. Thus, two-point shots not near the rim are usually bad shots* (all our data is from `Basketball-Reference.com`). As you will see, the Rockets understand this better than any other team.

	B	C	D	E	F	G	H	I	J	K	L	M	N	O	P
1						Shot					Shooting				
2						Frequency					Percentage				
3					Pts on shot		2	2	2	2	3				
4	How Good	How well		Actual Pts	Expected Points per										
	our shots	we shoot	Team	Per Shot	shot	0-3	3-10	10-16	16 to 3	3pt	0-3	3-10	10-16	16 to 3	3P
5	-0.01	-0.04	Chicago Bulls	1.00	1.03	0.25	0.17	0.10	0.14	0.35	0.62	0.39	0.39	0.38	0.36
6	-0.01	0.10	Golden State Warriors	1.14	1.04	0.27	0.11	0.14	0.14	0.34	0.71	0.42	0.49	0.46	0.39
7	0.05	0.01	Houston Rockets	1.10	1.09	0.29	0.10	0.06	0.04	0.50	0.67	0.37	0.45	0.43	0.36
8	0.02	0.02	Toronto Raptors	1.08	1.06	0.29	0.16	0.10	0.07	0.38	0.68	0.41	0.43	0.42	0.36
9	-0.03	0.03	Washington Wizards	1.05	1.02	0.24	0.16	0.14	0.15	0.31	0.67	0.42	0.44	0.41	0.38
10			League Average	1.04	1.04	0.28	0.16	0.11	0.12	0.34	0.66	0.39	0.42	0.40	0.36
11				0		0-3	3-10	10-16	16 to 3	3pt	0-3	3-10	10-16	16 to 3	3P
12					0 mean										
13					1.04										

Figure 38.2: 2017–2018 NBA shooting

In many of the following calculations, we used Excel's great SUMPRODUCT function (see the "Excel Calculations" section later in this chapter).

We first want to calculate how many points per shot a team's shooting is better or worse than the league average and then proceed as follows:

1. Determine (based on the league average shooting percentage for each distance and shooting frequency from each distance) the league average points per shot. For 2017–2018, the League Average Points per Shot = 1.04.

2. Based on a team's frequency of shots by distance, determine how many points per shot the team would get if they shot league average percentages from each distance. This is the team's Expected Points per Shot.

3. Compute for each team their *actual* points per shot.

Now we can deconstruct each team's shooting into two parts:

- How Good Are Our Shots = (Expected Points Per Team Shot if team made their shots at a league average percentage) – (League Average Points Per Shot).

- How Well We Shoot = (Actual Team Points Per Shot) – (Expected Points Per Team Shot if team made their shots at league average percentage).

The following steps illustrate the calculations by focusing on the 2017–2018 Houston Rockets:

1. Compute the league average points per shot:

$$(1)\, \text{League Average Points per Shot} = 2*(.281)*(.658) + 2*(.156)*(.394)$$

$$+2*(.106)*(.415) + 2*(.12)*(.4) + 3*(.337)*(.362) = 1.04 \text{ points per shot.}$$

To illustrate the logic behind these (and all subsequent) computations, consider 100 representative shots. How many points will come from shots at 0-3 feet? 100*(.281) of these shots will be from 0-3 feet, and each of those shots has a .658 chance of going in. Therefore, on 100 representative shots, an average NBA team can expect to score 2*(.281)*(.658)*100 points on 0-3 foot shots. Per shot, this yields 2*(.281)*(.658) points contributed by 0-3 foot shots. Therefore, summing each term in (1) yields expected points per shot (1.04) for an average NBA team.

2. Compute each team's points per shot assuming that from each distance they shot like an average shooter.

Cells G7:K7 of Figure 38.2 give the fraction of Houston's shot from each distance. Therefore, if the Rockets shot their shots like the average NBA shooter, they would expect to score an average of 2*(.288)*(.658) + 2*(.103)*(.394) + 2*(.062)*(.415) + 2*(.044)*(.4) + 3*(.503)*(.362) = 1.09 points per shot. This indicates that the Rockets' shots were on average 1.09 – 1.04 = .05 points better than average shots.

3. Compute each team's actual average points per shot.

Using the data in row 7, we find that the Rockets' actual average points per shot equals 2 * (.288) * (.669) + 2 * (.103) * (.369) + 2 * (.062) * (.454) + 2 * (.044) * (.43) + 3 * (.363) = 1.10.

Since average shooters would score 1.09 points per shot on the Rockets shots, and the Rockets scored 1.10 points per shot, the Rockets shot 1.10 – 1.09 = 0.01 points better than average shooters on the shots they took.

We can now interpret Columns B and C of Figure 38.2:

- The Bulls shots were only .01 points per shot worse than average, but they shot .04 points per shot worse than expected on the shots they took.

- The Warriors shots were .01 points per shot worse than average, *but they shot an amazing .10 points per shot better than expected on those shots.* No other team shot more than .04 points per shot better than expected!

- The Rockets shots were .05 points per shot better than average, but the Rockets shot only .01 points better than average on the shots they took. No other team took shots that were more than .03 points per shot better than average.

- The Toronto Raptors took shots that were .02 points per shot better than average, and they shot .02 points per shot better than expected.

- Surprisingly, the hapless Wizards shot .03 points better than expected on their shots, but they canceled this out by taking shots that were .03 points worse than average.

Zach LaVine Battles the Bulls' Analytics Department

Before the start of the 2019–2020 NBA season, the Bulls' analytics department told forward Zach LaVine to take fewer mid-range shots (see `chicago.suntimes.com/bulls/2019/10/11/20910675/the-bulls-zach-lavine-is-not-thrilled-with-his-analytics-department`). From the data shown in Figure 38.3, you can calculate that during the 2017–2018 and 2018–2019 seasons, LaVine took around one-third of his shots between 3 feet and three-point land. In 2017–2018, he averaged 0.54 points per shot on these shots, and in 2018–2019, he averaged 0.64 points per shot on these shots. So LaVine's team gave up at least 0.4 points per shot on these mid-range twos. LaVine shot around the league average on three-point shots and a little below the league average on 0–3-foot shots, so these were reasonably good shots. No wonder the Bulls' analytics department recommended fewer mid-range shots. Midway through the 2019–2020 season, LaVine had reduced his mid-range twos to 23%, but his percentage on mid-range twos has dropped back down to an abysmal 27%.

	C	D	E	F	G	H	I	J	K	L	M
5	Season	0-3	3-10	10-16	16-3pt	3P	0-3	3-10	10-16	16-3pt	3P
6	2014-15		0.276	0.117	0.066	0.292	0.247	0.631	0.316	0.333	0.354	0.341
7	2015-16		0.277	0.09	0.055	0.249	0.33	0.677	0.349	0.302	0.351	0.389
8	2016-17		0.272	0.061	0.049	0.182	0.437	0.637	0.419	0.343	0.411	0.387
9	2017-18		0.318	0.121	0.059	0.155	0.346	0.549	0.233	0.381	0.255	0.341
10	2018-19		0.396	0.127	0.067	0.127	0.283	0.653	0.264	0.303	0.382	0.374
11	2019-20		0.36	0.09	0.051	0.093	0.406	0.62	0.146	0.234	0.4	0.388
12	Career		0.324	0.1	0.058	0.179	0.339	0.638	0.279	0.307	0.365	0.377

Figure 38.3: Zach LaVine's shooting statistics

Conclusion

The best teams in NBA history play around 10 points per game better than average. The Rockets took 84 shots per game during the 2017–2018 season, so their shot quality made them .05 * 84 = 4.2 points better than average. That is almost half the distance from average to greatness.

The file RocketsShooting.xlsx has an analysis of the shooting performance of all teams during both the 2017–2018 and 2018–2019 seasons.

Excel Calculations

If you type =SUMPRODUCT(row _ range _ 1, row _ range _ 2, row _ range _ 3) in a cell, and the three row ranges of cells have the same size, Excel will multiply the cells pairwise. For example, in the worksheet 5 teams of the workbook RocketsShooting.xlsx, the formula =SUMPRODUCT($G$3:$K$3,G7:K7,$L$10:$P$10) in cell F7 computes

$$2*(.288)*(.658)+2*(.103)*(.394)+2*(.062)*(.415)+2*(.044)*$$
$$(.4)+3*(.503)*(.362)=1.09$$

This is the number of points per shot an average shooting team would score on the Rockets shots. SUMPRODUCT can also be applied to column ranges, but a row range cannot be paired with a column range. Also, between 2 and 255 cell ranges can be used as arguments for the SUMPRODUCT function.

CHAPTER 39

Why Have Sacrifice Bunts and Intentional Walks Nearly Disappeared?

Michael Lewis's mega best seller *Moneyball* (Norton, 2003) inspired an Oscar-nominated movie and increased the use of analytics in sports and other areas. The application of analytics to baseball is often called *sabermetrics* (named after the Society for American Baseball Research). By 2017, every Major League Baseball Team (see `https://www.techrepublic.com/article/how-big-data-won-the-2017-world-series/`) used analytics as a tool in decisions such as lineup selection, which free agents to sign, which players to draft, and when to pull the starting pitcher.

Great websites, including `Baseball-reference.com`, `Fangraphs.com`, and `Baseballprospectus.com`, have produced thousands of pages of great sabermetrics analysis. In this chapter, we provide simple explanations of how the increased use of analytics has greatly reduced two tools that used to be favorites of managers: the sacrifice bunt (often abbreviated SH for sacrifice hit) and the intentional walk (often abbreviated IBB for intentional base on balls).

Using information from `Baseball-reference.com`, we graphed in Figure 39.1 the decline in sacrifice hits and intentional walks. For reasons that will become clear later in the chapter, we also graphed the increase in home runs (HRs). From the figure, you can see that sacrifice hits (use the axis on the right) have dropped from 0.37 bunts per game (for each team) to a mere 0.17 bunts per game. In 2019, the Oakland As, led by *Moneyball*'s main character, Billy Bean, had only 0.04

bunts per game. IBBs dropped from 0.27 to 0.16 per game for each team (use the axis on the right). On the other hand, home runs increased from 1.01 HRs to 1.39 HRs per game (use the axis on the left).

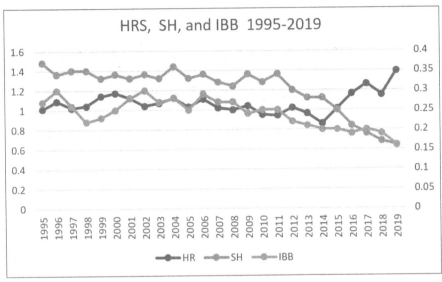

Figure 39.1: SH, IBB, and HR trends: 1995–2019

The Case Against Bunting

Bill James (watch a great *60 Minutes* portrait at www.cbsnews.com/news/the-red-sox-stat-man-and-the-numbers-game/) is often credited with creating sabermetrics during the late 1970s, but the real creator of sabermetrics is George Lindsey. In 1963, Lindsey published a brilliant analysis of baseball strategy ("An Investigation of Strategies in Baseball," *Operations Research*, vol. 11, no. 4, 1963, pages 477–501). On pages 484–488 of this article, Lindsey conducts a rather complex analysis that argues against average hitters bunting.

The key to analyzing baseball decisions is to understand that through most of a game (close games in the late innings are an exception), a team should make decisions that maximize the expected runs they will score in the current inning. To maximize the runs a team scores in an inning, we need a *run expectancy matrix*. As shown in Figure 39.2, in any inning there are eight possible on-base situations. In Figure 39.2, an x indicates that a base is not occupied. Thus, xxx indicates nobody on base, 1x3 indicates runners on first and third, and so on. Of course, for any of these eight on-base situations, there can be 0, 1, or 2 outs. A run expectancy matrix gives the expected number of runs that will be scored if an average offense is in any of these 8 * 3 = 24 situations. For the 2019 season, the great website Baseballprospectus.com gives the following run expectancy matrix.

	B	C	D	E
1				
2	Situation	0 outs	1 out	2 outs
3	xxx	0.5439	0.2983	0.1147
4	xx3	1.3685	0.9528	0.3907
5	x2x	1.1465	0.7134	0.3391
6	x23	1.9711	1.3679	0.6151
7	1xx	0.9345	0.5641	0.2422
8	1x3	1.7591	1.2186	0.5182
9	12x	1.5371	0.9792	0.4666
10	123	2.3617	1.6337	0.7426

Figure 39.2: 2019 run expectancy matrix

The entry of 0.5439 for nobody on base and 0 outs tells us that over all innings (every inning) that begin with nobody on and 0 outs, teams scored an average of 0.5439 runs. Similarly, the entry of 0.9345 for 1xx and 0 outs tells us that in all situations where a runner is on first with nobody out, teams score on average 0.9345 runs during the rest of the inning.

Let's now consider a situation with an average hitter batting and a runner on first with nobody out. Should we bunt? Many things can happen on an attempted bunt, but a bunt is termed successful if the batter is out and the runner on first makes it to second base. This puts us in a one out, x2x situation. In this situation, our expected runs drop to 0.7134. Thus, a successful bunt (trading an out for a base) costs us around 0.23 runs. No wonder the Oakland Athletics only had seven successful sacrifice hits in 2019.

Of course, if a bad hitter (like a typical National League pitcher) is at bat, then a bunt may very well make sense.

Bunting Against the Shift

The usual alignment of infielders is to position the SS (shortstop) and third baseman between second and third base and the first and second basemen between first and second base. It has long been known that most left-hand hitters hit ground balls much more often to the right side (between first and second base) of the infield than to the left side. Therefore, MLB teams now often shift the SS to the right side of the infield, leaving only the third baseman to cover the left side. For example, during 2019 against left-hand hitters, the Houston Astros shifted their infielders 77% of the time with only the third baseman protecting the left side of the infield (baseballsavant.mlb.com/visuals/team-positioning). Thus, this would make it seem easy for a hitter to lay down a bunt in an attempt to get a bunt single.

Andrew Kyne did a great analysis of this issue (see www.sportsinfosolutions.com/what-we-can-learn-from-rougned-odors-bunts-against-the-shift/). Kyne found that in 2018, Rougned Odor of the Texas Rangers bunted most (20 times) against the shift and batted .389 on 7 hits in 18 at bats (two plate appearances resulted in a sacrifice hit). On the whole, MLB hitters in 2018 got hits on 58.4% of all bunts against the shift (a .584 batting average). So, why don't batters try this more often?

- As Kyne points out, with fewer than two strikes, the third baseman usually plays in, thereby making it harder to bunt for a hit. With two strikes, almost nobody bunts for a hit because a foul ball results in a strikeout.

- A hitter's effectiveness is often measured by *OPS* (On Base + Slugging Percentage). Slugging Percentage is Total Bases / At Bats. In the formula, an HR generates four total bases, a triple as three total bases, a double as two total bases, and a single as one total base. The average major leaguer in 2018 had an OPS of .728, so for an average hitter even being successful on over half your bunts for a hit leads to less team benefit than hitting away.

- In a private conversation with an MLB analytics executive, I was told that hitters don't consider it "macho" to lay down a bunt when they are paid to hit home runs.

- In Chapter 59 "How do Baseball Teams decide where to shift fielders?", we give a detailed discussion of how MLB teams determine how to shift their fielder's based on the batter's hitting tendencies.

Why Are Intentional Walks on the Decline?

On August 4, 2019, *The Wall Street Journal* pointed out that during the 2019 season, the Astros had never issued an intentional walk (see www.wsj.com/articles/the-astros-give-a-hard-pass-to-the-free-pass-11564940857). The Astros did complete the season without issuing any IBBs. IBBs are most often used with a runner on second, or runners on second and third, with a great hitter up and a lesser hitter on deck. The idea is that you don't have to face the great hitter and you set up the possibility of the double play. In 2019, however, the fraction of at bats resulting in ground balls hit its lowest level since 2002, so the chance of turning a double play has dropped. Also, during 2019, forty-five percent of all runs scored (the most ever) were scored on HRs. Issuing an IBB can turn a two-run HR into a three-run HR, so the increased scoring on HRs also reduces the attractiveness of the IBB. I am sure the number of IBBs will continue to decline.

Do NFL Teams Pass Too Much and Go for It Often Enough on Fourth Down?

If, like most of America, you follow the NFL, you have surely noticed two things:

- Teams pass a lot more than they used to. Do NFL teams pass too much?
- Your favorite team often annoys you when they punt or try a field goal on fourth down and short yardage. Is the coach smarter than you?

In this chapter, we will try to convince you that even though teams pass a lot, it's not enough. We also will try to convince you that teams do not go for it often enough on fourth down.

The Ascent of Passing

Figure 40.1 and the cell range E8:F57 of the workbook `PlayMix.xlsx` (with data from the great site `Pro-football-reference.com`) shows the fraction of plays from scrimmage that are passing plays. You can see that in the five years before 1978, an average of 44% of plays were passes. In the years 1978–1987, the fraction of passing plays averaged 52%. This is probably because in 1978, the NFL prohibited defensive backs from making contact with receivers more than 5 yards from scrimmage. From 2015 to 2019, an average of 59% of all plays were pass attempts.

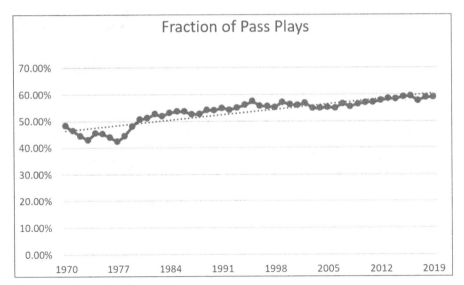

Figure 40.1: Fraction of pass plays

It seems that NFL play calling has stabilized with 50% more pass attempts than rushes. Still, many analysts think NFL teams should pass more (see Josh Hermsmeyer's great post at `fivethirtyeight.com/features/for-a-passing-league-the-nfl-still-doesnt-pass-enough/`). To make this case, look at Figure 40.2 (data again from `Pro-football-reference.com`). We summarized average points per play (refer to Chapter 16, "What's Wrong with the NFL QB Rating?") that were added on rushing and passing attempts for the 2015–2019 seasons (see the cell range O7:Q12 of the workbook `Playmix.xlsx`). In each season, passing plays added on average between 0.14 and 0.19 more points per play than rushing plays. If teams passed more, the defenses would adjust to expect more passing, but a few more passes should still result in passing plays averaging more points than running plays.

	O	P	Q
7	Points per Play Pass	Points per Play Rush	Difference
8	0.12	-0.03	0.15
9	0.13	-0.01	0.14
10	-0.01	-0.18	0.17
11	0.08	-0.11	0.19
12	0.11	-0.05	0.16

Figure 40.2: Average points added on rushing and passing attempts 2015–2019

Hermsmeyer makes a more detailed case for more passing. He points out that during the 2017 season, on first and 10, teams averaged 0.12 more points per play on passing attempts than rushes. Despite the obvious superiority of the pass, teams rushed 59% of the time on first down. On second down and long (7 to 10 yards needed for a first down), teams went 50-50 on the run-pass mix but *passes averaged 0.30 more points per play than rushing.*

Fourth Down Strategy

Since 1978, analysts who study the NFL have believed that coaches should more often eschew the field goal or punt on fourth down and go for the first down (see Virgil Carter and Robert Machol, "Note—Optimal Strategies on Fourth Down," *Management Science*, vol. 24, no. 16, 1978, pages 1758–1762). Let's look at some evidence in favor of going for it more often on fourth down.

The Yale Undergraduate Fourth Down Study

In 2015, the Yale Undergraduate Sports Analytics Group (YUSAG) looked at all fourth down and 1 yard to go plays (3,181 in all) from 1998 to 2016 (see `sports.sites.yale.edu/success-short-yardage-play-types-fourth-down`). They found that teams made the first down on 66% of all plays. Teams made the first down on 68% of all running plays and 58% of all passing plays. *Amazingly, teams were successful on 83% of all quarterback sneaks.* Of course, QB sneaks subject the QB to increased injury risk.

YUSAG also analyzed the expected points gained on fourth down and 1 yard to go on each type of play. As shown in Table 40.1, QB sneaks are by far the best choice on fourth and 1. If coaches were going for it on fourth and 1 as often as they should, then you would anticipate that expected points added would be near 0, so it is safe to conclude that teams should go for it more often on fourth and 1.

Table 40.1: Expected points added on fourth and 1

TYPE OF PLAY	EXPECTED POINTS ADDED
QB sneaks	1.61
Non-QB sneak runs	0.83
Passes	0.86

Are Coaches Going for It More Often on Fourth and Short?

Ahmed Cheema's great post (www.thespax.com/nfl/message-to-nfl-coaches-stop-being-stupid-on-fourth-downs/) contains many important insights into the fourth down debate:

- In 2011, NFL coaches went for it on fourth down and less than 3 yards to go only 27.5% of the time, and in the years 2012–2018, this percentage increased each year to 44.2% in 2018.

- ESPN's top NFL analyst (and former Navy fighter pilot) Brian Burke's analysis (based on expected points) indicates that on fourth down and less than 3 yards to go, teams should go for it unless they are inside their own 15-yard line. In fact, with fourth and 11 yards to go on the opponent's 38, teams should go for it. After all, a punt will in all likelihood gain your team 20 yards or less, and a missed field goal will have the same result as failing to convert the first down (the opponent gets the ball at the line of scrimmage).

- Cheema suggests that coaches choose the less risky field goal or punt strategy because they are conservative and fear a failed fourth down conversion may cost them their job. I don't know how to prove this assertion, but I am confident that coaches, like most people, are risk averse. To see if you are risk averse, ask yourself if you would accept the following one-time gamble: flip a coin, and if the coin comes up heads you win $30,000, and if the coin comes up tails you lose $25,000. Most of my students would not accept this gamble. But on average, you will win .5 * ($30,000) + .5 * (–$25,000) = $2,500, so if you reject this gamble you are not maximizing your expected winnings. Similarly, many coaches may prefer the less risky punt or field goal attempt.

New Data Partially Vindicates the Coaches

For years, all MLB stadiums and NHL and NBA arenas have used cameras to track the location of the players and the ball or puck multiple times per second. Now the NFL has RFID (radio-frequency identification) chips that are placed inside the football and inside each player's shoulder pads. The RFID chips collect 10 times per second the location of each player and the football. Some interesting results from this data can be found at nextgenstats.nfl.com. For example, based on the type of passes he threw in 2019, Titans QB Ryan Tannehill's passes resulted in 8% more completions than would be expected for an average NFL QB. This was the best in the NFL. Michael Lopez, Skidmore College professor and NFL Director of Football Data and Analytics, used Next Gen Stats to revisit the fourth down debate (see "Analyzing the NFL Is Challenging, but Player Tracking Data Is Here to Help," available at www.semanticscholar. org/paper/Analyzing-the-National-Football-League-is-but-data-Lopez/ 9cb5e1815cc5b0e4c851af46f76691ad77a92ea9).

I (and probably many other NFL fans) did not realize that when the TV says it is fourth down and 1 yard to go, the team can have anywhere between *1 and 71.99 inches to go for a first down*. Thus, not all fourth and 1 situations are created equal. Coaches, of course, have a much better idea of the actual distance needed for the first down. Lopez found that teams that went for it on fourth and 1 were an average of 0.78 yards from a first down, and when they did not go for it, an average of 0.99 yards were needed for a first down. Figure 40.3 (from Lopez's paper, reproduced with permission) shows that teams are less likely to go for it when more distance is needed and less likely to convert when more distance is needed. This figure shows that coarse calculations by NFL analysts based on classification of a fourth down situation as fourth and 1 or fourth and 2, are ignoring important information available to coaches. From Figure 40.3, we find that on fourth and inches, teams converted the first down 82% of the time, but in long fourth and 1 situations, they converted only 55% of the time. Thus, distance matters, and much analytics work did not use the actual distance needed for a first down.

Incorporating the actual distance needed for a first down into his analysis, Lopez found that coaches with incorrect fourth down decisions cost them an average of 0.14 wins over the course of a 16-game season. Lopez found that when the less accurate integer distances (fourth and 1, fourth and 2, etc.) are used, coaches with incorrect fourth down decisions cost twice as many (0.27) wins per season.

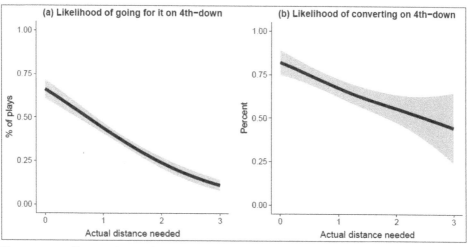

Figure 40.3: Chance of going for first down and converting on fourth down based on actual distance needed, Used by Permission of Michael Lopez, NFL Director of Data Analytics and Statistics

Teams Should Go for Two More Often

If you are down by 8 points and score a touchdown on the last play of the game, you clearly go for a 2-point conversion to tie the game; otherwise, you lose. All teams have a chart that recommends when going for 2 gives you a better chance to win than kicking the 1-point conversion (see Benjamin Morris's great work at `fivethirtyeight.com/features/when-to-go-for-2-for-real/`).

During recent seasons, however, things have changed. In 2015, the NFL made the 1-point conversion equivalent to a 32- or 33-yard field goal attempt. Now kickers miss 6% of all 1-point conversions. Data from `Pro-football-reference.com` shows us that during the 2017–2019 seasons, 51% of 2-point conversions were successful. This means that teams average more (1.02 is larger than 0.94) points on 2-point conversions. Thus, early in the game if you want to maximize expected points. you should always go for 2. Of course, going for 2 has a higher risk than going for 1, but I believe that during the first half you should always go for 2. Going for 2 more often also gives you more chances to improve your red zone offense, which should lead to more wins.

What Caused the 1854 London Cholera Outbreak?

Epidemiology is the branch of medicine and public health that attempts to determine the causes and risk factors that result in people getting diseases. English physician John Snow (1813–1856) is considered by many to be the founder of modern epidemiology (see `www.ph.ucla.edu/epi/snow/fatherofepidemiology.html`). In this chapter, we will explore John Snow's incredible work that showed that water contaminated with the bacterium *Vibrio cholerae* caused terrible cholera epidemics in nineteenth-century England.

Cholera

Cholera is a dreaded infectious disease that causes severe diarrhea. If left untreated, cholera can lead to dehydration and death. Cholera is treated with intravenous fluids, antibiotics, and zinc supplements. There are still between one million and four million cases per year of cholera. Before the amazing work of Dr. Snow, many doctors believed in the *Miasma theory*, which posited the existence of particles in the air, miasmata, that traveled through the air and infected people with cholera (see `www.ph.ucla.edu/epi/snow/choleratheories.html`). Snow believed (correctly) in the *germ theory*, which states that cholera entered an individual through drinking infected water or eating infected food. Then, cholera spread through germ cells. As you will see, Dr. Snow collected data that tipped the scales in favor of the germ theory.

Snow and the Broad Street Pump

In late August 1854, a terrible cholera outbreak hit the Soho district of London (see www.ph.ucla.edu/epi/snow/broadstreetpump.html). Between August 31 and September 2, a total of 127 people died of cholera, and by September 10, five hundred people had died. At nearby Middlesex Hospital, the famous Florence Nightingale (see page 181 of Sandra Hempel's excellent book, *The Strange Case of the Broad Street Pump*, University of California Press, 2007) treated many cholera patients. As you will see, most of the deaths were near the Broad Street water pump. The death rate in some areas around the Broad Street water pump reached 12.8%. On September 7, Snow used a microscope to examine some water from the Broad Street pump and saw "white flocculent particles." This convinced Snow that the water from the Broad Street pump was contaminated. Later it was found that pipes connected to toilets had leaked into the Broad Street well, contaminating the water (Hempel, page 233).

Snow became convinced that he needed to make the case that polluted water could cause cholera. He doggedly tracked down the address of each person who died in the cholera outbreak and plotted their locations on a *disease map*. Robin Wilson's great blog post (see blog.rtwilson.com/john-snows-cholera-data-in-more-formats/) gives us a mapping of the deaths combined with modern street addresses (see Figure 41.1). The map makes it clear that the deaths clustered around the Broad Street pump.

From Wilson's site, I downloaded into Excel the latitude and longitude of the addresses of each person who died, as well as the latitude and longitude of the eight pumps in the area. I found the closest pump to each address where a person(s) died. Then I used a PivotTable to sum up the number of deaths classified by the closest pump. Figure 41.2 summarizes the results in a bubble chart (see the workbook Deaths.xlsx). The "Excel Calculations" section describes how to create a bubble chart. The x-axis gives the longitude of each pump, the y-axis gives the latitude of each pump, and the area of each bubble is proportional to the number of deaths that were closest to each pump (there were no deaths closest to Pumps 4 and 7, but I changed the value to 1 so that the locations of those pumps would show up). Figure 41.2 shows that many more deaths were closer to the Broad Street pump (Pump 1 in the spreadsheet) than any other pump. Also, there were no deaths for which the two pumps that were furthest from the Broad Street pump (Pump 4 and Pump 7) were the closest pump.

There were many anomalies that did not fit the Broad Street pump theory, but the persistent Dr. Snow explained most of these. For example:

- A widow and her niece died and did not live near the Broad Street pump. However, Dr. Snow found out that they liked the taste of the Broad Street pump water so much that they had people bring them Broad Street pump water.

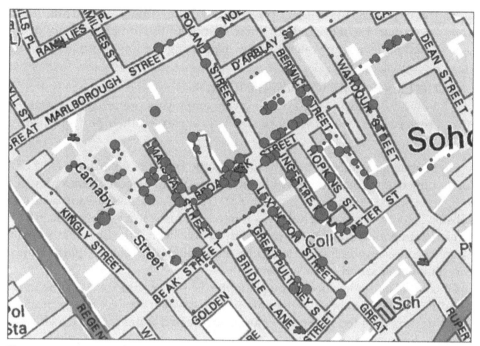

Figure 41.1: Location of 1854 cholera deaths

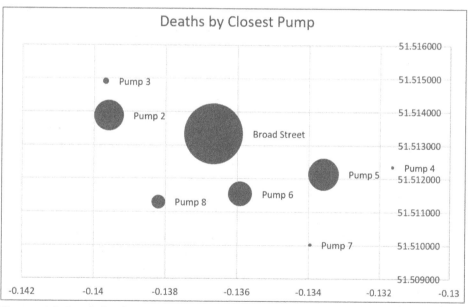

Figure 41.2: Deaths by closest pump

- There were 535 inmates at a prison around the corner from the pump and fewer than 1% of them died. Snow found out the inmates did not drink Broad Street pump water, thereby explaining the low death rate among the inmates.

- The Lion Brewery was near the Broad Street pump and none of the 70 brewery employees died. The brewery employees preferred beer, and the brewery had its own water pump. This explained their perfect survival rate.

On September 7, 1854, Dr. Snow spoke to the Board of Guardians (sort of a town council) and convinced them to remove the pump handle the next day (see www.ph.ucla.edu/epi/snow/removal.html). The epidemic had already begun to subside before the pump handle was removed. This was probably caused by a reduction in population density caused by people fleeing the Broad Street area. Therefore, it is impossible to determine how much the removal of the pump contributed to the end of the epidemic.

Of course, as we learned in our Chapter 37 ("Does Smoking Cause Lung Cancer?") discussion of cigarette smoking, *association does not prove causation*. Many doctors doubted Dr. Snow's view that infected water caused cholera. For example, Snow mentions (see www.ph.ucla.edu/epi/snow/snowbook3.html) that a Dr. Baly (no first name listed) pointed out that the districts of Westminster and Belgrave both received the same water, but Westminster endured 68 deaths per 10,000 people and Belgrave only 26 deaths per 10,000 people. If the water caused cholera, how can this discrepancy be explained? Dr. Snow realized that the population density was much greater in poor Westminster than upper-class Belgrave. Since Snow believed the disease could spread person to person (he was right!), the discrepancy in population density could explain the difference in mortality rate between the two districts. To prove causality, Snow needed a randomized controlled trial (see Chapter 19, "Evidence-Based Medicine"). Fortunately, Snow was able to perform a close equivalent to a randomized controlled trial (RCT).

Snow's Randomized Controlled Trial

If Snow's germ theory was correct, factors such as population density and poverty might affect the cholera death rate. Snow needed to "block out" the influence of these and other socioeconomic factors. It turned out that in many London streets, pipes from two different water companies (Southwark Vauxhall and Lambeth) served the street and the luck of the draw for each home (not income or any other variable) determined which company served the home. For nearly 67,000 homes, Snow found the water company serving the home and the cholera mortality rate. Snow examined the cholera deaths for the first four weeks of an 1853–1854 cholera epidemic on streets served by both companies. He found that in the 40,146 homes served by Southwark Vauxhall, 286 cholera deaths occurred, and in the 26,107 homes served by Lambeth, only 14 deaths occurred. This implies that the death rate for homes served by Southwark Vauxhall was 20 times the death rate for homes served by Lambeth. Using the resampling techniques discussed in Chapter 19, under the assumption that cholera mortality was identical in water from both companies, there is less than 1 chance in 100,000 that a discrepancy this large in death rates could occur.

Southwark Vauxhall received its water from the Thames, downstream from London's sewers, and Lambeth received its water upstream from London's sewers. Since homes next to each other are expected to be similar in socioeconomic variables, Snow in effect had conducted an RCT with the only varying factor being the quality of the water supplied to the homes. This brilliant emulation of an RCT confirmed beyond a shadow of a doubt that water tainted by sewage caused cholera and forever discredited the Miasma theory of disease spread.

Conclusion

Even in today's data-driven world, it would be hard to duplicate Snow's work. Imagine how hard it was to conduct his analysis in the 1850s!

John Snow made many other contributions to medicine. For example, he pioneered the use of ether and chloroform in anesthesia. (He delivered the last two of Queen Victoria's children.) In a March 2003 poll [by the now defunct *Hospital Doctor* magazine, John Snow was named the G.O.A.T. (Greatest of All Time) of physicians, even beating out the great Hippocrates (see https://www.ncbi.nlm.nih.gov/pmc/articles/PMC539667/).

As pointed out by Donald Cameron and Ian Jones ("John Snow, the Broad Street Pump, and Modern Epidemiology," *International Journal of Epidemiology*, vol. 12, no. 4, 1983, pages 393–396), Snow's contribution to epidemiology consisted of the following:

- Find a public health problem (cholera) and develop a theory on how the problem spread (germ theory).

- Use all methods and data available to confirm your theory. As we have seen, Snow went to Herculean lengths to obtain data that confirmed his theory.

- Once the theory is confirmed, advocate to the public and appropriate authorities strategies that will eliminate or mitigate the problem.

I am personally in awe of Dr. Snow's amazing accomplishments. We are all in his debt for pioneering a field that has greatly increased life expectancy and quality of life.

Excel Calculations

To create the bubble chart shown in Figure 41.2, proceed as follows:

1. Open the workbook `Deaths.xlsx` and select the cell range AC21:AE29, which contains for each pump, the longitude, latitude, and number of deaths closest to the given pump.

2. Select the Scatter Chart icon (last one in the bottom row) from the Insert tab, and then choose the first Bubble chart option (based on Area).

3. Select all the points in the chart and choose Data Labels, More Options from the Chart Elements icon (the + sign to the right of the chart).

4. In the Format Data Labels pane, under Label Contains, choose Value From Cells, and then choose the range AB22:AB29 for the cell labels.

CHAPTER 42

What Affects the Sales of a Retail Product?

If a brick-and-mortar retailer wants to survive in today's highly competitive environment, they need to understand what factors affect sales of their products. In this chapter, we show how to develop a simple yet powerful model that can be used to understand the factors that drive product sales.

Painter's Tape

The workbook `PaintersTape.xlsx` contains two years of weekly sales data for Painter's Tape at a local hardware store. As shown in Figure 42.1, for each week, we are given the following information:

- Units sold (Sales column)
- Quarter of the year (1 = January–March; 2 = April–June; 3 = July–September; 4 = October–December)
- Was the product on display that week? (1 = display; 0 = not on display)
- Was there a coupon for the product in the Sunday paper? (1 = there was a coupon; 0 = no coupon)
- The ratio of the hardware store's price to the product's price at the store's only competitor

	G	H	I	J	K	L	M	N	O	P
1							SSE	16410.35		RSQ
2	Week	Quarter	Display	Coupon	Price Ratio	Sales	Prediction	Squared Error		0.944999
3	1	1	0	1	0.97	71	79.33857	69.53179		
4	2	1	1	0	0.93	105	108.958	15.66562		
5	3	1	1	0	1.04	54	62.40879	70.70775		
6	4	1	0	1	1.08	42	46.44448	19.75336		
7	5	1	1	0	1.04	62	62.40879	0.167109		
8	6	1	1	0	1.1	51	47.1867	14.54122		
9	7	1	1	1	0.98	98	91.7106	39.55659		
10	8	1	0	1	0.96	80	83.54461	12.56423		
11	9	1	1	1	1.02	76	75.13	0.756904		
12	10	1	1	0	1.08	54	51.70625	5.261283		

Figure 42.1: Painter's tape data

For example, Week 1 was in Quarter 1; 71 units were sold; the product was not on display; there was a coupon in the local paper; and the hardware store's price was 3% lower than the competitor's price.

Assuming these are the only variables that influence unit sales, the usual model used by a marketing analyst to predict sales is

$$(1) \text{Predicted Sales} = (\text{Constant}) * (\text{Seasonal Index}) * (\text{Display Factor}) *$$

$$(\text{Coupon Factor}) * (\text{Price Ratio})^{-\text{elasticity}}$$

We now explain the unknowns in equation (1):

- Constant is used to scale (1) so that the predictions are accurate.

- Each quarter has a seasonal index, and the seasonal indices must average to 1. For example, if the seasonal index for Q2 = 1.3 and the seasonal index for Q4 = 0.6, then (after adjusting for other variables), we expect weekly sales during Quarter 2 to be 30% above average and weekly sales during Quarter 4 to be 40% below average. Our seasonal indices must average to 1.

- Display factor measures the bump in sales (after adjusting for all other variables) generated by placing the product on display. For example, a display factor of 1.2 means that a display increases weekly sales by 20%. In a week where the product is not on display, the display factor equals 1.

- Coupon factor measures the bump in sales (after adjusting for other variables) generated by putting a coupon in the Sunday paper. For example, a coupon factor of 1.3 means that a coupon in the Sunday paper increases weekly sales by 30%. In a week where the product does not have a coupon in the Sunday paper, the coupon factor equals 1.

- Elasticity measures the sensitivity (in percentage terms) of sales to a percentage change in the relative price of the painter's tape. For example, if elasticity = 5, then a 1% increase in the relative price of the painter's tape results in (after adjusting for other variables) a sales reduction of 5%.

Figure 42.2 shows the values of these unknown quantities that best fit the sales data (more later, on how we found these values).

	A	B
1		
2	avg	1
3	Quarter	
4	1	0.62
5	2	1.18
6	3	1.39
7	4	0.81
8	display	1.22
9	coupon	1.09
10	elasticity	4.98
11	constant	101.22

Figure 42.2: Optimal painter's tape parameters

For example, given these parameter estimates, our predicted sales (computed in Column M) for Weeks 1, 2, and 11 are computed as follows:

- Week 1 Prediction = $(101.22) * (0.62) * (1.09) * (.97)^{-4.98} = 79.34$
- Week 2 Prediction = $(101.22) * (0.62) * (1.22) * (0.93)^{-4.98} = 108.96$
- Week 11 Prediction = $(101.22) * (0.62) * (0.96)^{-4.98} = 76.45$

Estimating the Model Parameters

We could, of course, choose any values for the parameters in B4:B11 and see how well those values predict actual sales. As described in the "Excel Calculations" section later in this chapter, we want Excel to choose the parameter values that minimize the sum over all 104 weeks of (Actual Sales – Predicted Sales)^2. We do not minimize the sum of errors, because then positive and negative errors would cancel out. Excel's marvelous GRG Multistart Solver option (again, see the "Excel Calculations" section) can find the parameter values that minimize the sum of squared errors. We find that our best prediction for sales is given by

$$(2)\,101.22 * (1.09 \text{ if coupon}) * (1.22 \text{ if display}) * (\text{Price Ratio})^{-4.98} *$$
$$(.62 \text{ if Q1}; 1.18 \text{ if Q2}; 1.39 \text{ if Q3}; .81 \text{ if Q4})$$

These parameter values may be interpreted as follows:

- A coupon increases sales by 9%.
- Putting the product on display increases sales by 22%.
- Increasing our Price Ratio by 1% reduces sales by 4.98%.
- In the first quarter, sales are 38% below an average quarter; in the second quarter, sales are 18% above average; in the third quarter, sales are 39% above average; and in the fourth quarter, sales are 19% below average.

All these interpretations are *ceteris paribus* (all other variables being equal).

The hardware store owner can use these parameters to help them maximize the store's profit from Painter's Tape. For example, suppose that without a display, predicted sales from equation (2) are 100 units and profit per unit is $5. If it costs $50 to put the product on display for a week, then a display would increase sales to 1.22 * 100 = 122 units. This increases profit by $5 * 22 = $110, which outweighs the cost of putting the product on display, so putting the product on display would be a good idea.

Excel Calculations

In order to use Excel Solver to predict sales, you need to install Excel Solver:

1. Select the File tab on the ribbon and then choose Options.
2. Choose Add-ins ⇨ Go.
3. Select Solver Add-in from the list of add-ins available and click OK.

When you click the Data tab, you should see Solver in the Analyze group. With Solver installed, the steps to estimate the "best fit" parameters for equation (1) are as follows:

1. Select the range A8:B11 and from the Formulas tab, select Create From Selection in the Defined Names group. This gives the name display to B8, the name coupon to B9, the name elasticity to B10, and the name constant to B11. Using the F3 key, you can refer to these names in formulas. When a cell or range of cells is named, it performs as if it is absolute. (The cell reference does not change when you copy a formula.)
2. Create the predicted sales for each week by copying from M3 to M4:M106 the formula

$$= \text{constant} * \text{VLOOKUP}(H3, \$A\$4 : \$B\$7, 2) * \text{IF}(I3 = 1, \text{display}, 1) *$$
$$\text{IF}(J3 = 1, \text{coupon}, 1) * K3 \wedge (-\text{elasticity})$$

The VLOOKUP(H3,$A$4:$B$7,2) portion of the formula "looks up" the seasonal index by matching the quarter number in Column A and picking the seasonal index from Column B. The ^ character is used in Excel to raise a number to a power.

3. Copy from N3 to N4:N106 the formula =(L3-M3)^2 to compute the squared error for each week.

4. In cell N1, we compute the sum of squared errors for the current parameter values with the formula =SUM(N3:N106).

5. Choose Solver from the Data tab. Fill in the Solver Parameters dialog box, as shown in Figure 42.3. We want to minimize the sum of squared errors (cell N1) by changing our model parameters (cells B4:B11).

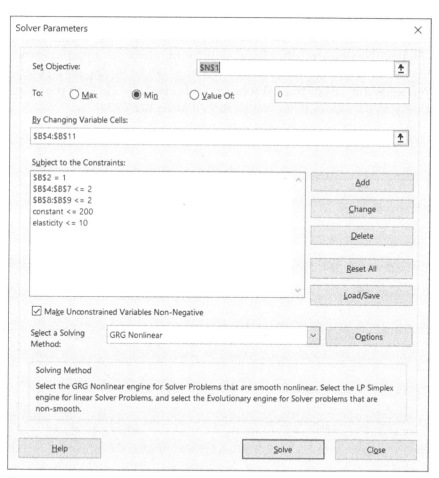

Figure 42.3: Solver Parameters dialog box settings

Constraints are restrictions on changing cells. The constraint B2=1 ensures that the average of the seasonal indices equals 1. The other constraints are upper bounds on each changing cell. *These are needed for the GRG Multistart option to efficiently search for the optimal values of the changing cells.* Solver likes "tight" upper and lower bounds on changing cells. This is because tight bounds reduce the size of the region over which Solver searches for an optimal solution. It's fine to say each changing cell is non-negative, which we ensure by selecting the Make Unconstrained Variables Non-Negative check box. Since Solver likes tight bounds, we don't just say each changing cell is less than a large number like 10,000. We assume that each seasonal index and the display and coupon effects are less than or equal to 2. *If Solver finds an optimal value near an upper or lower bound*, then you should relax the bound. We assume the elasticity is less than or equal to 10, and the constant is less than or equal to 200.

6. Choose Options, and from the GRG Nonlinear tab, select the Use Multistart check box. This ensures that Excel will try to minimize squared errors using 100 different combinations of starting values for the parameters. Excel keeps the best of the 100 solutions it finds. Now, clicking the Solve button yields the parameter values shown in Figure 42.2.

CHAPTER 43

Why Does the Pareto Principle Explain So Many Things?

The great nineteenth-century Italian economist Vilfredo Pareto (1848–1923) was the first to discover the *80/20 rule* (later also known as the *Pareto principle*), which emphasizes the importance of few items in explaining a total. For example:

- 20% of a company's products generate 80% of its revenue.
- 20% of a company's customers generate 80% of its profit.
- 20% of people have 80% of the income.
- 20% of websites get 80% of the hits.
- 20% of computer code contains 80% of the errors.
- Around 15% of all major league baseball players create 85% of their team's wins.
- 20% of criminals commit 80% of the crimes.
- 20% of people incur 80% of health care costs.

In this chapter, we show how the concept of a power law explains the widespread presence of the Pareto principle.

Power Laws

Consider an unknown quantity, X, which we suppose must equal a positive integer. Examples include a person's income, number of units purchased by a customer, and number of hits on a website. Then X follows a *power law* if the fraction of observations (X = x) that equal x is given by

$$(1)\, P(X = x) = C * x^{-\alpha}$$

In equation (1), α >1 and C is chosen to make the sum of the probabilities equal to one. In the rest of this chapter, we will discuss the prevalence of power laws and how power laws lead to the importance of few items explaining a total. The seminal reference on power laws is M. E. J. Newman's terrific study of power laws ("Power Laws, Pareto Distributions, and Zipf's Law," *Contemporary Physics*, vol. 46, no. 5, 2005, pages 323–351).

Twenty Percent of Customers Generate 80% of Sales

Let's assume that each of our company's 100 customers purchase between 1 and 1,000 units, and the probability that a customer buys x units is given by the following power law:

$$(2)\, \text{Probability customer buys x units} = 0.532 * x^{-1.8}$$

The constant 0.532 ensures that the sum of the probabilities of a customer ordering between 1 and 1,000 units equals 1. In the worksheet Units Sold of the workbook PowerLaws.xlsx, we show the probability that a customer buys between 1 and 20 units (see Figure 43.1).

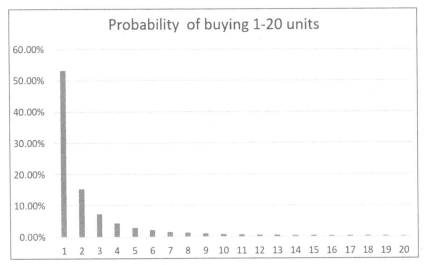

Figure 43.1: Probability customer buys between 1 and 20 units

You can see that there is over a 50% chance that a customer buys only one unit, and the probability of buying more units decreases quickly. We used these probabilities to randomly generate the number of units bought by 100 customers. We assumed each customer's probability of buying x units was governed by equation (2). We used Excel's Pareto chart option (see the "Excel Calculations" section later in this chapter) to summarize the units purchased by each customer (see Figure 43.2), sorted in descending order. The curved line gives the cumulative percentage of units purchased. You can see that our top 20 customers purchased around 80% of the total units, exactly as suggested by the Pareto principle.

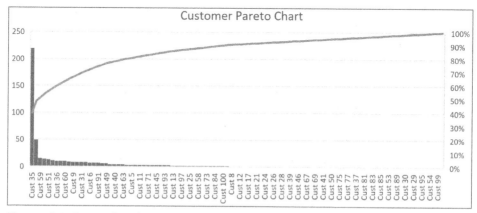

Figure 43.2: Pareto chart for units bought by 100 customers

Power Laws with α = 2

Power laws with α = 2 have an amazing property (see page 72 of Scott Page's wonderful book *The Model Thinker*, Hachette Books, 2018). When the power law exponent is 2, then

$$(3)\, n * \left(\text{Value of the nth largest item} \right) = \text{constant}$$

This implies that the second-largest item should be half as large as the largest item, the third-largest item should be one-third as large as the largest item, and so on.

Zipf's law perfectly illustrates equation (3). Zipf's law describes the relative frequency of the most frequently used word in the English (or any other) language. The most frequently used word in the English language is "the," which is used 7% of the time. The second most frequently used word is "of," which is used half as often as "the" (see plus.maths.org/content/mystery-zipf). The third most frequently used word, "to," is used 39% (compared to the theoretical 33.3%) as often as "the."

The population of the largest U.S. cities also is well described by equation (3). Figure 43.3 (based on data from the U.S. Census) shows that for the five largest cities, the product of the city's rank and population is approximately 8 million.

	C	D	E	F
7	Rank	City	2018 Population	Rank*Population
8	1	New York	8,398,748	8,398,748
9	2	Los Angeles	3,990,456	7,980,912
10	3	Chicago	2,705,994	8,117,982
11	4	Houston	2,325,502	9,302,008
12	5	Phoenix	1,660,272	8,301,360

Figure 43.3: Rank * Population for five largest U.S. cities

Power Laws and the Long Tail

Chris Anderson's bestseller, *The Long Tail* (Hyperion, 2006), argues that together the (very) many products with low sales volume can make up a large portion of the market. To illustrate the long tail, consider a brick-and-mortar Barnes & Noble bookstore (our town's store closed!) that stocks 100,000 titles. Erik Brynjolfsson, Michael D. Smith, and Yu (Jeffrey) Hu ("Consumer Surplus in the Digital Economy: Estimating the Value of Increased Product Variety at Online Booksellers," *Management Science*, vol. 49, 2003, pages 1580–1596) estimated that 40% of Amazon.com book sales would be from books not stocked by the Barnes & Noble store.

In the worksheet Long Tail of the workbook PowerLaws.xlsx, we assumed the 675 million U.S. book sales in 2018 followed a power law with $\alpha = 2$, and 1 million books were available. We used equation (3) to determine the sales for each book. The best-selling book would sell 46 million books, the second best-selling book would sell 23 million copies, and so on. We found that the 100,000 best-selling books accounted for 84% of all sales, leaving the "long tail" with 16% of the book market.

Why Do Incomes Follow the Pareto Principle?

In Chapter 7, "Measuring Income Inequality with the Gini, Palm, and Atkinson Indices," we discussed the worldwide trend toward increased income inequality. Charles I. Jones ("Pareto and Piketty: The Macroeconomics of Top Income and Wealth Inequality," *Journal of Economic Perspectives*, vol. 29, no. 1, 2015, pages 29–46) explains the relationship between power laws and the fact that incomes tend to follow the Pareto principle. If income follows a power law with exponent α, then for any income y

$$(4)\,\text{Prob}\big(\text{Income} > y\big) = y^{-1/\eta},\text{ where } \eta = 1/(\alpha - 1)$$

Jones states that for the U.S. economy, $\eta = 3/5$, which implies $\alpha = 8/3$. Jones shows that the fraction of income going to the top 1% is $(100)^{\eta-1}$. Thus, Jones estimates the fraction of U.S. income going to the top 1% as $(100)^{-2/5} = 15.8\%$. Again, we see the few (the top 1%) comprises a significant portion of a total (all income).

Jones proposes a simple mechanism that would generate a power law for income. Assume that income depends on a parameter (call it age). Assume age follows an *exponential distribution*—that is

$$(5)\,P\big(\text{Age} > x\big) = e^{-\beta x}$$

The exponential distribution has the *constant failure rate property*, which implies that at any age, the chance you die in a short length of time (say 1 day) does not depend on your age.

Next, assume that income increases with age according to the equation

$$(6)\,\text{Income} = e^{\mu x}$$

Together, Jones shows that equations (5) and (6) imply that

$$\text{Prob}\big(\text{Income} > y\big) = y^{-\beta/\mu}$$

This reduces to equation (4) with $\eta = \mu/\beta$.

Of course, this model is overly simplistic, but Jones and Jihee Kim have developed more realistic models that also imply that income follows a power law (see www.nber.org/papers/w20637). This implies, of course, that a small fraction of people will have a preponderance of the income.

Why Do a Few Websites Get Most of the Hits?

According to ahrefs.com/blog/most-visited-websites/, the five most visited websites in the United States are YouTube, Wikipedia, Facebook, Twitter, and Amazon. Together, these websites have more hits than the next 95 websites. Again, we see the importance of a few items in explaining a total. M. E. J. Newman gives a great description of how the "rich get richer" theory explains why a few websites dominate web traffic. Newman estimates that in 2005, the chance that a website received x hits is given by (1) with $\alpha = 2.4$.

To illustrate the simple intuition behind the rich-get-richer theory, suppose there are two social networks: SN1 and SN2. A new person is considering signing up for one of the two networks. It seems reasonable to assume a new person is more likely to sign up with the network that currently has more members. To model this idea, assume that if SN1 has f1 followers and SN2 has f2 followers, then the chance the next person joining a network will choose SN1 is f1 / (f1 + f2). For example, if we begin with f1 = 50 and f2 = 100, then there is a 50 / (50 + 100) = 1/3 chance that the next person joins SN1 and a 2/3 chance they join SN2. In the workbook `RichGetRicher.xlsx`, we assume that SN2 begins with 100 members and vary the number of beginning members for SN1 between 5, 10, 15,. . ., 95, 100. The workbook plays out 1,000 times the next 1,000 people who join a network (see the "Excel Calculations" section for details). For example, if SN1 begins with 50 members, the next person to join has a 1/3 chance to join SN1 and a 2/3 chance to join SN2. If the first person joins SN1, then the next person has a 51/151 chance of joining SN1 and a 100/151 chance of joining SN2. The workbook calculates for SN1 starting with 5–100 members the chance that SN1 ends with more members than SN2. Figure 43.4 shows that unless SN1 starts with nearly as many members as SN2, then SN1 has little chance of ending up with more members than SN2. Thus, a small initial edge in members usually leads to a larger long-run edge in members.

The rich-gets-richer idea makes it very surprising that Google beat out Yahoo! and that Microsoft Office beat out Lotus and WordPerfect. See `www.theregister.co.uk/2013/01/31/when_lotus_met_excel/` for a great explanation of how Excel beat out Lotus.

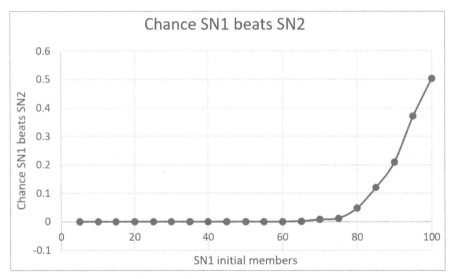

Figure 43.4: Chance SN1 beats out SN2

Excel Calculations

In this section, we create the Pareto chart shown in Figure 43.2 and model the rich-get-richer theory.

Creating a Pareto Chart

To create a Pareto chart (Figure 43.2) that summarizes unit sales, simply select the range P5:Q104 (Units sold worksheet in the `PowerLaws.xlsx` file) that contains the customer number (1–100) and the number of units purchased by each customer. Then (for Excel 2016 or newer), from the Insert tab, choose the Insert Statistic Chart option (second icon in the second row), and then choose the right-hand chart on the Histogram row.

Modeling the Rich-Get-Richer Theory

To simulate 1,000 people sequentially joining SN1 and SN2, proceed as follows in the workbook `RichGetRicher.xlsx`:

1. Copy from G3 to G4:G1002 the function =RAND(). This generates 1,000 numbers that are equally likely to assume any value between 0 and 1. If you press F9, all the numbers will change.

2. Copy from F3 to F4:F1002 the formula =IF(G3<=H2/(H2+I2),1,2). This ensures that each new person joins SN1 or SN2 with the rich-get-richer probability. For example, in cell F3, the formula ensures that a random number < = 1/3 results in the first person joining SN1 and a random number >1/3 results in the first person joining SN2.

3. Copy from H3 to H4:H1002 the formula =IF(F3=1,H2+1,H2). This adds one member to SN1 if and only if the new member joins SN1. Copying from I3 to I4:I1002 the formula =IF(F3=2,I2+1,I2) adds one member to SN2 if and only if the new member joins SN2.

4. Now we can use an Excel two-variable data table to "play out" our spreadsheet 1,000 times. Enter the integers 1–1000 in L5:L1004 and the numbers 5, 10, . . ., 95, 100 in the range M4:AF4.

5. In cell L4, enter the formula (=H1002), which we want Excel to calculate 1,000 times. Cell H1002 is just the ending number of members of SN2. This formula is the data table's *output cell*.

6. Before performing the simulation (with a two-variable data table), go to the Formulas tab and choose Calculation Options from the Calculations group, and then choose Automatic Except For Data Tables. Otherwise, your data table will slow down your worksheet. With this setting, you need to press F9 when you want the data table to recalculate.

7. Select the table range L4:AF1004, and from the Forecast group on the Data tab, choose What-If Analysis, and then choose Data Table. In the Data Table dialog box, specify cell H2 as the Row input cell, and for the Column input cell, choose any blank cell. After clicking OK and pressing F9 (be

patient), Excel will, in each column, place the row 4 entry in cell H2 (the initial number of SN1 members). The column input cell being a blank cell "tricks" Excel so that in each row of the data table, the random numbers recalculate. This is equivalent to playing out our model 1,000 times. Each row of results is called an *iteration*.

8. Copy from M2 to N2:AF4. This computes, based on initial SN1 members, one-half the total number of ending members. For example, if SN1 starts with 50 members, then when 1,000 new people join a network, the larger network will have at least .5 * (100 + 50 + 1000) = 575 people.

9. Copy from M1 to N1:AF4 the formula =COUNTIF(M5:M1004,">"&M2)/1000. This computes the fraction of our 1,000 iterations for which SN1 has more members than SN2.

CHAPTER 44

Does Where You Grow Up Matter?

Consider a child named Anna whose parents are low income (25th percentile of income for U.S. families). Anna grows up in the Roxbury neighborhood of South Boston. How would moving to the nearby Savin Hill neighborhood (three miles away from Roxbury) affect Anna's future income? The average adult income in Savin Hill is nearly double ($40,000 vs. $23,000) the average adult income in Roxbury. As Raj Chetty points out in his notes (see Lecture 2 notes at `opportunityinsights.org/course/`) for his great Stanford course "Using Big Data to Solve Economic and Social Problems," the effects of the move to Savin Hill on Anna's future greatly depend on Anna's age when she moves to Savin Hill. The earlier that Anna moves, the higher her future income. Table 44.1 shows Anna's expected income at age 26 if her family moves when Anna is 2, 10, or 20.

Table 44.1 shows that if Anna's family moves early, Anna can capture most of the income difference between Roxbury and Savin Hill, whereas a later move makes much less difference for Anna. Chetty estimates that a child's adult income converges to the income in the destination at an average rate of 4% per year lived in the higher income neighborhood. Thus, if a child spends 20 years in a neighborhood where the average income ranks 1% higher than their birth neighborhood, then the child's expected adult income picks up 80% of the difference between the average income in the two neighborhoods.

Raj Chetty and Nathaniel Hendren found that among the 100 most populous counties in the United States, DuPage County (the Western suburbs of Chicago) had the best outcomes for lower-income children and nearby Cook County

Table 44.1: Effect on Anna's income based on age she moves

AGE MOVED FROM ROXBURY TO SAVIN HILL	ANNA'S EXPECTED AGE 26 INCOME
2	$38,000
10	$33,000
20	$27,000

Lecture 2 notes at `opportunityinsights.org/course/`)

(Chicago) had the worst outcomes for low-income children ("The Impacts of Neighborhoods on Intergenerational Mobility II: County Level-Estimates," *The Quarterly Journal of Economics*, vol. 133, no. 3, August 2018, pages 1163–1228). The authors estimate that moving at birth from Cook County to DuPage County would increase a child's adult income by an average of 29%.

Quasi-Experimental Design vs. Randomized Controlled Trials

To determine the effect of moving to a higher-income area on a child's adult income, the gold standard (see Chapter 19, "Evidence-Based Medicine") would be to flip a coin each year to randomly choose which families move to a higher-income neighborhood from a lower-income neighborhood. This design would allow us to isolate how the difference in the adult income of the children who moved was influenced by their age when their families moved and the difference in income between the lower- and higher-income neighborhoods. Obviously, a randomized trial is impossible in this situation.

Instead of a randomized controlled trial (RCT), Chetty and Hendren used a *quasi-experimental design*, in which they collected deidentified tax data on three million families with children who moved during the 1997–2010 period. Chetty and Hendren ran regressions to predict the child's adult income from the age the children moved, and the difference in average income between the lower- and higher-income neighborhoods. These regressions could be biased, however, if variables that affect a child's future income were correlated with the age at which the families move. The fact that other variables affecting a child's future income are uncorrelated with the age the families move is an *identification assumption*. Chetty and Hendren verified their identification assumption as follows:

- Running baseline regressions on families (with one child) who moved showed that each year in a better neighborhood resulted in the child capturing 4% of the income difference in the neighborhoods.

- Looking at families (with siblings) that moved, the authors found that after adjusting for the characteristics of each family, the regression results remained unchanged. This showed that the baseline results were not influenced by a correlation between the age a family moves and family differences on variables affecting a child's adult income.

- San Francisco and Boston children had similar average adult incomes, but the San Francisco children exhibit much higher variability in adult income than Boston children. This illustrates that the distributions, not the means, of adult income in different neighborhoods may differ. The predictions from the baseline regressions come close to matching the actual distribution of adult incomes in different locations. It would be impossible for this to happen if some omitted variables were explaining differences in adult income.

What Drives Neighborhood Differences in Upward Mobility?

Chetty and Hendren identified five factors that are most correlated with a neighborhood's degree of upward mobility:

- More segregated neighborhoods have less upward mobility.
- Neighborhoods with more income inequality have less upward mobility.
- Neighborhoods with better schools have more upward mobility.
- An increase in the fraction of single parent families correlates most strongly with poor upward mobility.
- To paraphrase Bloomington, Indiana's poet laureate John Mellencamp, "everyone needs a hand to hold on to." The concept of *social capital* was devised to measure the resources that a county has to help those in need. Anil Rupasinga, Stephan J. Goetz, and David Freshwater ("The Production of Social Capital in US Counties," *Journal of Socio-Economics*, vol. 35, no. 1, 2006 [with updates], pages 83–101), developed a measure of social capital for all U.S. counties that measures resources available to help people in need. Neighborhoods with higher social capital tend to have more upward mobility.

Their measure of a county's social capital is based on the following criteria:

- Number of religious organizations
- Number of establishments in business associations
- Number of establishments in political organizations

- Number of establishments in professional organizations
- Number of establishments in labor organizations
- Number of establishments in bowling alleys
- Number of establishments in fitness and recreational sports centers
- Number of establishments in golf courses and country clubs
- Number of establishments in sports teams and clubs
- Number of nonprofit organizations
- Voter turnout
- Census response rate

The first 10 criteria are, of course, measured on a per-capita basis.

How Can We Make Things Better?

If we want to increase intergenerational mobility and reduce future levels of inequality, Chetty and Hendren's findings suggest two paths forward:

- Make it easier for lower-income families to move to "higher opportunity" neighborhoods. For example, make it easier for families to move from Cook County to DuPage County.
- Make it easier to move up the economic ladder in "lower opportunity" neighborhoods. For example, are there government or privately financed programs for Cook County that would increase upward mobility? These types of programs are called *place-based programs for shared economic growth.*

Do Housing Vouchers Work?

From 1994 to 1998, the federal government conducted an RCT designed to determine if housing vouchers could increase intergenerational mobility. A total of 4,600 lower-income families living in Baltimore, Boston, Chicago, Los Angeles, and New York were randomly assigned to three groups:

- The Experimental group was given a voucher that required them to move to a higher-income neighborhood.
- The Section 8 group was offered a housing voucher for the same monetary value that allowed the family to move anywhere.
- The Control group did not receive a voucher.

Based on their other work, Chetty, Hendren, and Lawrence Katz realized that giving vouchers to families with older children would have little effect on the children's future (see www.nber.org/papers/w21156.pdf). Therefore, they restricted their analysis to measuring adult outcomes for children in the study who were 12 years of age or younger at the time their family entered the RCT. Table 44.2 shows their results.

Table 44.2: Results of housing voucher study

OUTCOME	CONTROL	SECTION 8	EXPERIMENTAL
Mean Adult Income	$11,270	$12,994	$14,747
Fraction Attending College	16.5%	18%	21.7%
Fraction Living in Poor Neighborhoods as an Adult	23.8%	21.7%	20.4%
Fraction of Single Mothers in Adult Neighborhood	33%	31%	23%

www.equality-of-opportunity.org/bigdatacourse_stanford/

Based on each of these measures, the Experimental program resulted in the best outcome, and for each measure there was less than a 5% chance that these differences were due to chance (p-value less than 5%).

Before looking at these results, I would have thought the Section 8 group would have performed best, because the Section 8 voucher gave more choices (unlimited) than the Experimental voucher. It seems that the implicit advice (move to a better neighborhood!) incorporated in the Experimental voucher "nudged" families into making better decisions. Still, there was a high degree of noncompliance with the program's requirements.

Moving is difficult for any family. Raj Chetty and his multi-university team realized that it is important to make it easier for lower-income families to take advantage of the voucher. In a pilot program, Chetty and his team worked with the Seattle and King County Housing authority to make it easier for families to take advantage of the voucher program (see www.npr.org/2019/08/05/747610085/in-seattle-a-move-across-town-could-be-a-path-out-of-poverty). Each family receiving a voucher was assigned a navigator to guide the family through the difficult process of moving to an entirely new neighborhood. *Initial results indicate that the assignment of a navigator increased the fraction of families actually using the voucher from 14% to 54%.*

Of course, housing vouchers and navigators are expensive, so it seems like a relative assessment of the benefits and costs of housing voucher programs is needed. Deven Carlson, Robert Haveman, Thomas Kaplan, and Barbara Wolfe (see "The Benefits and Costs of the Section 8 Housing Subsidy Program: A Framework and Estimates of First-Year Effects," *Journal of Policy Analysis and Management*, vol. 30, no. 2, 2011, pages 233–255) found that the Section 8 program created social benefits (such as improved education for children, improved children's health, and reduction in crime) that outweigh the cost of the program.

Place-Based Programs

Ryan Nunn, Jay Shambaugh, and Kristin McIntosh have a book-length study that discusses several types of programs designed to improve economic mobility in poorer neighborhoods (see `www.brookings.edu/blog/up-front/2018/10/19/placed-based-policies-for-shared-economic-growth/`). These programs include

- Job subsidies to reduce unemployment and provide higher-paying jobs. Pumping more income into the poorer neighborhoods should result in better schools, less housing blight, and many other benefits.
- Modify federal guidelines on funds given to states to ensure that more money is assigned to lower-income neighborhoods.
- Research universities are often near low-income areas (Johns Hopkins, MIT, Harvard, Notre Dame, etc.). Incentivize research universities to use their research to create high-tech and skilled manufacturing jobs in the nearby lower-income neighborhoods.
- Improve nutritional assistance and health-care programs in poorer neighborhoods.

The 2017 Tax Act created *opportunity zones,* which give developers tax incentives to invest in certain neighborhoods (most of which, though not all, are low income). You can go to `opportunitydb.com/tools/map/` and enter a zip code to see the opportunity zones near you. Many have criticized opportunity zones as simply a tax dodge to enable developers to gentrify poor neighborhoods (see `www.marketwatch.com/story/opportunity-zones-are-just-an-opportunity-for-the-rich-to-gentrify-poor-neighborhoods-2019-10-29/`).

It is far too early to access the effect that opportunity zones will have on intergenerational mobility, but this will surely be a fertile area to be mined by future researchers.

CHAPTER 45

The Waiting is the Hardest Part

I am sure everybody reading this thinks they spend too much time standing in line. Most people define the longest line at the supermarket as the line they are in. Things would be much worse, however, if Danish engineer A. K. Erlang (1878–1929) had not invented *queueing theory*, the mathematics of waiting lines, or queues. Erlang began working for the Copenhagen Telephone Company (CTC) in 1908. People would try to make phone calls, talk for an unknown time, and then hang up. Meanwhile, other people were trying to make calls. If CTC did not have enough phone lines or phone operators to connect the calls, callers would get very frustrated. Erlang figured out the mathematics for determining the number of operators and lines required to ensure that 99.99% of all callers could get through. Erlang's work marked the birth of queueing theory.

In this chapter, we will define the key terms in queueing theory and provide a spreadsheet that can be used to determine how a customer's time in the system and average number of customers present depends on the number of servers. We assume that all customers wait in a single line for the first available server. The idea of a single line began around 1970 (see `www.cnn.com/style/article/design-of-waiting-lines/index.html`), and many companies (including American Airlines, British Airways, and Wendy's) claim to have originated the single line (also known as the *serpentine line*). The serpentine line maximizes the utilization of servers, prevents jockeying between servers, and also seems fairer because everyone is in the same line.

Which Factors Influence the Performance of a Queueing System?

The following three factors determine the performance of a queueing system:

- *The number of servers*—Clearly, the more servers, the less time on average customers wait in line and the fewer people on average will be waiting in line.

- *The mean and standard deviation of the time between arrivals*—The time between arrivals is called the interarrival time. If the average time between arrivals increases, then the number of arrivals decreases, which results in shorter waiting times and fewer people in the queueing system. As you will soon see, an increase in the standard deviation of interarrival times degrades the performance of a queueing system.

- *The mean and standard deviation of the time needed to complete service*—If the average service time increases, you will see an increase in the average time a customer spends in the system and an increase in the average number of customers present. As you will soon see, an increase in the standard deviation of service times increases the average time a customer spends in a queueing system and the average number of customers present.

Operating Characteristics of a Queueing System

When analyzing the average time people spend waiting in line, mathematicians talk about *steady-state characteristics* of a queueing system. Essentially, steady state means that a system has operated for a long time. More specifically, analysts want to know the value of the following quantities in the steady state:

- W = Average time a customer spends in the system
- W_q = Average time a customer spends waiting in line before the customer is served
- L = Average number of customers present in the system
- L_q = Average number of customers waiting in line

If we define λ = average number of arrivals per unit time, then a fundamental law of queueing (Little's law) tells us that

$$(1)\, L = \lambda W$$

and

$$(2)\, L_q = \lambda W_q$$

For the concept of a steady state to be meaningful, the following must be true:

- The mean and standard deviation of both the interarrival times and service times change little over time. The technical phrase is that the distribution of interarrival and service times is stationary over time. Of course, this assumption is often violated (think of restaurants and voting sites). There are more complex models that describe the operating characteristics of such nonstationary systems (see page 1131 of my book *Operations Research*, Cengage, 4th edition, 2004).

- If you let s = number of servers and μ = average number of services that can be completed per unit time, a steady state requires

  (3) $s\mu > \lambda$

Essentially, equation (3) implies that you can serve more people per unit time than are arriving. For example, suppose the average service time is 2 minutes, and the average time between arrivals is 30 seconds. Then equation (3) requires s * (1/2) > 1 / (1/2) = 2. This implies that in order to keep up with arrivals we need s > 4, or at least 5 servers. You might think that 4 servers would be enough to ensure a steady state; however, with 4 servers you serve customers as fast as they arrive, and with any random variation in interarrival or service times, eventually the system will fall behind and, in all likelihood, never catch up.

Queueing analysts define the *traffic intensity* $\rho = \lambda/s\mu$. Equation (3) can be restated as a steady state requires the traffic intensity be smaller than 1.

How Does Variability Degrade the Performance of a Queueing System?

To demonstrate that variability degrades the performance of a queueing system, consider a doctor's office where patients arrive in the morning every 15 minutes (8:00 a.m., 8:15 a.m., . . . 11:45 a.m.). If the doctor takes exactly 15 minutes to see a patient, there will never be more than one patient in the office. Now suppose that the doctor spends 5 minutes with half the patients and 25 minutes with half the patients. Suppose the doctor spends 5 minutes with the first patient and 25 minutes with the second patient. Then the first patient leaves at 8:05 a.m. and the doctor waits until 8:15 a.m. to see the second patient. The second patient leaves at 8:40 a.m. *Therefore, between 8:30 and 8:40 we have two patients present, which never happens when service times are known with certainty.*

Calculating the Operating Characteristics of a Queueing System

The worksheet Analysis in the workbook `Queues.xlsx` (see Figure 45.1) can be used to approximate (within 10% of their true value) the steady state values for L, W, L_q, and W_q.

	A	B	C
1			
2			
3	Arrival rate	0.077734	per second
4	Service rate	0.01297	per second
5	s(servers)	6	
6	Mean interarrival time	12.864	
7	Mean service time	77.102	
8	Standard deviation of interarrival times	4.43908	
9	Standard deviation of service times	48.05051	
10	CV arrive	0.119079	
11	CV service	0.388387	
12	u	5.993412	
13	ro	0.998902	
14	R(s,mu)	0.73554	
15	E_c(s,mu)	0.996956	
16	W_q	2960.658	
17	L_q	230.1434	
18	W	3037.76	
19	L	236.1368	

Figure 45.1: Queueing calculator

After you enter the following data in B3:B7, the worksheet computes L, W, L_q, and W_q.

- Cell B3: Number of servers
- Cell B4: Mean interarrival time
- Cell B5: Mean service time
- Cell B6: Standard deviation of interarrival times
- Cell B7: Standard deviation of service times

These parameters can be estimated using past data.

To illustrate the use of the model, suppose you have observed the interarrival times (in seconds) and service times at your local bank shown in the worksheet Queueing data (see Figure 45.2). Using the Excel AVERAGE and STDEV functions, we calculated the mean and standard deviation of the interarrival and service times. We found the mean interarrival time to be 12.864 seconds with a standard deviation of 4.439 seconds. We found the mean service time to be 77.102 seconds with a standard deviation of 48.05 seconds. In cells B1 and B2 of the Analysis worksheet, we compute the mean number of arrivals per second as 1 / 12.864 = 0.07773 and the mean number of service completions per second as

1 / 77.102 = 0.01297. To begin, we assume 6 servers and enter the other relevant data in B4:B7. We find that the system performs horribly with an average of 236 customers present, and an average of 3038 seconds (nearly 51 minutes) in the system. The reason for this poor performance is that with 6 servers, we can serve 6 * (0.01297) = 0.07782 customers per second and nearly this many (0.07773) customers arrive per second. Note that the traffic intensity can be computed as 0.07782 / (6 * 0.01297) = 0.9989. When the traffic intensity is near 1, adding just a little service capacity will result in a great improvement in system performance. *The key take-away from queueing is that when the traffic intensity is near 1, adding a small amount of capacity will greatly improve system performance.*

	A	B	C	D	E
1	mean	12.86440678	77.10169492 seconds!		
2	sigma	4.43908047	48.05051039		
3		Interarrival times	Service Time		Mean
4		5	95		=AVERAGE(B4:B62)
5		17	240		Sigma
6		12	71		=STDEV.S(B4:B62)
7		18	68		
8		9	90		
9		16	117		
10		15	291		
11		15	116		
12		10	107		
13		11	100		
14		9	28		
15		15	119		
16		19	98		
17		9	72		
18		16	127		
57		13	74		

Figure 45.2: Interarrival time and service time data

Using a one-way data table shown in Figure 45.3 (see also the "Excel Calculations" section), we see that adding only one more server will reduce the average line from 236 people to only 7! Adding three more servers won't even reduce the average line length by a single customer!

To see the impact of service time variability on the performance of a queueing system, suppose we keep the mean service time fixed and increase the standard deviation of the service time from 40 seconds to 80 seconds. Entering these values in cell B9 of the Analysis worksheet, we find that the average time a customer spends in the system triples from 2342 seconds to 7053 seconds!

	F	G	H
5		L	W
6	Servers	236.14	3037.76
7	6	236.14	3037.76
8	7	6.92	88.99
9	8	6.26	80.57
10	9	6.09	78.37
11	10	6.03	77.59

Figure 45.3: Sensitivity of L and W to number of servers

Excel Calculations

Every model has inputs and outputs. *Sensitivity analysis* attempts to determine how changes in model inputs change model outputs. In our queueing model, we will focus on how a change in one input (the number of servers) affects two outputs (L and W).

A *one-way data table* enables you to easily determine how changes in a single input affects multiple outputs. To see how changing the number of servers affects L and W, we created a one-way data table in the worksheet Analysis:

1. Enter the values of the inputs (6 through 10 servers) in F7:F11.

2. Go up one row from the first input value and one column to the right and enter the formulas for your desired outputs (=B17 in G6 and =B16 in H6).

3. Select the table range F6:H11.

4. From the Data tab, select What-If Analysis from the Forecast group, and then choose Data Table.

5. Leave the Row input cell blank (there is no input in the first row of the table range) and enter **B3** as the Column input cell.

6. After clicking OK, you will see that Excel has substituted the numbers 6, 7, 8, 9, and 10 in cell B3, and as the number of servers vary, Excel computes the values of L and W.

We see that increasing the number of servers from six to seven greatly improves system performance, but adding more than seven servers provides little improvement in system performance.

CHAPTER 46

Are Roundabouts a Good Idea?

Carmel, Indiana has the second-highest median income in Indiana (trailing Zionsville; see `www.homesnacks.net/richest-places-in-indiana-126056/`). The Carmel High School Girls Swim Team has won 34 consecutive state championships, the longest active string in any high school (boys or girls) sport. What we are interested in, however, is the fact that Carmel is the roundabout capital of the United States. Carmel has more than 125 roundabouts (see `carmel.in.gov/department-services/engineering/roundabouts`). In this chapter, we will explore the pros and cons of roundabouts versus traffic lights, two-way stops, and four-way stops. One of Carmel's roundabouts is shown in Figure 46.1.

On a lighter note, on October 13, 2015, Carmel resident Oran Sands set a World Record (verified by Recordsetter.com) by driving around a single roundabout for 3 hours and 34 minutes (`www.roadandtrack.com/car-culture/news/a27318/64-year-old-hero-sets-world-record-for-driving-around-a-roundabout/`).

Figure 46.1: A roundabout in Carmel, Indiana

What Is a Roundabout?

As Figure 46.1 illustrates, a *roundabout* is a circular intersection in which traffic travels in a counterclockwise direction around a center island. Usually there are four roads that allow drivers to enter and leave the roundabout. In theory, vehicles arriving at the entry roads should yield to those already in the roundabout. The origin of this rule is traced to the United Kingdom in 1966. As you will see, roundabouts can be almost as polarizing as U.S. politics.

History of Roundabouts

According to Wikipedia, one of the first U.S. roundabouts was built in San Jose, California in 1907, and the first British roundabout was built in 1909 in Letchworth Garden City. Again according to Wikipedia, over half the world's roundabouts are in France. Florida has more roundabouts than any other state, but per capita, Maryland has the most roundabouts—one out of every 363 intersections have a roundabout. On the other hand, in South Dakota, only one out of every 22,806 intersections is a roundabout (`www.citylab.com/transportation/2016/03/america-traffic-roundabouts-street-map/408598/`).

Benefits of Roundabouts

In many situations, roundabouts create three types of benefits:

- Reduced congestion
- Fewer and less serious accidents
- Reduced operating cost

Reduction in Traffic Congestion

Most studies have found that roundabouts result in a large decrease in traffic congestion. Eugene Russell, Margaret Rys, and Srinivas Mandavilli used the following five metrics to measure the effectiveness of roundabouts (see (`www.researchgate.net/publication/228684063_Operational_Efficiency_of_Roundabouts`):

- **95% Queue Length:** Measured in feet, 5% of the time the average length of all queues entering the roundabout will exceed the 95% Queue Length
- **Average Intersection Delay:** Measured in seconds, the average vehicle delay for all vehicles entering the roundabout
- **Maximum Approach Delay:** Measured in seconds, the average vehicle delay for the roundabout entry road with the highest average delay
- **Proportion Stopped:** The fraction of vehicles required to stop due to vehicles already in the intersection
- **Maximum Proportion Stopped:** For the intersection with the highest fraction of vehicles stopped, the fraction of vehicles required to stop due to vehicles already in the intersection

Russell, Rys, and Mandavilli examined four Kansas intersections that were converted from four-way stops to roundabouts and found the range of improvement in traffic congestion shown in Table 46.1.

Table 46.1: Improvement in Traffic Congestion Due to Roundabouts

MEASURE	RANGE OF IMPROVEMENT
95% Queue Length	44% to 87% reduction
Average Intersection Delay	50% to 87% reduction
Maximum Approach Delay	55% to 91% reduction
Proportion Stopped	35% to 82% reduction
Maximum Proportion Stopped	36% to 73% reduction

Paul Hoglund ("Case Study: Performance Effects of Changing a Traffic Signal Intersection to Roundabout," in Brilon, Werner (ed.) *Intersections without Traffic Signals II*. Springer-Verlag, Berlin, Heidelberg, 1991) found that in Jönköping, Sweden, changing a traffic signal to a roundabout reduced the time needed to negotiate the intersection an average of 55%.

If you have ever spent 30 seconds or so waiting at a red signal when nobody else is at the intersection, you can understand why roundabouts are appealing. If you are the only car at the roundabout, you don't need to stop. At traffic lights, there is always a lot of downtime during which *no cars* move, whereas roundabouts encourage continuous traffic flow. Roundabouts seem to work best when the traffic volume from different directions is relatively equal. In this situation, almost every car needs to stop at a four-way stop, whereas at a roundabout a far greater proportion of cars don't need to stop. Most sites claim that roundabouts are less effective (`www.acsengineers.com.au/2016/08/22/roundabouts-vs-traffic-lights/`) when the "major road" has much more traffic volume than a "minor road." This is because the roundabout always requires traffic on the major road to slow down, and without the roundabout, the traffic on the major road rarely needs to stop. I am not sure this analysis is justified. Several roundabouts near my home fit the major-minor road situation. Before conversion from a two-way stop to a roundabout, the traffic on the minor road would often wait several minutes for an opening. For example, in our Bloomington, Indiana Renwick-Moore's Pike roundabout, I would estimate that 90% of the traffic on this roundabout travels on Moore's Pike. The roundabout delays the Moore's Pike traffic around 2 seconds, but the average Renwick vehicle waits at least 30 seconds less on average. This implies that the roundabout increases average travel time by $0.9 * (2) + 0.1 * (-30) = -1.2$ seconds per vehicle. Thus, this roundabout reduces average travel time by an average of 1.2 seconds per vehicle and also improves equity.

Reduction in Accidents

Many accidents occur at traffic signals (with at least one car traveling at high speed) when a car tries to make a left turn or a car rushes though a yellow or red light. When driving in Houston, drivers often honked at me when I stopped at a yellow light. This was probably because stopping at a yellow light on Westheimer Road usually caused me to sit through five red lights in a row, whereas rushing through the yellow light resulted in five consecutive green lights! I quickly got the message to speed through the yellow lights. At roundabouts, these causes of accidents are eliminated, and in most cases, the cars involved in the accident are traveling at lower speeds and (hopefully) in the same direction.

The Insurance Institute for Highway Safety (IIHS) has collected the results of many studies that show the safety improvements that have resulted from conversion of intersections from stop signs or traffic signals to roundabouts (www.iihs.org/topics/roundabouts):

- In the United States, the conversion of an intersection to a roundabout reduces injury crashes 72%–80% and overall crashes 35%–47%.

- In Europe and Australia, the conversion of an intersection to a roundabout reduced injury crashes 25%–87% and reduced all crashes 36%–61%.

- It is estimated that converting 10% of all U.S. intersections to roundabouts would save 231 lives per year!

Reduced Cost

The costs of building roundabouts and traffic signals are about equal (www .wsdot.wa.gov/Safety/roundabouts/benefits.htm). Since roundabouts don't need electricity, roundabouts are between $5,000 and $10,000 per year cheaper than traffic signals. Unlike traffic lights, power outages or signal malfunctions do not affect roundabouts.

Disadvantages of Roundabouts

As Joni Mitchell wrote in her great song "Both Sides Now," "something's lost and something's gained in living every day." Along those lines, roundabouts have some disadvantages:

- Roundabouts usually require more space than other intersections.

- Older drivers (including my mother-in-law) often have difficulty adjusting to multilane roundabouts.

- Pedestrians often complain that it is difficult to cross roundabouts. Most multilane roundabouts have crosswalks and drivers are required to yield to pedestrians who are within the roundabout or waiting to cross. A Minnesota study found that 45% of drivers did not yield to pedestrians (see www.dot.state.mn.us/research/TS/2012/2012-28.pdf).

Probably the best way to evaluate roundabouts is to compare public approval of roundabouts before and after their construction. Richard Retting, Sergey Kyrychenko, and Anne McCartt ("Long-Term Trends in Public Opinion Following Construction of Roundabouts," *Transportation Research Record: Journal of the Transportation Research Board*, vol. 10, 2019, pages 219–224) found that before a roundabout was constructed, support ranged from 22%–44%, and several years after, support increased to 57%–87%.

Roundabout Capacity

According to the Wisconsin Department of Transportation (see page 20 of `wisconsindot.gov/rdwy/fdm/fd-11-26.pdf`), a single-lane roundabout has a capacity of up to 25,000 vehicles per day and a two-lane roundabout has a capacity of 25,000 to 45,000 vehicles per day. There are many complex formulas (see Chapter 4 and Appendix A of Bruce Roberts, *Roundabouts: An Informational Guide*, University of Michigan Libraries, 2000) used to estimate roundabout capacity. Rather than try to explain these complex formulas, we provide a simple example to illustrate how, in theory, a two-lane roundabout can have a surprisingly high capacity.

Consider a two-lane roundabout with four entries—North, South, East, and West—in which each entry has a right-turn lane. Assume that once a car enters the roundabout, it takes two seconds for the car to reach the next entry. For example, a car entering the North entry takes two seconds to reach the West entry. Also assume that each driver needs an "acceptable gap" of two seconds before they will enter the roundabout. Now suppose that cars arrive at the roundabout as shown in Table 46.2. Unless otherwise stated, assume the car travels through three exits and then exits the roundabout.

Table 46.2: Arrivals to a Roundabout

TIME	ARRIVALS
0	North, South, North turning right
4	East, West, West turning right, East Driver gets off at West exit
8	North, South, North turning right
12	East, West, West turning right, East Driver gets off at West exit

Assume that the arrivals at 16 seconds are the same as those at 8 seconds, the arrivals at 20 seconds are the same as those at 12 seconds, and so on. Assuming the 2-second acceptable gap, here's what will happen:

- At 2 seconds, the North turning right driver exits.
- At 4 seconds, the time 0 North driver will be at South exit, and the time 0 South driver will be the North exit. This means the East and West arrivals can enter.
- At 6 seconds, the time 4 West driver turning right, and two of the time 0 arrivals exit.
- At 8 seconds, the time 4 East driver will be at the West exit, and the time 8 West driver will be at the East exit. This allows the time 8 arrivals to enter, and the cycle continues.

In our utopian roundabout, three cars per 4 seconds (or 45 cars per minute) can pass through the roundabout. This is equivalent to 45 * 60 = 2,700 cars per hour. Of course, arrivals will not be deterministic, and not all drivers will enter with exactly a 2-second gap. A key assumption in our simple example was that the exits were 2 seconds apart. For this assumption to be met, the size of the roundabout and the speed of the drivers must be analyzed. Most drivers I observe at our two-lane roundabout will enter at the time when a driver enters the previous entrance (for example, a driver will enter the East entrance at the same time a driver enters the South entrance). If the roundabout were not large enough, this type of driver behavior would be a recipe for disaster.

We have a two-lane roundabout a mile from our home. The busiest time at the roundabout is between 7:30 and 8 a.m., when parents drop their children off at middle school. I observed this roundabout and found at this peak time, an average of 1,900 cars per hour (equivalent to 45,600 cars per day) passed through the roundabout. It also appeared that my 2-second acceptable gap assumption approximated reality. I also interviewed several dog walkers, and they said cars usually stopped for them.

Roundabouts and Revolutions

In researching this chapter (and others), I heavily used Amazon.com's one-click button (they own a patent on it) to buy books on roundabouts that I thought would help me learn more about the math behind roundabouts. One book I purchased was Eyal Weizman's *The Roundabout Revolutions* (Sternberg Press, 2015). When I ordered this book, I did not see the "s" at the end of the word Revolutions. This made me think the book would discuss how roundabouts can revolutionize the design of traffic intersections. This amazing book described, with dozens of amazing photos, how many revolutions around the world were catalyzed by protesters gathering in roundabouts. Revolutions described include the following:

- The 1980 Gwangju protest in South Korea that helped overthrow South Korea's military government.
- The Tahrir Square 2011 protest in Cairo that helped overthrow Egyptian President Hosni Mubarak grew to 300,000 protesters.
- A 1965 protest in Bahrain at the Pearl Roundabout resulted in the British leaving Bahrain.
- A 2009 protest in Azadi Square in Tehran was suppressed by the Iranian government.

■ The Arab Spring began in late 2010, when Tunisian street vendor Mohamed Bouazizi set himself on fire to protest the government's economic policies. The roundabout square Place du 7 Novembre 1987 in Tunis, was the starting point for many of the protests that resulted in the resignation of President Ben Ali on January 14, 2011. The square is now named January 14, 2011.

Weizman believes that many protests occur in roundabouts because closing a roundabout in a city's center can paralyze traffic throughout the city, making it easier for large protests to occur. Since many roundabouts contain monuments that are symbols of the current regime, it is easy to motivate protesters to congregate in the hope that they can destroy the monuments.

CHAPTER 47

Red Light, Green Light, or No Light?

Since 1999, I have made over 50 trips to Redmond, Washington, to consult or teach classes for Microsoft. During each trip, I drive on I-405 from Sea-Tac Airport to my hotel in downtown Bellevue. The ramps on I-405 have *ramp meters*, which are traffic signals that cycle between green and red. When the light is green, a car is allowed to attempt to merge onto I-405. The first ramp meter in the United States was installed in 1953 on the Eisenhower Parkway in Chicago. In this chapter, we will explain how ramp meters can lessen freeway congestion and why some people oppose them. The U.S. Department of Transportation *Ramp Management and Control Handbook* is probably the most complete reference discussing ramp meters (ops.fhwa.dot.gov/publications/ramp_mgmt_handbook/manual/manual/pdf/rm _ handbook.pdf).

What Causes Traffic Jams?

Clearly, if there are too many cars on the freeway, traffic will have to slow down. By increasing the fraction of time that ramp meters are red, traffic controllers can reduce the inflow of cars to the freeway during times of peak congestion. As pointed out by Gabor Orosz, R. Eddie Wilson, Robert Szalai, and Gábor Stépán ("Exciting Traffic Jams: Nonlinear Phenomena Behind Traffic Jam Formation on Highways," *Physical Review*, vol. 80, no. 4, 2009, 046205), a mile-long traffic jam (the article calls it a *backward traveling wave*) can begin when one driver hits the brakes hard, thereby causing the driver behind them to hit the brakes, and so it goes. Without ramp meters, a platoon of vehicles can attempt to merge. This will almost surely cause a driver in the right lane to brake or attempt to switch into the second lane, and then people attempt to switch into the third lane. Without the ramp meters, the freeway drivers' adjustments are much more likely to cause a backward traveling wave.

As mentioned in Chapter 45, "The Waiting is the Hardest Part" increasing variability in interarrival times increases queue length and time in the system. Ramp meters decrease the variability in the time between cars merging onto the freeway. In his number-one bestseller *Traffic* (Knopf, 2008), Tom Vanderbilt gives two great examples to explain why increased variability can increase highway congestion:

- Take a liter of rice, and quickly pour it down a funnel. It takes 40 seconds to pass through the funnel. Then pour a liter of rice more slowly through the funnel at a constant rate; it takes only 27 seconds for the rice to pass through the funnel. When you pour the rice quickly, the rice particles pile up because the particles are arriving at a faster rate than the funnel's capacity. As the particles pile up (like cars on the freeway), they interfere with each other, thereby slowing down the rice—just like nearby cars slow down other cars. The moral here is that slow and steady yields less congestion. Also, the rice analogy indicates that ramp meters should yield fewer accidents (like fewer rice particles bumping into each other).

- The Holland Tunnel under the Hudson River connects Manhattan and Jersey City, New Jersey. When no restrictions were placed on cars entering the tunnel, 1,176 cars per hour passed through the two-lane tunnel. (Cars cannot change lanes in the tunnel.) As an experiment, police regulated the entry of cars in the tunnel to 44 cars per two minutes by making cars wait, if needed. Now 44 * 30 = 1,320 cars per hour passed through the tunnel. By separating the groups of entering cars, the police limited the length of the backward traveling wave, resulting in the increased throughput.

How Should We Set the Lights?

There are three approaches used to determine how time is allocated between green and red lights for ramp meters (see *Ramp Metering: A Proven, Cost-Effective Operational Strategy—A Primer,* at ops.fhwa.dot.gov/publications/fhwahop14020/sec1.htm).

Pre-timed Metering With pre-timed metering, the fraction of the time the light is green is preset based on the historical average traffic levels at that time. For example, during peak times the meters might be set to allow 300 cars per hour to enter and at nonpeak times be set to allow 600 cars per hour to enter. This is the simplest and cheapest system, but it ignores the current level of freeway congestion.

Local Traffic Responsive Metering   This method sets the fraction of the time the light is green based on *the current level of traffic and traffic conditions near the ramp*. Of course, this method requires sensors that continually monitor the traffic flow and speed near each ramp.

Systemwide Traffic Responsive Metering   This method sets the fraction of the time the light is green at each ramp using information of traffic flow and speed on the *entire freeway*. This method uses complex algorithms that attempt to estimate how the green-red allocation controlling southbound entry at say the I-405 Exit 12 in Bellevue should be determined based on the amount of traffic between Bellevue and Sea-Tac Airport. Of course, this method will require the most information and incur the highest cost. When correctly implemented, this method should yield the most improvement in freeway traffic flow, average speed, and reduce accidents.

Ramp Meters and Equity

Even if ramp meters improve freeway performance (more on this later), they may make some commuters worse off. Motorists who have longer suburban commutes often enter the freeway in a less congested location that has no ramp meters, whereas commuters who live closer to the destination city will have to suffer through the ramp meters. Thus, some analysts believe that ramp meters promote suburban sprawl. Also, ramp meters can cause ramp traffic to back up onto city streets, upsetting nonfreeway travelers. David Levinson and Lei Zhang ("Ramp Meters on Trial: Evidence from the Twin Cities Metering Holiday," *Transportation Research Part A*, vol. 40, 2006, pages 810–828) confirmed that ramp meters benefit travelers who travel more than three exits, whereas many travelers making trips with fewer than three exits are hurt by ramp meters.

Lei Zhang and David Levinson propose a clever method to trade-off equity and travel time reduction (pdfs.semanticscholar.org/251d/74a34f8dfd6ea5574b 8389f01cd30996c0b9.pdf). They propose that the ramp meters be set to minimize average travel time based on a weighted average of traveler waiting times in which travelers who wait longer on the ramps have their travel times weighted more. For example, a traveler who waits eight minutes on a ramp could have their travel time given twice the weight of a traveler who waits four minutes on a ramp.

Measuring the Impact of Ramp Meters

Traffic engineers use four metrics to measure the improvement due to ramp meters (see `ops.fhwa.dot.gov/publications/fhwahop14020/sec1.htm`):

- Increase in average traffic speed
- Average percentage reduction in trip length
- Percentage decrease in collisions
- Percentage decrease in emissions

The preceding reference gives statistics on these metrics for the Minneapolis-St. Paul, Long Island, Portland, Denver, and Seattle areas. Traffic speed improvement ranged from 5% in Long Island to 170% in Portland. Travel time reduction ranged from 10% in Long Island to 150% in Portland. The percentage decrease in collisions ranged from 8% in Long Island to 40% in Denver. Improvement in emissions ranged from 15% in Denver to 40% in Minneapolis-St. Paul.

The Twin Cities Metering Holiday

In 1999, Minnesota Senate Republican leader Dick Day proposed a "Freedom to Drive" plan that called for shutting off all ramp meters, using the left lane as only a passing lane, and allowing all drivers to use the high-occupancy vehicle (HOV) lanes. During 2000, the Minnesota State Legislature debated "Freedom to Drive" and passed a bill that included, in part, a two-month "ramp meter holiday," which turned off all ramp meters for two months. This provided a great opportunity to test the effectiveness of ramp meters. David Levinson and Lei Zhang ("Ramp Meters on Trial: Evidence from the Twin Cities Metering Holiday," *Transportation Research Part A*, vol. 40, 2006, pages 810–828) summarized the results from the holiday. On Highway TH169, they found that ramp metering decreased average travel time per mile from 167 seconds to 106 seconds and increased average travel speed from 30 to 44 miles per hour.

After the ramp meter holiday, some adjustments were made to the ramp meters. The meters were altered so that nobody has to wait more than four minutes to enter the freeway, and queues cannot back up to reach city streets.

How Do I Make Good Things Happen?

In This Part

How Can We Improve K–12 Education?

Every nation needs a great precollege (in the United States, K–12) education system. In the United States, adults without a high school diploma earn 26% less than adults whose highest education is a high school diploma. Those with a bachelor's degree earn an average of 69% more than adults whose highest education is a high school diploma (see www.oecd-ilibrary.org/education/ education-at-a-glance-2018/indicator-a4-what-are-the-earnings-advantages- from-education _ eag-2018-10-en). This shows how important it is to get kids through high school and get college students to graduate.

If we consider test scores to be an important output of an education system, then the U.S. K–12 system does not deliver good results from the enormous resources the country devotes to education. The Programme for International Student Assessment (PISA) test measures math, reading, and science achievement in different countries (see data.oecd.org/pisa/mathematics-performance-pisa. htm#indicator-chart for 2018 math results and https://data.oecd.org/pisa/ reading-performance-pisa.htm#indicator-chart for 2018 reading results). In the file PISA.xlsx, I averaged the 2018 math and reading scores for boys and girls in all participating countries. Figure 48.1 shows how the United States ranks on the math and reading averages among OECD (Organisation for Economic Co-operation and Development) countries. OECD includes most European countries as well as Japan, Australia, and New Zealand. Figures 48.1 and 48.2 show 2018 average math and reading scores, respectively. On math, number one Japan performs 1.22 standard deviations above average, whereas at number 33 (out

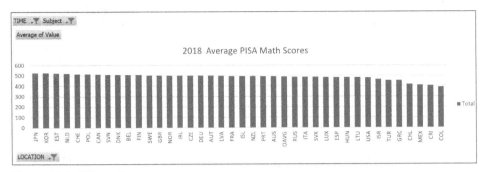

Figure 48.1: PISA math scores

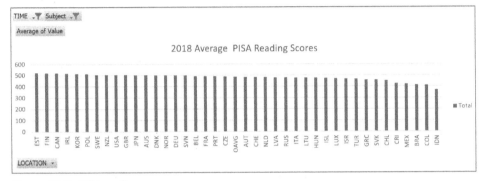

Figure 48.2: PISA reading scores

of 40!), the United States performs 0.27 standard deviations below average. On reading, the United States fares much better, ranking number 9 and performing 0.74 standard deviations better than average.

Figures 48.3 and 48.4 show the 2015 spending per student in U.S. dollars on primary and secondary education, respectively. You can see that the United States ranks second in per-capita primary school spending and fourth in per-capita secondary school spending. You don't have to be a rocket scientist to realize that the high level of U.S. spending is not producing satisfactory results (see `data.worldbank.org/indicator/SE.XPD.TOTL.GD.ZS`).

School systems have lots of data on student and teacher performance. Schools should be able to use this data to improve student performance. In this chapter, we will explore two examples of how data-driven decision making can improve educational outcomes:

- Do smaller class sizes justify the additional expense?
- Can predictive analytics increase enrollment and improve performance in eighth-grade Algebra I?

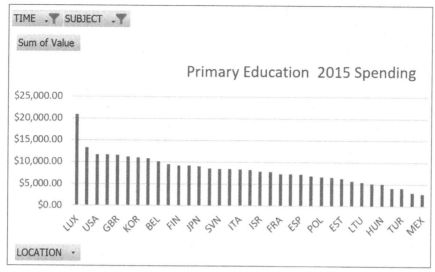

Figure 48.3: Primary education spending (2015)

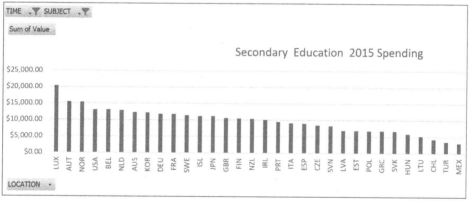

Figure 48.4: Secondary education spending (2015)

Tennessee's STAR Study on K–2 Class Size

In the early 1980s, Tennessee Governor (soon to become senator) Lamar Alexander made improving K–12 education a priority for his administration. In 1985, a total of 79 Tennessee elementary schools entered a randomized trial to test whether a reduction in class size in grades K–2 would improve test scores. The 79 schools were classified as inner-city, suburban, urban, or rural schools. Each school had a one-third chance of being assigned one of the following classroom strategies:

- Regular-sized class (22–23 students) without a teacher's aid
- Regular-sized class with a teacher's aide

▪ Class one-third smaller (an average of 15 students) than a regular-sized class with no teacher's aide

Within each school, students and teachers were randomly assigned to each of the three classroom strategies. Performance was measured by scores on standardized reading and math tests. The results of the STAR (Student/Teacher Achievement Ratio) experiment and two follow-up studies (the Lasting Benefits Study and Project Challenge) were reported by legendary statistician Frederick Mosteller ("The Tennessee Study of Class Size in the Early School Grades," *The Future of Children*, vol. 5, no. 2, 1995, pages 113–127).

In the STAR randomized trial, Mosteller found that the first-grade students in the smaller class performed around 0.25 standard deviations better than students in the regular-sized classes (with or without a teacher's aide). Assuming that test scores are normally distributed, an improvement of 0.25 standard deviations would move an average student from the 50th percentile to the 60th percentile (see the "Excel Calculations" section later in this chapter). The STAR study also found that minority students experienced almost twice the benefit received by nonminority students!

The Lasting Benefits follow-up to the STAR study showed that the benefit of the smaller K–2 class sizes persisted as children grew older. Averaged across six subjects, students performed 0.2 standard deviations better in fifth grade.

Based on the performance benefits experienced by minority students, in 1989, Tennessee instituted Project Challenge, which reduced class sizes for K–3 students in the 17 poorest Tennessee school districts. Before Project Challenge, second graders in these school districts ranked 95th among 139 districts in reading and 85th in math. By 1993, the second graders in these 17 districts ranked 78th in reading and 56th in math!

Cost–Benefit Analysis

Of course, the smaller class sizes incur the additional expense of higher teacher salaries. The economic benefits of the smaller class size are less clear. The late great economist Alan Krueger (see "Economic Considerations and Class Size," *Economic Journal*, vol. 113, 2003, pages F34–F63) estimated that the benefit of a one standard deviation improvement in age 7 test scores resulted in 8% higher adult salaries. Then Krueger conducted a *cost–benefit analysis*, which is an attempt to determine if the financial benefits of smaller class sizes (higher adult salaries) justify the increased teacher's salaries. Cost–benefit analysis is often used to evaluate public policy decisions such as building a new highway, building the San Francisco mass transit system, and the building of outdoor recreation facilities.

After discussing the important concept of the time value of money, we will attempt to update Krueger's cost–benefit analysis on class size.

The Time Value of Money: Net Present Value and Internal Rate of Return

As the old saying (from John Ray's *Handbook of Proverbs*, 1670) goes, "a bird in the hand is worth two in the bush." An example of this idea is the fact that if someone owes us $1, we would prefer to have them pay us back today instead of one year from now. The concept of the *time value of money* recognizes that money received later is worth less than money received now. Many public policy analysts believe that the annual rate used to discount future cash flows should be the *real* return on 10-year Treasury bonds (see www.env-econ.net/2005/08/discount_rates_.html). The real rate is the annual rate on 10-year bonds reduced by the expected annual inflation rate. In early 2020, the average real rate of return during the last 10 years was an anomalous –0.46% (see www.multpl.com/10-year-real-interest-rate), but for the period 1999–2017 we calculated in the workbook RealReturns.xlsx that the real rate of return on 10-year bonds was 3.4%. To keep the math simple, let's assume that the appropriate discount rate for a government cost–benefit analysis is 5%. This means that

$$\$1 \text{ now} = \$(1.05) \text{ a year from now}$$

or

$$\$1 / 1.05 \text{ now} = \$1 \text{ a year from now}$$

The *net present value* (NPV) of a sequence of cash flows is the value in today's dollars of the sequence of cash flows. To determine the NPV of a sequence of cash flows, we multiply the cash flow one year from now by 1/1.05, multiply the cash flow two years from now by $1/1.05^2$, and so on.

Figure 48.5 and the worksheet NPV in the workbook CostBenefit.xlsx illustrate the concept of NPV. Today (the beginning of Year 1), Investment 1 incurs a cash outflow of $10,000, and at the beginning of each of the next four years, Investment 1 brings in a cash inflow of $2,800. Investment 2 incurs a cash flow of $10,000 today and brings in a cash flow of $11,000 one year from now. Ignoring the time value of money, the total cash flow from Investment 1 is +$1,200, and the total cash flow from Investment 2 is +$1,000. This would indicate that Investment 1 is superior. Note, however, that Investment 2's cash inflows come in much earlier than Investment 1's cash inflows. When we use Excel's NPV function (see the "Excel Calculations" section), we find that using an annual discount rate of 5%, for the same cash outflow, Investment 1 has an NPV of –$71.34 (the cash inflows don't cover the cash outflows), whereas Investment 2 has an NPV of $476.19. Thus, when we consider the time value of money, Investment 2 is better.

	D	E	F	G	H
4	Year		Investment 1	Investment 2	
5		1	-$10,000.00	-$10,000.00	
6		2	$2,800.00	$11,000.00	
7		3	$2,800.00	$0.00	
8		4	$2,800.00	$0.00	
9		5	$2,800.00	$0.00	
10	NPV		-$71.34	$476.19 =E5+NPV(0.05,E6:E9)	
11	IRR		4.69%	10.00% =IRR(E5:E9)	
12	Total cash flow		$1,200.00	$1,000.00 =SUM(E5:E9)	

Figure 48.5: Example of NPV and IRR

Of course, experts will differ on the appropriate discount rate. The concept of *internal rate of return* (IRR) skirts the issue of a discount rate. The IRR of a project is the discount rate that makes the project's cash flows have an NPV of 0. If a project's cash flows change sign exactly once, a project is guaranteed to have a unique IRR. An IRR of 10%, for example, means that the project is essentially "earning" 10% per year on its cash outflows. In the worksheet NPV (see Figure 48.6), we used the Excel IRR function to find that Investment 1 has an IRR of 4.69%, and Investment 2 has an IRR of 10%. There is a simple relationship between NPV and IRR:

NPV > 0 if and only if IRR > discount rate.

NPV < 0 if and only if IRR < discount rate.

	D	E	F	G
2		IRR	9.77% =IRR(F5:F64)	
3				
4		Age	Cost	
5		6	-$1,271	
6		7	-$1,271	
7		8	-$424	
8		9	$0	
9		10	$0	
10		11	$0	
11		12	$0	
12		13	$0	
13		14	$0	
14		15	$0	
15		16	$0	
16	Mean Salary	17	$0	
17	$18.0	18	$360	
18	$18.0	19	$360 = D18*1000*(1+benefit)-D18*1000	

Figure 48.6: Cost–benefit analysis of smaller classes

Note that Investment 1's NPV is less than 0, and its IRR is less than 5%. Investment 2's NPV is positive, and its IRR exceeds the discount rate.

We can now conduct a crude cost–benefit analysis (see Figure 48.6 and the worksheet Class Size in the workbook `CostBenefit.xlsx`) that estimates the IRR of reducing class size in grades K–2. Krueger estimates that the typical student spent 2.33 years with a reduced class size. The average annual teacher salary is $60,000 (see `www.forbes.com/sites/niallmccarthy/2019/04/02/the-evolution-of-u-s-teacher-salaries-in-the-21st-century-infographic/#10954d6377f0`). To estimate the annual cost of reduced class size, consider an elementary school with 110 students and 5 classes of 22 students. This will cost 5 * ($60,000) = $300,000 per year in salaries. If we reduce the class size to 15 students, we would need 110 / 15 = 7.33 teachers, which will cost ($60,000) * 7.33 = $439,800 per year. Per student, the reduced class size costs ($439,800 – $300,000)/110 = $1,271 per student. As shown in Figure 48.6, we entered costs of $1,271 at ages 6 and 7 and one-third that amount at age 8.

Coupling Krueger's estimate that the benefit from one standard deviation in test scores is an 8% increase in salary with the STAR study's estimate that smaller class sizes in K–2 increase test scores by 0.25 standard deviations, we use a 0.25 * 8% = 2% increase in annual salary as the wage benefit per student during their working years (ages 18–65) (obtained from `smartasset.com/retirement/the-average-salary-by-age`). For example, at age 29, the average salary was $45,500, so the benefit from the reduced class size is estimated as .02 * (45,500) = $910. Using Excel's `IRR` function, we find the IRR of the incremental cash flows per student to be 9.77%. If we assume minority students receive double the overall benefit (4% increase in annual salary vs. 2% annual increase in salary), then we get an estimated IRR of 13.26%. Both these IRRs greatly exceed the discount rates used in evaluating most public expenditures, so reducing class size seems like a slam dunk.

In our conservative analysis, we ignore two factors that would increase the IRR of reducing class size:

■ We are ignoring the role of increased productivity in raising wages. During the period 1947–2019, U.S. productivity increased by at least 1% per year (see `www.bls.gov/lpc/prodybar.htm`).

■ Improving students' school performance will lead to a decrease in crime (see `www.economics.handels.gu.se/digitalAssets/1439/1439011 _ 49-55 _ research _ lochner.pdf`).

Of course, these two factors would tilt the scales even more in favor of reducing K–2 class size.

Can Predictive Analytics Increase Enrollment and Performance in Eighth-Grade Algebra I?

Students who take Algebra I in eighth grade are on track to take calculus in high school. The U.S. Department of Education believes that success in high school math is strongly correlated with success in college and the ability to succeed in a STEM career (see www2.ed.gov/rschstat/research/pubs/toolboxrevisit/toolbox.pdf).

Wake County is North Carolina's largest school district. Wake County used predictive analytics to triple enrollment in eighth-grade Algebra I, with 95% of students passing a proficiency exam at the end of the course (see "Middle School Math Acceleration and Equitable Access to 8th Grade Algebra: Evidence from the Wake County Public School System," *Educational Evaluation and Policy Analysis*, vol. 37, no. 15, 2015, pages 80S–101S).

Based on standardized test results, SAS (Statistical Analysis System) used a proprietary algorithm to estimate at the end of the fifth grade each student's probability of successfully completing Algebra I. Students whose predicted success probability was at least 70% were recommended to take pre-algebra classes during sixth and seventh grade. During the second year of the program, the Algebra I pass rate was 97%. The program doubled the fraction of low-income students taking Algebra I from 20% to 40%.

Before analytics-based placement was introduced, placement was based on subjective recommendations given by teachers and guidance counselors. Of course, each student's grades factored prominently into the recommendation decision. Wake Forest-Rolesville Middle School Principal Elaine Hanzer realized that grades often (especially for low-income students) reflected attributes such as class participation and turning in homework. Though important, these attributes are more likely to hurt the grades of low-income students. Increasing the importance of math achievement in the placement decision greatly improved outcomes for low-income students.

Excel Calculations

In this section, we begin by showing how to use Excel's NORM.S.DIST function to convert standard deviation improvements to percentile improvements. Then we describe the Excel NPV and IRR functions and show how they can be used to help perform the cost–benefit analysis on reduced class size.

The *NORM.S.DIST* Function

For any x, the formula =NORM.S.DIST(x,True) gives the probability that any normal random variable is <= x standard deviations above average. Thus, in cell E7 of the worksheet Sigma to Percentile in the workbook CostBenefit.xlsx, the formula =NORM.S.DIST(0.25,TRUE) returns the chance that a normal random variable will be at most .0.25 sigma above the mean is 59.8%. Of course, an average student scores 0 standard deviations above average and ranks at the 50th percentile. This analysis shows that for an average student, the smaller class size raises the student's rank on standardized tests by around 10%.

The NPV and IRR Functions

Entering the formula =NPV(rate, range of cash flows) computes the NPV of a range of cash flows, assuming that cash flows occur at the end of each period. The NPV function ignores blanks, so make sure to enter 0s for periods with no cash flow. In the worksheet NPV of the workbook CostBenefit.xlsx, the formula =E5+NPV(0.05,E6:E9) in cell E10 computes the NPV (–$71.34) for Investment 1. We separated out the first cash flow, because the cash flows for this investment are at the beginning, not the end, of the first year.

The formula =IRR(cell range) computes the IRR of a range of cash flows. In cell E11, the formula =IRR(E5:E9) computes the IRR (4.69%) for Investment 1. Copying the formula =SUM(E5:E9) from cell E12 to F12 computes the total cash inflow (ignoring the time value of money) from each investment.

Cost–Benefit Evaluation of Smaller Class Sizes

In the worksheet Class Size of the workbook CostBenefit.xlsx, we entered in cells F5:F7 the cost of the smaller class sizes. Copying from F17 to F18:F64, the formula =D17*1000*(1+Benefit)-D17*1000 computes each year's increment in wages due to the smaller class size. In cell M3 (named Benefit), we assumed a 2% (0.25 * 8%) growth in annual income due to the smaller class size. Finally, the IRR (9.77%) of the smaller class sizes is computed in cell F2 with the formula =IRR(F5:F64).

Can A/B Testing Improve My Website's Performance?

If your company has a website, there are many decisions you need to make. *A/B testing* (sometimes called *split testing)* allows a website to test whether changes in a website will increase revenue, click-through rates, or other metrics. The basic idea is simple and is a special case of randomized controlled trials (RCTs). Call the changed website design the Challenger and the current website design the Status Quo. Table 49.1 shows some examples of commonly considered changes in website design for a shopping site.

Table 49.1: Examples of A/B tests

STATUS QUO	CHALLENGER
Purchase button is on upper-left portion of page.	Put purchase button on upper-right portion of page.
Purchase button is red.	Make purchase button blue.
Show a picture of product.	Show a video of a person using the product.

If desired, you can compare more than two alternatives. For example, you could compare how red, blue, and green purchase buttons influence the chance that a potential customer purchases the product.

To use A/B testing for comparing two alternatives, you create two versions of your site at the same URL: one version with the Status Quo and one version with the Challenger. Each visitor to your URL has a 50% chance of being sent to each version of the site. The randomization ensures that the potential customers sent to each version should be virtually identical on all attributes influencing the likelihood of purchase, so any difference in website performance should be due to the change in website design.

Many examples of successful A/B tests are given in Stefan Thomke's book *Experimentation Works* (Harvard Business Review Press, 2020).

- ▪ `Bookings.com` allows you to book hotel rooms, restaurants, airline tickets, and rental cars. In 2017, their revenue was $13 billion. Every day, they test more than 1,000 changes in their website design in the hopes of finding changes that will increase revenue. For example, they found that displaying the checkout date when a potential customer entered the number of children staying in a room significantly increased revenue.

- ▪ Microsoft's Bing search engine found that having search results load 100 milliseconds quicker increased revenue 0.6% ($18 million per year).

- ▪ Bing experimenters also found that showing more information (such as types of flowers on a search for 1-800-FLOWERS) on a single line increased revenue 12% ($500 million extra revenue per year).

In the rest of this chapter, we walk through a statistical analysis (using fictitious data) comparing three alternative fundraising designs for Barack Obama's 2008 fundraising web page. For the reader interested in learning more about A/B testing, I recommend watching Facebook's instructive videos on split testing at `www.facebookblueprint.com/student/path/187637-split-testing`.

Improving Obama's Fundraising in 2008

Early in his successful 2008 presidential campaign, then-Senator Barack Obama was having trouble raising funds. As described in *Experimentation Works*, Obama's advisers thought that showing a campaign video would yield the most donations. After testing 24 different website designs on 300,000 different visitors to the website, the campaign found that showing a picture of the Obama family with a Learn More button increased the sign-up rate 41% over the page with the campaign video.

To illustrate how you evaluate alternatives using A/B (in this case, A/B/C) testing, let's suppose 100 visitors to Obama's website were directed to a page with a video, 90 visitors were directed to a page with a picture of the Obama family, and 86 visitors were directed to a website that simply had a Donate button. The file `ObamaWebsite.xlsx` (see a subset of the data in Figure 49.1) shows the donation results.

⬛	A	B	C	D
2				
3	Average donation per visitor	$14.64	$18.92	$12.24
4	Visitor	Video	Family	Donate
5	1	$0	$0	$0
6	2	$0	$112	$0
7	3	$0	$0	$0
8	4	$0	$76	$60
9	5	$0	$0	$0
10	6	$0	$121	$55
11	7	$0	$0	$0
12	8	$0	$0	$56
13	9	$0	$0	$0
14	10	$51	$0	$0
15	11	$0	$113	$0
16	12	$0	$0	$0

Figure 49.1: Obama donation results

You see that the family image generated the most money per visitor. The question, of course, is how significant these results were. Like Facebook (see www.facebook.com/business/learn/lessons/how-to-evaluate-split-test-ad-results), we will evaluate our A/B/C test using *resampling* and find that if you ran the test again, based on the observed data, there would be a 78% chance that the Obama family image would generate the most money.

The Mechanics of Resampling

Resampling involves drawing repeated samples from the original data. We sample with replacement. For example, to generate one iteration of resampling from the visitors who saw the video, we generate 100 resampled donation amounts from the observed donations made by visitors who saw the video. *Each new resampled donation amount has a 1/100 chance of being one of the observed donation amounts, and an original donation amount may be repeated.* For example, in theory the 10th person's donation amount of $51 could occur 100 times in the resampled donation amounts. In a similar fashion, we resample 90 observations from visitors who saw the Obama family image and resample 86 observations from visitors who saw the Donate button. The results, to this point, constitute one iteration of resampling. Next, we generate many (say 1,000) iterations and trace the fraction of the time each website design generated the largest amount of the donations. As shown in Figure 49.2, we found that the Obama family picture won 78% of the time, the video won 17% of the time, and the Donate button won only 5% of the time (details in the "Excel Calculations" section). Our limited A/B/C test data does not provide overwhelming proof that the family picture is best. Most practitioners demand a 95% chance that the Challenger beats the Status Quo before deciding that the Challenger has dethroned the Status Quo. Usually A/B/C testing involves thousands of people, and with such large sample sizes, one of the tested alternatives will usually be a clear winner.

	M	N	O	P
5				
6		Video	Family	Donate
7	Total Brought in	$12.46	$26.69	$14.70
8	Chance Best	17.20%	78.10%	4.70%

Figure 49.2: Results of A/B/C Obama website test

Excel Calculations

We now describe the mechanics of conducting 1,000 iterations of resampling for our A/B/C test of the website design for Obama's 2008 website.

1. Copying from F5 to F6:F104, the formula =RANDBETWEEN(1,100) chooses the 100 resampled donation amounts for Video from the 100 observed amounts. This function is equally likely to return any integer between 1 and 100. If, for example, 10 is returned twice, then two of our resampled values will equal the amount donated by the 10th person to observe the video ($51).

2. Copying from G5 to G6:F94, the formula =RANDBETWEEN(1,90) chooses the 90 resampled donation amounts from the 90 observed donation amounts for the Obama family image.

3. Copying from H5 to H6:H90, the formula =RANDBETWEEN(1,86) chooses the 86 resampled donation amounts from the 86 observed donation amounts for the Donate button.

4. Next, we need to transform the observation numbers into donated amounts. Copying the formula =VLOOKUP(F5,$A$5:$D$104,J$1) from J5 to K5:L5 generates the first resampled amount for each version of the website. As shown in Figure 49.3, the first resampled value for Video will be the 49th video observation ($0); the first resampled value for the Obama family image will be the 48th family image observation ($72); and the first re-sampled value for the Donate button will be the 12th observed donation amount for the Donate button ($0). Then we copy the formula in J5 down 99 rows to generate 100 resampled donation amounts for the people who saw the video. In a similar fashion, we copy the formula in K5 down 89 rows to generate 90 resampled donation amounts for people who saw the family image, and copy the formula in L5 down 85 rows to generate 86 resampled donation amounts for people who saw the Donate button.

F	G	H	I	J	K	L
1				2	3	4
2 Observation Number				Resampled		
3						
4 Video	Family	Donate		Video	Family	Donate
5 49	48	12		$0	$72	$0
6 97	53	64		$0	$0	$0
7 78	4	74		$73	$76	$63
8 99	67	66		$0	$55	$0
9 21	61	61		$0	$0	$0
10 90	77	11		$0	$0	$0
11 43	23	35		$0	$0	$60
12 5	43	7		$0	$0	$0
13 87	76	36		$51	$0	$0
14 50	10	75		$0	$0	$0
15 30	51	56		$0	$0	$0

Figure 49.3: One iteration of resampling

5. Copying from N7 to O7:P7, the formula =SUM(J5:J104)/COUNT(J5:J104) computes for the resampling iteration shown the average donation amounts for each website demand.

6. Next, we will use a one-way data table to "play out" our resampling 1,000 times. We enter the numbers 1–1000 in the cell range N16:N1015. To efficiently accomplish this, enter a **1** in N16 and with the cursor in N16, from the Home tab, select Fill from the Editing group, and then choose Series. Then, select Columns and enter a Stop Value of **1000**.

7. Now we need to tell Excel which cells to recalculate 1,000 times. Copying from O15 to P15:Q15, the formula =N7 ensures that our data table will compute 1,000 times the resampled average donation amount for each website demand.

8. Select the Data Table range N15:Q1015.

9. To activate the Data Table feature, select What-If Analysis from the Forecast group on the Data tab, and choose Data Table.

10. Leave the Row input cell box in the Data Table dialog box blank, and choose *any blank cell* for the Column input cell.

11. After clicking OK, press F9. Excel will place the numbers 1–1000 in your chosen blank cell and recalculate for each website design the average donation amount for one iteration of resampling. *When Excel places an integer between 1 and 1000 in a blank cell, all our* RANDBETWEEN *functions recalculate.* This generates different donation results for each resampling iteration. Each time you press F9, you get a different set of 1,000 iterations.

An example of the 1,000 iterations generated by the data table is shown in Figure 49.4.

12. Copying from R16 to R17:R1015, the formula =IF(O16=MAX(O16:Q16),"Video", IF(P16=MAX(O16:Q16),"Family","Donate")) tracks for each iteration the "winning design." For example, for the first two iterations shown in Figure 49.4, the family image won, but for the third iteration, the video design won.

13. Finally, copying from N8 to O8:P8 the formula =COUNTIF($R$16:$R$1015, N6)/1000 computes (as shown in Figure 49.2) the fraction of iterations in which each design won.

◢	M	N	O	P	Q	R
6		Video	Family	Donate		
7	Total Brought in	$16.89	$22.38	$12.09		
8	Chance Best	17.20%	78.10%	4.70%		
9						
10						
11						
12						
13						
14			Video	Family	Donate	
15			$16.89	$22.38	$12.09	What Wins
16		1	$12.45	$16.93	$10.30	Family
17		2	$11.96	$26.09	$12.67	Family
18		3	$12.92	$12.51	$12.63	Video
19		4	$16.12	$16.46	$12.72	Family
20		5	$12.13	$16.97	$14.37	Family
21		6	$10.29	$19.69	$13.14	Family
22		7	$15.59	$23.13	$16.07	Family
23		8	$10.30	$23.61	$13.67	Family
24		9	$16.01	$18.88	$7.77	Family

Figure 49.4: 1,000 iterations of resampling

How Should I Allocate My Retirement Portfolio?

If you have money to invest, how should you allocate your money among possible investments? The key tool in asset allocation is *portfolio optimization*. Economist Harry Markowitz (1927–) came up with the basic ideas behind portfolio optimization in 1954, and in 1990, was awarded the Nobel Prize in Economics. In a 2008 interview (www.altavra.com/docs/thirdparty/interview-with-nobel-laureate-harry-markowitz.pdf), Markowitz stated that the main ideas underlying his Nobel Prize research came to him in a single afternoon!

Markowitz realized that an investor wants to simultaneously maximize expected portfolio return and minimize portfolio risk. His key contribution was to determine a mathematical model that enables an investor to manage the risk-return trade-off. In this chapter, we will use actual data on annual returns for five asset classes: REITs (real estate investment trusts), gold, U.S. stocks (the Standard & Poor's index), 90-day Treasury bills, and bond funds (consisting of a mix of bonds, with a duration between 10 and 30 years) to illustrate the mechanics of portfolio optimization.

The Basic Portfolio Optimization Model

In Chapter 32, "Guess How Many Are Coming to Dinner?," we used Excel's Solver to find the parameters of a forecasting model that best forecasted daily customer count at a local restaurant. In Chapter 42, "What Affects the Sales of a Retail

Product?," we used Solver to derive the most accurate forecasts of painter's tape sales. In this chapter, we describe the basics of Markowitz's portfolio optimization model. We begin by describing the three parts of an optimization model.

What Is an Optimization Model?

An optimization model allows you to determine the best way to accomplish a goal subject to constraints. An optimization model consists of three parts: the objective or target cell, changing variable cells, and constraints.

Objective or Target Cell

You must have an objective you want to maximize or minimize. In Markowitz's model, the goal is to minimize the risk (measured by the variance or standard deviation) of the portfolio's annual return. The portfolio standard deviation counts upside variance (returns above the expected return) equal to downside variance (returns below the expected return), so standard deviation is flawed as a measure of portfolio risk. Despite this fact, we will assume the portfolio objective is to minimize the standard deviation of the annual portfolio return.

Changing Variable Cells

In any optimization problem, there are cells (called *changing variable cells*) that a decision maker can change to optimize the objective cell. In Markowitz's model, the changing cells are the fraction of your assets invested in each investment class.

Constraints

Constraints are restrictions on the changing cells. In Markowitz's model, the constraints are as follows:

- The fraction invested in each asset class must be non-negative. This rules out short sales (betting that an investment will drop in value).
- The sum of the fraction of your assets allocated to each investment must equal 1.
- Choose a desired expected annual return—for example, 8%. The chosen asset allocation must then generate an annual return of at least 8%.

Solution to the Portfolio Optimization Model

The worksheet Trial Solution in the workbook PortfolioFinal.xlsx contains annual returns on REITs, gold, U.S. stocks, 90-day Treasury bills, and bonds for the years 1972–2019. A subset of the data is shown in Figure 50.1. You can see that stocks had the highest annual mean return; gold had the highest standard deviation; and T-bills had the lowest mean and lowest standard deviation. Markowitz's model also requires the correlation matrix (see Figure 50.2), which shows the correlations between each pair of assets. Note that stocks and REITs exhibit the most positive correlation, whereas gold returns are negatively correlated with stock returns. This tells us that when stocks go down in value, gold tends to increase in value, providing a good hedge against a decline in stock prices. Note that T-bills and bonds are virtually uncorrelated with non-fixed-income asset classes. The correlation matrix is needed to compute the variance of a portfolio. If all your investments exhibit a high positive correlation, the positive correlations will increase the riskiness of your portfolio. Introducing negatively correlated investments into your portfolio will drive a decrease in the riskiness of your portfolio. The "Excel Calculations" section explains the detailed steps used to find the optimal asset allocation.

Cells B4:F4 contain the weights, or the fraction of our assets allocated to each investment. You can start with any trial solution. We began by allocating 20% of our assets to each investment class (see Figure 50.1 and worksheet Trial Solution). Given the weights chosen in cells B4:F4, cell C2 computes the annual variance of the annual portfolio return, cell D2 computes the annual standard deviation of the portfolio return, and cell E2 computes the expected annual return. Thus, we see that an equal asset allocation results in an expected annual return of 9.2%, with a standard deviation of 8.2%.

	A	B	C	D	E	F	G
1	mean	=AVERAGE(B8:B55)	variance	sigma	mean		Required
2	sigma	=STDEV(B7:B55)	0.0067523	0.0821723	0.0924654	>=	0.08
3	wts*sigma		4.0%	5.9%	3.4%	0.7%	1.9% Total Invested
4	wts		20.0%	20.0%	20.0%	20.0%	20.0%	1.00
5	mean		11.8%	10.7%	12.0%	4.6%	7.1%
6	sigma		20.0%	29.3%	17.1%	3.4%	9.5%
7		REIT		Gold	Stocks	Bills	Bonds
8	1972		11.2%	46.5%	18.8%	4.0%	2.8%
9	1973		-27.2%	76.6%	-14.3%	6.7%	3.7%
10	1974		-42.2%	61.2%	-25.9%	7.8%	2.0%
11	1975		36.3%	-24.1%	37.0%	6.0%	3.6%
12	1976		49.0%	-3.0%	23.8%	5.0%	16.0%
13	1977		19.1%	23.9%	-7.0%	5.1%	1.3%
14	1978		-1.6%	34.7%	6.5%	6.9%	-0.8%
15	1979		30.5%	146.1%	18.5%	9.9%	0.7%

Figure 50.1: Portfolio optimization model: trial solution

◢	I	J	K	L	M	N
8		REIT	Gold	Stocks	Bills	Bonds
9	REIT	1.00	-0.13	0.58	-0.03	0.07
10	Gold	-0.13	1.00	-0.20	0.07	-0.12
11	Stocks	0.58	-0.20	1.00	0.04	0.01
12	Bills	-0.03	0.07	0.04	1.00	0.23
13	Bonds	0.07	-0.12	0.01	0.23	1.00

Figure 50.2: Correlation matrix: trial solution

The worksheet Optimal Solution displays the minimum variance asset allocation that has an expected return of at least 8% (see Figure 50.3). Allocating 6.9% to REITs, 10.3% to gold, 20.6% to stocks, 32.6% to T-bills, and 29.6% to bonds yields an 8% expected annual return and an annual standard deviation of 5.8%.

◢	A	B	C	D	E	F	G
1	mean	=AVERAGE(B8:B55)	variance	sigma	mean		Required
2	sigma	=STDEV(B7:B55)	0.0033761	0.0581045	0.08 >=		0.08
3	wts*sigma	1.4%	3.0%	3.5%	1.1%	2.8%	Total Invested
4	wts	6.9%	10.3%	20.6%	32.6%	29.6%	1.00
5	mean	11.8%	10.7%	12.0%	4.6%	7.1%	
6	sigma	20.0%	29.3%	17.1%	3.4%	9.5%	
7		REIT	Gold	Stocks	Bills	Bonds	
8	1972	11.2%	46.5%	18.8%	4.0%	2.8%	
9	1973	-27.2%	76.6%	-14.3%	6.7%	3.7%	
10	1974	-42.2%	61.2%	-25.9%	7.8%	2.0%	
11	1975	36.3%	-24.1%	37.0%	6.0%	3.6%	
12	1976	49.0%	-3.0%	23.8%	5.0%	16.0%	
13	1977	19.1%	23.9%	-7.0%	5.1%	1.3%	
14	1978	-1.6%	34.7%	6.5%	6.9%	-0.8%	
15	1979	30.5%	146.1%	18.5%	9.9%	0.7%	

Figure 50.3: Portfolio optimization model: optimal solution

The Efficient Frontier

There is no particular reason that an investor should require an 8% annual return. Markowitz suggested varying the desired annual return and plotting for each desired expected return the minimum annual standard deviation (obtained by solving the optimization problem described in the "Excel Calculations" section) on the x-axis and the desired expected return on the y-axis. Varying the desired expected return between 6% and 12% yields the *efficient frontier*, as shown in Figure 50.4 (see also the worksheet Efficient Frontier). Depending on an investor's risk-return trade-off, they should choose one of the points on the efficient frontier. All points on the efficient frontier are attainable, because they are solutions to an optimization problem that finds the minimum risk portfolio for a given expected return (see Figure 50.5). Any point below the efficient frontier, say (0.08, 0.04), is inferior to the point directly above it on the efficient frontier, because the point on the efficient return is attainable and has the same risk and a larger expected annual return. Any point above the efficient frontier, say (0.02, 0.08), is not attainable. For example, if (0.02, 0.08) were attainable by some asset allocation solving for the minimum risk portfolio associated with an 8% expected annual return, then we would have found an annual standard deviation of 0.02—and the best that could be found was 0.058.

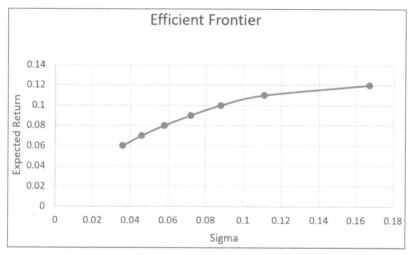

Figure 50.4: Efficient frontier

Note that the efficient frontier curve gets flatter (has a smaller slope) as the standard deviation increases. This implies that each additional 0.01 of annual standard deviation allowed results in a smaller increase in expected annual return. Figure 50.5 shows risk minimizing asset allocations for required expected annual returns varying from 6% to 12%.

	A	B	C	D	E	F	G
2							
3							
4	Sigma	Mean	REITS	GOLD	STOCKS	TBILLS	BONDS
5	0.036	0.06	3.83%	4.01%	7.58%	72.03%	12.55%
6	0.046	0.07	5.35%	7.14%	14.08%	52.33%	21.10%
7	0.058	0.08	6.86%	10.27%	20.58%	32.64%	29.65%
8	0.072	0.09	8.38%	13.41%	27.08%	12.94%	38.20%
9	0.088	0.1	11.18%	16.86%	35.67%	0.00%	36.29%
10	0.111	0.11	16.45%	20.92%	48.24%	0.00%	14.39%
11	0.167	0.12	7.94%	0.00%	92.06%	0.00%	0.00%

Figure 50.5: Optimal asset allocation

Difficulties in Implementing the Markowitz Model

In our formulation of Markowitz's portfolio optimization model, we used past expected returns, past standard deviations, and past correlations as inputs. Unfortunately, in finance, past is not always prologue and using past data to create an optimal asset allocation will not be very successful if the distribution of past returns does not look much like the distribution of future returns. Modifying the Markowitz model to correct for this flaw is beyond the scope of this book. Often, the *Black-Litterman* model (see Chapter 13 of the late Simon Benninga's outstanding *Financial Modeling*, MIT Press, 4th edition, 2014) is used to develop a model to predict future investment returns. This method combines past data with an investor's opinion about future returns.

Excel Calculations

In this section, we outline the steps needed to implement Markowitz's model. The model is implemented in the worksheet Optimal Solution of the workbook `PortfolioFinal.xlsx`.

1. Enter the trial values of your asset allocation in cells B2:F2 of the worksheet Optimal Solution.

2. Enter the formula `=SUMPRODUCT(wts,means)` in cell C2. This computes the expected return on a portfolio by weighting the past mean return on each investment by the fraction of your portfolio in each investment.

3. For each investment, compute the product of the fraction allocated to the investment times the portfolio's annual return standard deviation by copying from B3 to C3:F3 the formula `=B4*B6`.

4. In cell C2, compute the variance of the portfolio by typing the formula `=MMULT(B3:F3,MMULT(correlationmatrix,TRANSPOSE(B3:F3)))` and then pressing Ctrl+Shift+Enter. This formula is an *array formula*.

   If you have the newest version of Office 365, you will not need to press Ctrl+Shift+Enter. Explaining why this formula computes the variance of a portfolio is beyond the scope of this book; see `www.riskprep.com/all-tutorials/36-exam-22/58-modeling-portfolio-variance` for an explanation.

5. In cell G4, add the total fraction of assets allocated with the formula `=SUM(B4:F4)`.

6. From the Data tab, choose Solver from the Analyze group. The Solver Parameters dialog box appears, as shown in Figure 50.6.

7. Set the Objective cell to minimize the variance of the portfolio's annual returns (cell C2).

8. Enter the changing variable cells as the weights in the range B4:F4.

9. Select the Make Unconstrained Variables Non-Negative check box to ensure the changing cells will be non-negative.

10. Add the constraint $E$2 >= $G$2 to ensure that the chosen asset allocation has an expected annual return of at least 8%.

11. Add the constraint $G$4 = 1 to ensure that the total fraction of assets allocated equals 1.

12. Choose the GRG Nonlinear method from the Select A Solving Method drop-down list.

13. Click Solve. This causes Solver to efficiently search for the minimum variance asset allocation fractions over all combinations of asset allocations that meet the constraints.

14. Enter the formula `=SQRT(C2)` in cell D2 to find the standard deviation of the portfolio.

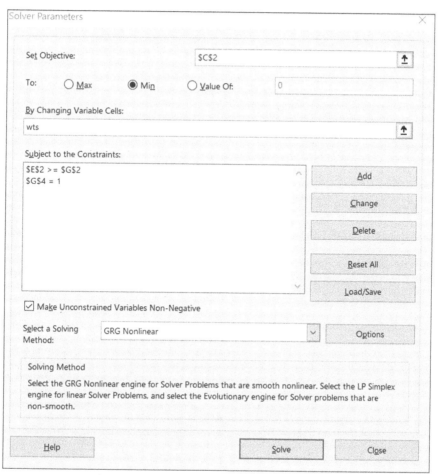

Figure 50.6: Solver model for portfolio optimization

How Do Hedge Funds Work?

As I'm writing this chapter in March 2020, the market lost nearly 8% in one day due to fears about the spread of the coronavirus (specifically, COVID-19). As we all know, market volatility can result in wild market swings. Investment strategies that greatly decrease the risk of exposure to market volatility and result in slightly lower than average returns appeal to many (particularly wealthy) investors. *Hedge funds* use trading strategies that are supposed to reduce risk (mainly due to the volatility in equities) and hopefully even increase average returns.

In this chapter, we will give brief explanations of several commonly used hedge fund strategies:

- Long/short and market-neutral equity strategies
- Convertible arbitrage
- Risk arbitrage
- Global macro

We will also look at the performance of hedge funds during the years 2007–2017, which was analyzed by Nicola Metzger and Vijay Shenai (see "Hedge Fund Performance during and after the Crisis: A Comparative Analysis of Strategies 2007–2017," *International Journal of Financial Studies*, vol. 7, no. 1, March 2019, pages 1–31).

Growth in Hedge Funds and Hedge Fund Fee Structure

Most hedge funds require the investor to put in at least $500,000. The most common fee structure is 2 *and* 20, which means that the hedge fund takes a flat fee of 2% plus a 20% performance fee on profits above a set target. For example, if the target is an 8% annual return and the hedge fund earns a 15% return, then the hedge fund performance fee would be $0.20 * (0.15 - 0.08) = 1.4\%$ of the amount invested in the fund. The amazing Renaissance Technology Fund (see Chapter 22, "Does a Mutual Fund's Past Performance Predict Future Performance?") averaged a 72% return during the period 1994–2015, which enables them to demand a 44% performance fee. See Gregory Zuckerman's great book *The Man Who Solved the Market* (Portfolio, 2019) if you want to peel back the curtain behind the success of the Renaissance Technology Fund.

By the way, if high finance, soap opera machinations, and political deal making interest you, watch the great series *Billions* on Showtime and follow the ups and downs of the Axe Capital Hedge Fund, which has a 3 and 30 fee structure!

In 1997, U.S. hedge funds had $118 billion invested (see Metzger and Shenai), and by 2018, this amount had grown to $3 trillion.

Shorting a Stock

Hedge funds often short a stock, currency, or commodity such as oil. Shorting a stock, means the investor is betting that the stock price will drop. For example, suppose you want to short 100 shares of a stock that currently sells for $10 per share. You "borrow" 100 shares and receive $10 * 100 = $1,000. Suppose a year later the stock has dropped to $9. You can buy back the 100 shares at a cost of $9 * 100 = $900. A person who bought the stock made a return of $(900 - 1000) / 1000 = -10\%$. Since our original amount spent was really –$1,000, the profit on the short sale is $(-100) / (-1000) = 10\%$. Even though we originally spent no money, it is correct to calculate our return as 10%. If you buy a stock, the most you can lose is 100%. If you short a stock, however, there is no upper limit on how much you can lose. For example, if the stock price increases to $100, you have lost $90 * 100 = $9,000!

In reality, if you short sell, you need to maintain a margin account (let's assume 50% of the purchased stock current value is margin + the current value of the borrowed shares) to ensure that if the stock price increases, money is available to guarantee that the borrowed shares are covered by real money.

Long/Short and Market-Neutral Strategies

In Chapter 50, "How Should I Allocate My Retirement Portfolio?," you saw that the mean annual return on stocks was 12% with a standard deviation of 21%. The rule of thumb implies that normal variation for stock returns is between –30% and 54%. Hedge funds want to reduce this enormous potential variation in equity returns for their investors. Let's assume a hedge fund's analysts are good at picking both overvalued and undervalued stocks. As you will soon see, a hedge fund with these talented analysts can reduce equity risk by buying (going long) undervalued stocks and shorting overvalued stocks. Let's suppose Stock 1 and Stock 2 each sell for $20, and our crack analyst Taylor Kim believes Stock 1 is undervalued and Stock 2 is overvalued. Also, suppose we have $100 in cash. Following our analysts' recommendations, we buy 5 shares of Stock 1 and short 5 shares of Stock 2. Also, assume that money left in a money market fund earns 2% interest per year. Shorting the 5 shares of Stock 2 gives us $100, which we use to buy the 5 shares of Stock 1. Consider the two scenarios shown in Table 51.1.

Table 51.1: Stock market scenarios for long/short strategy

STOCK MARKET RETURN	STOCK 1 RETURN	STOCK 2 RETURN
Up 8%	Up 10%	Up 5%
Down 8%	Down 5%	Down 10%

In each scenario, Stock 1 (as expected by Taylor) does better than the market and Stock 2 performs worse. If each market scenario occurred with equal probability, then on average, an investor entirely invested in stocks would earn no return on their money. Table 51.2 shows how our Long/Short portfolio will perform.

Table 51.2: Returns from long/short strategy

SCENARIO	CASH VALUE	LONG VALUE	SHORT VALUE	TOTAL VALUE
Current situation	$100	$100	–$100	$100
Market up 8%	$102	$110	–$105	$107
Market down 8%	$102	$95	–$90	$107

If the market goes up, our long position increases in value by 10%, and if the market goes down, our long position decreases by 5% in value.

If the market goes up, our short position decreases in value by 5%, and if the market goes down, our short position increases in value by 10%.

Our $100 in cash always increases to $102.

From Table 51.2, we see that whether the market goes up or down, our Long/ Short portfolio earns 7% and is uncorrelated with the market! Of course, this result depends on Taylor being very good at stock valuation.

Convertible Arbitrage

Suppose a company raises money by issuing a 10-year bond that pays $1,000 in 10 years and pays $90 (9%) in interest each year. The company might want to raise money with a bond that pays a lower interest rate. Suppose the company's current stock price is $40. The company might offer investors a *convertible bond* that pays $1,000 in 10 years and pays only $50 (5%) in interest each year. To compensate for the reduced interest rate, the company might offer a convertible option that allows the investor to redeem the bond for 20 shares of the company's stock. This option will be exercised only if the price of the stock increases.

Why are convertible bonds of interest to hedge funds? If the stock goes up, the convertible bond will capture most of the increase in the stock's value, but if the stock goes down in value, the convertible bond still pays interest, so it does not drop in value (percentage-wise) as much as the stock. With this in mind, hedge funds often go long on the convertible bond and short the stock. This is an example of a *convertible arbitrage* strategy. For a specific example, suppose that Table 51.3 gives the percentage change in value for the stock and convertible bond for three different scenarios.

Table 51.3: Scenario returns on convertible bonds and stocks

CHANGE IN STOCK PRICE	DOWN 10%	UNCHANGED	UP 10%
Return on stock	−10%	0%	+10%
Return on convertible bond	−2%	+5%	+8%

Note that the convertible bond captures most of the upside when the stock increases in value, and when the stock declines 10%, the convertible does not lose much because it is still paying interest.

If the hedge fund goes long fifty $1,000 bonds and shorts 625 shares of stock, they have $25,000 tied up in stock, which is one-third of their investment. Figure 51.1 (see the worksheet Convertible Arb of the workbook HedgeFund.xlsx) shows what happens to the hedge fund's portfolio for nine years, during which each scenario occurs three times. We computed the mean, sigma, and Sharpe ratio (assuming risk free rate = 0%) for our Long/Short portfolio, 100% short in stocks, and 100% long in bonds.

	A	B	C	D	E
1		unit value	$40.00	$1,000	
2		total initial value	$25,000.00	$50,000.00	
3		how many	625	50	
4			0.333333333	0.666666667	
5			Stock	Bond	Long Short Return
6			-10.00%	-2.00%	2.00%
7			-10.00%	-2.00%	2.00%
8			-10.00%	-2.00%	2.00%
9			0.00%	5.00%	3.33%
10			0.00%	5.00%	3.33%
11			0.00%	5.00%	3.33%
12			10.00%	8.00%	2.00%
13			10.00%	8.00%	2.00%
14			10.00%	8.00%	2.00%
15		Mean	0.00%	3.67%	2.44%
16		Sigma	8.66%	4.44%	0.67%
17		Sharpe	0.00	0.83	3.67
18				Mean	=AVERAGE(E6:E14)
19				Sigma	=STDEV(E6:E14)
20				Sharpe	=E15/E16

Figure 51.1: Analysis of convertible bond arbitrage

During any year in which the stock drops 10% in value, the following returns ensue:

- The 100% short in stocks earns a 10% return.
- The 100% long in bonds loses 2%.
- The Long-Short portfolio returns (⅓) * 10% + (⅔) * (–2%) = 2%.

During any year in which the stock increases 10% in value, the following returns ensue:

- The 100% short in stocks earns a –10% return.
- The 100% long in bonds earns an 8% return.
- The Long/Short portfolio returns (⅓) * (–10%) + ⅔ * (8%) = (2%).

During any year in which the stock price remains unchanged:

- The Short Stock portfolio returns 0%.
- The Long Bond portfolio returns 5%.
- The Long/Short portfolio returns (⅓) * 0% + (⅔) * 5% = 3.33%.

Recall from Chapter 5, "How Did Bernie Madoff Keep His Fund Going?," that the Sharpe ratio is a risk-adjusted measure of portfolio return. For simplicity, we assume the risk-free rate is 0%. Then a portfolio's Sharpe ratio is simply the (portfolio mean) / (portfolio standard deviation). We see that the Short Stock portfolio has a Sharpe ratio of 0, the Long Bond portfolio has a Sharpe ratio of 0.83, and the Long/Short portfolio has an amazing Sharpe ratio of 3.67.

Merger Arbitrage

In 2018, AT&T tried to acquire Time Warner. AT&T offered $110 per Time Warner share, yet the Time Warner price was $86.74. The reason for this wide discrepancy or spread was the fact that investors felt there was a good chance that regulators would cause the deal to not go through, and then the price of Time Warner would plummet. The deal did eventually go through, although the Trump administration tried to block it.

On the other hand, in 2016, Microsoft tried to acquire LinkedIn for $196 per share. When the prospective acquisition was announced, LinkedIn's price increased from $131.08 to $192.21. The narrow spread between the offer price and the LinkedIn price was because investors felt this deal was sure to go through.

Many hedge fund firms invest in *merger arbitrage*. They attempt to estimate the chance a merger will go through and buy shares of the target company. If the deal goes through, the hedge fund will profit by the spread, but if the deal does not go through, the hedge fund will lose because the price of the target company will surely drop. Hedge funds believe that profits on merger arbitrage (often called *risk arbitrage*) trades are uncorrelated with the market. If this is the case, then merger arbitrage will "hedge" away some market risk.

Let's suppose our merger arbitrage specialist Chuck Axelrod wants to determine for the Time Warner and LinkedIn mergers whether to buy shares of the target. Chuck needs to estimate the chance that the merger will go through and the percentage loss (due to a drop in the Time Warner or LinkedIn stock price) that will occur if the merger does not go through. Based on Chuck's estimates of these two parameters, Chuck can determine the expected percentage return on a purchase of shares of the target company. To convert the expected return to an annual return, Chuck must also estimate the length of time the merger will take to close. We illustrate the approach by analyzing merger arbitrage for the Time Warner deal. We note that often the hedge fund will go long the target and short the acquiring company, but we will not pursue analysis of that strategy.

Suppose Chuck's estimates for this merger are as follows:

- There is a 60% chance the merger will go through, earning an expected return of (110 − 86.74) / 86.74 = 26.8%.

- If the merger does not go through, the Time Warner price will drop 25%.

- If successful, the merger will take six months to complete.

The expected percentage return from the merger is then

$$0.6*(0.268)+0.4*(-0.25)=6.1\%$$

Since the merger is expected to take six months to close, the expected annual return is 12.2%. Thus, if Chuck is good at estimating the key inputs to analysis, his company should buy Time Warner. In reality, Chuck cannot be certain about these parameters, and he should probably model them as random variables and determine the probability that the purchased shares of the target company will earn an annual return above a desired threshold, say 10%. If that probability is high, then the hedge fund should purchase Time Warner.

Ben Branch and Taewon Yang ("The Risk Arbitrage Performance: Failed Attempts," *Quarterly Journal of Business and Economics*, vol. 45, no. 1/2, Winter–Spring 2006, pages 53–68) found that on average, the target company's stock price dropped 16% after a failed merger.

Global Macro Strategy

A hedge fund that uses a *global macro strategy* attempts to use macroeconomic principles to build models that look at the world's economic environment and attempts to find trades that appear to be favorable. Ray Dalio, author of the bestseller *Principles* (Simon & Schuster, 2017), is founder co-chairman and co-chief investment officer of Bridgewater Associates, a company that runs many hedge funds. Bridgewater's "All Weather Fund" is supposed to perform well in all economic environments. For the years 2010–2019, the All Weather Fund has averaged a 7.77% return with an annual standard deviation of 5.48%. According to www.lazyportfolioetf.com/allocation/ray-dalio-all-weather/, the returns of the All Weather Fund during those years was closely duplicated with the following asset allocation:

- 30% stocks
- 40% 20+ year bonds
- 15% 3–7-year bonds
- 7.5% gold
- 7.5% commodity index

Dalio has used the concept of *risk parity* to help determine his asset allocation strategy (see towardsdatascience.com/ray-dalio-etf-900edfe64b05#:~:text=). The risk parity asset allocation ensures that each asset class contributes an equal amount of risk to the entire portfolio. Further discussion of this ingenious approach is beyond the scope of this book. For a detailed explanation of the risk parity approach, see Sébastien Maillard, Thierry Roncalli, and Jérôme Teiletche, "On the Properties of Equally-Weighted Risk Contributions Portfolios," *Journal of Portfolio Management*, vol. 36, no. 4, Summer 2010, pages 60–70.

Steven Drobny's excellent book *Inside the House of Money* (Wiley, 2014) contains a detailed discussion of many successful global strategies. For example, billionaire George Soros made between $1 billion and $2 billion by shorting the British pound in 1992. Soros knew that in order to participate in the single European currency (the Euro), the United Kingdom would have to keep the pound worth approximately 2.95 deutsche marks. Soros knew the UK economy was not strong enough to justify this exchange rate. Therefore, Soros and other investors shorted the pound. The UK could not buy enough pounds to maintain the pound's high valuation, and finally the pound dropped to 2.16 deutsche marks per pound, and Soros and other short sellers made a fortune.

Hedge Fund Performance

Metzger and Shenai conducted an extensive analysis of hedge fund performance during the period June 2007–January 2017. Here we summarize some of their interesting results:

- Convertible arbitrage, long/short funds and event-driven (includes merger arbitrage funds) all have a correlation greater than 0.5 with market returns, so these strategies do not come close to eliminating market risk.
- After adjusting for risk, over the entire period, only global macro funds and multi-strategy funds (funds using multiple strategies) outperformed equities.

The George Costanza Portfolio

If you watched *Seinfeld*, you surely know that George Costanza was very paranoid. So if you think the world is against you, how should you invest? The workbook `MaxWorstCase.xlsx` contains my approach. For the years 1985–2019, stocks had their worst year in 2008, when they dropped 37%. If I were George's financial adviser, I would ask him to specify a desired expected return, and choose an asset allocation (short sales allowed) that would maximize the worst return during 1985–2019 while yielding George's desired expected return. The "Excel Calculations" section provides the details, but Table 51.4 shows for 6%, 8%, and 10% required returns, the asset allocations, worst case, and correlation with stocks. Note that for each scenario, the worst case is much better than 1 100% stock porttfolio's 2008 return of –37%. If George will settle for a 6% expected return, our recommended portfolio did not lose money in any of the years 1985–2019.

Table 51.4: George's maxmin portfolio

REQUIRED RETURN	REIT	GOLD	STOCKS	T-BILLS	BONDS	WORST CASE	CORRELATION TO STOCKS
6%	5%	–1%	8%	67%	22%	1%	0.51
8%	–6%	19%	27%	34%	27%	–1%	0.41
10%	20%	24%	18%	–7%	45%	–4%	0.44

Excel Calculations

Figure 51.2 shows our George Costanza model for a 6% required expected return. We constructed the optimal 6% portfolio as follows:

1. In cells B3:F3 of the Six Percent worksheet in the `MaxWorstCase.xlsx` workbook, we enter trial asset allocations, and in cell G3, we sum the asset allocations.

2. In cell H8, the formula `=SUMPRODUCT(wts,means)` computes the mean return for the given asset allocations.

3. Copying from G7 to G8:G54, the formula `=SUMPRODUCT(wts,B7:F7)` computes the actual return for each year.

4. In cell H4, the formula `=MIN(G7:G54)` computes the worst year's return.

▲	A	B	C	D	E	F	G	H
1								
2	wts*sigma	0.01	0.00	0.01	0.02	0.02	Total	
3	wts	0.05	-0.01	0.08	0.67	0.22	1.00	worst case
4	mean	0.12	0.11	0.12	0.05	0.07		0.01
5	sigma	0.21	0.31	0.18	0.03	0.10		
6	1971	REIT	Gold	Stocks	Bills	Bonds	Port return	
7	1972	0.11	0.47	0.19	0.04	0.03	0.05	Mean
8	1973	-0.27	0.77	-0.14	0.07	0.04	0.02	0.06
9	1974	-0.42	0.61	-0.26	0.08	0.02	0.01	
10	1975	0.36	-0.24	0.37	0.06	0.04	0.10	Correlation
11	1976	0.49	-0.03	0.24	0.05	0.16	0.11	0.51
12	1977	0.19	0.24	-0.07	0.05	0.01	0.04	
13	1978	-0.02	0.35	0.07	0.07	-0.01	0.04	
14	1979	0.31	1.46	0.19	0.10	0.01	0.08	
15	1980	0.28	0.06	0.32	0.11	-0.03	0.11	
16	1981	0.09	-0.33	-0.05	0.14	0.08	0.12	
17	1982	0.32	0.13	0.20	0.11	0.33	0.17	

Figure 51.2: George Costanza 6% portfolio

5. In cell H11, the formula `=CORREL(G7:G54,D7:D54)` computes the correlation between the annual return on our portfolio and the annual return on stocks.

6. From the Data tab, choose Solver, and fill in the Solver Parameters dialog box as shown in Figure 51.3. Select the Options button, and then from the GRG Nonlinear tab, select Use Multistart (because the ordinary GRG Solver has difficulty solving this problem).

7. The Changing Variable Cells are the asset allocations in cells B3:F3. Set the Objective cell to maximize the worst year's return, which is computed in cell H4.

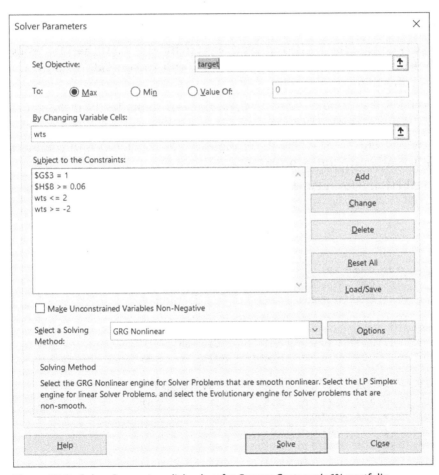

Figure 51.3: Solver Parameters dialog box for George Costanza's 6% portfolio

8. Since we are allowing short sales, we deselect the Make Unconstrained Variables Non-Negative check box. This allows changing cells to assume negative values. The GRG Multistart algorithm requires upper and lower bounds on changing cells. It is unlikely that more than 200% of our assets would be placed long or short in an asset, so we bounded our weights between –2 and 2.

9. We added the constraint H8 > = .06 to ensure that the mean return is at least 6%. The constraint G3 = 1 ensures 100% of our capital is allocated.

CHAPTER 52

How Much Should We Order and When Should We Order?

Suppose you are the manager of your local Target store. You sell thousands of items (often called SKUs, or stock keeping units.) For each SKU (to be specific, let's focus on an Xbox game console), you face two key decisions:

> When I place an order for Xbox consoles, how many should I order?

> How low should I let my inventory level go before I order more Xbox consoles?

In this chapter, you will learn how the *economic order quantity* (EOQ) model is used to determine the optimal order size. Then you will learn how the concept of *service level* is used to determine the *reorder point*, which is the inventory level that triggers the reordering of a product.

The Economic Order Quantity Model

In 1913, Ford Harris (1877–1962) of Westinghouse developed the EOQ model, which is widely used to determine the cost-minimizing order quantity. The size of an order that minimizes the sum of the annual inventory and ordering costs can be determined after the following parameters are known:

- K = Cost of placing an order (does not depend on size of the order)
- h = Cost of holding one unit in inventory for a year
- D = Annual demand for a product

We assume that orders arrive the instant the order is placed. It turns out (see the "Excel Calculations" section later in this chapter) that the order quantity minimizing the sum of annual inventory and annual ordering costs is given by

$$EOQ = \sqrt{\frac{2KD}{h}}$$

When you use the EOQ, keep the following points in mind:

- If you receive quantity discounts, then the EOQ is no longer valid because with quantity discounts, the annual purchase cost depends on the order size.

- The EOQ assumes that demand for a product occurs at a relatively constant rate throughout the year. The EOQ should not be used for products that exhibit seasonal demand.

- The main component of holding cost is not the cost of storing a product. It is the opportunity cost of the capital tied up in your inventory. Usually the annual holding cost is assumed to be between 20% and 30% of the cost of producing a unit (www.investopedia.com/terms/c/carryingcostofinventory.asp#:~:text=).

- Note that as expected, an increase in order cost or demand increases the EOQ, while an increase in holding cost decreases the EOQ.

The worksheet EOQ in the workbook `EOQ.xlsx` (see Figure 52.1) gives an example of how the EOQ is calculated. Given the following assumptions, we determine the optimal order size when ordering Xbox consoles:

- Order cost: K = $10.00

- Cost of holding 1 Xbox in inventory for one year: h = $20.00

- Annual demand: D = 10,400

From Figure 52.1 you see that each order should be for 102 (rounding up 101.98) units, and 10,400 / 102 = around 102 orders should be placed each year. Note that the Annual Order Cost = Annual Holding Cost. *If a company orders the EOQ, this will always be true.*

	B	C	D
2	K	$10.00	
3	h	$20.00	
4	D	10400	
5	EOQ	101.98039	=SQRT(2*K*D/h)
6	annhc	$1,019.80	=0.5*EOQ*h
7	annoc	$1,019.80	=K*annorders
8	anncost	$2,039.61	=annhc+annoc
9	annorders	101.98039	=D/EOQ

Figure 52.1: Computation of EOQ

The Power of Two Rule

Target stores rarely, if ever, receive a delivery truck that delivers only a single item. Let's suppose Target orders four types of video consoles, and they come on a truck for a single supplier. Robin Roundy's amazing *Power of Two Rule* (see "98%-Effective Integer-Ratio Lot-Sizing for One-Warehouse, Multi-Retailer Systems," *Management Science,* vol. 31, 1985, pages 1416–1430) makes it easy to coordinate deliveries. The Power of Two Rule states that for some n ordering a product every 2^n days will never result in a cost more than 6% higher than the cost for the EOQ. The Power of Two Rule is illustrated in the worksheet Power of 2 of the workbook EOQ.xlsx, as shown in Figure 52.2 (see the "Excel Calculations" section for further details). The annual cost of ordering every 1, 2, 4, 8, . . .256 days is given in the range B13:B20. We see that the minimum Power of Two Ordering Cost of $2,052.23 is obtained by ordering every four days. Ordering every four days results in an annual cost less than 1% higher than the EOQ associated annual cost.

	A	B	C	D	E	F	G
1							
2	cost/order	K	$10.00				
3	annual holding cost per unit	h	$20.00				
4	annual demand	D	10400				
5	order quantity	Order Quantity	113.9726	=D/C9			
6	holding cost per year	annhc	$ 1,139.73	=0.5*EOQ*h			
7	order cost per year	annoc	$ 912.50	=K*annorders			
8	total annual cost (excluding purchasing)	anncost	$ 2,052.23	=annhc+annoc			
9	orders per year	annorders	91.25	=365/C10			
10		days between orders		4 Enter days between orders in C10.			
11							
12			$2,052.23				
13		1	$3,934.93				
14		2	$2,394.86				
15		4	$2,052.23				
16		8	$2,735.70				
17		16	$4,787.03				
18		32	$9,231.87				
19		64	$18,292.65				
20		256	$72,956.72				

Figure 52.2: The Power of Two Rule

Suppose Target orders four types of video game consoles that are delivered from a single supplier. Suppose the optimal Power of 2 order interval for the four consoles are 4, 8, 16, and 32 days. Then a truck can be sent every four days, with Console 1 always on the truck. Every other truck will contain Console 2; every 4th truck will contain Console 3; every 8th truck will contain Console 4. Without the Power of Two Rule, it would be difficult to efficiently coordinate shipments of the consoles.

Reorder Points, Service Levels, and Safety Stock

In reality, demand during any time period is uncertain. When demand is uncertain, a natural question is how low to let inventory go before placing an order. The inventory level at which an order is placed is called the *reorder point*. Clearly, a high reorder point will decrease shortages and increase holding costs. Similarly, a low reorder point will increase shortages and decrease holding costs. It is difficult to estimate the cost of a shortage. Sometimes a sale is lost, and sometimes it is not. Sometimes the customer gets upset with a shortage and will not return in the future. Given the difficulty of determining shortage costs, most companies use a *service-level* approach to determine a reorder point. For example, a 95% service level means that you set the reorder point at a level that ensures that an average of 95% of all demand will be met on time. The workbook ServiceLevel.xlsx (see Figure 52.3) contains an example of computing a reorder point.

	A	B	C	D	E	F
1	Service level	SL	0.99			
2	cost/order	K	$50.00			
3	annual holding cost per unit	h	$10.00			
4	mean annual demand	D	1000			
5	order quantity	EOQ	100			
6	orders per year	annorders	10			
7	annual sigma	annsig	200			
8	mean lead time	meanLT	0.0833			
9	sigma lead time	sigmaLT	0.0192			
10	mean lead time demand	meanLTD	83.333			
11	sigma lead time demand	sigmaLTD	60.854			
12	reorder point	ROP	189.44			
13	standardized reorder point	SROP	1.7436			DIFF
14	normal loss for stand. ROP	NLSTANDRO	0.0164 =		0.016	4E-10
15	safety stock	SS	106.1			

Figure 52.3: Computation of reorder point for 95% service level

The following inputs are needed to compute a reorder point:

- K = Cost of placing an order (does not depend on the order size).
- h = Cost of holding one unit in inventory for a year.
- D = Average annual demand. We'll assume average annual demand for Xbox consoles is 1,040.
- Annual Sigma = Standard deviation of annual demand. We will assume the annual standard deviation of demand is 200. Assuming demand follows a normal random variable (often a valid assumption), this means that we are 95% sure demand during a year will be within two standard deviations of 1,040 (between 640 and 1,440 units).

- Mean Lead Time = The average time it takes for an order to arrive. We assume that on average, it takes one month (1/12 year) for an order to arrive.

- Lead Time Standard Deviation = The standard deviation of the time it takes for an order to arrive. We assume the standard deviation of the lead time is 1/2 month (1/24 year).

- Desired Service Level = The percentage of all demand that should be met on time. To begin we will assume a Desired Service Level of 95%.

To determine the reorder point for a given set of inputs, you simply enter the inputs in cells C1:C4 and C7:C9. Then from the Data tab, choose Solver from the Analyze group, and in the Solver Parameters dialog box, specify the inputs and click Solve. You will find a reorder point of 165.01.

Safety stock is the inventory kept on hand to handle shortages. It may be computed with the formula

Reorder Point – Average Demand During Leadtime

For our 95% service level, we find

$$Safety\ Stock = 165.01 - (1/12)*1040 = 78.35$$

Table 52.1 gives the reorder point and safety stock for several other scenarios.

Table 52.1: Examples of service level and reorder point

SIGMA LEAD TIME	SERVICE LEVEL	REORDER POINT	SAFETY STOCK
0	90%	119.7	33
1/24	90%	137.7	51
0	95%	142.6	56
1/24	95%	165	78.3
0	99%	185.6	99
1/24	99%	216.9	130.2

Table 52.1 shows that changing the lead time from a certain value of 1 month to a mean of 1 month with a standard deviation of 0.5 months increases safety stock at least 30%. Also, for any value of the standard deviation of lead time, increasing the service level from 95% to 99% requires a much larger increase in safety stock than an increase in service level from 90% to 95%. This shows that obtaining near perfection in service level requires a large increase in holding costs.

Excel Calculations

In this section, we will derive the EOQ formula (calculus is required), illustrate the Power of Two Rule, and explain how to install the Excel Solver.

Deriving the EOQ Formula

If each order you place is for Q units, then your average inventory level will be 0.5Q. To illustrate this idea, suppose Q = 1,000. As shown in Figure 52.4, your inventory will equal 1,000 when an order arrives, and then decline at a rate of 200 (10,400 / 52 = 200) units per week until the inventory level hits 0 and the next order arrives. This picture shows that average inventory level will equal Q/2 (500, in this case). Since demand D must be met each year, the number N of orders per year must satisfy N * Q = D or N = D / Q. Thus, the annual sum of ordering and holding costs is given by

$$(1)\, TC = Total\ Cost = KD\,/\,Q + .5*Q*H$$

To minimize total cost, we need the slope or derivative of (1) to equal 0:

$$(2)\, Slope\ of\ Total\ Cost = -KD\,/\,Q^2 + .5H = 0$$

Solving for Q, we find

$$Q = \sqrt{\frac{2KD}{H}}$$

To check that this value of Q minimizes (and does not maximize) TC, we need to show the second derivative of TC evaluated at the EOQ is >0:

$$2nd\ Derivative\ of\ TC = 2KD\,/\,Q^3 > 0$$

This shows that the EOQ minimizes total annual cost.

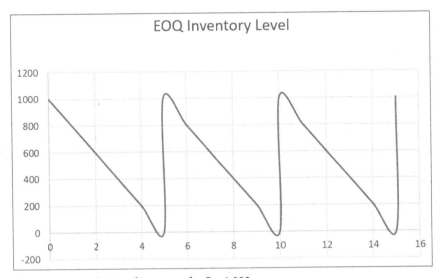

Figure 52.4: Evolution of inventory for Q = 1,000

Illustrating the Power of Two Rule

In the worksheet Power of 2 of the workbook EOQ.xlsx, we determine how the annual sum of order and holding costs varies as we change the time between orders. We begin with a copy of the EOQ worksheet and modify it as follows:

1. In cell C10, enter a trial number for the number of days between orders. (We chose 4 days.)

2. Assuming 365 days per year, in cell C9, we compute the number of orders per year with the formula =365/C10.

3. In cell C5, compute the order quantity with the formula =D/C9. (We have assigned the name D to the cell (D4) containing the value of annual demand.)

4. We can now use a one-way data table to show how total annual cost varies as the time between orders changes. In cells A13:A19, we enter various power of 2 order intervals (1, 2, 4, . . . 256).

5. In cell B12, enter **=anncost** to tell Excel the formula that should be recalculated for the different Power of 2 reorder times.

6. Select the table range A12:B20, and from the Data tab, choose What-If Analysis and then Data Table from the Forecast group.

7. In the Data Table dialog box, leave the Row input cell blank, enter cell C10 as the Column input cell, and then click OK. Excel places the values 1, 2, 4, . . . 256 in cell C10, and for each time between orders, computes the annual total cost.

We find that ordering every four days minimizes total annual cost. As previously mentioned, if you order every four days, then your total annual cost is within 1% of the total annual cost if you use the EOQ policy.

Installing the Excel Solver

In Chapter 32, we showed how to install Solver. For convenience, we repeat those steps here:

1. Select Options from the File tab on the ribbon. The Excel Options dialog box opens.

2. Choose Add-ins and then click the Go button.

3. From the Add-ins Available list in the Add-ins dialog box, check the Solver Add-in and click OK. On the Data tab, you should see the Solver command displayed in the Analyze group.

4. Click Solver to activate the Solver add-in.

You can now run the Solver model (the settings are shown in Figure 52.5) to determine the reorder point that results in the desired service level.

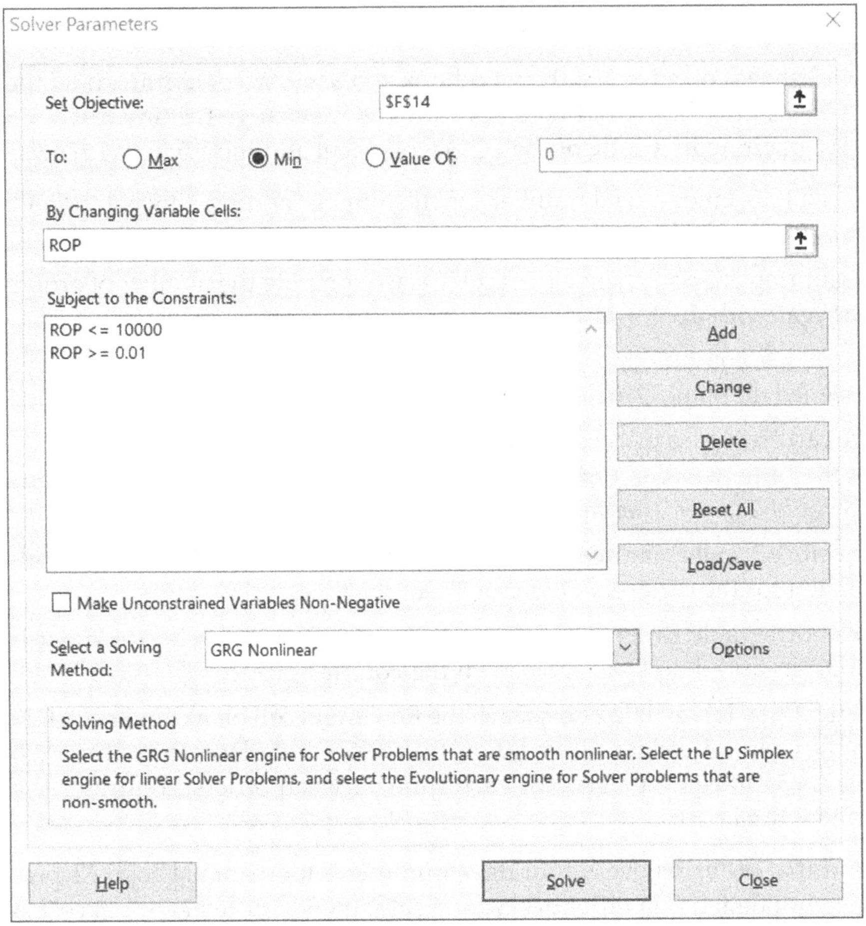

Solver Parameters   ✕

Se_t Objective: $F$14   ⬆

To: ○ _M_ax   ◉ Mi_n_   ○ _V_alue Of: 0

_B_y Changing Variable Cells:

ROP   ⬆

S_u_bject to the Constraints:

ROP < = 10000   _A_dd
ROP > = 0.01

       _C_hange

       _D_elete

       _R_eset All

       Load/Save

☐ Ma_k_e Unconstrained Variables Non-Negative

S_e_lect a Solving   GRG Nonlinear   ⌄   O_p_tions
Method:

Solving Method

Select the GRG Nonlinear engine for Solver Problems that are smooth nonlinear. Select the LP Simplex
engine for linear Solver Problems, and select the Evolutionary engine for Solver problems that are
non-smooth.

     _H_elp   _S_olve   Cl_o_se

Figure 52.5: Solver settings

How Does the UPS Driver Know the Order to Deliver Packages?

Tom Vanderbilt (author of the great book *Traffic*, discussed in Chapter 47, "Red Light, Green Light, or No Light?") tells us that if each UPS driver drove one less mile per year to deliver their packages, UPS would save $50 million (see `longitudes.ups.com/unhappy-truckers-and-algorithms/#:~:text=`). Vanderbilt also tells us that on an average day, a UPS driver delivers 130 packages. In theory (but not in practice), determining the order in which packages should be delivered that results in the fewest miles traveled is an example of the famous *Traveling Salesperson Problem* (TSP).

To define the TSP, suppose you are given a starting city and a list of cities to visit. You know the distance between each pair of cities, and you need to visit each city exactly once and return to the starting point. What sequence of visiting the cities requires the smallest distance?

In this chapter, we will show how Excel can quickly solve a 30-city TSP. You will also learn about the struggles UPS had in their attempts to use the TSP to help drivers deliver packages. A University of Waterloo web page (`www.math.uwaterloo.ca/tsp/index.html`) contains a lot of great information on the TSP, including maps of solutions to many TSPs, including an optimal pub crawl through 49,687 pubs in the United Kingdom. To date, the largest TSP solved involved 85,900 cities (see `www.math.uwaterloo.ca/tsp/pla85900/index.html`).

Why Is the Traveling Salesperson Problem So Hard?

A possible solution to a TSP is called a *tour*. Suppose, for example, that you live in City 1 and the TSP involves four cities. Table 53.1 shows all possible tours. We assume that for any two cities i and j, the distance between City i and City j is dij and that traveling from City i to City j involves the same distance as traveling from City j to City i. For example, d43 and d34 both equal the distance between cities 3 and 4.

Table 53.1: All tours for 4-city TSP

TOUR	TOTAL DISTANCE
1-2-3-4-1	d12+d23+d34+d41
1-4-3-2-1	d14+d43+d32+d21
1-3-2-4-1	d13+d32+d24+d41
1-4-2-3-1	d14+d42+d23+d31
1-3-4-2-1	d13+d34+d42+d21
1-2-4-3-1	d12+d24+d43+d31

Since dij = dji, the first two tours are really the same and require the same distance. This is also true for the third, fourth, fifth, and sixth listed tours. Therefore, there are actually 6 / 2 = 3 possible tours.

Suppose there are n cities and we start in any city (pick City 1). How many tours are possible? The next city can be one of n – 1 cities, the next city one of n – 2 cities, and so on. Therefore, there are (n – 1) × (n – 2) × (n – 3) * ... 2 * 1 = (n – 1)! (read as n – 1 factorial) possible tours. As Table 53.1 demonstrated (instead of six possible tours, there are actually 6 / 2 = 3 possible tours), we should divide (n – 1)! by 2 to obtain the total number of possible solutions.

The Excel function FACT(n) returns n!. Figure 53.1 (see the worksheet Tours in the workbook TSP.xlsx) uses this function to show how quickly the number of possible tours grows as the number of cities increases. The number of tours is written using scientific notation. For example, with 30 cities, there are 4.42×10^{30} possible tours. That is 442 followed by 28 zeroes.

In order to solve the TSP, an algorithm must find the tour that results in the smallest distance traveled. For a 30-city problem, suppose that in one second the computer could evaluate the distance traveled for one trillion tours. Then the algorithm would need more than 100 billion years to evaluate the distance traveled on each tour. Fortunately, computer scientists have developed efficient algorithms that can solve reasonably sized (up to 85 cities) TSPs. See William Cook's *In Pursuit of the Traveling Salesman Problem: Mathematics at the Limits of*

Computation (Princeton University Press, 2011) for a lucid explanation of algorithms used to solve TSPs.

◢	A	B	C	D
1	Cities	Tours		
2	3	1	=FACT(A2-1)/2	
3	4	3	=FACT(A3-1)/2	
4	5	12	=FACT(A4-1)/2	
5	10	181440	=FACT(A5-1)/2	
6	20	6.0823E+16	=FACT(A6-1)/2	
7	30	4.4209E+30	=FACT(A7-1)/2	
8	40	1.0199E+46	=FACT(A8-1)/2	
9	50	3.0414E+62	=FACT(A9-1)/2	
10	60	6.9342E+79	=FACT(A10-1)/2	
11	70	8.5561E+97	=FACT(A11-1)/2	
12	80	4.473E+116	=FACT(A12-1)/2	
13	90	8.254E+135	=FACT(A13-1)/2	
14	100	4.666E+155	=FACT(A14-1)/2	

Figure 53.1: Number of tours as a function of number of cities

Solving the Traveling Salesperson Problem

To illustrate how Excel can be used to solve a 30 city-TSP, the worksheet TSP in the workbook TSP.xlsx contains the distance (in miles) between every pair of NBA arenas. (I refuse to admit the Seattle Sonics moved to Oklahoma City!) Suppose you live in Indianapolis (the location of the Indiana Pacers' arena) and want to visit each arena once and then return to Indianapolis. To travel the smallest total distance, in what order should you visit the arenas? You might think that simply visiting the closest city you have not visited (called the *nearest neighbor approach*) might yield the minimum distance tour, but that does not work for our problem. The nearest neighbor approach would first visit Chicago and next visit Giannis Antetokounmpo and the Bucks, but we will see that the minimum distance tour does not include this possible leg of the trip.

Basically, the TSP is a sequencing problem. Each tour corresponds to a reordering of the integers 1–30. It is not necessary that Indianapolis (City 11) be first in the reordering. For example, consider the sequence placing even-numbered cities first followed by odd-numbered cities:

2-4-6-8-10-12-14-16-18-20-22-24-26-28-30-1-3-5-7-9-11-13-15-17-19-21-23-25-27-29-2

To see the order in which cities are visited with this sequence, just start wherever City 11 is placed in the sequence. Then, this tour goes Indiana, LA Lakers, Miami Heat,…Seattle, Utah, loop to Boston on the top, Chicago,…Denver, Golden State, Indiana.

The "Excel Calculations" section later in this chapter shows how to set up our NBA TSP in a manner that allows the Excel Solver to efficiently consider all possible tours and find the minimum distance tour. Figure 53.2 (see the worksheet TSP in the workbook TSP.xlsx) shows the minimum distance tour found by Excel.

	A	B	C
1	City	Order	Distance
2	LA Clippers	12	358.7708
3	LA Lakers	13	0
4	Golden State	9	339.786
5	Sacramento	25	68.192
6	Portland	24	482.7207
7	Seattle	27	144.1444
8	Utah	29	700.3238
9	Denver	7	365.0766
10	Minnesota	17	702.0942
11	Milwaukee	16	299.0443
12	Chicago	4	80.7875
13	Memphis	14	481.2537
14	Indiana	11	383.1551
15	Detroit	8	240.0075
16	Cleveland	5	113.1587
17	Toronto	28	191.3496
18	Boston	2	431.3524
19	New York	20	188.4763
20	New Jersey	18	8.3216
21	Philadelphia	22	85.5789
22	Washington	30	121.7231
23	Charlotte	3	328.3485
24	Atlanta	1	226.7853
25	Orlando	21	401.4298
26	Miami	15	203.5529
27	New Orleans	19	669.4139
28	Houston	10	317.7427
29	Dallas	6	224.7778
30	San Antonio	26	251.554
31	Phoenix	23	847.9026
32		Total	9256.8247

Figure 53.2: Solution to NBA TSP

From Indiana we first visit Detroit, then Cleveland,...,San Antonio, Phoenix, LA Clippers, LA Lakers,...,Chicago, Memphis, and finally back home again in Indiana. The total distance traveled is 9,256.8 miles.

The Traveling Salesperson Problem in the Real World

As described by Tom Vanderbilt, UPS has worked hard to turn the math behind the TSP into a tool that UPS drivers would embrace and use to sequence their deliveries. The result is ORION (On-Road Integrated Optimization and Navigation). Consider a driver who has 130 packages to deliver today. With the advent of modern GPS systems, UPS certainly knows the distances (and times) between each pair of addresses. It would be simple to print out the TSP optimal package delivery sequence, and tell the drivers to use it. Unfortunately, there are many factors that render the bare-bones TSP solution virtually useless:

- Many packages must be delivered by 10:30 a.m., so the TSP must be modified to penalize tours that do not deliver all these packages on time. This is easy to implement. For example, if Package 10 is not delivered by 10:30 a.m., simply add 1 hour to the total time of the tour. The act of optimizing the new Objective cell will ensure that Package 10 is delivered on time.

- A delivery schedule must build in lunch and break times.

- A driver in Northern Indiana might have part of their route in the Eastern Time Zone and part of their route in the Central Time Zone. Good luck with that!

- Drivers may have certain roads that they don't want to use on their route. This can be handled by giving each driver their own personalized matrix of distances. For instance, since I value my life, in Houston I would rather take Westheimer from the Galleria to the University of Houston, than the 45 Freeway. Therefore, my time of traveling from the Galleria to U of H might be 35 minutes, whereas for most people it would be 15 minutes.

Despite these difficulties, Vanderbilt believes most UPS drivers are very happy with ORION. One driver in Gettysburg, Pennsylvania saw his daily travel distance decrease from 150 to 126 miles.

Excel Calculations

In this section, we explain how Excel was used to solve our NBA TSP problem. The model is in the worksheet Sample of the workbook TSP.xlsx. The worksheet TSP contains the optimal solution.

To find the minimum distance tour for our NBA distance example, we proceed as follows:

1. Enter a trial sequence in cells B2:B31. We chose the even numbers 2, 4,....30 in sequence, followed by the odd numbers in sequence 1, 3,...29.

2. We must compute the distance traveled on each leg of the trip. In cell C2, the formula =INDEX(Distances,B31,B2) computes the distance between the last city listed and the first city. The name Distances represents the cell range F2:AI31. The INDEX function picks off the entry in the Distances matrix that is the distance traveled from the last city listed to the first city listed. In the Sample worksheet (see Figure 53.3), this distance of 2,099 miles is the distance traveled from City 29 (Utah) to City 2 (Boston).

	A	B	C
1	City	Order	Distance
2	Boston	2	2098.7672
3	Chicago	4	852.9186
4	Dallas	6	803.3595
5	Detroit	8	995.3916
6	Houston	10	1104.4521
7	LA Clippers	12	1374.9023
8	Memphis	14	1604.6884
9	Milwaukee	16	555.7017
10	New Jersey	18	726.5283
11	New York	20	8.3216
12	Philadelphia	22	85.3486
13	Portland	24	2412.8864
14	San Antonio	26	1719.53
15	Toronto	28	1441.1172
16	Washington	30	352.737
17	Atlanta	1	541.7573
18	Charlotte	3	226.7853
19	Cleveland	5	434.1983
20	Denver	7	1232.1416
21	Golden State	9	933.2864
22	Indiana	11	1938.8731
23	LA Lakers	13	1811.0135
24	Miami	15	2340.3118
25	Minnesota	17	1511.4905
26	New Orleans	19	1051.0509
27	Orlando	21	534.0803
28	Phoenix	23	1845.8577
29	Sacramento	25	634.8503
30	Seattle	27	623.548
31	Utah	29	700.3238
32		Total	32496.2193

Figure 53.3: Starting solution to NBA TSP

3. Copying from C3 to C4:C31, the formula =INDEX(Distances,B2,B3) computes the distance for each other leg of the trip. For example, the formula in C3 computes the distance of 853 miles between the first team listed (Boston) and the second team listed (Chicago).

4. In cell C32, we compute the total distance traveled on the listed tour with the formula =SUM(C2:C31).

5. Choose the Excel Solver from the Data tab, and fill in the Solver Parameters dialog box as shown in Figure 53.4.

6. We set the total distance traveled on the tour (cell C32) as the Objective cell and the cells defining the tour (B2:B31) as the Changing Variable cells.

7. From the Select A Solving Method drop-down list, we choose the Evolutionary Solver method and add a constraint that the cell range $B$2:$B$31 containing the changing cells must satisfy AllDifferent. This ensures that Solver only considers changing cells values in which each of the integers 1–30 appears exactly once in $B2:$B31.

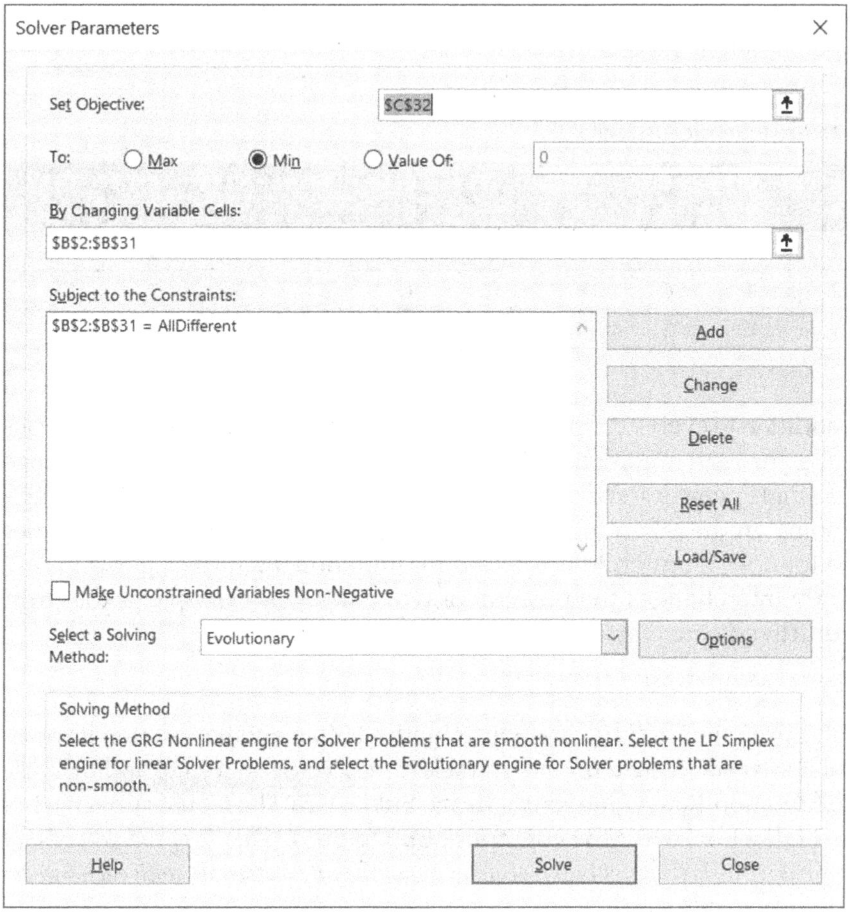

Figure 53.4: Solver settings for NBA TSP

The Evolutionary Solver approach (often called *genetic algorithms*, invented by former Michigan Professor John Holland [1919–2008]), uses a mathematical version of Darwin's survival of the fittest idea to solve the TSP. A great description of this approach is given by Eric Stoltz (see towardsdatascience.com/evolution-of-a-salesman-a-complete-genetic-algorithm-tutorial-for-python-6fe5d2b3ca35).

Excel begins with a Population of 100 randomly chosen tours. Then the value of the Objective cell is determined for each member of the Population. Two members of the Population are chosen to "breed." The better the Objective cell value (in this case, the smaller the total distance traveled), the larger the probability that the member of the population is involved in breeding. To explain how the breeding works, consider a 10-city TSP and assume the following two tours are chosen to breed. A random part of the Pop 1 tour is chosen (let's suppose 123 is chosen). Then, 123 is "mated" with the remaining cities listed in the order they occur in Pop 2. This yields the child shown in Table 53.2.

Table 53.2: Two tours breed a "child"

TOUR	CITY 1	CITY 2	CITY 3	CITY 4	CITY 5	CITY 6	CITY 7	CITY 8	CITY 9	CITY 10
Pop 1	1	2	3	4	5	6	7	8	9	10
Pop 2	2	4	6	8	10	1	3	5	7	9
Child	1	2	3	4	6	8	10	5	7	9

In addition to evolving through a survival of the fittest mechanism, species evolve through mutation. In biology, a mutation corresponds to a change in a single gene or the deletion or resequencing of part of a living thing's genome. In the TSP, a mutation occurs by randomly swapping two cities in a tour. So, if our child is selected for mutation, then the algorithm randomly interchanges the position of two cities. For example, if the third and fifth city are chosen, our child would become

1-2-6-4-3-8-10-5-7-9

I have used the Evolutionary Solver method often and have found it works best if after selecting Options, you select the Evolutionary tab and increase the Mutation Rate value to 0.5. In the Subject To The Constraints part of the dialog box, enter the constraint **$B$2:$B$31**. *This tells the Solver that your changing cells must be a resequencing of the integers 1–30, with each integer occurring exactly once.*

8. Increase the maximum time without improvement to 5. This causes the Solver to run until 5 minutes elapse without obtaining a tour with a smaller total distance.

9. Click Solve. After several minutes, Solver should find the solution shown in Figure 53.2 and the worksheet TSP of the workbook TSP.xlsx. *We have no guarantee that this is the best solution,* but if we listed every possible tour (which would take years!), experience with solving TSPs indicates that our solution is likely the minimum distance tour.

CHAPTER 54

Can Data Win a Presidential Election?

Jim Rutenberg's *New York Times Magazine* article "Data You Can Believe In" (June 20, 2013) described how Barack Obama's 2012 presidential campaign used sophisticated analytics and huge databases as powerful tools to defeat Mitt Romney. In 2016, Hillary Clinton's campaign failed to understand the power of social media as well as Donald Trump's director of digital media, Brad Parscale. Andrew Marantz's *New Yorker Magazine* article "The Man Behind Trump's Facebook Juggernaut" (March 9, 2020) describes in great detail how Parscale's mastery of Facebook advertising played a key role in Trump's upset victory. In this chapter, we will describe the use of analytics by Democrats and the GOP in recent presidential campaigns.

Democratic Presidential Analytics

As described by Eitan Hersh in his book *Hacking the Electorate* (Cambridge, 2015), Obama's 2012 campaign made extensive use of the Catalist voter database. As of March 2020, Catalist contains information on 185 million registered voters and 55 million unregistered voters (see www.catalist.us/about/). Hersh describes how most of this data comes from publicly available data, with the most used source being voter registration data. In different states, this contains different types of data. Usually the voter registration data will contain the voter's name, address, party registration, voting history, age, and gender. In seven southern states and Pennsylvania, race is required on the voter registration guide [form] (see whowhatwhy.org/2018/10/31/ asking-voters-about-race-helpful-tool-or-roadmap-for-suppression/).

Once your address is known, a party can use U.S. Census data to get more detailed information about people who live in your neighborhood. For example (see www.incontext.indiana.edu/2001/july01/spotlight.asp), for any neighborhood, census data describes living arrangements, ages, income, educational attainment, commuting patterns, and occupations. It also describes characteristics of the residences, in terms of age of home, number of rooms, value, whether it has complete kitchen and plumbing facilities, the availability of telephones and automobiles, and the type of home-heating fuel used.

The government keeps publicly available databases such as teaching, law, nursing, accounting, medical, pilot, hunting, and fishing licenses. They also have data on farmers receiving subsidies.

Catalist puts this data together and sells the data to progressive or liberal candidates.

NGP VAN (Voter Activation Network) allows Democratic campaign operatives to efficiently query databases like Catalist. An example of a query might be to bring up every African American registered voter over 60; who lives in Monroe County, Indiana; who did not vote early; and who is not on the Do Not Call Registry. These voters would likely be for Obama and would likely need a ride to the polls. Volunteers would probably make good use of their time calling the people on this list and offering them a ride to the polls.

For each person in the database, VAN's VoteBuilder tool outputs several "scores" (see madisondems.org/wp-content/uploads/2017/06/DNC-Scores-in-VoteBuilder.pdf for an example). These scores measure the following:

- Likelihood the person supports the National Democratic Party
- Likelihood the person will vote in the next election
- Likelihood the person is wealthy
- Likelihood the person has a college degree
- Likelihood the person lives in a household with children
- Likelihood the person is married
- Likelihood the person is Catholic, Evangelical, Other Christian denomination, or non-Christian

Computing VAN Scores

VAN uses over 100 variables to compute these scores. The workbook Democrats. xlsx (see Figure 54.1) shows a simplified example (see the "Excel Calculations" section later in this chapter for more details) that uses *logistic regression* to estimate the probability that an individual is a Democrat based on the follow-ing independent variables:

- Age.

- Gender (for simplicity, we assumed Gender is binary, with M = Male or F = Female).

- Race (NW = Non-White, W = White). In reality, we would also have categories for African American, Asian American, and Hispanic.

- Education (C = College graduate, NC = Not a college graduate). In reality, we would also have categories for some college, high school graduate, and non–high school graduate.

- Evangelical Christian (Y = Evangelical Christian, N = Not an Evangelical Christian). In reality, we would have many more categories for religion.

For 5,000 individuals, we have listed these variables and whether they are a Democrat. For example, the first person was a 67-year-old non-white male Democrat who graduated college and was not an Evangelical. The coeffi-cients in cells G2:L2 are used to compute a score for everyone. A higher score indicates the person is more likely to be a Democrat. We compute a person's score by adding the following:

- The constant of –1.04.

- Multiply age by –0.175. This means older people are less likely to be Democrats.

- Add 1.81 if the person is a female. This means women are more likely to be Democrats.

- Add 3.86 if the person is non-white. This means non-whites are more likely to be Democrats.

- Add 0.028 if the person is a college graduate. This means that college graduates are slightly more likely to be Democrats.

- Subtract 2.52 if the person is an Evangelical. This means that Evangelicals are much less likely to be a Democrat.

After computing a person's score, we convert the score to a probability of the person being a Democrat with the formula

$$\frac{e^{Score}}{1+e^{Score}}$$

For example, the 1st Person's score is –1.04 + 3.86 + 0.03 = 2.85. Then our estimated probability that the person is a Democrat is

$$\frac{e^{2.85}}{1+e^{2.85}}=0.945$$

	F	G	H	I	J	K	L	M	N	O	P
1		constant	Age	Gender	Race	College	Evangelical			Sum Ln Likelihood	
2		-1.03826	-0.17503	1.811657	3.857932	0.028018	-2.52323			-2014.991827	
3	ID	Democrat?	Age	Gender	Race	College	Evangelica	Score	Prob	Ln Likelihood	
4	1 D		67	M	NW	C	N	2.847686	0.945199	-0.056359845	
5	2 Not		23	M	W	C	Y	-3.53347	0.028375	-0.028784979	
6	3 D		25	F	W	NC	N	0.773393	0.684254	-0.379425627	
7	4 D		24	M	W	C	N	-1.01025	0.266932	-1.320762596	
8	5 Not		78	M	W	NC	Y	-3.56149	0.027612	-0.028000712	
9	6 Not		67	F	W	NC	N	0.773393	0.684254	-1.152818179	
10	7 Not		70	M	W	NC	N	-1.03826	0.261485	-0.303113991	
11	8 Not		39	M	W	NC	N	-1.03826	0.261485	-0.303113991	
12	9 D		35	F	W	NC	Y	-1.74984	0.148068	-1.910084232	
13	10 D		28	F	W	NC	N	0.773393	0.684254	-0.379425627	
14	11 Not		27	M	W	C	Y	-3.53347	0.028375	-0.028784979	
15	12 Not		75	F	W	NC	N	0.773393	0.684254	-1.152818179	
16	13 D		46	M	W	NC	N	-1.03826	0.261485	-1.341378005	
17	14 Not		18	F	W	NC	Y	-1.74984	0.148068	-0.160248467	
18	15 Not		78	F	W	C	N	0.80141	0.690276	-1.172073965	
19	16 Not		24	F	W	C	Y	-1.72182	0.151637	-0.164446837	

Figure 54.1: Data to predict whether a person is a Democrat

Analytics and the Obama 2012 Campaign

The Obama campaign created scores (updated daily) that would estimate the chance a voter would vote for Obama or Romney. The campaign also received a daily estimate of the chance a voter would turn out on Election Day. Voters with a high predicted chance of voting for Romney can be ignored. Voters with a high predicted chance of voting for Obama and a low predicted chance of turning out should be offered a ride to the polls. Voters with a near 50-50 chance of voting for Obama need to be persuaded to vote for Obama. Rutenberg points out that the Obama campaign had identified 15 million of these "toss-up" voters. Political scientist Amy Gershkoff obtained access to 20 million cable boxes that helped the campaign learn what TV shows these toss-up voters watched. Gershkoff's team found ads on the afternoon show *Judge Joe Brown* and late-night reruns of the news show *The Insider* reached these toss-up voters at a much lower cost per voter than ads on prime time or evening news shows. The Obama campaign ran twice as many cable ads as the Romney campaign. Obama's campaign spent $90 million less than the Romney campaign and ran 40,000 more ads!

Obama analytics team member Rayid Ghani came up with a way to use Facebook to reach toss-up voters. Ghani proposed asking people who signed into the Obama campaign website whether they would allow the campaign to scan their friends list. This approach identified 15 million toss-up voters in swing states that could now receive Obama campaign information through Facebook.

The Democrats in 2020 and Beyond

Even if you have not given money to a candidate, I am sure most readers of this book have received at least one text message from a political candidate. The DNC

(Democratic National Committee) announced in January 2020 (see democrats
.org/news/dnc-announces-new-national-cell-phone-purchase/) the purchase
of cell phone numbers for *every eligible voter*. This purchase includes a provision that ensures that the cell phone numbers remain accurate in the future. Of
course, these phone numbers are being merged with the DNC's eligible voter
database. The DNC also announced a predictive analytics model, Sonar, that is
supposed to increase the efficiency of donor solicitation by 35%.

The GOP Strikes Back

In her informative *60 Minutes* interview (www.cbs.com/shows/60_minutes/
video/elHhrLFmOS2ZYFqRG68KQPAu0_aUKPKC/who-is-brad-parscale-/) with Brad
Parscale, Leslie Stahl points out that although Brad Parscale is not well known, he
played a key role in Trump's stunning 2016 win over Hillary Clinton. Marantz's
outstanding profile of Parscale details his vital role in Trump's victory. In honor
of the Americans who died fighting Mexico at the Alamo, Parscale named his
work for Trump "Project Alamo." During the 2016 campaign, Trump's campaign
paid Parscale's company $94 million. Most of this money was used to buy
millions of Facebook ads. Project Alamo made extensive use of *microtargeting*
to design ads that would be most likely to persuade a voter to vote for Trump.
Microtargeting uses data about the individual (usually gleaned from Facebook)
to determine the type of ad that will appeal to a potential voter. For example,
in the *60 Minutes* interview, Parscale describes how he found Rust Belt voters
who cared deeply about America's crumbling infrastructure and sent them
ads showing how Trump would fix roads and bridges. See the 1:20 mark of
www.realclearpolitics.com/video/2016/08/08/trump_promises_infrastructure_
we_will_put_new_american_metal_into_the_spine_of_this_nation.html for
an example of Trump's infrastructure appeal.

Project Alamo conducted extensive A/B testing (see Chapter 49, "Can A/B
Testing Improve My Website's Performance?"). The day of the third presidential
debate, Project Alamo ran 175,000 variations of a single ad! If you count variations of ads used in A/B testing as separate ads, then Trump ran 5.9 million
Facebook ads, whereas the Clinton campaign ran only 66,000 Facebook ads. As
Parscale pointed out in his *60 Minutes* interview, some voters prefer a green
button to a red button and some voters prefer to make a contribution with a
button that says Donate rather than Contribute.

Parscale made extensive use of Facebook's *Lookalike Audience* feature. He
would put together in Excel a *custom list* containing as much information as he
had about 300,000 people that the Trump campaign had successfully targeted.
Then, the Lookalike Audience (see www.pbs.org/wgbh/frontline/article/
brad-parscale-trumps-2020-campaign-manager-calls-facebook-ad-policy-a-gift/)

feature (probably using some of the collaborative filtering ideas we explored in Chapter 29, "How Does Netflix Recommend Movies and TV Shows?") spits out 300,000 new Facebook members who are most similar to the custom list. For example, if you give Facebook a list of 300,000 people in Ohio who think the wall should be built, then Facebook will spit out 300,000 more people who are likely to support the wall. Then, Parscale would send those people an ad showing how Trump will build the wall.

Clients (like the Trump campaign) that spend a lot of money on Facebook ads are entitled to have a Facebook employee on site who tells the client the tricks that will improve the efficiency of their advertising. Facebook sent Jim Barnes (known as an *embed*) to the Trump campaign. As an example, Barnes designed a Facebook ad that cost $328,000 and brought in $1.32 million in funds. The Clinton campaign was offered an embed and declined.

Parscale claims that the Trump campaign has 215 million voter records (with cell phone numbers) and hopes to send out a billion texts before the 2020 election.

Russia's Use of Social Media in the 2016 Election

Russia's Internet Research Agency (IRA) bought over 3,000 Facebook ads in 2016 before the election (`www.nytimes.com/2017/09/06/technology/facebook-russian-political-ads.html`). Democrats from the House Intelligence Committee released a list of the ads (`intelligence.house.gov/social-media-content/`). More than 11 million Americans were exposed to these ads.

The House Intelligence Committee Democrats also reported that in 2016, some 36,000 Russian bot accounts sent out over 130,000 tweets. These tweets showed up 288 million times in someone's Twitter feed.

The House Intelligence release shows that most of the Russia-sponsored social media content emphasized divisive issues, such as the Second Amendment, race relations, gender identity, and immigration. Of course, the key question is whether Russia's social media efforts swung the election to Trump. Trump carried Wisconsin, Pennsylvania, and Michigan by a total of 107,000 votes. Flip those states to Clinton, and she wins the election. Without knowing the individual identities of the targeted Facebook users (and we don't), it would seem impossible to know how many votes were changed by Russia's social media activity. Former Facebook Product Manager Antonio García Martínez said (see Brian Feldman's article "Did Russia's Facebook Ads Actually Swing the Election?" at `nymag.com/intelligencer/2017/10/did-russias-facebook-ads-actually-swing-the-election.html?utm_source=nym&utm_medium=f1&utm_campaign=feed-part`) the theory that Russia social media efforts swung the election to Trump was "utter bull____."

Cambridge Analytica and the 2016 Election

Cambridge Analytica was a British firm that managed to illegally obtain information on 87 million Facebook users. The history of Cambridge Analytica is detailed in Chapter 16 of Steven Levy's history of Facebook (*Facebook: The Inside Story*, Blue Rider Press, 2020).

David Stillwell of Nottingham University developed the myPersonality app, which could determine your personality type: introvert, extrovert, etc. Eventually, 6 million people completed the test. Michał Kosiński of Cambridge University became interested in the myPersonality data and asked Stillwell to work with him, scraping the likes of many Facebook users. For 60,000 volunteers, Kosiński and Stillwell determined how to use a person's likes to predict many aspects of a personality. They found, for example, that based on a person's likes, they could predict a person's political party with 85% accuracy. Kosiński and Stillwell claimed that based on 300 likes, they would know more about you than your spouse.

In 2013, data scientist Aleksandr Kogan began working with Kosiński and Stillwell. Kogan wrote a successor to myPersonality, called This Is Your Digital Life (TIYDL). Only 270,000 people used the app (see www.newscientist.com/ article/2166435-how-facebook-let-a-friend-pass-my-data-to-cambridge-analytica/). *Using the app gave Kogan access to each user's friends' (without their permission!) Facebook information.* It is estimated that this approach harvested 87 million Facebook users' information.

In 2013, Kogan met Alexander Nix, the head of a British political consulting firm SCL (Strategic Communication Laboratories). Kogan was enticed into allowing SCL to have access to his data. Then Nix had a meeting with Steve Bannon (former head of the conservative Breitbart News and eventually Trump's White House chief strategist), where they discussed how to use Kogan's data to influence voter behavior. Bannon brought wealthy (estimated to be worth $900 million; see www.townandcountrymag.com/society/money-and-power/a13143108/ robert-mercer-net-worth/) conservative Renaissance Technology manager Robert Mercer to meet with SCL. Mercer agreed to underwrite the use of Kogan's data for political purposes, and Cambridge Analytica was born.

Mercer backed Ted Cruz for president in 2016, and the Cruz campaign used Cambridge Analytica's data early in his campaign. Nix took some credit (see www .texasmonthly.com/politics/cambridge-analytica-helped-ted-cruz-win-iowa-now-may-haunt-reelection/) for Cruz's surprising victory in the Iowa caucuses. Eventually, the Trump campaign paid Cambridge Analytica $5 million (see www.cnn.com/2018/03/21/politics/trump-campaign-cambridge-analytica/index .html). In Marantz's article, Parscale denied that the Cambridge Analytica data was useful, a notion seconded by Daniel Kreiss, a political communications professor at the University of North Carolina.

As I write this chapter, nobody associated with Cambridge Analytica has been convicted of any crimes.

Excel Calculations

The following steps show how logistic regression was used to predict the likelihood that an individual was a Democrat based on age, gender, race, education, and religion. Our work is in the workbook `Democrats.xlsx`.

1. Enter trial values for the constant and weights for age, gender, race, education, and religion in cells G2:L2.

2. Copying from M4 to M5:M5003 the formula `=constant+Age*H4+IF(I4="F", Gender,0)+ IF(J4="NW",Race,0)+IF(K4="C", College,0)+IF(L4="Y",Evange lical,0)` computes for any set of trial weights each individual's score.

3. Copying from N4 to N5:N5003 the formula `=EXP(M4)/(1+EXP(M4))` computes for any set of trial weights the probability that the person is a Democrat.

4. The logistic regression approach calculates for any set of weights the probability that the 5,000 observed party affiliations occur. This is obtained by multiplying for each Democrat the implied probability that they are Democrats and for each non-Democrat the probability that they are not Democrats. The *method of maximum likelihood* chooses the weights that maximize this product. Since this product is incredibly small, we maximize the natural logarithm of this product. The natural logarithm of a product of numbers is the sum of the natural logarithm of the individual numbers. Therefore, we copy from O4 to O5:O5003 the formula `=LN(IF(G4="D",N4,1-N4))`.

5. In cell O2, we add up O4:O5003.

6. We now use the Excel Solver to find the weights and constant that maximize the natural logarithm of the probability of our 5,000 observed party affiliations. The Solver settings are shown in Figure 54.2. Set the Objective cell to maximize cell O2, which is the log likelihood of the observed party affiliations. Our changing variable cells are the constant and the weights (cells $G$2:$L$2). If you don't put bounds on the changing cells, you may receive an error message. Therefore, we bound all changing cells between −10 and +10. If the Solver hits a bound, then the bound should be relaxed. We choose the GRG Nonlinear Solver method from the Select A Solving Method drop-down list in the dialog box.

The Solver yields the weights shown in Figure 54.1.

Solver Parameters   ✕

Se_t Objective: $O$2   ⬆

To: ⦿ _M_ax   ◯ Mi_n_   ◯ _V_alue Of: | 0 |

_B_y Changing Variable Cells:

| $G$2:$L$2 | ⬆ |

S_u_bject to the Constraints:

$G$2:$L$2 <= 10 ⌃		Add
$G$2:$L$2 >= -10		
		_C_hange
		_D_elete
		_R_eset All
⌄		_L_oad/Save

☐ Ma_k_e Unconstrained Variables Non-Negative

S_e_lect a Solving | GRG Nonlinear   ⌄ | | O_p_tions |
Method:

Solving Method

Select the GRG Nonlinear engine for Solver Problems that are smooth nonlinear. Select the LP Simplex engine for linear Solver Problems, and select the Evolutionary engine for Solver problems that are non-smooth.

| _H_elp | | _S_olve | | Cl_o_se |

Figure 54.2: Solver settings for logistic regression

CHAPTER 55

Can Analytics Save Our Republic?

In 1787, at the end of the Constitutional Convention, Benjamin Franklin was asked what type of government the Founding Fathers had just created. He's alleged to have replied, "A Republic, if you can keep it." Whatever your political views, most Americans believe the Republic is in peril. In March 2020, a Pew Research survey (see www.pewresearch.org/fact-tank/2020/03/04/far-more-americans-see-very-strong-partisan-conflicts-now-than-in-the-last-two-presidential-election-years/) found that 71% (up from 47% in 2012) of Americans believe very strong partisan conflicts exist between Democrats and Republicans, and 20% believe strong conflicts exist between Democrats and Republicans.

Another way to see the increase in polarization is to look at how many laws Congress passes when one party controls the House and the other party controls the Senate and the presidency. The 98th Congress (1983–1985 during the Reagan administration) passed 667 laws, whereas the 112th Congress (2010–2012 during the Obama administration) passed only 283 laws (see theconversation.com/congress-used-to-pass-bipartisan-legislation-will-it-ever-again-107134).

What has caused this increased partisanship and polarization? I believe it is the fact that the party primaries that choose the Democratic and Republican nominees are dominated by voters who are more liberal or more conservative than most voters. In 2016, only 29% of eligible voters participated in the primaries (www.pewresearch.org/fact-tank/2016/06/10/turnout-was-high-in-the-2016-primary-season-but-just-short-of-2008-record/).

A Brookings Institution survey (www.brookings.edu/research/the-2018-primaries-project-the-ideology-of-primary-voters/) found that 87% of 2018 Republican primary voters thought they were more conservative than the typical voter in their congressional district, whereas 81% of the Democratic primary voters felt they were more liberal than the typical voter in their district. I believe these statistics show that under the current system, the more extreme members of the electorate are determining who are on the ballot in November. This results in an implicit disenfranchisement of moderate voters. A Gallup Poll (news.gallup.com/poll/275792/remained-center-right-ideologically-2019.aspx) found that since 1992, the fraction of moderates (including the author) has remained constant at 35%, so the primary system appears to exclude a substantial number of eligible voters.

Of course, we have not mentioned gerrymandering (discussed in Chapter 18), which results in a House of Representatives that is not representative of the American electorate, and the Electoral College, which has resulted in two presidents (Donald Trump and George W. Bush) winning the election when they lost the popular vote.

So, can analytics come up with some ideas that will increase the likelihood that we can keep our Republic?

Stanford University's 1972 Nobel Prize winner Kenneth Arrow's (1921–2017) Impossibility Theorem showed that no "perfect" voting system exists. After a brief discussion of Arrow's Result, we will discuss three alternatives to "the most votes wins" criteria, which currently decide most U.S. elections:

➤ Ranked choice voting

➤ Approval voting

➤ Quadratic voting

Arrow's Impossibility Theorem

Consider a country with at least three candidates running for office and at least two voters. Each voter ranks the candidates.

Arrow ("A Difficulty in the Concept of Social Welfare," *Journal of Political Economy*, vol. 58, no. 4, 1950, pages 328–346) stated three axioms that should be satisfied by a fair voting system based on all voters' ranking of a candidate:

▪ **No dictator:** No single voter should be able to determine the winning candidate.

▪ **Independence of irrelevant alternatives:** Suppose more voters prefer A to B. Suppose voters change their ranking of other candidates but no voter changes their relative ranking of A and B. After these changes, the system should still prefer A to B.

▪ **Pareto optimality:** If every voter prefers A to B, then the voting system cannot prefer B to A.

These axioms seem reasonable, but Arrow proved that no voting system based on rank ordering can satisfy all three axioms!

It's Not Easy to Pick a Winner!

W. D. Wallis's *The Mathematics of Elections and Voting* (Springer, 2014) is an outstanding reference (requiring no advanced math) on the mathematical issues involved in elections. Wallis gives a great example where 120 voters rank five candidates, as shown in Table 55.1.

Table 55.1: Five candidates, six results

HOW MANY VOTERS	36	24	20	18	8	4
1st choice	A	B	C	D	E	E
2nd choice	D	E	B	C	B	C
3rd choice	E	D	E	E	D	D
4th choice	C	C	D	B	C	B
5th choice	B	A	A	A	A	A

Amazingly, six seemingly reasonable voting systems each give a different result:

■ If the winner must receive a *majority*, then there is no winner.

■ If the candidate with the most votes wins (*plurality voting*), then Candidate A wins.

■ A *runoff election* could be held between the top two candidates (A and B). 24 + 20 + 18 + 8 + 4 = 74 of the 110 voters prefer B to A, so B is the winner.

■ *Ranked-choice voting* (RCV) begins by eliminating the candidate with the fewest votes and allocating their votes to the most preferred of the remaining candidates. Next, the remaining candidate with the fewest votes is eliminated and their votes are reallocated to the most preferred of the remaining candidates. This continues until one candidate has a majority. Table 55.2 summarizes the ranked choice voting process. Note that C received the third-most votes but that C wins in a landslide (74-36) with ranked-choice voting!

■ The *Borda count* gives each candidate 1 point for a first-place vote, 2 points for a second place vote, . . . , 5 points for a 5th-place vote. Then the voter with the fewest points wins. As shown in the file Borda.xlsx (see Figure 55.1), Candidate D ekes out a 4-point victory over Candidate E. The "Excel Calculations" section later in this chapter explains the method we used to implement the Borda count.

Table 55.2: Ranked voting example

WHO'S OUT	VOTES FOR A	VOTES FOR B	VOTES FOR C	VOTES FOR D	VOTES FOR E
All in	36	24	20	18	12
E out	36	24 + 8 = 32	20 + 4 = 24	18	0
D and E out	36	32	24 + 18 = 42	0	0
B, D, and E out	36	0	42 + 32 = 74	0	0

◢	A	B	C	D	E	F	G	H	I
5			How Many Voters	36	24	20	18	8	4
6		1	1st choice	A	B	C	D	E	E
7		2	2nd choice	D	E	B	C	B	C
8		3	3rd choice	E	D	E	E	D	D
9		4	4th choice	C	C	D	B	C	B
10		5	5th choice	B	A	A	A	A	A
11	Points	Candidate							
12	406	A	A Points	1	5	5	5	5	5
13	348	B	B Points	5	1	2	4	2	4
14	336	C	C Points	4	4	1	2	4	2
15	278	D	D Points	2	3	4	1	3	3
16	282	E	E Points	3	2	3	3	1	1
17		B12 fomula	=SUMPRODUCT(D12:I12,$D$5:$I$5)						
18		E12 formula	=MATCH($B12,D$6:D$10,0)						

Figure 55.1: Candidate D wins by Borda count

- A *Condorcet winner* is a candidate who gains a majority of votes when paired against each other candidate. It would be wonderful if ranked-order voting would guarantee a Condorcet winner. Unfortunately, consider the three-voter, three-candidate example in Table 55.3. In a vote between A and B, A wins 2-1; in a vote between A and C, C wins 2-1; in a vote between B and C, B wins 2-1. Therefore, in this example there is no Condorcet winner.

For the data given in Table 55.1, Candidate E beats everyone in a pairwise evaluation and is, therefore, a Condorcet winner.

- Against A, E wins with 110 − 36 = 74 votes.

- Against B, E wins with 110 − 24 − 20 = 66 votes.

- Against C, E wins with 110 − 20 − 18 = 72 votes.

- Against D, E wins with 110 − 36 − 18 = 56 votes.

Table 55.3: No Condorcet winner

VOTER	FIRST CHOICE	2ND CHOICE	3RD CHOICE
1	A	B	C
2	B	C	A
3	C	A	B

Wallis's amazing example shows that seemingly reasonable voting systems each lead to results where anyone (or nobody!) can win. Our only hope is to look for flawed systems that seem to work better in practice than the most widely used system: *plurality voting,* or most votes win.

Ranked-Choice Voting

In the previous section, we gave an example of RCV. Ranked-choice voting (often called *instant runoff voting*) has been used in Australia, Maine, Minneapolis, and parts of California (such as Oakland). In Oakland's 2010 mayoralty race, Jean Quan (see `www.oaklandmagazine.com/November-2016/Opinion-Why-Ranked-Choice-Voting-Matters-in-Oakland/`) trailed Dom Perata 33% to 24% after the first iteration of RCV but won 51% to 49% in the final RCV, because she was the second or third choice of many voters.

A century of RCV in Australia has increased the number of major parties from three to seven. As pointed out by Bangor, Maine reporter Benjamin Reilly, in 1 out of 11 Australian districts (see `bangordailynews.com/2018/08/28/opinion/contributors/a-century-of-ranked-choice-voting-in-australia-offers-lessons-for-maine/`), the first round leader did not win. Reilly also points out that Australia's RCV has resulted in "increased social harmony by delivering centrist politics." RCV also encourages candidates to connect with all voters, because voters' second or third choices may well decide the election.

On February 1, 2020, Bernie Sanders appeared way ahead in the 2020 campaign to become the Democratic nominee. *The Economist* (my favorite!) magazine (`www.economist.com/graphic-detail/2020/02/01/under-ranked-choice-voting-left-wing-purism-would-aid-joe-biden`) used a national poll to determine what would happen on that date if RCV had been used. They found that Biden would have narrowly defeated Elizabeth Warren. In the first round, Biden had 32%, Sanders 21%, and Warren 22%, but in the final RCV tally, Biden narrowly beat Warren 53% to 47%, because Warren was the second or third choice of many Democratic voters.

States (such as Maine) can easily adopt RCV without a constitutional amendment, and I hope the future will see more states adopt RCV.

Approval Voting

With approval voting, voters simply list any number of candidates they approve. The winner is the candidate with the most "approvals." To illustrate approval voting, suppose there are three candidates (A, B, and C) and 10 voters. Suppose four voters approve only A, three approve only B, and three approve both B and C. Then, with six approvals, B is declared the winner. In 2018, Fargo, North Dakota became the first location in the United States to favor approval voting by a 64% to 36% margin (see `ballotpedia.org/Fargo,_North_Dakota,_Measure_1,_Approval_Voting_Initiative_(November_2018)`).

In practice, approval voting can encourage voters to suppress approvals of candidates to help their first-choice candidate. An example from `FairVote.org` illustrates the problems that may arise with approval voting (see `www.fairvote.org/new_lessons_from_problems_with_approval_voting_in_practice`).

Suppose there are 10 voters and three candidates: Jill, Jack, and Harry. Seven voters strongly support Jill and only three strongly support Jack. Five of Jill's backers hate Harry and are naive, so they approve of both Jack and Jill. Three of Jack's strong backers think Jill is fine but want Jack to win. Being sophisticated, they realize nobody likes Harry, and to increase the chances that Jack wins, these five voters only approve Jack. Now Jack beats Jill 8-7, despite the fact that Jill is the most satisfactory candidate.

Dartmouth College used approval voting for several years (see `www.fairvote.org/the_troubling_record_of_approval_voting_at_dartmouth`) to choose the alumni president. By 2016, some 98% of the voters engaged in "bullet voting," voting only for a single candidate. Before the 2017 election, Dartmouth returned to plurality voting, which simply declares the winner to be the candidate with the most votes.

Quadratic Voting

As we pointed out in Chapter 18, "Gerrymandering," the U.S. Congress is very unpopular. In March 2020, Congress had a 20% approval rating (see `www.realclearpolitics.com/epolls/other/congressional_job_approval-903.html`). For comparison, in 2017, some 17% of Americans approved of polygamy (see `www.usnews.com/news/national-news/articles/2017-07-28/us-acceptance-of-polygamy-at-record-high-and-tv-might-explain-why`).

As we previously discussed in this chapter, increased partisanship has made it harder for Congress to pass meaningful legislation. This is probably an important reason for Congress's low approval rating. One problem with the legislative process or voting for candidates is that individuals who care deeply about an issue can cast only one vote on that issue. For example, one voter may feel gun control is the most important issue, another might feel Medicare for All is the most important issue, and a third voter might feel having Mexico pay for the wall is the most important issue. *Quadratic voting* is an elegant approach that allows legislators or voters to express the strength of their feelings on an issue.

Probably the best way to explain quadratic voting is to look at its use by Colorado's Democratically controlled state legislature. The legislature had $40 million to spend and $120 million in requests. Each member of the legislature was given 100 "tokens" they could use to cast votes on 15 bills. The key to quadratic voting is that you can cast more than one vote on an issue, but casting N votes costs you N^2 tokens. Thus, casting two votes costs four tokens, three votes costs nine tokens, four votes costs 16 tokens, and so on (see `coloradosun.com/2019/05/28/quadratic-voting-colorado-house-budget/`).

Basically, quadratic voting incentivizes you to "spend" your tokens based on your willingness to pay. Let's use dollars instead of tokens. If you think, for example, that a bill is worth $10, how many dollars will you spend on it? Four votes costs you $16 and the fifth vote will cost you an additional $5^2 - 4^2 = 9, so you will buy the fifth vote. The sixth vote, however, would cost $6^2 - 5^2 = 11, so you would stop at five votes. As shown in the "Excel Calculations" section, calculus can be used to show that with quadratic voting, if a vote is worth $N to you, you will purchase N / 2 votes. Therefore, the number of votes you will purchase for a bill is directly proportional to the value you place on passing the bill. This approach allows legislatures or voters to either cheaply spread their votes across many bills or give stronger support to fewer bills. For example, if I were given 100 votes I could buy one vote on 100 bills or buy seven votes on two bills and one vote on two other bills).

If it costs C(V) dollars to purchase V votes, it can be shown that only quadratic voting will induce people to purchase votes for bills directly proportional to the strength of their preference for the bill. This ensures that the number of votes a bill receives accurately represents the sum of the preferences voters have for the bill. The thought-provoking book *Radical Markets* by Glen Weyl and Eric Posner (Princeton University Press, 2018) contains further discussion of quadratic voting and many other interesting proposals that might help save our Republic.

Excel Calculations

In this section, we show how we calculated the Borda count and use calculus to show that quadratic voters who place a value N on a bill will purchase N / 2 votes.

Calculating the Borda Count

We used the following steps to calculate the Borda count for each candidate shown in Figure 55.1 (see the workbook `Borda.xlsx`):

1. Copying the formula =MATCH($B12,D$6:D$10,0) from D12 to D12:I16 computes the rank of each candidate in each of the six voter segments. These formulas find the position that matches the candidate's name (A, B, C, D, or E) in the desired column. For example, in cell E15, the formula matches D in the range E6:E10 and returns 3 because D occurs in E8.

2. Copying the formula =SUMPRODUCT(D12:I12,$D$5:$I$5) from A12 to A13:A16 computes each candidate's Borda count. For example, in cell A12, the formula multiplies the number of voters in each column times Candidate A's ranking in each column ($36 * 1 + 24 * 5 + 20 * 5 + 18 * 5 + 8 * 5 + 4 * 5 = 406$). We find that Candidate D has the smallest Borda count and would be declared the winner.

If a Vote Is Worth $N to You, Why Does Quadratic Voting Induce You to Buy N / 2 Votes?

If a vote is worth $N to you and it costs V^2 to buy V votes, then you should purchase the number of votes maximizing the benefit B(V) of buying V votes. Now $B(V) = NV - V^2$. We denote the first derivative of B(V) by B'(V) and the second derivative of B(V) by B"(V). If B"(V) < 0, the maximum benefit will be obtained when B'(V) = 0. Now B'(V) = N - 2V = 0 for V = N / 2. Also B"(V) = −2 < 0, for all values of V, so if you value a vote at $N, quadratic voting (and it turns out no other function) will incentivize you to purchase a number of votes for a bill directly proportional to your valuation of the bill.

Why Do I Pay Too Much on eBay?

In 2018, eBay had 168 million active buyers. Most people are elated when their bid wins the item they covet. Fans of professional sports teams are thrilled when their team signs a top free agent. Oil companies are happy when their high bid gives them rights to an offshore oil lease. Being a pessimist by nature, this chapter is devoted to explaining to you why the winning bid often exceeds the value of what the bidder obtains. Nobel Prize winner Richard Thaler has written the definitive survey article ("Anomalies: The Winner's Curse," *The Journal of Economic Perspectives*, vol. 2, no. 1, Winter 1988, pages 191–202) on the winner's curse.

To gain some intuition for the winner's curse, assume there is a painting that has a true value of $100,000. Suppose five people are going to bid on the painting and on average (see Chapter 33, "Can Prediction Markets Predict the Future?" on prediction markets), the bidders get the value right. A set of bids that might plausibly occur would be $60,000, $80,000, $100,000, $120,000, and $140,000. These bids average to the true value of $100,000, but the winning bid of $140,000 is $40,000 too high.

How Many Pennies in the Jar?

Many economics teachers attempt to replicate Max Bazerman and William Samuelson's experiment ("I Won the Auction but Don't Want the Prize," *Journal of Conflict Resolution*, vol. 27, no. 4, 1983, pages 618–634). The authors filled jars with coins or objects like paper clips and the value of each jar was $8. Boston University MBAs were asked to bid on the jars and were told that the highest bidder would win the jar. Also, a $2 prize was offered to the student who came closest to guessing the true $8 value of the jar's contents. The experiment was repeated 48 times, and the average bid was much lower ($5.13) than the true value. Even though student estimates were too low, the average winning bid (in agreement with the winner's curse) was much more ($10.01) than the true value.

The Importance of Asymmetric Information

William Samuelson and Max Bazerman ("The Winner's Curse in Bilateral Negotiations," *Research in Experimental Economics*, vol. 3, 1985, pages 105–137) came up with an interesting example of the winner's curse.

Suppose Vivian Winston is a top-notch entrepreneur. If she buys any company, the stock price of the company will instantly increase by 50%. Vivian has her eyes on acquiring WidgetCo. WidgetCo's true value is equally likely to be anywhere between $0 and $200, and *WidgetCo, not Vivian*, knows the true value of the company. How much should Vivian bid for the company?

At first glance, Vivian might reason that on average, WidgetCo will be worth $100. Since she can increase the value of the company by 50%, a bid a little less than 1.5 * ($100) = $150 seems logical. However, this argument ignores the *asymmetric information* involved in the situation. WidgetCo has more information than Vivian. They know exactly the value (call it B) of their company. If WidgetCo accepts bid B, then the value to them must be at most B and on average B/2. Then if Vivian buys WidgetCo for $B, even after increasing its value, on average she will gain 1.5 * (B/2) – B = –0.25B. Thus, the more she bids, the more (on average) she loses. Samuelson and Bazerman report 90% of all participants make a non-zero bid, and more than half the bids are between $100 and $150.

The Winner's Curse and Offshore Oil Leases

Ed Capen, Robert Clapp, and William Campbell ("Competitive Bidding in High-Risk Situations," *Journal of Petroleum Technology*, vol. 23, no. 6, June 1971, pages 641–653) were the first to find an actual example of the winner's curse. The authors were petroleum engineers working for Atlantic Richfield. They found that oil companies that won bids for offshore oil leases in the Gulf of Mexico on the average lost money. When the article was written, the authors did not know how all the oil leases panned out. In 1983, Walter Mead, Asbjorn Moseidjord, and Philip Sorensen ("The Rate of Return Earned by Lessees under Cash Bonus Bidding of OCS Oil and Gas Leases," *Energy Journal*, vol. 4, no. 4, 1983, pages 37–52) reported the results from 1,223 Gulf of Mexico oil leases. They found that

- 62% of all leases were dry and returned no revenues.

- Using a 12.5% annual discount rate, 16% of the leases lost money.

- With a 12.5% discount rate, 22% of leases were profitable.

With a 12.5% annual discount rate (the authors deemed this the correct discount rate given the riskiness of the leases), the leases had an average net present value of –$192,128. (See Chapter 48, "How Can We Improve K-12 Eduation?" for an explanation of net present value.)

Sports Free Agents and the Winner's Curse

James Cassing and Richard Douglas ("Implications of the Auction Mechanism in Baseball's Free Agent Draft," *Southern Economic Journal*, vol. 47, no. 1, July 1980, pages 110–121) concluded that Major League Baseball (MLB) teams overpaid for free agents. Of course, in the last 20 years, all pro sports have become much more sophisticated with regard to analytics. To determine if the winner's curse presently exists in pro sports, I found, for each NBA free agent signed in July 2018, their salary for the 2018–2019 season. Then I used ESPN's Real Plus-Minus estimate of Wins Generated for each of these players to generate an estimate of the value created by each free agent during the 2018–2019 season. NBA teams pay around $3 million for each win. In the workbook FreeAgents.xlsx, we calculated that 47 free agents were paid $502 million and generated $492 million of value. This small study seems to indicate that the increased sophistication of sports management has mitigated the winner's curse.

Can You Avoid the Winner's Curse?

It seems logical that you might avoid the winner's curse if you bid a little below your expected valuation of the object in question. This type of analysis requires assumptions about the behavior of the other bidders. For example, will other bidders bid their believed valuation, or will they also reduce their bid? In this section, we provide a simple example that illustrates how we might avoid the winner's curse. Our work is in the file FixWinnersCurse.xlsx (see Figure 56.1). The model is explained in the next section, "Excel Calculations." Our assumptions follow:

- Our best guess is the object is worth $100, but it is equally likely to be worth anything between $80 and $120.

- Our one competitor is equally likely to bid any amount between 70% and 130% of the object's true value. *This means our competitor has more information about the object's true value than we do.*

We had Excel simulate this situation 5,000 times. Figure 56.1 shows the first few iterations. All iterations shown assume we bid $90.

- On the first iteration, we were outbid.

- On the second iteration, we outbid the competitor for an object worth $94 and earned a $4 profit.

- On the third iteration, we outbid the competitor for an object worth $83 and lost $7.

	A	B	C	D	E	F	G	H
1	ourbid	$90.00						Mean Profit
2								$1.53
3			Iteration	True Value	Competitor's Bid	My Profit		
4			1	$101.00	$125.24	$0.00		
5			2	$94.00	$75.20	$4.00		
6			3	$83.00	$89.64	-$7.00		
7			4	$80.00	$77.60	-$10.00		
8			5	$91.00	$65.52	$1.00		
9			6	$110.00	$123.20	$0.00		
10			7	$102.00	$76.50	$12.00		
11			8	$118.00	$113.28	$0.00		
12			9	$109.00	$118.81	$0.00		
13			10	$80.00	$74.40	-$10.00		

Figure 56.1: Avoiding the winner's curse

Figure 56.2 shows our average profit over all 10,000 iterations as a function of our bid. We see that a bid of $82 earns the maximum expected profit ($2.13). Also note that bids of $95 or more result, on average, in negative profit.

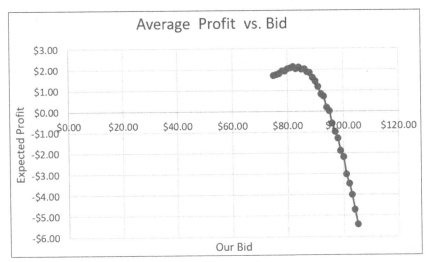

Figure 56.2: Bidding $82 maximizes expected profit.

Thus, in this simple example, bidding less than our best estimate ($100) of the object's value removes the winner's curse.

Excel Calculations

In this section, we show how we determined that a bid of $82 maximizes expected profit and produces, on average, a positive profit. Our work is in the file `FixWinnersCurse.xlsx`.

1. Enter a trial bid in cell B1. (We tried $90.)

2. Copy from D4 to D5:D10003 the formula =RANDBETWEEN(80,120). This generates 10,000 true values for the object. The Excel function RANDBETWEEN(a,b) is equally likely to generate any integer between a and b.

3. Copy from E4 to E5:E10003 the formula =RANDBETWEEN (70,130)*D4/100. This generates 10,000 competitor's bids. Each competitor bid is equally likely to assume any value between 70% and 130% of the object's true value.

4. Copy from F4 to F5:F510003 the formula =IF(ourbid>E4,D4-ourbid,0). This computes our profit for each iteration. If our bid is higher than the competitor, we win and our profit equals Object's Value – Our Bid; otherwise, our profit is 0.

5. Enter in cell H2 the formula **=AVERAGE(F4:F10003)**. This computes the average profit over all 10,000 iterations.

6. We now use a one-way data table to vary our bid between $75 and $105. Enter in cell J5 the formula for average profit (=H2) that we want to compute for each of our bids. Select the table range I5:J36, and from the Forecast group on the Data tab, select What-If Analysis, and then Data Table. Choose B1 as the Column input cell. This causes Excel to compute the average profit for each bid.

7. Select the range I6:J36, and choose a Scatter chart with lines and markers to create the chart shown in Figure 56.2.

CHAPTER 57

Can Analytics Recognize, Predict, or Write a Hit Song?

I love trivia. Here's a great music trivia question. Of all albums recorded between 2000 and 2009, which album by a solo artist sold the most copies in the United States? The answer is Norah Jones's debut album *Come Away With Me*, which sold 11.02 million copies (rateyourmusic.com/list/abyss89/the_100_biggest_ selling_albums_of_the_2000s__usa_/). When Jones recorded this album, she was unknown in the music world, but the computer program Hit Song Science used artificial intelligence (AI) to accurately predict that the album would be a huge hit (www.nytimes.com/2003/12/14/magazine/2003-the-3rd-annual-year-in-ideas-hit-song-science.html).

The key to using computers to recognize, predict, or write a hit song is to create an *acoustic fingerprint* of a song. Stripped to its essence, a song is a sound wave. The acoustic fingerprint of a song (or any sound) identifies at some (or all) points in time many attributes of a song, including

➤ Beats per minute (tempo).

➤ Frequency. For example, the top note on a guitar is 1,000 cycles per second, whereas a typical adult female singer sings a frequency between 165 and 255 cycles per second.

➤ During any part of a song, different frequencies (a guitar and a singer, for example) are combined, so you need to know at different points in time the *amplitude* of the song in different frequency ranges. *Spectral flatness* is used to measure at a point in time whether a song's sound is more like a pure tone or white noise (equal amplitude at different frequencies). Spectral flatness ranges between 0 and 1, with a value of 0 indicating all the sound is at a single frequency and a value of 1 indicating white noise.

Describing the acoustic fingerprint of a song requires huge amounts of data; therefore, to digitize a song, music geeks usually "sample" the music around 44,000 times a second. If you want to understand the math of music digitization, read Christophe's truly wonderful post on Shazam (see `coding-geek.com/how-shazam-works/`). As you will see, Shazam's secret sauce involves sampling a song 100 times a second.

In this chapter, we will discuss three interesting topics involving the interface of music and analytics:

➤ How does Shazam know what song you are listening to?

➤ How did Hit Song Science know Norah Jones's album would be a smash?

➤ Can artificial intelligence write a good song?

How Does Shazam Know What Song You Are Listening To?

I am sure many of our readers have heard a song they did not recognize, and after pressing the Shazam button on their phone, held their phone toward the music. Fifteen seconds later, Shazam amazingly tells you the title of the song. Fiona Harvey ("Name That Tune," *Scientific American*, vol. 288, June 2003, page 84–86) wrote a short, nontechnical explanation of the key idea behind Shazam.

At present Shazam has a library of 8 million songs, so when you are listening to a song (say, Don McLean's masterpiece "American Pie"), Shazam must determine which song in its library is most like "American Pie." In a three-minute song ("American Pie" is much longer), the possible songs number around *30 trillion* (see `https://www.wired.com/2015/03/many-different-songs-can/`. If Shazam tried to match the exact sequence of musical notes in "American Pie" to a song in its library, it could not quickly find an exact match in its library. The genius behind Shazam, Avery Wang (see `www.ee.columbia.edu/~dpwe/papers/Wang03-shazam.pdf` for a technical explanation of Wang's genius), figured out that in order to uniquely identify a song, you only need to record 100 times a second for 15 seconds the highest level and lowest level of each frequency. Then, Shazam gets 1,500 (15 * 100) of these data points from your phone. Like a person's fingerprints, these 1,500 pieces of data serve to uniquely identify a song. Using sophisticated computer programming, Shazam can quickly find the one in 8 million songs that matches the 1,500 pieces of information from "American Pie!"

The key lines of "American Pie" reference the following:

- "While the king was looking down" (Elvis)

- "The jester stole his thorny crown" (Bob Dylan)

- "While sergeants played a marching tune" (The Beatles' *Sgt. Pepper's Lonely Hearts Club Band* album, which was the first album that came with a lyrics sheet)

- "Eight miles high and falling fast" (an album by the Birds)

- "No angel born in Hell could break that Satan's spell" (The Rolling Stones played a rock concert December 6, 1969 at Altamont and the Stones kept playing while the Hell's Angels stabbed Meredith Hunter to death.)

- "There we were all in one place" (the 1969 Woodstock concert)

- "I met a girl who sang the blues" (Janice Joplin)

- "The day the music died" (On February 3, 1959 a plane crashed, killing Buddy Holly, Richie Valens, and "The Big Bopper.")

How Did Hit Song Science Know Norah Jones's Album Would Be a Smash?

Hit Song Science utilizes *cluster analysis*, so before discussing Hit Song Science in detail, a brief introduction to cluster analysis is in order.

Cluster analysis takes a large set of objects and classifies each object into clusters such that the objects classified in each cluster are similar and are substantially different from the objects in other groups. The math utilized in cluster analysis is beyond the scope of this book, but an example from the author's *Marketing Analytics* book (Wiley, 2014) should clarify how cluster analysis can aid you in making sense of a complex data set.

For the largest U.S. cities, I found the following six pieces of demographic data about each city:

- Percentage of population that is black

- Percentage of population that is Hispanic

- Percentage of population that is Asian

- Median age

- Unemployment rate

- Median per capita income

I found that four clusters well represented the 49 cities. Each cluster has an "anchor" that best represents the cities in the cluster. I found the following anchors:

- San Francisco cluster: Represents older, rich, highly Asian cities like Seattle and Honolulu.

- Memphis cluster: Represents highly black cities with high unemployment rates. Other cities in this cluster include Atlanta and Baltimore.

- Los Angeles cluster: Young, highly Hispanic with high unemployment rate. Other cities in this cluster include Houston and Dallas.

- Omaha cluster: Average income cities with few minorities. This cluster also includes Indianapolis and Jacksonville.

Hit Song Science was discussed in the *New Yorker Magazine* by mega-bestselling author Malcolm Gladwell ("The Formula," *New Yorker Magazine*, vol. 79, October 16, 2006, pages 138–149). Hit Song Science downloaded the acoustic fingerprint of thousands of songs. Then they focused on all songs that were Billboard Top 30 hits and found 60 clusters among these hit songs. Hit Song Science was confident that songs whose fingerprint was not near a cluster would not be a hit. Nine of the 14 songs on the album *Come Away with Me* were classified as having hit potential—and the rest is history.

Hit Song Science classified Gnarls Barkley's song "Crazy" as a likely hit. Hit Song Science's president, Michael McCready, placed "Crazy" in the same hit cluster as Ashanti's hit song "Baby" and Mariah Carey's megahit "One Sweet Day." (Carey has the most number one songs of any individual!) "Crazy" hit #2 in the United States and was #1 in England for nine weeks. *Rolling Stone* magazine (see `en.wikipedia.org/wiki/Crazy_(Gnarls_Barkley_song)#:~:text=`) named "Crazy" the best song of the 2000–2009 decade. As of this writing, the official YouTube video (see `www.youtube.com/watch?v=-N4jf6rtyuw`) has over 32 million views.

If McCready does not predict that a song will be a hit, all is not lost. Hit Song Science can tell a song producer how to change a song to move it closer to the center of a hit cluster. For example, the producer may be told to change the bassline (the lowest notes in the song) or adjust the song's decibel level. (The normal conversation is 60 decibels; a lawn mower is 90 decibels.) Hit Song Science is owned by a company named Platinum Blue Music Intelligence, which claims to predict hit songs with 80% accuracy. Of course, what we really want to know is (see Chapter 30, "Can We Predict Heart Attacks in Real Time?") Platinum Blue Music's sensitivity (probability they say a song is a hit given it turned out to be a hit) and specificity (probability they say a song is not a hit given the song did not turn out to be a hit).

Can Artificial Intelligence Write a Good Song?

In Roberta Flack's #1 song "Killing Me Softly with His Song," Flack referred to Don McLean's "American Pie" and said, "I heard he sang a good song." We know that computers can beat humans at Chess, Go, and Jeopardy! So, will a soulless computer put songwriters out of business? If you want to hear a sample of AI music, listen to "Daddy's Car," a song in the style of the Beatles, created by Sony's Flow Machine Research Laboratory (see www.google.com/search?q= flow+machine+daddy%27s+car&rlz=1C1CHBD_enUS733US733&oq=flow+machine+ daddy%27s+car&aqs=chrome..69i57j33.6695j0j4&sourceid=chrome&ie=UTF-8).

An easy-to-use AI music site is Amper Music (www.ampermusic.com). After creating a free account, you tell Amper Music the desired length of the music. Then, after telling the site the type of music you want (such as romantic, modern, or folk), several snippets of AI music appear. Former "American Idol" contestant Taryn Southern used Amper Music (see www.theverge.com/2018/8/31/17777008/ artificial-intelligence-taryn-southern-amper-music) to get started with her 2017 single "Break Free." (Listen to it here: www.youtube.com/watch?v=XUs6CznN8pw; I think it's really good!) On March 13, 2020, the YouTube version had over 2 million views.

The math behind computer efforts to write good music is really hard. At present, the most comprehensive reference is Jean-Pierre Briot, Gaëtan Hadjeres and François-David Pachet's *Deep Learning Techniques for Music Generation, Computational Synthesis and Creative Systems* (Springer, 2019). Pachet previously worked for Flow Machine and is currently director of creative technology for the streaming service Spotify. We will now describe two relatively simple algorithmic approaches to writing music:

- The Markov chain approach
- The evolutionary algorithm approach

Describing anything near the state of the art in computer-generated music is well beyond the scope of this book.

The Markov Chain Approach

A *Markov chain* describes a sequence of possible events, such as the daily closing price of a stock or the sequence of chords in a song. At any point in time, the Markov chain is in a state. For example, the closing stock price might be $50. A sequence of events is a Markov chain if the location of the next state only depends on *the most recent state* and not the previous states in the sequence. So, in our stock example, the closing price of the stock the day after it closed at $50 is not influenced by how the stock price reached $50. Whether the stock went up 10 straight days or down 10 straight days makes no difference. As described by

Alexander Osipenko (see `towardsdatascience.com/markov-chain-for-music-generation-932ea8a88305`), a Markov chain can be used in a simplistic fashion to compose a song. To begin, you need a *corpus*, or collection of music. Suppose your corpus is all music by Bach, Beethoven, Mozart, and Chopin. Think about each piece of music as a sequence of chords. It's easy to look at your corpus and figure out for a given chord the probability mass function of the next chord. For example, Osipenko found the probability mass function for the next chord after an F chord, as shown in Table 57.1.

Table 57.1: Probability Mass Function for Next Chord After an F

NEXT CHORD	PROBABILITY
F	0.167
G7	0.056
Fsus4	0.111
A7sus4	0.222
C	0.222
Em7	0.222

So, to compose a piece of music, pick any chord to start, and then use the probability mass function for that chord to generate the next chord, and so on. Of course, this approach ignores the fact that your opinion of how a given chord sounds depends on much more than just the previous chord, so don't expect the Markov chain approach to generate great music.

The Evolutionary Algorithm Approach

Of course, just looking at chords cannot completely describe a piece of music. Many researchers (see, for example, `data-x.blog/projects/maia-ai-for-music-creation/`) try to summarize a piece of music at a given time by quantifying three elements:

- *Duration*—This measures how long a note or tone lasts.
- *Pitch*—Pitch is like frequency, which is measured in cycles per second. In contrast, pitch refers to how high or low the music sounds when you listen to it.
- *Dynamics*—Dynamics refers to the volume of the music. Static dynamics refers to the volume at a given point in time. Dynamics can also refer to changes in volume.

We discussed evolutionary algorithms in Chapter 53, "How Does the UPS Driver Know the Order to Deliver Packages?" With a set of rules, you can define a "target cell" that is optimized by choosing a musical sequence that violates the rules as little as possible. Calvin Pelletier (see "Music Composition Using Recurrent Neural Networks and Evolutionary Algorithms," at `www.ideals.illinois.edu/bitstream/handle/2142/99544/ECE499-Su2017-pelletier.pdf?sequence=2&isAllowed=y`) used evolutionary algorithms to compose music. He penalized a piece of music based on the following:

- Penalize the music when successive notes are far apart in semitones. (A semitone is the interval between two successive notes on a 12-tone scale.)

- Penalize the music when a given note is not within the chord being played.

- Penalize the music when a given note is not within the key being played.

- As a surrogate for rhythm, the music is penalized when the beat within a measure starting a note is a downbeat.

These penalties are measured over the song's entirety, so you would expect this approach to generate better music than the Markov chain approach. For example, the Markov chain approach could easily result in a string of four or five identical chords, which would sound pretty bad.

Pelletier asked 15 people to rate his evolutionary algorithm music against human-composed music and found that the evolutionary music's average rating was 2.9 on a 5-point scale, as compared to a 3.9 average rating for the human-composed music. The human-composed music rating is around 3 standard deviations better than the evolutionary algorithm rating.

The use of computers to write music is a rapidly evolving field. Again, we refer the interested and technically savvy reader to *Deep Learning Techniques for Music Generation* and encourage readers to use their favorite search engine using the search term "neural networks and music composition."

CHAPTER 58

Can an Algorithm Improve Parole Decisions?

In 2019, the American prison system had 2.3 million people in jail (www.pris-onpolicy.org/reports/pie2019.html). The United States has 4.4% of the world's population but 22% of the world's prisoners. In 2016, the United States had 4.5 million people on parole or probation. (www.bjs.gov/index.cfm?ty=pbdetail&iid=6188). In 2018, there were 91,600 parole officers (www.bls.gov/ooh/community-and-social-service/probation-officers-and-correctional-treatment-specialists.htm), so on average a parole officer supervises around 50 people on parole or probation.

A 2018 Department of Justice (DOJ) study followed for nine years prisoners who were released in 2005 (www.bjs.gov/content/pub/pdf/18upr9yfup0514.pdf). This, of course, includes prisoners who were released but not paroled. The DOJ study found that 83% of all prisoners released in 2005 committed a crime within nine years of their release. (Eighty-seven percent of blacks were arrested compared to 83% of whites.)

In recent years, sophisticated data science algorithms have been widely applied to aid the U.S. government, cities, and states in their parole decisions. Common inputs to these algorithms include information similar to the information collected by the government on the Post Conviction Risk Assessment (PCRA) (see Jennifer Skeem and Christopher Lowenkamp's article "Risk, Race, and Recidivism: Predictive Bias and Disparate Impact," *Criminology*, vol. 54, no. 4, 2016, pages 680–712). PCRA uses the following information (and logistic regression; see Chapter 54, "Can Data Win a Presidential Election?") to assign a *risk score* that assigns each potential parolee a low, low/moderate, moderate, or high risk of committing a crime if released:

➤ Age

➤ Number of arrests

➤ Level of education

➤ Social networks (unmarried, family problems, lack of social support)

➤ Recent drug or alcohol problems

➤ Low motivation to change

Many people have criticized the use of these algorithms. For example, University of Michigan professor Sonja Starr points out that young black men are six times more likely to be arrested than young white men (`www.abajournal.com/magazine/article/algorithm_bail_sentencing_parole`). Therefore, using inputs such as arrests may have *disparate impact* by increasing the differences between the times whites and blacks spend in prison. Critics of risk scores equate this disparate impact to a lack of fairness. Critics of the algorithms also argue arrests may be racially biased, and at least the analysts should use conviction history instead of arrest history. The problem is, according to University of Pennsylvania criminology professor Richard Berk, "arrests predict better than convictions" (`thepenngazette.com/black-box-justice/`).

This chapter is organized as follows:

➤ We use *logistic regression* to construct a simple example that illustrates the "classic" approach to calculating risk scores.

➤ We discuss the widely cited ProPublica searing criticism of risk scores.

➤ We discuss how Skeem and Lowenkamp showed that PCRA does not exhibit significant test bias.

➤ We introduce the important concept of *machine learning* and discuss Professor Berk's use of machine learning to create risk scores for prospective parolees.

An Example of Risk Scores

The worksheet Base of the workbook `Parole.xlsx` contains fictitious data that we will use, combined with logistic regression to create risk scores. A subset of the data is shown in Figure 58.1. For each of 5,000 prisoners who were paroled, we are given the following information:

▪ Age at first arrest

▪ Number of prior arrests

- Race (1 = black, 0 = white)
- Whether they committed a crime in the first two years after release (1 = committed crime, 0 = no crime committed)

	E	F	G	H	I	J	K	L	M
5			constant	0.102					
6			age	-0.029					
7			arrests	0.283					
8								Total Ln Likelihood	
9								-3319.120376	
10									
11	Person	Race	Age		Arrests	Score	Prob	Commits Crime	Ln Likelihood	Bias
12	1	0	17		2	0.182	0.545	1	-0.606	0.455
13	2	0	26		2	-0.075	0.481	1	-0.732	0.519
14	3	0	21		2	0.067	0.517	0	-0.727	-0.517
15	4	0	27		3	0.179	0.545	0	-0.786	-0.545
16	5	1	27		6	1.027	0.736	0	-1.333	-0.736
17	6	1	24		2	-0.018	0.495	1	-0.702	0.505
18	7	1	27		2	-0.104	0.474	1	-0.746	0.526
19	8	1	17		2	0.182	0.545	0	-0.788	-0.545
20	9	0	30		4	0.376	0.593	1	-0.523	0.407

Figure 58.1: Calculation of risk scores with logistic regression

Using logistic regression (see Chapter 54), we used Age and Number of Prior Arrests to estimate a probability that each person would commit a crime during their first two years out of prison. *Note we did not use Race as a predictor of likelihood to commit a crime.* We found

Score = 0.102 − 0.029 * AGE + 0.283 * PRIORARRESTS

Then, logistic regression implies our estimate of the probability that a person commits a crime during the first two years out is $e^{Score}/(1 + e^{Score})$. Our data indicates that the likelihood that a person commits a crime decreases as the AGE at first arrest increases and increases with the number of PRIORARRESTS. Here are some examples of our results:

- Person 1 is white, first arrested at age 17, with two prior arrests. They committed a crime, and we estimated a 54.5% chance they would commit a crime.
- Person 5 is black, first arrested at age 27, with six prior arrests. They did not commit a crime, and we estimated a 73.6% chance they would commit a crime.

Are Our Predictions Unbiased?

As shown in Table 58.1, for whites and blacks, our predictions are on average very accurate.

Table 58.1: Average prediction for chance of crime vs. actual crime percentage

RACE	AVERAGE ESTIMATED PROBABILITY OF COMMITTING CRIME	FRACTION COMMITTING A CRIME
Black	56.7%	56.8%
White	44.6%	44.4%

We can also evaluate bias by calculating for each person:

(1) Commit Crime (a 1 or 0) – Estimated Probability of Committing a Crime

If our forecasts are unbiased, then for each race and range of risk scores, the average of equation (1) should be near 0. As shown in Figure 58.2, this is indeed the case. For each range of risk scores and race, the average of equation (1) is very close to 0. The exception is for whites with risk scores greater than 0.7, but this group only contained 12 parolees.

	O	P	Q
20	Average of Bias	Column Label	
21	Row Labels	0	1
22	0-0.5	0.00457	-0.00651
23	0.5-1	-0.01981	0.00519

Figure 58.2: Risk score bias vs. risk score

Does Adding Race Improve Our Predictions?

We can check whether adding race to our model improves our forecasts. In the worksheet Add Race, we incorporated race into our predictive model by adding three variables to our Score equation:

- **Race:** A positive coefficient for race in our score equation would indicate that after adjusting for AGE and PRIORARRESTS, race would increase our estimate of the probability a person would commit a crime.

- **Race*AGE:** The coefficient of this variable indicates the degree of *interaction* between RACE and AGE. This measures the degree to which the influence of AGE on our prediction is different for blacks and whites.

- **RACE*PRIORARRESTS:** The coefficient of this variable indicates the degree of interaction between RACE and PRIORARRESTS. This measures the degree to which the influence of PRIORARRESTS on our prediction is different for blacks and whites.

As shown in cell M10 of the worksheet Add Race, adding these three variables on average changed each person's predicted chance of recidivism by a mere 0.006. This means that after incorporating AGE and PRIORARRESTS into our model, adding information about a prisoner's race has little additional predictive value.

Are Our Predictions Fair?

This is such a hard question! Our predictive model is accurate, but as shown in Table 58.1, the average prediction of a black person's probability for committing a crime is 12% higher than the average prediction for a white person. Thus, if parole is based on our predictions, a much larger percentage of blacks will be denied parole. For example, if a predicted probability of 0.5 for recidivism is the cutoff for parole, then 69% of blacks and only 25% of whites would be denied parole. To see why, note from Figure 58.3 that blacks averaged twice as many prior arrests than whites, and their first arrest averaged three years earlier than for whites. Together these facts explain the higher average of our estimated probabilities of recidivism for blacks. Of course, the key question is to what degree the racial differences in crime rates are due to racism and factors beyond the control of the prisoners. As summarized by Steven Barkan (see page 56 of *Race, Crime and Justice*, Oxford University Press, 2017), the academic consensus is that most of the racial difference in crime rates is explained by the fact that African Americans are much more likely than whites to be exposed to environmental factors that lead to crime such as poverty, unemployment, and family disruption.

	O	P	Q
28	Row Labels	Average of Age	Average of Arrests
29	0	26.05	1.48
30	1	23.01	2.99

Figure 58.3: Age at first arrest and number of arrests by race

ProPublica Criticizes Risk Scores

If you type into Google a search for "are parole risk scores biased?" the first two results lead you to ProPublica's study on this issue (www.propublica.org/article/machine-bias-risk-assessments-in-criminal-sentencing). According to their website, ProPublica is a journalistic site whose mission is

> To expose abuses of power and betrayals of the public trust by government, business, and other institutions, using the moral force of investigative journalism to spur reform through the sustained spotlighting of wrongdoing.

ProPublica analyzed risk scores developed by Northpointe (now Equivant) that were used *at time of trial* to forecast the likelihood of recidivism. Since this data was not collected at the time of parole, its relevance to our discussion of parole and algorithms is compromised. The Correctional Offender Management Profiling for Alternative Sanctions (COMPAS) algorithm used the following variables to calculate for each defendant a 1–10 score, where a higher score means the defendant was more likely to commit another crime:

- Age at first arrest
- History of violence
- Vocational education
- History of noncompliance

These scores were used to classify each defendant as high, moderate, or low risk of committing a future crime.

ProPublica obtained data for nearly 5,000 defendants in Broward County, Florida. (Remember them from our discussion of the 2000 election?) A great analysis of ProPublica's assessment of this data was done by the *Washington Post* (www.washingtonpost.com/news/monkey-cage/wp/2016/10/17/can-an-algorithm-be-racist-our-analysis-is-more-cautious-than-propublicas/). In the *Post* analysis, four Stanford and Berkeley data scientists analyzed the scores for accuracy and fairness.

Are COMPAS Scores Accurate?

The *Post* analysts found defendants with the highest risk score committed another crime 81% of the time, whereas, as expected, the defendants with the lowest scores committed another crime only 22% of the time. More importantly, the *Post* analysts found that for a risk score between 1 and 10, *whites and blacks reoffended at almost exactly the same rate*. For example, blacks with a risk score of 5 reoffended 51% of the time, and whites with the same risk score reoffended 48% of the time. The small average difference between the reoffending rate for each test score indicates that COMPAS exhibits little or no test bias.

Are COMPAS Scores Fair?

As shown in Figure 58.4 (reading off the *Post*'s summary chart of the ProPublica data), we *approximated* the results for the 5,000 defendants.

	A	B	C
7	Black	Reoffended	Did not Reoffend
8	Low Risk	464	857
9	High Medium Risk	1179	643
10			
11	White		
12	Black	Reoffended	Did not Reoffend
13	Low Risk	393	1000
14	High Medium Risk	393	250

Figure 58.4: Actual ProPublica data

From this data, we find that $643 / (643 + 857) = 42.8\%$ of non-reoffending blacks were misclassified with high or medium risk scores and $250 / (250 + 1000) = 20\%$ of whites who did not reoffend were misclassified with high or medium risk scores. Also, we find that $(464 + 1179) /(464 + 1179 + 857 + 743) = 52\%$ of blacks and $(393 + 393) / (393 + 393 + 1000 + 250) = 39\%$ of whites reoffended.

ProPublica correctly found that among defendants who did not reoffend, 42% of blacks and only 22% (from the chart, we got 20%) of whites were classified as medium or high risk. This would imply that black defendants who went straight would, based on their higher risk scores, be treated more harshly by the court system.

It also turns out, however, that 52% of blacks and only 39% of whites reoffended. Given that for each risk score the COMPAS scores are accurate and the fact that a higher percentage of blacks reoffend, Jon Kleinberg, Sendhil Mullainathan, and Manish Raghavan prove that *it must be the case that blacks who do not reoffend will be classified as riskier than whites who do not reoffend* (see arxiv.org/abs/1609.05807). Their work shows the inherent trade-off between accuracy and fairness.

As with PCRA and our hypothetical example, the inputs to COMPAS are in all likelihood influenced by racial bias and unequal opportunity. To paraphrase Shakespeare's immortal line from *Julius Caesar*, "the fault is probably not in our algorithms, but most likely in the inequality created by our society." In a 2019 Pew Research Center study (www.pewsocialtrends.org/2019/04/09/race-in-america-2019/), 56% of Americans felt that being black hurt a person's prospects of getting ahead. Perhaps by implementing some of the remedies discussed in Chapters 44 and 48, reducing inequalities between neighborhoods and schools provides a long-term solution. After watching HBO's fantastic *Watchmen* miniseries and seeing the horrible experiences Hooded Justice lived through (Google the Tulsa 1921 Massacre), and viewing the tragic, needless, and horrible death of George Floyd, I am in favor of reparations for a quicker fix.

Skeem and Lowenkamp and PCRA

In their analysis of how well the PCRA predicted the likelihood of a potential parolee committing another crime, Skeem and Lowenkamp followed 48,475 offenders for at least one year after their release. Based on the data (previously described) on the PCRA, they classified each offender as low, low/moderate, moderate, or high risk of committing another crime. For each classification, the authors found that the fraction of blacks and whites predicted to commit a crime during the follow-up period was virtually identical. For example, whites classified as high risk committed crimes 66% of the time and 66% of blacks classified as high risk committed a crime.

Like our fictitious example, the authors found that after incorporating the data on an offender's PCRA test, adding variables for race into their model left classifications virtually unchanged. With regard to fairness, the authors point out that some of an offender's criminal history may be due to socioeconomic status, but the criminal history is needed for accurate prediction. They point out that blacks score an average of .56 standard deviations worse on risk scores than whites, and this may result in a disparate impact.

Machine Learning and Parole Decisions

A recent development is the use of *machine learning* in parole decision modeling. Machine learning uses sophisticated algorithms to find patterns in data. Throughout this book, we have created plausible models (such as our Chapter 32 model used to predict customer count at a restaurant) that use input variables to predict an output of interest. In Chapter 32, our inputs were the day of the week, week of the year, and special day (if any), and the output was daily customer count. Our model was

Daily Customer Count = Constant + Day #* (Daily Trend)

+ (Day of the Week Effect) + (Week of the Year Effect)

+ (Adjustment due to Special Day)

This model did well in forecasting daily customer count. For all models we have fit to data, we have used Excel to see if the model provides satisfactory predictions. With machine learning, you give a computer package (often the statistical programming package R or Python programming language) the inputs and outputs and say please find a pattern in the inputs (not specified by the user) that does a good job forecasting the outputs. Machine learning is needed when we can't specify a model that provides satisfactory results.

A Brief Introduction to Machine Learning

The classic XOR (exclusive or model) data set provides a simple example of why we need machine learning. The worksheet XOR of the workbook `Parole.xlsx` contains eight observations with two inputs, X1 and X2, and a single output, Y. The rule used to determine Y is that Y = 1 when both X1 and X2 are 0 or 1, and Y = 0 when only one of X1 and X2 equal 1. We tried to fit a multiple linear regression model to predict Y from X1 and X2. Our R^2 = 0, and multiple linear regression simply yields as its best prediction for Y the simple but useless prediction that Y = 0.5. In short, linear regression is useless in this situation. Any human or machine learning algorithm would quickly recognize the pattern in this data. The importance of machine learning is that the many techniques utilized in machine learning can easily and quickly find complex patterns in data. (See John Paul Mueller and Luca Massaron's *Machine Learning for Dummies*, Wiley, 2016 for an excellent introduction.)

We now give a brief description of three important applications of machine learning.

- Your email system tries to classify email messages as *spam* or *not spam*. One common set of inputs is the frequency of various words used in the email. For example, most emails containing the word "Viagra" turn out to be spam. The output for each email is whether the email is spam or not. As we all know, spam filters make mistakes, but after feeding a large number of emails to a machine learning algorithm, the algorithm is usually pretty accurate at detecting spam. For example, M. Tariq Banday and Tariq Jan fed 8,000 emails into a variety of machine learning algorithms (arxiv.org/ftp/arxiv/papers/0910/0910.2540.pdf). Forty-five percent of these emails were spam, but even the simplest machine learning techniques correctly classified 97% of the emails correctly.

- Google used machine learning to classify 18,000 mammograms as either breast cancer or not breast cancer (medcitynews.com/2020/01/googles-ai-beats-humans-at-detecting-breast-cancer-sometimes/). Google's algorithms resulted in 6% fewer false positives (saying a woman has breast cancer when she does not) and 9% fewer false negatives (saying a woman does not have breast cancer when she does) than the average radiologist.

- *Driverless or autonomous cars* use data from cameras in the car to form a map of the car's surroundings (see www.synopsys.com/automotive/what-is-autonomous-car.html). To collect data useful for developing driverless cars, Google's Waymo subsidiary has driven driverless cars more than 20 million miles (fortune.com/2020/01/07/googles-waymo-reaches-20-million-miles-of-autonomous-drihving/). Based on what the car's cameras "see," computers record the acceleration and direction that a good driver has used. Machine learning recognizes how the inputs from the camera influence the behavior of the driver. Then, at every instant, the car's cameras are processed through the patterns learned from data like Waymo's. The driverless cars then can (in theory) determine at any instant desired acceleration and car direction based on the insights gleaned from all this driving.

  At present, driverless cars make mistakes. See www.theguardian.com/technology/2016/jan/12/google-self-driving-cars-mistakes-data-reports for a description of errors made by Waymo's cars. Perhaps the most tragic mistake made by driverless cars occurred in 2018, when a car powered by driverless car technology (with an actual driver at the wheel, however) killed Elaine Herzberg of Tempe, Arizona as she walked across the street in darkness (see www.azcentral.com/story/news/local/tempe/2019/03/17/ one-year-after-self-driving-uber-rafaela-vasquez-behind-wheel-crash-death-elaine-herzberg-tempe/1296676002/).

Richard Berk, Machine Learning, and Parole Decisions

For many years, logistic regression was the state of the art in predicting whether a paroled offender would reoffend. Criminology professor Richard Berk of the University of Pennsylvania has pioneered the use of machine learning to improve parole decision making. Berk's basic tool is a *classification tree*. An example of a classification tree is shown in Figure 58.5. We are trying to predict if a parolee is high (H), moderate (M), or low risk (L) based on age at first arrest and number of prior offenses. Our simple classification tree would classify parolees as follows:

- For those under 25 at time of first arrest, classify a parolee as low risk with 0 prior arrests, medium risk with 1 prior arrest, or high risk with at least 2 prior arrests.

- For those 25 or over at time of first arrest, classify a parolee as low risk with less than or equal to 2 arrests, medium risk with 3 or 4 arrests, and high risk with at least 5 arrests.

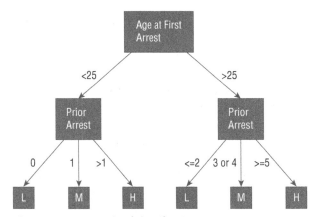

Figure 58.5: Example of classification tree

When you use many predictors, to paraphrase Carl Sagan, the late creator of TV's *Cosmos*, "there are billions and billions of possible classification trees." Berk uses (www.law.upenn.edu/live/files/2258-berk-bakeoff.pdf) the advanced machine learning tool of random forests to zero in on one of these classification trees that excels at classification. (See towardsdatascience.com/understanding-random-forest-58381e0602d2 for an introduction to random forests.) In Berk's work with the Philadelphia parole system, he found that the random forests performed much better than logistic regression.

Berk points out (thepenngazette.com/black-box-justice/) that in parole decisions, most governments consider the cost of a false negative (saying a parolee will not commit a crime when they do) to be much higher than the cost of a false positive (saying a parolee will commit a crime when they do not). As Berk says, most governments feel that "it's much more dangerous to release Darth Vader than it is to incarcerate Luke Skywalker" (www.bloomberg.com/features/2016-richard-berk-future-crime/).

We now use Berk's example from www.law.upenn.edu/live/files/2258-berk-bakeoff.pdf to illustrate how random forests outperform logistic regression. Using data from 25,000 parolees, Berk used the following variables to try to determine if a parolee would be arrested for a serious crime within two years of release:

- Age
- Prior arrests for violent crimes as an adult
- Age of first arrest as an adult
- Total number of prior arrests as an adult
- Earliest age charged as a juvenile
- Total number of prior charges as a juvenile
- Number of charges for drug crimes as an adult
- Number of sex crimes as an adult

With the cost of a false negative set at five times the cost of a false positive, logistic regression obtained the results shown in Table 58.2. A table that shows each combination of predicted and actual outcomes is called a *confusion matrix*.

Table 58.2: Logistic regression confusion matrix

RESULT	CRIME PREDICTED	CRIME NOT PREDICTED	PERCENTAGE ERROR
Committed serious crime	378	302	44.4%
Did not commit serious crime	1,385	2,935	32.1%

Using his random forest approach, Berk obtained the confusion matrix shown in Table 58.3.

Table 58.3: Random forest confusion matrix

RESULT	CRIME PREDICTED	CRIME NOT PREDICTED	PERCENTAGE ERROR
Committed serious crime	427	253	37.2%
Did not commit serious crime	1,196	3,124	27.7%

From these tables, we see that the random forest approach reduced the fraction of false negatives by 7% and the fraction of false positives by 5%. Berk points out that each year, the agency he worked with manages 40,000 ex-offenders on probation. Approximately 5,000 of these people are arrested for a serious crime within two years. This implies that classification by random forests versus logistic regression would prevent 0.07 * 5,000 = 350 serious crimes. Berk stated that the agency found this to be a significant improvement.

Of course, the classification results are heavily influenced by the "Darth Vader/Luke Skywalker" trade-off ratio. The Black Box Justice article states that the Philadelphia parole agency reduced the cost ratio from 10-1 to 2.5-1 because they could not handle the increased number of high-risk offenders left in prison based on the 10-1 ratio.

With regard to fairness, random forests can be modified (at the cost of reduced accuracy) to incorporate fairness restrictions, such as the fraction of false positives for blacks and whites should be equal.

The title of this chapter is "Can an Algorithm Improve Parole Decisions?" I think the answer is that until we reduce the socioeconomic disparity between blacks and whites and eliminate racism, we must make difficult trade-offs between accuracy and fairness.

CHAPTER 59

How Do Baseball Teams Decide Where to Shift Fielders?

During 1894–1907, Hall of Fame outfielder William Henry "Wee Willie" Keeler played for all three New York teams (Yankees, Dodgers, and Giants). His advice to hitters was "Keep your eye clear and hit 'em where they ain't." Today, most major league teams position fielders with the philosophy "put them where they hit." In this chapter, we explore how the increased use of the shift has changed baseball.

The Debut of the Shift

The great left-handed hitter Ted Williams usually hit the ball to the right side of the field. On July 14, 1946, the Cleveland Indians player-manager Lou Boudreau decided to play all four infielders, the right fielder, and center fielder on the right side of the field. During the rest of Williams's great career (interrupted by military service in the Korean War), teams used the shift during most of his plate appearances. Williams estimated that the shift cost him 15 points in batting average. Figure 59.1 illustrates the difference between today's most common shift (three infielders between first and second base) and the normal alignment of fielders.

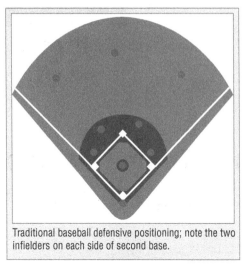

Traditional baseball defensive positioning; note the two infielders on each side of second base.

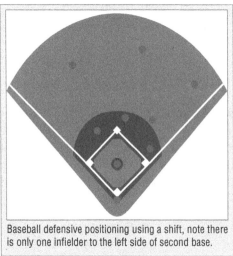

Baseball defensive positioning using a shift, note there is only one infielder to the left side of second base.

Figure 59.1: Comparison of the shift and normal fielding alignments

The Return of the Shift

After a 50+ year hiatus, the shift has returned with a vengeance. In 2010, teams shifted on 3% of plate appearances, and in 2019, teams shifted on 15% of all plate appearances (41% of the time against left-hand hitters). Now that teams know where each hitter tends to hit the ball against different types of pitchers, it is a relatively easy mathematical exercise to determine where to place the fielders to minimize the batter's effectiveness. As an example, consider the worksheet Shift in the file Shift.xlsx (see Figure 59.2), which contains made-up data about where a hitter hits the ball on their ground ball at bats. A 1 in Column C means the ball is hit between first and second, and a 2 in Column C means the ball is hit between second and third. Column E gives the actual distance of the batted ball from first base. For example, on the first at bat, the ball was hit 67.65 feet of the way between first and second, and on the second at bat, the ball was hit 64.76 feet of the way between second and third. In L6:L9, we determined where to put the four infielders to maximize the chance of successfully fielding the ball. We assume the play results in an out if the fielder was positioned within 5 feet of where the ball is hit. We added a constraint that the first baseman must be positioned within 10 feet of first base and a constraint to ensure that one fielder is stationed between second and third base. By using the Excel Solver (see the "Excel Calculations" section at the end of the chapter), we found that placing the first basemen 3 feet from first base, the second basemen 51 feet from first base, the shortstop 60 feet from first base, and the third basemen 151 feet from first base, we can successfully field 67% of all ground balls. Note that 87% of all balls were hit between first and second.

	C	D	E	F	G	H	I	J	K	L	M
1	The shift				Made up data for left hand pull hitter						
2	Data: Where hitter hits ball in infield				Assume success if fielder within 5 feet of hit						
3	defined by distance between 1st and 2nd and second and third							Fraction fielded			
4									0.67 First baseman within 10 feet of bag		
5	Base	distance	changed distance	Distance to 1	Distance to 2	Distance to 3	Distance to 4	Fieldit		Optimal Position	Default
6	1	67.65	67.65	64.59	17.04	6.96	82.95	0	1	3.0586	8
7	2	64.76	154.76	151.71	104.16	94.07	4.17	1	2	50.60358	78
8	1	61.70	61.70	58.64	11.10	1.01	88.89	1	3	60.69059	130
9	1	57.93	57.93	54.87	7.33	2.76	92.67	1	4	150.5954	170
10	1	47.13	47.13	44.07	3.47	13.56	103.47	1			
11	1	52.00	52.00	48.94	1.40	8.69	98.60	1			
12	2	54.78	144.78	141.72	94.17	84.09	5.82	0			
13	2	59.69	149.69	146.63	99.08	89.00	0.91	1			
14	2	41.29	131.29	128.23	80.69	70.60	19.31	0			
15	1	60.46	60.46	57.40	9.86	0.23	90.13	1			

Figure 59.2: The power of the shift

As shown in the worksheet No Shift (see Figure 59.3), if the infielders were positioned in their normal position, only 19% of the ground balls would have been fielded.

	C	D	E	F	G	H	I	J	K	L	M	N
1	The shift				Made up data for left hand pull hitter							
2	Data: Where hitter hits ball in infield				Assume success if fielder within 5 feet of hit							
3	defined by distance between 1st and 2nd and second and third							Fraction fielded				
4									0.19 First baseman within 10 feet of bag			
5	Base	distance	changed distance	Distance to 1	Distance to 2	Distance to 3	Distance to 4	Fieldit		Optimal Position	Default	
6	1	67.65	67.65	61.07	2.35	62.35	102.35	1	1	6.579027	8	
7	2	64.76	154.76	148.19	84.76	24.76	15.24	0	2	70	78	
8	1	61.70	61.70	55.12	8.30	68.30	108.30	0	3	130	130	
9	1	57.93	57.93	51.35	12.07	72.07	112.07	0	4	170	170	
10	1	47.13	47.13	40.55	22.87	82.87	122.87	0				
11	1	52.00	52.00	45.42	18.00	78.00	118.00	0				
12	2	54.78	144.78	138.20	74.78	14.78	25.22	0				
13	2	59.69	149.69	143.11	79.69	19.69	20.31	0				
14	2	41.29	131.29	124.71	61.29	1.29	38.71	1				

Figure 59.3: Not shifting fails

Empirical Evidence on the Shift

It is difficult to determine how well shifting works, but the shift surely destroyed Ryan Howard's career. Great writer Rob Arthur of `FiveThirtyEight.com` gives us the sad details (see `fivethirtyeight.com/features/ryan-howards-career-is-dead-the-shift-killed-it/`).

First, we define OPS (On Base + Slugging Percentage), a standard measure of a hitter's productivity. OPS is computed as

Fraction of Time Hitter Reaches Base + Average Number of Total Bases

Per At Bat (Single = 1 total base, Double = 2 total bases, Triple

= 3 total bases, Home Run = 4 total bases)

During 2010–2016, the great left-handed Philly slugger recorded an OPS of .975 when teams did not shift and a mediocre .643 OPS (compared to the 2019 major league average .758 OPS) when teams shifted. Sadly for Howard, teams shifted against him nearly 90% of the time.

Also, through June 2017, Chicago Cubs World Series hero and left-handed hitter Kyle Schwarber only hit .180 on ground balls, largely due to the shift (see `wrigleyville.locals.baseballprospectus.com/2017/06/04/schwarber-and-the-shift/`).

MLB.com writer Mike Petriello analyzed the 2017 batting average of all hitters who saw at least 100 pitches against the shift and not against the shift (see `www.mlb.com/news/9-things-you-need-to-know-about-the-shift-c276706888`). Petriello found these hitters got hits 28.1% of the time against the shift and got hits 29.9% of the time without the shift. Therefore, the shift costs hitters 18 points of batting average on balls in play.

As another measure of the effectiveness of the shift, ESPN found that in 2019, shifts by several teams (Rays, Yankees, and Diamondbacks) saved over 20 runs, which results in two more wins per season (see `www.espn.com/mlb/story/_/id/24049347/mlb-hitters-explain-why-just-beat-shift`).

Why Not Just Beat the Shift?

When a left-hand hitter is at bat against the shift, there is only one infielder between second and third base. It seems like the hitter could just lay down a bunt and reach first base. ESPN asked three left-hand hitters why they don't try this strategy (see `www.espn.com/mlb/story/_/id/24049347/mlb-hitters-explain-why-just-beat-shift`). They had several answers:

- Kyle Seager of the Mariners said it's hard to lay down a successful bunt off a 90+ mph fastball.

- Daniel Murphy of the 2019 World Champion Nationals pointed out that three infield singles won't score a run but a double and single will, so why try and lay down a bunt?

- Matt Carpenter of the Cardinals suggested just outlawing the shift by requiring two infielders to be positioned on either side of second base.

I had lunch with a top MLB executive who told me hitters don't want to bunt because that's not what they get paid for. Also recall that during 2019, the average OPS was .758. Therefore, for a hitter to match this level of effectiveness, their bunts would have to be successful 76% of the time, which is impossible.

Excel Calculations

We now show how to use Excel's Evolutionary Solver (see Chapter 53, "How Does the UPS Driver Know the Order to Deliver Packages?") to determine the optimal position of fielders given made-up data that describes where a left-hand hitter hits the ball. The needed steps are as follows:

1. In cells L6:L9 of the worksheet Shift of the workbook `Shift.xlsx`, enter trial positions for each fielder.

2. Copy from F6 to F6:J295 the formula `=ABS(E6-$L$6)`. This computes the distance of the first baseman from the location of the batted ball. Similar formulas in Columns G through I calculate the distance of the other fielders from the batted ball.

3. We assume that the ball is successfully fielded if there is a fielder within 5 feet of the batted ball. Copy from J6 to J7:J295 the formula `=IF(MIN(F6:I6)<=5,1,0)`. This returns a 1 if the ball will be successfully fielded and a 0 otherwise. For example, we see the first batted ball was not successfully fielded by the second baseman, whereas the second batted ball was successfully fielded.

4. Enter in cell J4, the formula `=SUM(J6:J295)/COUNT(J6:J295)` to compute the fraction of batted balls successfully fielded.

5. From the Data tab, select Solver from the Analyze group to bring up the Solver Parameters dialog box shown in Figure 59.4.

6. Choose Max and enter in the Set Objective portion of the dialog box cell J4 (the fraction of balls fielded).

7. In the Changing Variable Cells portion of the dialog box, enter cells L6:L9 (the fielder's positions). Note that Excel automatically places dollar signs

on any cell references entered in any section of the dialog box.

8. The MIN function is involved in our objective, and this requires the use of the Evolutionary Solver. Like the GRG Multistart Solver, the Evolutionary Solver requires upper and lower bounds on each changing cell. The lower bound on each changing cell is 0. The first baseman must be within 10 feet of first base, so we require L6<=10. We also require L6:L9<=180. To ensure at least one fielder between second and third base, we added the constraint L9>=100.

9. To ensure that the GRG Multistart Solver is used, click Options and then choose the Use Multistart option from the GRG tab.

10. Click Solve to yield the optimal solution.

Figure 59.4: Solver parameters for optimal shift

The optimal positioning of the fielders results in 67% of all batted balls being fielded. The positioning of the fielders is as follows:

- First baseman 3.1 feet from first base
- Second baseman 50.6 feet from first base
- Shortstop 60.7 feet from first base
- Third basemen 150.6 feet from first base

Did Analytics Help the Mavericks Win the 2011 NBA Title?

During the 2000–2001 through the 2010–2011 seasons, Mark Cuban's Dallas Mavericks averaged 56 wins per season, second only to the San Antonio Spurs' 58 wins. During most of those years, my friend Jeff Sagarin (creator of the widely respected *USA Today* sports ratings posted at Sagarin.com) and I were privileged to provide analytic support to the Mavericks. As Mark graciously points out (see video.search.yahoo.com/yhs/search?fr=yhs-pty-pty_packages&hsimp=yhs-pty_packages&hspart=pty&p=mark+cuban+jeopardy+wayne+winston+video#id =1&vid=b8a9ca147a084c09bf35f35bff383da9&action=click), Jeff and I were the first data scientists to aid an NBA team. Of course, the players and the coaches deserve the lion's share of the credit for the Mavericks' great decade and 2011 NBA title, but in this chapter, I hope to pull back the curtain and show you how our analytic work played a small role in the Mavs' decade-long success. I'd also like to note that when Jeff and I provided similar services for the Knicks' great GM, Glen Grunwald, the Knicks won 54 games, their most wins since 1997.

How Can You Evaluate a Basketball Player?

NBA box scores give you plenty of data on players, but not much data on a player's defensive ability. Our view was that basketball players should be evaluated based on how the score of the game moves when the player is on or off the court. As an example, legendary Celtics coach Red Auerbach noted that guard

K. C. Jones (`www.talkbasket.net/47445-red-auerbach-on-k-c-jones-he-didnt-come-to-play-he-came-to-win`) "didn't come to play, he came to win." Jones had horrible box score stats. For example, he shot 39%, and his career Player Efficiency Rating (a well-respected box-score metric) was 10.4, which during the 2019–2020 season, would have ranked 61st among 70 point guards. Jones is in the Basketball Hall of Fame, so he must have done something right that was missed by the box score (probably on defense).

Our approach is based on basketball's +/– statistic (now included in NBA and college box scores). The +/– statistic originated in hockey in the 1950s, and simply measured the number of goals by which a player's team outscored the opponent while the player was on the ice (ignoring power plays, empty net goals, or penalty shots). In the NBA, +/– is usually measured per 48 minutes. *It is important to note that a player's +/– rating is influenced equally by offense and defense. Giving up one more point hurts your +/– as much as scoring one more point helps your +/–.* During the 2018–2019 season, MVP Giannis Antetokounmpo of the Bucks had the league's best +/– rating, with 12.8 points per 48 minutes. That means that when he was on the court, the Bucks outscored their opponents by 12.8 points per 48 minutes. The problem with using raw +/– as a measure of player ability is that almost everyone with a good +/– is on a good team. During the 2018–2019 season, for example, the only player on a team with a losing record to rank in the top 50 on raw +/– was New Orleans Pelican guard Jrue Holiday (#47 with a +/– of 4.6 points per 48 minutes).

Recognizing the flaws of raw +/–, Jeff wrote a Fortran program (yes, Fortran!) to download who was on the court every minute of the NBA season and how the score moved. Each row of the data (let's call it a lineup segment) contained the 10 players on the court, the length of time the players were on the court, whether the game was home or away, and the number of points by which the home team outscored the away team. In a typical season, there are more than 30,000 lineup segments. Jeff and I came up with the idea of *adjusted +/–*, as described by *New York Times* columnist David Leonhardt (see `www.nytimes.com/2003/04/27/sports/pro-basketball-mavericks-new-math-may-be-an-added-edge.html`). Adjusted +/– uses advanced math (not just an ordinary multiple regression) to adjust each player's raw +/– based on the nine other players he shared the court with and whether the game was home or away. (Home teams usually win by an average of 3 points per game.) Over the course of several years, I believe adjusted +/– (and its successors, such as ESPN's Real +/– at `www.espn.com/nba/statistics/rpm` and `538.com`'s RAPTOR ratings at `projects.fivethirtyeight.com/2020-nba-player-ratings/`) gives you a better idea of a player's ability (especially defensive ability) than box score metrics.

To test the merits of adjusted +/–, write down (before you look at Tables 60.1 and 60.2) who you think were the top five players of the decades 2000–2009 and 2010–2019. Our adjusted +/– lists are shown in Tables 60.1 and 60.2. To interpret these numbers, let's take the often underrated (great actor in *Uncut Gems*!) Kevin Garnett's rating of 11.0, which tells us that if Garnett played with four other average NBA players against a team of five average NBA players, we would expect his team to win by 11 points per game.

Table 60.1: Top 5 NBA Players 2000–2009

PLAYER	ADJUSTED +/– RATING
LeBron James (played only 7 years)	11.5
Kevin Garnett	11.0
Tim Duncan	10.7
Dirk Nowitzki	10.5
Kobe Bryant	9.1

Table 60.2: Top 5 NBA Players 2010–2019

PLAYER	ADJUSTED +/– RATING
LeBron James (again!)	12.9
Steph Curry	11.2
Chris Paul	11.1
Dame Lillard (7 years)	10.5
Kevin Durant	9.4

When I ask NBA fans how they would modify my 2000–2009 list, they sometimes suggest Dwayne Wade (he comes in #6) or Steve Nash. Nash's Phoenix years would place him at #7, but with the Mavs, his poor defense reduced his rating. For my 2010–2019 list, many fans would be angered by omission of James Harden. His performance for 2014–2019 would place him at #4 but prior to joining the Rockets, you must remember he played on the Oklahoma City Thunder with Russell Westbrook and Kevin Durant, and the team did not have amazing success (one trip to the finals where the Heat destroyed them). During the abbreviated 2019–2020 season, Chris Paul (our #3 player for the decade) has been amazing, leading OKC to fifth place in the tough Western Conference (Harden's Rockets were 6th).

From Player Ratings to Lineup Ratings

Once a team has set their season roster, a big part of a coach's job is to figure out which lineups work. Often adding up the ability of the five players in a lineup will not accurately predict a lineup's performance. Often the whole is greater or less than the sum of its parts. I think our most important work for the Mavericks was our accurate evaluation of a lineup's ability. The average NBA team plays over 400 different lineups in a season. You can think of a coach's varying of NBA lineups as A/B experimentation (see Chapter 49, "Can A/B Testing Improve My Website's Performance?") on steroids (but good steroids). By varying lineups and looking carefully at data, coaches can make better decisions for the all-important NBA playoffs.

Rating the Warriors' Death Lineup

To illustrate how we rate lineups, let's consider the 2015–2016 Golden State Warriors, who had the best regular season record (73-9) in history but were defeated (yay!) in the NBA finals by LeBron's Cleveland Cavaliers. How good was the Warriors' famed "Death Lineup" of Klay Thompson, Steph Curry, Harrison Barnes, Andrew Iguodala, and Draymond Green? This lineup played 297 minutes and outscored opponents by around 26 points per 48 minutes. We estimated that the strength of the lineups opponents played against the Death Lineup was 8 points better than average, so we rated the Death Lineup an amazing 26 + 8 = 34 points per game better than an average NBA lineup. This lineup averaged playing around 3 minutes per game, and I have no clue why the Warriors did not play this lineup more often.

Spurs-Mavericks 2006 Western Conference Semifinal

We also computed an adjusted +/− for each player broken down by opponent. To see how this could be useful, let's look at the Dallas Mavericks' surprising journey to the NBA finals during the 2006 playoffs. Few analysts gave the Mavs any chance against the World Champion Spurs. A key coaching move during this series was the insertion of guard Devin Harris into the starting lineup in place of Adrian Griffin. This surprise decision enabled the Mavs to "steal" game 2 at San Antonio, and the Mavs went on to win the series in seven games by winning an overtime thriller game 7 at San Antonio. Our team-by-team adjusted +/− ratings were an important input into this coaching decision. Devin Harris's overall 2005–2006 rating was −2.1 points. Against the Spurs, Harris's rating was +9.4 points. Against the Spurs, Griffin had a −5 point rating. More importantly, Griffin had a −18-points offense rating. This indicates that against the Spurs, Griffin reduced the Mavs' scoring ability by 18 points per game. Given this data, it seems clear that Harris should have started in lieu of Griffin. So, how did Harris do? During the playoffs, we do a two-way lineup calculator that shows how the Mavs perform with any combination of Mavs players on or off court against any combination of opponent players on or off court. For the 2005–2006 regular season, our data indicated that Harris could outplay future Hall of Famer Tony Parker. So, what happened during the first six games of the Spurs-Mavs series? With Harris on the court against Parker, the Mavs (excluding game 2, in which the Mavs took the Spurs by surprise by starting Harris) beat the Spurs by an average of 102-100 per 48 minutes. With Parker on the floor and Harris out, the Mavs lost by an average of 96-81 per 48 minutes!

As the series progressed, we learned other interesting things. When Marquis Daniels was on the court against Manu Ginobili, the Mavs lost by an average score of 132-81 per 48 minutes! When Ginobili was on the court and Daniels was out, the Mavs won by an average of 94-91 per 48 minutes. By the way, Daniels did not play in game 7 of the series.

Next, the Mavs played the Suns in the 2006 Western Conference finals. Here we knew Devin Harris would not be as effective because he has trouble with Steve Nash. For this series, when the Harris Jason Terry backcourt played against Nash, the Mavs were down by 113-90 per 48 minutes. The Terry and Jerry Stackhouse backcourt (with Harris out) was up 116-96 per 48 minutes with Nash in. The Mavs used this information to adjust their rotation to play the more effective combination more often.

Analytics Helps the Mavericks Become 2011 World Champions!

At the start of the 2011 NBA playoffs, Las Vegas gave the Miami Heat (with their Big 3 of LeBron James, Dwayne Wade, and Chris Bosh) a 60% chance to win the series. The Dallas Mavericks upset the Heat, and lineup analysis played a huge role. During the regular season, the Mavericks' best lineup was Jason Terry, Jason Kidd, Dirk Nowitzki, Shawn Marion, and Tyson Chandler. During the regular season, this lineup played an average of only 2 minutes per game, but during the regular season, this lineup played 28 points per game better than average. Recognizing the greatness of this lineup, the Mavs increased the lineup's playing time to 8 minutes per game during the playoffs, and this lineup played an incredible 46 points per game better than average!

One of the most important decisions a coach must make is determining the optimal lineup to play when their star player (in this case, Dirk Nowitzki) is out. During the three Western Conference playoff series, the Mavericks rested Nowitzki by inserting Peja Stojaković. In the 126 minutes Stojaković replaced Nowitzki, the Mavs played 3 points per game better than average. If you can rest your star and still play above average, you are doing great!

In the first three games of the NBA finals against the Heat, the Mavs continued to insert Stojaković for Nowitzki. Unfortunately, in these games the Mavs lost by 24 points in 18 minutes. All these games were close, so something needed to be done. In game 4, the Mavs benched Stojaković and began to use Brian Cardinal to replace Nowitzki. In games 4-6 of the finals, the Mavs lost by only

3 points in 24 minutes with Cardinal replacing Nowitzki. This lineup change improved the Mavs' performance by 7 points per game.

In the first three games of the series, the Mavs' starting lineup of Kidd, Nowitzki, Chandler, Marion, and DeShawn Stevenson was –7 points in 28 minutes, while with guard J. J. Barea in, the Mavs were –14 points in 51 minutes. During the first three games of the series, Barea came off the bench and was usually matched up against Mario Chalmers. This matchup did not go well for the Mavs. During the first three games, Chalmers owned Barea (Mavs –31 points in 21 minutes with both in). On the other hand, during the first three games, Barea owned Heat starter Mike Bibby (Mavs +17 points in 33 minutes with both in). Based on this information, Rick Carlisle inserted Barea into the starting lineup, replacing Stevenson. This new lineup was +8 points in 28 minutes in games 4 and 5. Starting Barea placed Barea more often against Bibby than against Chalmers. The Heat finally figured out that starting Barea was hurting them, and in game 6, the Heat started Chalmers. This rendered the Mavs' new starting lineup ineffective, but the damage had been done and the Mavs were world champions!

The 2012–2013 New York Knicks

As previously mentioned, during the 2012–2013 NBA season, Jeff and I were consultants to the New York Knicks. On March 17, 2017, the Knicks lost their fourth game in a row. All season, our lineup data indicated that the Knicks played more than 10 points per game better than average when 35-year-old Argentinian rookie Pablo Prigioni and veteran Raymond Felton were the backcourt. After the March 17th loss, the Knicks started Prigioni and Felton and won 13 games in a row. (Just coincidence?) The Knicks went on to win their first playoff series since 2000, and were (in my opinion) one missed goaltending call on Roy Hibbert away from making the Eastern Conference Finals.

In Sports, Analytics Needs a Champion!

Most coaches do not have a mathematics or statistics background. For analytics to help a team, I think the "geeks" need a person with respected basketball expertise to interpret the numbers. With the Mavs, the wonderful Del Harris (Kobe Bryant's first NBA coach) interpreted our numbers for head coach Avery Johnson. With the Knicks, their director of analytics Mike Smith came up with a great format to distill the lineup information for head coach Mike Woodson. After each game, we would email Mike Smith an updated summary of how every frontcourt and backcourt combination performed. I think the lesson from our successes with the Mavs and the Knicks is that a straightforward and clear presentation of key insights is needed for data to improve an organization's decision making.

Who Gets the House in the Hamptons?

Sadly, the marriage of rich New Yorkers Denny and Irene is ending in divorce. As shown in Figure 61.1 and worksheet 50_50 of the workbook DivorceNYCStyle. xlsx, the couple needs to divide the following assets (for convenience, we will classify Custody as an asset):

- ➤ Home in the Hamptons

- ➤ NYC home

- ➤ Ferrari

- ➤ Bank account

- ➤ Family jewels

- ➤ Custody of their daughter

Can analytics come up with a fair division in this situation? Political scientists Steven Brams and Alan Taylor (*The Win-Win Solution*, Norton, 1999) came up with an elegant solution to this problem. Their solution can be used to settle many other conflicts between two parties (such as labor and management, the Palestinians and the Israelis, and so forth).

	A	B	C	D	E	F
1						Worst
2				50	50	50
3	Denny	Irene		Denny	Irene	
4	0.5	0.5	Hamptons Home	16	9	
5	0.5	0.5	NYC Home	16	14	
6	0.5	0.5	Ferrari	9	5	
7	0.5	0.5	Bank Account	28	25	
8	0.5	0.5	Jewels	6	10	
9	0.5	0.5	Custody	25	37	

Figure 61.1: Denny and Irene's assets

The Basic Idea

To begin, we ask Denny and Irene to allocate a total of 100 points to the assets. From Figure 61.1, we see that Denny places the most value on the bank account, and Irene places the most value on custody. For now, we assume all assets are divisible. We need to determine the fraction of each asset assigned to each party. One possible solution is to simply assign half of each asset to each person. As shown in Figure 61.1, this solution gives Denny and Irene 50 points. Clearly, giving a greater percentage of custody to Irene and more of the bank account to Denny would make both better off (see Figure 61.2 and the worksheet First Try). We see that giving 70% of the bank account to Denny and 70% of the custody to Irene increases Denny's points to 50.6 and Irene's to 52.4. What we need is a systematic method to search all possible asset divisions and choose the "best" asset division.

	A	B	C	D	E	F
1						Worst
2				50.6	52.4	50.6
3	Denny	Irene		Denny	Irene	
4	0.5	0.5	Hamptons Home	16	9	
5	0.5	0.5	NYC Home	16	14	
6	0.5	0.5	Ferrari	9	5	
7	0.7	0.3	Bank Account	28	25	
8	0.5	0.5	Jewels	6	10	
9	0.3	0.7	Custody	25	37	

Figure 61.2: A better division

What Asset Division Is Best?

We first met Italian economist Vilfredo Pareto (1848-1923) in our Chapter 43 ("Why Does the Pareto Principle Explain So Many Things?") discussion of the Pareto principle. Pareto realized that there are many situations, such as allocation of property in a divorce, that involve trade-offs. In such situations, Pareto came up with the idea of a *Pareto optimal* solution. In our divorce example, a Pareto optimal solution is a division of assets in which you cannot make one person better off without making the other person worse off. The solution shown in Figure 61.2 makes both people better off. This shows that the 50-50 solution is not Pareto optimal.

To find a Pareto optimal division of assets, we use the Excel Solver to change the fraction of each asset given to Denny. For each asset, Irene simply gets what is left over. So, if Denny gets 70% of the bank account, Irene gets $1 - 0.70 = 30\%$ of the bank account. Our objective is to

$$\text{Maximize}\big[\text{Minimum}(\text{Denny's Points and Irene's Points})\big]$$

The "Excel Calculations" section of this chapter shows the details of our Solver setup. The Pareto optimal asset division is shown in Figure 61.3 (see worksheet Basic). Denny and Irene each get 57.34 points (14% more than the 50-50 allocation).

	A	B	C	D	E	F
1						Worst
2				57.3416	57.3416	57.3416
3	Denny	Irene		Denny	Irene	
4	1	0	Hamptons Home	16	9	
5	0.7631	0.237	NYC Home	16	14	
6	1	0	Ferrari	9	5	
7	0.719	0.281	Bank Account	28	25	
8	0	1	Jewels	6	10	
9	1E-07	1	Custody	25	37	

Figure 61.3: Pareto optimal solution with divisible assets

Some assets are not divisible. In our example, suppose that each home, the Ferrari, and the jewels are not divisible. Then the optimal solution is shown in Figure 61.4 (see the worksheet Binary). The non-divisibility of assets slightly reduces (from 57.34 to 56.98 points) each person's points.

	A	B	C	D	E	F
1						Worst
2				56.9772	56.9772	56.97719
3	Denny	Irene		Denny	Irene	
4	1	0	Hamptons Home	16	9	
5	1	0	NYC Home	16	14	
6	1	0	Ferrari	9	5	
7	0.5245	0.4755	Bank Account	28	25	
8	0	1	Jewels	6	10	
9	0.0516	0.9484	Custody	25	37	

Figure 61.4: Pareto optimal solution with non-divisible assets

Excel Calculations

In this section, we show how to use the Excel Solver to find a Pareto optimal division of assets for the case where all assets are divisible and the case where some assets are not divisible. In both cases, the Evolutionary Solver engine (introduced in Chapter 53, "How Does the UPS Driver Know the Order to Deliver Packages?") is used to find the Pareto optimal division. Note that the Efficient Frontier discussed in Chapter 50 ("How Should I Allocate My Retirement Portfolio?") consisted of Pareto optimal points that traded off portfolio risk versus portfolio expected return.

Pareto Optimal Solution for Divisible Assets

The following steps (see the worksheet Basic) find a Pareto optimal solution when the assets are divisible:

1. Enter trial asset fractions from Denny in the cell range A4:A9.

2. Compute the fraction of assets going to Irene in the cell range B4:B9 by copying the formula =1-A4 from B4 to B5:B9.

3. Copy the formula =SUMPRODUCT(D4:D9,A4:A9) from D2 to E2 to compute each person's total points. This formula computes A4 * D4 + A5 * D5 + . . ., A9 * D9.

4. Enter in cell F2 the formula =MIN(D2:E2). This computes the total points for the person who receives the fewer points.

5. Fill in the Solver Parameters dialog box, as shown in Figure 61.5, to yield the Pareto optimal asset allocation. The Target cell is to maximize F2, and the changing variable cells A4:A9 are constrained to be less than or equal to 1. The Target cell involving a MAX and MIN requires the use of the Evolutionary Solver, so we select the Evolutionary solving method.

This solution assigned 57.34 points to Denny and Irene. To see that the solution is Pareto optimal, suppose there is a solution that would make Irene better off (say, 58 points). This solution cannot reduce Denny below his current value of 57.34, because that would yield a Target cell smaller than 57.34 and would not maximize our Target cell. If this new solution kept Denny at 57.34, then just reduce Irene's fraction of each asset a tiny bit and keep Irene over 57.34 and raise Denny above 57.34. This new solution would contradict the optimality of the solution found by the Solver.

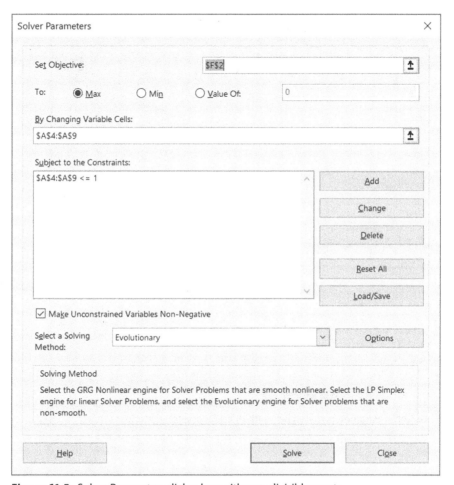

Figure 61.5: Solver Parameters dialog box with non-divisible assets

Pareto Solution for Non-divisible Assets

The only change needed from our previous Solver model is to add constraints that the changing cells for each house, the Ferrari, and the jewels are binary. When the Solver is told that a changing cell is binary, then the changing cell will be set equal to 0 or 1. The new Solver Parameters dialog box is shown in Figure 61.6. We find that Denny and Irene's points drop slightly to 56.98, and Denny gets both houses and the Ferrari, whereas Irene gets the jewels and most of the custody.

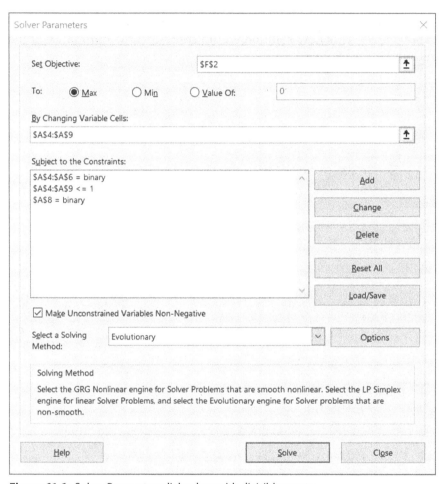

Figure 61.6: Solver Parameters dialog box with divisible assets

Index